Revenue Statistics in Latin America and the Caribbean 2024

1990-2022

Please cite this publication as:
OECD et al. (2024), *Revenue Statistics in Latin America and the Caribbean 2024*, OECD Publishing, Paris, https://doi.org/10.1787/33e226ae-en.

ISBN 978-92-64-58537-9 (print)
ISBN 978-92-64-36526-1 (PDF)
ISBN 978-92-64-92271-6 (HTML)
ISBN 978-92-64-66864-5 (epub)

Revenue Statistics in Latin America and the Caribbean
ISSN 2410-4728 (print)
ISSN 2410-4736 (online)

Photo credits: Cover © some of the graphic elements in the main cover illustration were adapted from Freepik.com.

Corrigenda to OECD publications may be found on line at: www.oecd.org/about/publishing/corrigenda.htm.

Foreword

Revenue Statistics in Latin America and the Caribbean 2024 is a joint publication by the Organisation for Economic Co-operation and Development (OECD) Centre for Tax Policy and Administration, the OECD Development Centre, the United Nations Economic Commission for Latin America and the Caribbean (UN - ECLAC), the Inter-American Center of Tax Administrations (CIAT) and the Inter-American Development Bank (IDB), with financial support from the Spanish Agency for International Development Cooperation (AECID). It presents detailed, internationally comparable data on tax revenues for 27 Latin American and Caribbean (LAC) economies, four of which are OECD members.

Revenue Statistics in Latin America and the Caribbean 2024 is based on the well-established classification of revenues set out in the OECD Interpretative Guide. In this publication, the term "taxes" is confined to compulsory, unrequited payments to general government. As outlined, taxes are "unrequited" in the sense that benefits provided by government to taxpayers are not normally in proportion to their payments. The OECD methodology classifies a tax according to its base: income, profits and capital gains (classified under heading 1000); payroll (heading 3000); property (heading 4000); goods and services (heading 5000); and other taxes (heading 6000). Compulsory social security contributions paid to general government are treated as taxes and classified under heading 2000. Greater detail on the tax concept, the classification of taxes and the accrual basis of reporting is set out in the Interpretative Guide in Annex A.

Extending the OECD methodology to countries in Latin America and the Caribbean (LAC) enables comparisons of tax systems on a consistent basis across this region as well as with OECD countries and with all countries included in the *Global Revenue Statistics* database. In a few cases, this methodology differs from the approach used by UN-ECLAC, CIAT and IDB; these differences are noted in the text and in the tables.

The report provides an overview of the main taxation trends in the LAC region. It examines changes in the level and the composition of tax revenue plus the attribution of tax collection by sub-level of government between 1990 and 2022. The report includes two special features: the first examines fiscal revenues from non-renewable natural resources in the LAC region in 2022 and 2023; the second discusses equivalent fiscal pressure, a complementary revenue indicator for the LAC region.

Acknowledgements

Revenue Statistics in Latin America and the Caribbean 2024 was jointly produced by the Organisation for Economic Co-operation and Development (OECD) Centre for Tax Policy and Administration, the OECD Development Centre, the United Nations Economic Commission for Latin America and the Caribbean (UN - ECLAC), the Inter-American Center of Tax Administrations (CIAT) and the Inter-American Development Bank (IDB). This publication benefited from the financial support of the Spanish Agency for International Development Cooperation (AECID) in the framework of the activities aimed at improving fiscal systems in Latin America and the Caribbean (LAC).

The staff from these organisations with responsibility for producing the publication were: Emmanuelle Modica of the OECD Centre for Tax Policy and Administration, under the supervision of the Director, Manal Corwin, the Deputy Director David Bradbury, the Acting Head of the Tax Policy and Statistics Division Kurt Van Dender, and the Acting Head of the Tax Data and Statistical Analysis Unit, Alexander Pick; Jingjing Xia and René Orozco of the OECD Development Centre, under the supervision of the Director, Ragnheiður Elín Árnadóttir, Deputy Director Federico Bonaglia, and the Head of the Latin America and the Caribbean Unit, Sebastian Nieto Parra; Michael Hanni of the Economic Development Division of UN-ECLAC, under the supervision of Director Daniel Titelman and the Chief of the Fiscal Affairs Unit, Noel Pérez Benítez; Julio Alberto López from the CIAT Tax Studies and Research Directorate, under the supervision of Director Santiago Díaz de Sarralde; and Alejandro Rasteletti, Lead Specialist and Knowledge Coordinator at the IDB Fiscal Management Division at the IDB and Ubaldo González de Frutos, Sector Lead Specialist in Tax Administration. Michael Hanni of UN-ECLAC authored the special feature on fiscal revenues from non-renewable natural resources in the LAC region (Chapter 2); Santiago Díaz de Sarralde and Dalmiro Morán of CIAT, with inputs by Alejandro Rasteletti of IDB, authored the special feature on the equivalent fiscal pressure in the LAC region based on a report by Dalmiro Morán and Marco Solera (Chapter 3).

The authors would like to thank other staff at the OECD Development Centre and the Centre for Tax Policy and Administration for their invaluable support in completing and enhancing the 2024 edition of this publication. Karena Garnier and Antonia Vanzini from the OECD Centre for Tax Policy and Administration, Delphine Grandrieux and Elizabeth Nash from the OECD Development Centre's Communications and Publications team, and Damian Garnys from the OECD Directorate for Communications, ensured the production of the publication, in both paper and electronic form. Michael Sharratt from the OECD Centre for Tax Policy and Administration provided invaluable assistance with the databases, website and other dissemination tools. Nicolas Miranda from the OECD Centre for Tax Policy and Administration and Laura Gutierrez of the OECD Development Centre provided precious help in proof-reading the Spanish content. The authors would also like to thank Ivonne González and Elisa Araneda from the Economic Development Division of UN-ECLAC for translating the special feature on fiscal revenues from non-renewable natural resources in the LAC region.

Finally, the OECD Centre for Tax Policy and Administration and the OECD Development Centre would like to thank our colleagues working in national entities, with whom we have consulted regularly in preparing this report. In particular, we are grateful to Eduardo Rodriguez from the Ministry of Finance of Argentina;

Fidelia Raulina Pérez Castillo and Mariam Ortiz from the Dominican Republic's Finance Ministry; Luis Alberto Canjura Vásquez, from the Ministry of Finance of El Salvador; David Fernando Pineda Pinto from the Revenue Administration Service and Kervin Andre Sánchez Valle and Neffy Noel Velásquez Sagastume from the Secretary of Finances in Honduras; Andrea Gregory from Jamaica's Tax Administration and Customs agencies; Emma Isaza from Panama's Finance Ministry; and Óscar Gustavo Núñez Del Arco Mendoza and Jorge Rivera Calderón from Peru's Ministry of Economy and Finance.

Table of contents

FIGURES

TABLES

Executive summary

Between 2021 and 2022, tax-to-GDP ratios increased in more than three quarters of countries in Latin America and the Caribbean (LAC), while the average tax-to-GDP ratio for the LAC region rose by 0.3 percentage points (p.p.) to 21.5%, still slightly below its pre-pandemic level (21.6%). The increase in the regional average was driven by corporate income tax (CIT) amid higher profits by oil companies, although this was partially offset by a decline in revenue from excises, due to lower demand as well as the adoption of a range of policy measures by countries to mitigate the impact of energy and food inflation on households and firms.

Revenue Statistics in Latin America and the Caribbean 2024 provides internationally comparable data on tax levels and tax structures for 27 LAC countries: Antigua and Barbuda, Argentina, the Bahamas, Barbados, Belize, Bolivia, Brazil, Chile, Colombia, Costa Rica, Cuba, the Dominican Republic, Ecuador, El Salvador, Guatemala, Guyana, Honduras, Jamaica, Mexico, Nicaragua, Panama, Paraguay, Peru, Saint Lucia, Trinidad and Tobago, Uruguay and Venezuela. The LAC average represents the unweighted average of 26 countries included in this publication, excluding Venezuela due to data issues.

In this publication, "taxes" are defined as compulsory, unrequited payments to general government. Compulsory social security contributions (SSCs) paid to general government are classified as taxes. More information on the tax classification is set out in the Interpretative Guide in Annex A.

Tax-to-GDP ratios in the LAC region in 2022

Tax-to-GDP ratios ranged from 10.6% in Guyana to 33.3% in Brazil in 2022. Against a backdrop of an ongoing recovery from the COVID-19 shock and high commodity prices, tax-to-GDP ratios increased in twenty countries between 2021 and 2022 and declined in six.

The largest increases were observed in Chile (whose tax-to-GDP ratio rose by 1.7 p.p.), the Bahamas (1.6 p.p.) and Ecuador (1.5 p.p.). The increase in Chile was mainly driven by higher CIT revenue, while growth in tourism in the Bahamas led to strong VAT receipts. In Ecuador, the increase was driven by the oil sector and the introduction of taxes on net wealth. The largest decreases in 2022 occurred in Caribbean countries, as strong GDP growth in this sub-region outpaced the rise in tax revenue, particularly in Guyana, where the tax-to-GDP ratio fell by 6.3 p.p. between 2021 and 2022.

In 2022, revenue from CIT increased by 0.6 p.p. on average across the LAC region from the previous year while revenue from personal income tax (PIT) was unchanged as a share of GDP. Meanwhile, revenue from taxes on goods and services declined by 0.3 p.p. Within this category, revenue from excises fell by 0.4 p.p. as sharp increases in the cost of essential items caused demand to fall and prompted governments to reduce taxes (mostly on fuel products). In contrast, VAT revenues remained unchanged in 2022 relative to 2021.

Average tax-to-GDP ratios in the Caribbean, Central America & Mexico and South America stood at 21.7%, 19.4% and 23.5% respectively in 2022. Tax revenue increased by 1.0 p.p. and 0.3 p.p.

respectively in South America and in Central America & Mexico, while the Caribbean's tax-to-GDP ratio decreased by 0.6 p.p. If Guyana is excluded, the Caribbean's average tax-to-GDP ratio rose by 0.2 p.p.

Evolution of tax-to-GDP ratios in the LAC region since 1990

The average tax-to-GDP ratio for the LAC region rose by 6.9 p.p. between 1990 and 2022 largely due to increases in revenue from VAT and from taxes on income and profits (of 3.8 p.p. and 3.1 p.p., respectively). The gap between the LAC and OECD average tax-to-GDP ratios narrowed over this period, from 16.2 p.p. in 1990 to 12.5 p.p. in 2022, although it has widened since 2010. On average, South America's tax-to-GDP ratio recorded the strongest growth among the sub-regions between 1990 and 2022.

Tax structures in the LAC region

In 2022, taxes on goods and services generated almost half of total tax revenue in the LAC region, compared with less than a third in the OECD (31.9% in 2021, the latest year available). VAT was the principal source of this revenue in the LAC region in 2022, accounting for 28.3% of total tax revenue on average and amounting to 6.1% of GDP.

On average, taxes on income and profits accounted for 30.1% of total tax revenue in the LAC region in 2022. CIT and PIT revenue accounted for 18.8% and 9.2% respectively of total tax revenue, compared with 10.2% and 23.7% in the OECD (2021 figures). The average share of SSCs in total tax revenue was 16.7% in the LAC region in 2022, below the OECD average of 25.6% (2021 figure).

Environmentally related tax revenue (ERTR) amounted to 0.8% of GDP on average in 2022 in the 23 LAC countries for which data are available, below the OECD average of 1.9%. ERTR in the LAC region was derived principally from taxes on energy, most commonly excises on diesel and petrol (0.5% of GDP on average). A reduction in energy-related tax revenue was behind the decline in ERTR of 0.1 p.p. between 2021 and 2022.

Special feature: Trends in fiscal revenues from non-renewable natural resources

Hydrocarbon-related revenue among major oil producers in the LAC region increased to 4.4% of GDP on average in 2022 from 2.6% of GDP in 2021 as oil prices surged in the first half of 2022 due to the impact of Russia's invasion of Ukraine and constrained global supply. Meanwhile average revenue from mining increased from 0.7% of GDP in 2021 to 0.8% of GDP in 2022 despite weakening prices and lower production. In contrast, both hydrocarbon-related revenue and mining revenue fell as a share of GDP in 2023, to an estimated 3.9% and 0.5% of GDP respectively as oil and mineral prices trended down.

Special feature: Equivalent fiscal pressure in the LAC region

Equivalent fiscal pressure (EFP) is an indicator of the tax burden that complements the tax-to-GDP ratio by adding contributions to private social security systems and non-tax revenue from the exploitation of natural resources to tax revenue. On average, EFP was 1.7% of GDP higher than the LAC region's tax-to-GDP ratio in 2021. In Chile and Mexico, which recorded the largest revenues from these additional components, the EFP was 5.9% and 5.5% of GDP higher respectively than the countries' tax-to-GDP ratios in 2021.

1 Tax revenue trends, 1990-2022

Introduction

After a strong rebound in 2021 from the shock of the COVID-19 pandemic the previous year, growth slowed in many countries in Latin America and the Caribbean (LAC) in 2022. External conditions were less favourable, public transfers were rolled back, monetary policy tightened and the effects of the reopening of economies dissipated (OECD et al., 2023[1]). Challenging socioeconomic conditions persisted, as poverty and extreme poverty in the region remained above pre-pandemic levels and inflation further eroded purchasing power. In 2022, 29% of the population was in poverty and 11.2% in extreme poverty in the LAC region (OECD et al., 2023[1]).

Despite recent consolidation efforts, fiscal space remains limited in the LAC region. To fund their development programmes, governments in the region need to enhance the targeting of public spending and mobilise additional resources through higher borrowing and by increasing public revenues. Fairer and more efficient tax systems are required: low tax revenues in most LAC countries limit the state's capacity to respond to citizens' demands and improve public services. In addition, by rebalancing the tax structure away from a dependence on consumption taxes and corporate income tax and by promoting further progressivity in the personal income tax, the region could reduce inequalities and minimise distortions that constrain entrepreneurship (OECD et al., 2023[1]). Tax reforms will also be needed to encourage a green and just transition (OECD et al., 2022[2]). In many LAC countries, a stronger fiscal pact between government, citizens and the private sector is required to ensure that political support for these reforms is sustained throughout what is likely to be a long-term process (OECD et al., 2021[3]).

Revenue Statistics in Latin America and the Caribbean 2024 provides a unique basis for such fiscal pacts. By providing internationally comparable data on tax revenues in 27 countries in the region, it serves both as a basis for countries' in-depth tax policy analysis and as a common starting point for knowledge sharing and capacity development across the LAC region. This chapter discusses the evolution of key tax indicators between 1990 and 2022, including the tax-to-GDP ratio, the tax mix and the share of tax revenue generated by different levels of government, as well as the efficiency of value-added tax in the region. It also analyses revenue from environmentally-related taxes. This analysis is complemented by special features on revenues from non-renewable natural resources (Chapter 2) and the equivalent fiscal pressure indicator (Chapter 3). Chapter 4 provides comparative tables for key tax indicators across the region, while Chapters 5 and 6 provide a detailed country-by-country breakdown of tax revenue.

Tax-to-GDP ratios: levels and annual changes in 2022

Tax-to-GDP ratios in 2022

The tax-to-GDP ratio measures tax revenue (including social security contributions paid to the general government) as a proportion of gross domestic product (GDP). The LAC average represents the unweighted average of 26 of the countries included in this publication; it excludes Venezuela due to a lack of data (see Box 1.1).

The average tax-to-GDP ratio in the LAC region was 21.5% in 2022 (Figure 1.1). The highest tax-to-GDP ratios were observed in Brazil (33.3%), Barbados (30.5%) and Argentina (29.6%), while the countries with the lowest tax-to-GDP ratio were Guyana (10.6%), Panama (13.1%) and Dominican Republic (13.9%). All countries in the LAC region recorded a tax-to-GDP ratio below the OECD average of 34.0% in 2022.[1]

Figure 1.1. Tax-to-GDP ratios in the LAC region, 2022

Total tax revenues as percentage of GDP

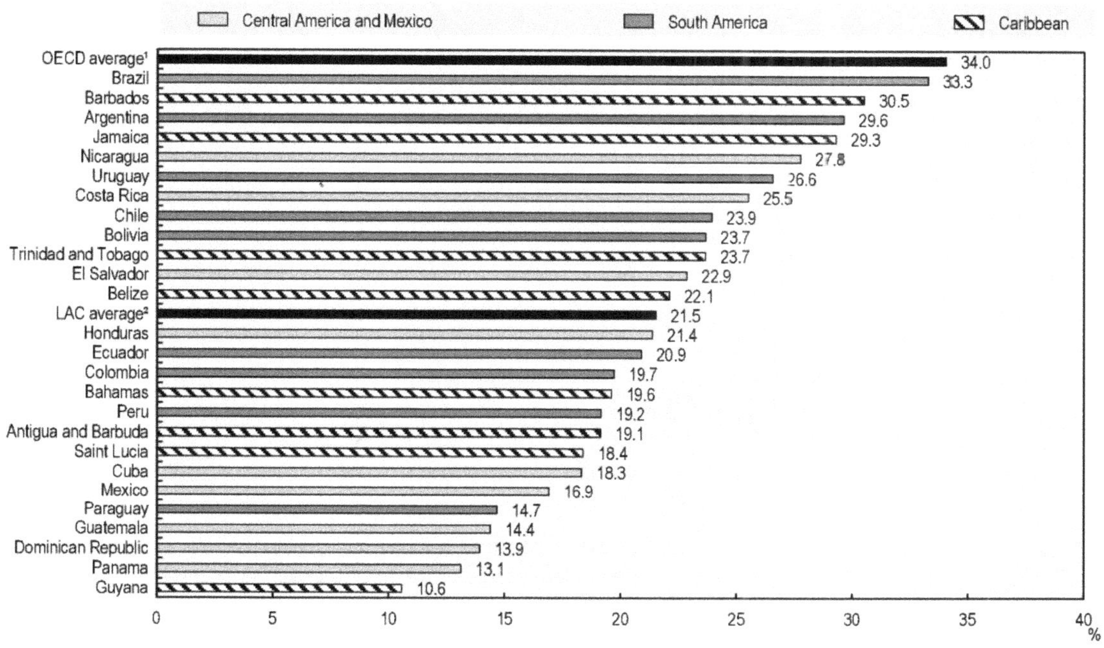

Note: The classification of countries into different sub-regions follows ECLAC's classification and is based on the spoken language of countries. The "Caribbean" includes English-speaking countries and Guyana, while "Central America and Mexico" covers Spanish-speaking countries including Dominican Republic and Cuba.

The figures exclude local government revenues for Antigua and Barbuda, Argentina (but include provincial revenues), The Bahamas, Barbados, Cuba, the Dominican Republic, Saint Lucia, Trinidad and Tobago, and Venezuela as data are not available.

1. Represents the unweighted average of the 38 OECD member countries. Chile, Colombia, Costa Rica and Mexico are also part of the OECD (38).

2. Represents the unweighted average of the 26 Latin American and Caribbean countries included in this publication, excluding Venezuela due to data availability issues.

Source : OECD et al. (2024[4]), Table 4.1.

StatLink https://stat.link/enrchl

In 2022, the average LAC tax-to-GDP ratio was 0.3 percentage points (p.p.) higher than in 2021 (21.3% of GDP). Changes in tax-to-GDP ratios between 2021 and 2022 varied across the region (Figure 1.2). Twenty countries recorded an increase in their tax-to-GDP ratio while six countries recorded a decline.

The increase in the tax-to-GDP ratio between 2021 and 2022 exceeded 1.0 p.p. in nine countries. Chile, The Bahamas and Ecuador recorded the largest increases, of 1.7p.p., 1.6 p.p. and 1.5 p.p. respectively. Over the same period, tax-to-GDP ratios in three LAC countries decreased by more than 1 p.p.: Guyana (6.3 p.p.), Barbados and Saint Lucia (both 1.4 p.p.). Although tax revenue grew strongly in nominal terms in these latter countries, their tax-to-GDP ratios declined between 2021 and 2022 because this growth was outpaced by the increase in nominal GDP (see Box 1.1).

Figure 1.2. Changes in tax-to-GDP ratios in the LAC region in 2021 and 2022

Year-on-year change, p.p.

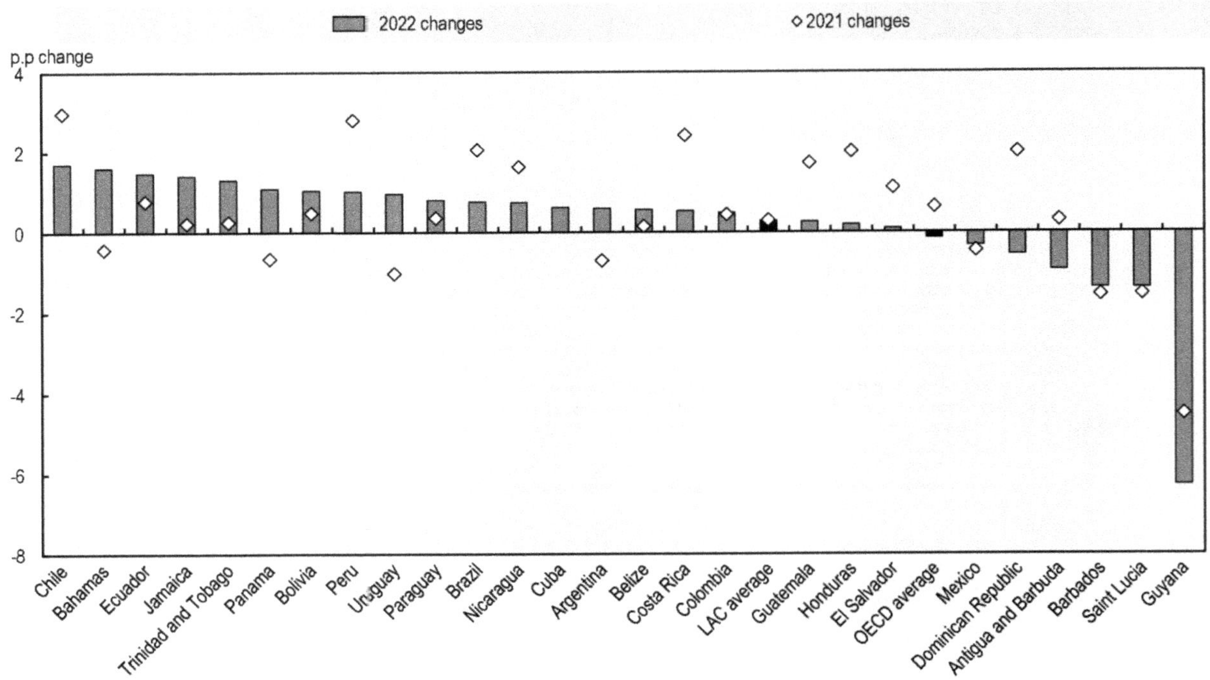

Note: The LAC average represents the unweighted average of 26 LAC countries included in this publication and excludes Venezuela due to data availability issues. The OECD average represents the unweighted average of the 38 OECD member countries. Chile, Colombia, Costa Rica and Mexico are also part of the OECD (38).
Source: Authors' calculations based on OECD et al. (2024[4]), Table 4.1.

StatLink https://stat.link/s5ht0z

Box 1.1. The tax-to-GDP ratio methodology

The tax ratios shown in this publication express aggregate tax revenue as a percentage of GDP. The value of this ratio depends on its denominator (GDP) and its numerator (tax revenue). Both the numerator and the denominator may be subject to historical revision. The tax-to-GDP needs to be treated with caution: nominal tax revenue and nominal GDP may change in the same direction (both increasing or both decreasing), but the tax-to-GDP ratio will go in the opposite direction over the same period if the change in nominal tax revenue is lower than the change in nominal GDP.

In 21 LAC countries, the reporting year coincides with the calendar year. The remaining six countries report on a fiscal year basis:

- The fiscal year in Barbados, Belize and Saint Lucia runs from April to March. This means that reporting year 2022 is Q2/2022-Q1/2023.
- The fiscal year in Trinidad and Tobago covers October to September. The reporting year 2022 spans Q4/2021-Q3/2022.
- The fiscal year for The Bahamas ends on 30 June. The reporting year 2022 runs from Q2/2021-Q2/2022.

The numerator (tax revenues)

This publication uses tax revenue figures that are submitted by focal points or published annually by national Ministries of Finance, tax administrations or statistics offices. Historical data are subject to revisions each year, with more important revisions in more recent years. Past figures may also change from one edition to the next when data are improved (for example, new data is obtained or classification is refined).

The denominator (GDP)

The GDP figures used in this publication are mainly sourced from the *World Economic Outlook* (WEO) published by the IMF. Using these GDP figures maximises consistency across countries, as well as international comparability. GDP figures are also revised and updated to reflect better data sources and improved estimation procedures, or to move towards new internationally agreed guidelines for measuring the value of GDP. The most recent available figures from the WEO were published in October 2023 (IMF, 2023[5]) and include GDP revisions. The GDP figures for the four LAC countries that are also members of the OECD – Chile, Colombia, Costa Rica and Mexico – are based on the OECD Annual National Accounts.

Nominal GDP figures in this edition were revised from those shown in last year's edition for 13 countries. Of these, the GDP of 11 countries was revised upwards (in ascending order Costa Rica, Nicaragua, Paraguay, Colombia, El Salvador, Brazil, The Bahamas, Uruguay, Belize, Panama, and Saint Lucia). Saint Lucia recorded the largest revision, of 11.3%. The resultant difference between the tax-to-GDP ratio for 2021 shown in the 2023 and 2024 editions of this report ranged from -2.0 p.p. in Belize and Saint Lucia to +0.7 p.p. in Costa Rica.

The average tax-to-GDP ratio for the LAC region in 2021 shown in the 2023 edition of *Revenue Statistics in Latin America and the Caribbean* was 21.7%. In this year's edition, it is 0.4 p.p. lower, at 21.3%, primarily because of the GDP revisions mentioned above. The increase in the LAC region's tax-to-GDP ratio between 2020 and 2021 has also been revised downwards, from 0.8 p.p. in the 2023 edition to 0.3 p.p. in this edition. The difference in the average-tax-to-GDP ratio for 2021 between the two editions is also due (to a lesser extent) to the inclusion of Cuba in the LAC average from 2021 in this year's edition. A monetary reform implemented in 2021 significantly altered Cuba's tax structure as well the level and relative weight of its tax and non-tax revenue. Cuba is only included in the LAC average from 2021 onwards because revenue data prior to 2021 is not comparable with data subsequent to the reform. (OECD et al., 2023[6])

Major changes in tax-to-GDP ratios in LAC countries in 2022

In 2022, the LAC region faced a challenging macroeconomic backdrop. Regional growth slowed to 4.0% in real terms from 7.0% in 2021. Inflation rose strongly in 2022 due partly to external factors such as trade disruptions and supply bottlenecks caused by the pandemic and compounded by Russia's invasion of Ukraine, which further affected commodity prices. As elsewhere in the world, governments in the LAC region implemented measures to mitigate the inflationary pressures on households and firms (see Box 1.2) (OECD et al., 2023[1]).

Against this backdrop, tax revenue grew as a percentage of GDP in most countries but these increases tended to be weaker than those observed in 2021. This section examines in greater detail the largest changes in tax-to-GDP ratios in LAC countries in 2022 relative to 2021. Two main factors explain the higher tax-to-GDP ratios in 2022: economic growth and higher prices and production levels in the oil and mineral sector, which led to higher tax revenue from non-renewable natural resources (see Chapter 2 (ECLAC, 2022[7])). However, measures to mitigate inflation resulted in lower revenue from consumption taxes.

- Chile recorded the largest increase in its tax-to-GDP ratio among LAC countries in 2022, at 1.7 p.p. The increase was primarily driven by a rise of 1.9 p.p. in revenue from corporate income tax (CIT) as the economy recovered from the impact of COVID-19.
- The Bahamas experienced the second-largest rise in tax revenue as a percentage of GDP (1.6 p.p.) amid an economic recovery, particularly in the tourism sector. The increase was driven by revenue from value-added tax (VAT), which rose by 1.9 p.p.in 2022 relative to 2021 even though the statutory VAT rate was reduced from 12% to 10% in January 2022 (ECLAC, 2023[8]).
- Ecuador's tax-to-GDP ratio recorded the third-largest increase between 2021 and 2022, of 1.5 p.p. Increases in revenue cut across different tax types: income tax, VAT, and property tax revenues (the latter shown in "other taxes" in Figure 1.3) increased by 0.4 p.p., 0.6 p.p., and 0.5 p.p., respectively. As well as benefiting from a stronger economic performance and high oil prices, Ecuador introduced measures to temporarily tax net wealth from individuals and companies, and it also improved the efficiency of its tax collection (IMF, 2022[9]).
- In Trinidad and Tobago, the tax-to-GDP ratio rose by 1.3 p.p. between 2021 and 2022. CIT revenue rose by 5.5 p.p. over the period due to a surge in oil and natural gas prices. This increase was partly offset by a drop in VAT revenue of 2.9 p.p. in 2022 relative to 2021, partly explained by enhanced VAT refunds (Ministry of Finance Trinidad and Tobago, 2022[10]).

Figure 1.3. Changes in tax-to-GDP ratios in LAC countries by main tax heading, 2022

Year-on-year change, p.p.

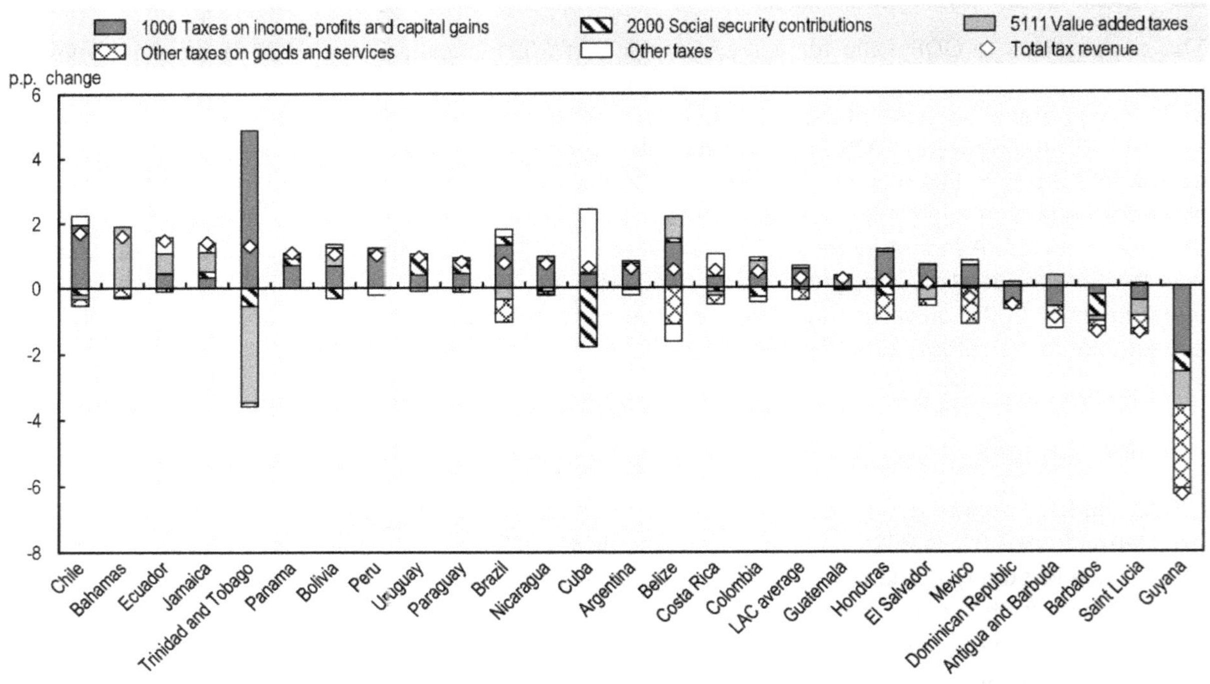

Note: The LAC average represents the unweighted average of 26 LAC countries included in this publication and excludes Venezuela due to data availability issues.
Source: Authors' calculations based on OECD et al. (2024[4]), Chapter 4.

StatLink https://stat.link/suxmp3

Six countries in the LAC region experienced a decline in their tax-to-GDP ratio between 2021 and 2022; in each case, the decrease was the result of nominal tax revenue increasing by less than nominal GDP. The largest declines occurred in four Caribbean countries: Guyana recorded the largest decline (of 6.3

p.p.), followed by Barbados and Saint Lucia (both 1.4 p.p.), and Antigua and Barbuda (0.9 p.p.) (Figure 1.4).

Guyana recorded an increase in nominal GDP of 83% (63% in real terms) between 2021 and 2022 while nominal tax revenue rose by 15% over the same period. GDP growth in Guyana was the highest in the world in 2022, resulting from strong growth in oil production and high oil prices. Several tax reforms contributed to the slower growth in tax revenue, including an increase in the value of personal income tax (PIT) thresholds to benefit lower-income households, the reduction and then removal of excise taxes on gasoline and diesel to mitigate high energy prices, and the calculation of customs duties, excise tax and VAT based on pre-pandemic freight costs for importers facing high shipping prices (ECLAC, 2023[11]).

Figure 1.4. Changes in nominal tax and nominal GDP by sub-regions, 2021-2022

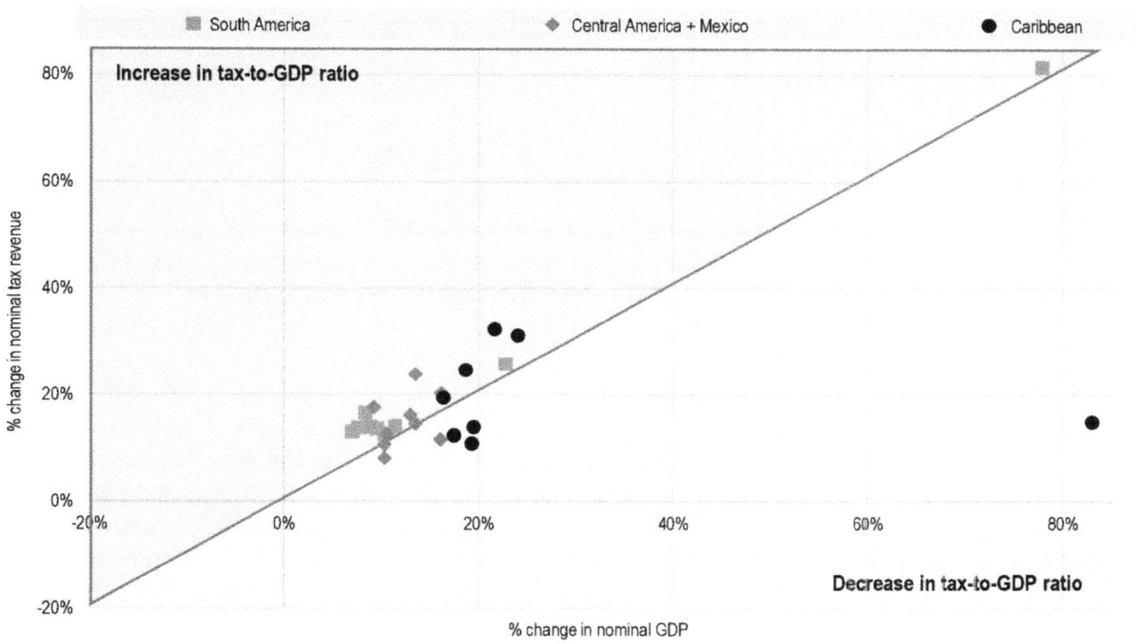

Note: The diagonal line across the graph represents the point at which the change in tax revenues and in GDP were of the same magnitude and therefore the point at which the tax-to-GDP ratio remained unchanged. Countries above the diagonal line had increases in their tax-to-GDP ratios; countries below it had falls.
Source: LAC figures are authors' calculations based on *OECD et al.* (2024[4])

StatLink https://stat.link/o245sz

Changes in tax revenues from different tax types in 2022

Increases in tax revenue across the LAC region in 2022 were driven by CIT, which was supported in a number of countries by high commodity prices. In contrast, revenue from taxes on goods and services contracted in 2022 amid high inflation and rising credit costs that affected households' purchasing power and led to a fall in private consumption. In addition, revenue from taxes and goods and services fell as a result to the adoption of measures to mitigate a surge in energy prices.

CIT revenue increased by 0.6 p.p. on average across the LAC region between 2021 and 2022. High oil and gas prices in 2021 strengthened companies' profits in 2022, especially in oil-producing countries. In contrast, revenue from PIT remained unchanged as a percentage of GDP over the same period despite an increase in wages due to inflation. Revenue from social security contributions (SSCs) decreased by 0.1 p.p. in 2022. (Table 1.1).

Within taxes on goods and services, VAT revenue was unchanged as a percentage of GDP between 2021 and 2022. Over the same period, revenue from other consumption taxes (OCT), which include excises, customs and imports duties, and non-VAT general taxes (such as sales taxes), decreased by 0.3 p.p. Falls in OCT revenue were driven by a decline of 0.4 p.p. in excise revenue, which was mainly due to cuts in fuel taxes by several countries in response to higher prices (see Box 1.2).

Table 1.1. Changes in tax revenues by main tax categories, 2021 and 2022

Year-on-year change, p.p.

	2021	2022
PIT	-0.1	0.0
CIT	0.1	0.6
SSCs	-0.2	-0.1
VAT	0.2	0.0
OCT	0.0	-0.3
Res.	0.1	0.1
Total tax	**0.3**	**0.3**

Note: The LAC averages represent the unweighted average of 26 LAC countries included in this publication and excludes Cuba (up to 2020) and Venezuela due to data issues. In addition, the PIT and CIT averages exclude Ecuador due to data quality issues.
Source: Authors' calculations based on OECD et al. (2024[4])

Tax-to-GDP ratios in LAC sub-regions

This report examines trends in tax revenue across three sub-regions: Central America and Mexico; the Caribbean; and South America. Average tax-to-GDP ratios in Central America and Mexico and South America increased for the second consecutive year in 2022 reaching 19.4% and 23.5% respectively while the Caribbean's tax-to-GDP ratio decreased (also for the second year) to 21.7%. South America and Central America and Mexico recorded an increase of 1.0 p.p. and 0.3 p.p., respectively between 2021 and 2022, while the Caribbean's tax-to-GDP ratio declined by 0.6 p.p. over the period.

Tax revenue and GDP both increased in nominal terms in all three sub-regions in 2022. However, for four of the eight Caribbean countries included in the report, GDP increased by more than tax revenue, leading to lower tax-to-GDP-ratios for these countries and for the Caribbean on average (Figure 1.4). This is particularly the case for Guyana, whose sharp decline in the tax-to-GDP ratio is discussed in the previous section; if Guyana is excluded, the Caribbean's average tax-to-GDP ratio increased by 0.2 p.p. in 2022.

GDP growth in the Caribbean region was particularly strong in 2022, growing by 13.1% in real terms in 2022, driven largely by the tourism sector. Nominal tax revenue in the Caribbean also increased, especially from VAT and taxes from international transactions (ECLAC, 2023[8]). Latin America's GDP grew at a slower rate, at 3.9% in real terms. As shown in Figure 1.4, all Caribbean countries in this publication recorded growth in nominal GDP of 16% or more between 2021 and 2022 while all but four Latin American countries recorded growth below this level.

Box 1.2. The tax policy response to inflation

In 2022, prices on energy and food surged internationally, a tendency exacerbated by Russia's invasion of Ukraine, causing difficulties for firms and households, especially those with low incomes (OECD et al., 2022[2]). In response, governments in the LAC region adopted a wide range of measures, including subsidies and transfers to households and businesses or price support measures, to reduce the impact of higher international prices on consumers. The price support measures included price controls and reductions or exemptions of taxes on goods and services, such as VAT and excises.

According to an IMF survey of 22 LAC countries, half of the measures adopted in the LAC region related to energy products, and most of them related to fuel (Amaglobeli et al., 2023[12]). Temporary reductions in excise taxes on petroleum products were the most frequently introduced measure, followed by decreases in the VAT/GST rate on fuel products, and in import duties to a lesser extent.

Countries that reduced excises on fuel included Belize, Brazil, Guyana, Honduras, Mexico and Peru:

- In Belize, tax cuts on fuel were implemented in April 2022; these reduced the excise tax on diesel and gasoline by 100% and 77% respectively (Government of Belize, 2022[13]).
- Brazil reduced rates of the Contribuição sobre Intervenção do Domínio Econômico (best known as CIDE) levied on imports and retail sale of gasoline, diesel fuel, fuel oil, aviation kerosene, LPG, other petroleum products and ethanol fuel (OECD, 2024[14]).
- Honduras reduced petrol and diesel prices, leading to a decline in revenue from the levy on fuel sales (called the contribution for social programmes and conservation of road assets). In addition, the government reduced taxes on imports of gasoline (by around 30%) and diesel (by around 50%) (ECLAC, 2023[8]; OECD, 2024[14]).
- Mexico introduced a tax credit on fuel excise duties, which fuel importers and producers could use to offset monthly CIT or VAT payments (OECD, 2022[15]).
- Gasoline and diesel, as well as selected goods that make up the basic family basket, were exempted from the excise tax in Peru (OECD, 2024[14]).

Some countries made changes to VAT, including Barbados, Brazil, Costa Rica, Guyana, Honduras and El Salvador:

- Barbados put a cap on VAT on gas and diesel (in US dollars) for six months (OECD, 2022[15]).
- A VAT exemption for electricity purchases intended for distribution was introduced by Costa Rica (OECD, 2022[15]).
- El Salvador temporarily reduced the VAT rate on fuels from April 2022 (OECD, 2022[15]).
- Honduras extended the discount on freight costs when calculating the VAT base on imports up to June 2022 (OECD, 2022[15]).

Figure 1.5 shows changes in excise and VAT revenue between 2021 and 2022. Policies to reduce excises or VAT on fuel products contributed to declines in those tax types. Excise revenue declined as a percentage of GDP in 19 countries; decreases of more than 1.0 p.p. occurred in The Bahamas, Belize, Guyana and Mexico. On average, excise revenue fell by 0.4 p.p. over the period. In contrast, revenue from VAT was unchanged as a percentage of GDP on average between 2021 and 2022 but declined in countries that reduced VAT rates to mitigate inflation; the declines were 0.1 p.p. in Barbados and Costa Rica, 0.3 p.p. in Brazil, 0.4 p.p in El Salvador and 1.0 p.p. in Guyana.

Figure 1.5. Changes in excise and VAT revenue in LAC countries between 2021 and 2022, % of GDP

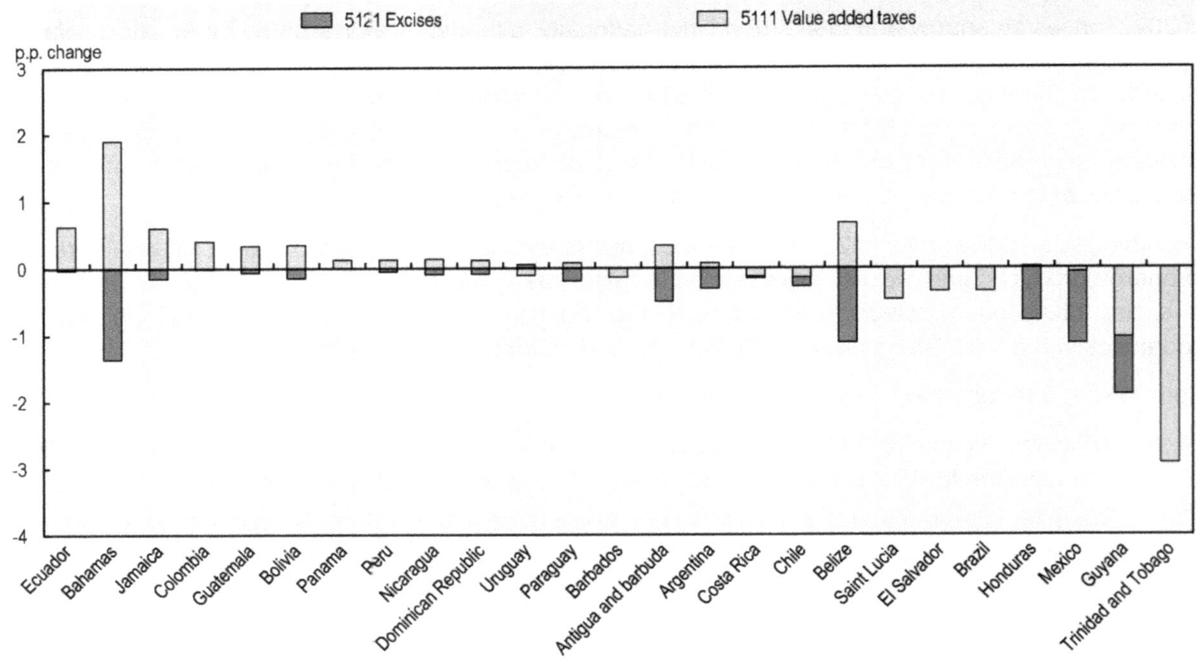

Source: Authors' calculations based on OECD et al. (2024[4]), Chapter 4.

StatLink https://stat.link/spt5wn

Table 1.2 presents annual changes in revenue for the Caribbean, Central America and Mexico, and South America by main tax type in 2022. Revenue from income taxes increased by 0.4 p.p. in the Caribbean, 0.5 p.p. in Central America and Mexico, and by 0.8 p.p. in South America. These increases were driven by CIT in all three cases. OCT revenue declined in all sub-regions. Changes in revenue from VAT, PIT and SSCs varied across the sub-regions; the Caribbean was the only sub-region where revenue from all three categories declined between 2021 and 2022.

- In the Caribbean, the largest decreases in revenue as a share of GDP in 2022 were recorded in OCT (-0.6 p.p.). Revenue from other categories except for CIT decreased to a lesser extent (by -0.2 p.p. for PIT, SSCs and property taxes in the 'residual' category and by -0.1 p.p. for VAT). CIT revenue grew 0.7 p.p., largely due to the increase in Trinidad and Tobago.
- In Central America and Mexico and in South America, the largest increases in revenue as a share of GDP in 2022 were recorded in CIT (0.4 p.p. and 0.7 p.p. respectively). Revenue from PIT increased by 0.1 p.p. in both sub-regions. VAT revenue increased in South America by 0.1% of GDP and was unchanged in Central America and Mexico. In South America, the only revenue category that recorded a decrease was OCT, which declined by 0.1 p.p. This category declined in Central America and Mexico (by 0.3 p.p.) as well, where SSCs also fell (by 0.2 p.p.).

Table 1.2. Changes in tax revenues by category as a share of GDP, LAC and sub-regions, 2022

Year-on-year change, p.p.

	LAC	Caribbean	Central America & Mexico	South America
PIT	0.0	-0.2	0.1	0.1
CIT	0.6	0.7	0.4	0.7
SSC	-0.1	-0.2	-0.2	0.1
VAT	0.0	-0.1	0.0	0.1
OCT	-0.3	-0.6	-0.3	-0.1
Res.	0.1	-0.2	0.3	0.1
Total tax	**0.3**	**-0.6**	**0.3**	**1.0**

Note: The averages exclude Venezuela due to data availability issues. Additionally, the PIT and CIT averages for LAC and the South America sub-region exclude Ecuador due to data quality issues.
Source: Authors' calculations based on OECD et al. (2024[4]).

Long-term trends in tax-to-GDP ratios

Evolution of tax-to-GDP ratios since 1990

Despite the declines in tax-to-GDP ratios caused by the global financial crisis (GFC) in 2009 and by COVID-19 in 2020 (of 0.8 p.p. and 0.7 p.p., respectively), the average tax-to-GDP ratio for the LAC region has increased significantly over the past three decades, rising from 14.6% in 1990 to 21.5% in 2022 (Figure 1.6). This trend contrasts with that of OECD countries, where the average tax-to-GDP ratio has been relatively stable since 1990 (although at a higher level than the LAC average); the OECD tax-to-GDP ratio reached 34.0% in 2022, 3.2 p.p. above its level in 1990. The difference between the LAC and OECD average tax-to-GDP ratio has thus reduced considerably over time, reaching 12.5% of GDP in 2022.

Figure 1.6. Tax-to-GDP ratios, LAC and OECD averages, 1990-2022

Percentage of GDP

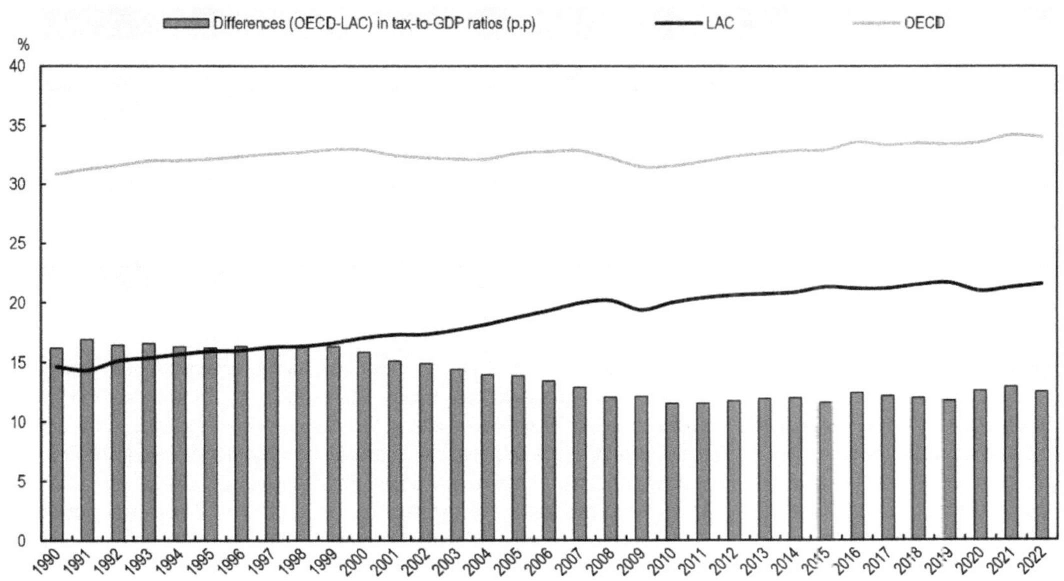

Note: The LAC average represents the unweighted average of 26 LAC countries included in this publication and excludes Cuba (up to 2020) and Venezuela due to data availability issues. The OECD average represents the unweighted average of the 38 OECD member countries. Chile, Colombia, Costa Rica and Mexico are also part of the OECD (38).
Source: Authors' calculations based on OECD et al. (2024[4]), Chapter 4.

StatLink https://stat.link/2tpcm6

Box 1.3. Factors influencing tax levels

Tax-to-GDP ratios are influenced by a range of economic and structural factors. Differences between the LAC and OECD average tax-to-GDP ratios are consistent with the tendency for countries at higher income levels to have higher tax-to-GDP ratios (Figure 1.7). Argentina, Barbados, Brazil and Uruguay show similar tax-to-GDP ratios and levels of income to some OECD countries. Empirical analysis suggests that stronger tax collection, accompanied by stronger institutions, education and skills, and economic diversification, allowed many OECD countries to evade the middle-income trap, in contrast to countries in the LAC region (Melguizo et al., 2017[16]).

The economic and structural factors that influence tax-to-GDP ratios include GDP per capita (a measure of a country's income level), openness to trade, natural resource endowments and the importance of agriculture in the economy. The capacity of tax administrations, levels of corruption and tax morale (the willingness of people to pay taxes) are also strongly linked to the level of tax revenue (OECD, 2014[17]; OECD, 2019[18]).

Figure 1.7. GDP per capita in PPP (USD) and tax-to-GDP ratios for countries in the LAC region, the OECD, and a group of African, Asian and Pacific economies, 2021

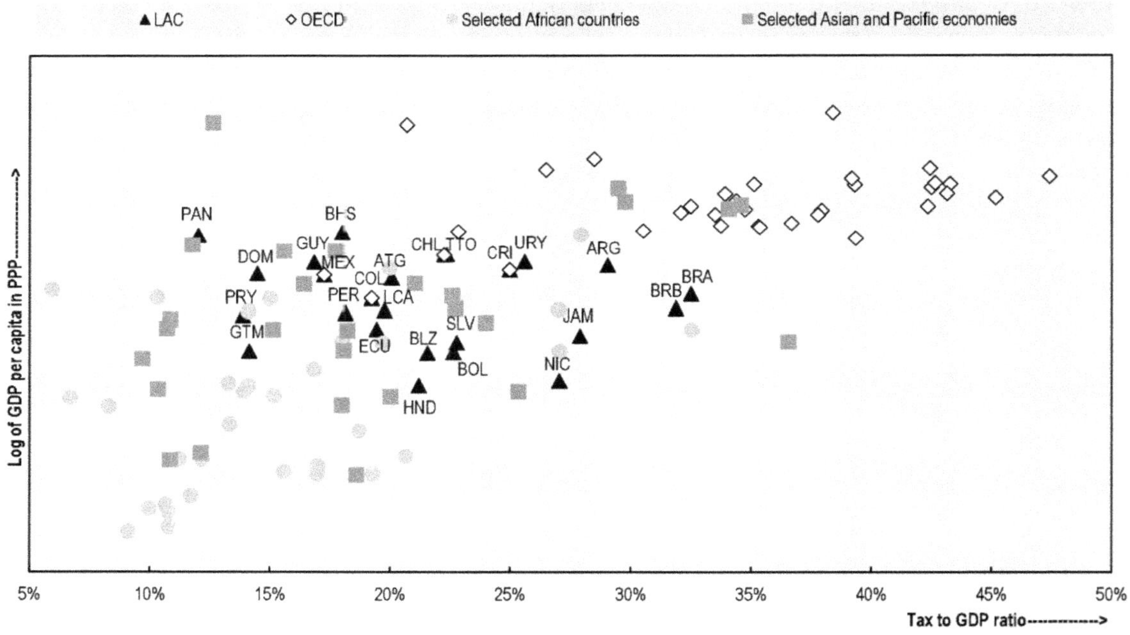

Note: The year of comparison is 2021 as data for tax-to-GDP ratios in 2022 is not available for the selected African, Asian and Pacific economies. Cuba and Venezuela are not included in this figure due to data issues. The purchasing-power-parity (PPP) between two countries is the rate at which the currency of one country needs to be converted into that of a second country to ensure that a given amount of the first country's currency will purchase the same volume of goods and services in the second country as it does in the first. The implied PPP conversion rate is expressed as national currency per current international dollar. An international dollar has the same purchasing power as the US dollar has in the United States. An international dollar is a hypothetical currency that is used as a means of translating and comparing costs from one country to the other using a common reference point, the US dollar (USD).

Source: IMF (2023) for figures of GDP per capita. Tax-to-GDP ratios are sourced from the *Global Revenue Statistics* Database (https://www.oecd.org/tax/tax-policy/global-revenue-statistics-database.htm).

StatLink https://stat.link/hjyfix

The tax-to-GDP ratio also reflects political choices regarding the role and size of the government. For example, the extent of state participation in financing social security is an important factor behind disparate tax ratios in the LAC region. From the 1980s onwards, many LAC countries, such as Chile, El Salvador and Mexico, privatised healthcare and pensions to greater or lesser degrees: these contributions to private institutions are not considered SSCs. In Colombia and Peru, private and public programmes compete, and employees opt between them (OECD et al., 2015[19]; OECD/IDB/The World Bank, 2014[20]). On the other hand, Argentina, Brazil and Uruguay follow a model where public and private systems are complementary. In these countries, substantial reforms were undertaken to extend coverage of social security systems to those previously excluded. This has also been instrumental in the increase of tax revenues (ECLAC, 2014[21]).

Informality is another factor that constrains tax collection in the LAC region by significantly reducing the tax base. Informal employment accounts for close to 60% of workers in Latin America and the Caribbean (OECD, 2020[22]).

The LAC region loses significant amounts of tax revenue to tax evasion and aggressive tax planning. Foregone tax revenue due to non-compliance in the region was estimated at 6.1% of GDP in 2018, mainly in income tax (3.8% of GDP) and VAT (2.3% of GDP) (ECLAC, 2020[23]).

In addition, geographic location and historical factors can influence tax-to-GDP ratios. For example, landlocked countries are less able to impose taxes on goods and services at a port of entry than coastal countries. Socio-demographic determinants, such as the level of education or female participation in the labour force are also important. Finally, international factors, including the tax policies of other countries, can impact tax-to-GDP ratios.

Figure 1.8 shows the evolution of the average tax-to-GDP ratio in the three LAC sub-regions since 1990. While tax levels in all three sub-regions have shown an upward trend during the last three decades, their trajectory shows notable differences:

- On average, South America recorded the strongest growth between 1990 and 2022, of 10.0 p.p. The sub-region recorded a strong increase in its tax-to-GDP ratio during the 1990s. Since 2015, however, South America's tax-to-GDP ratio has declined towards the LAC average, and from 2019 it has followed the LAC average trend. In 2022, South America' tax-to-GDP ratio stood at 23.5%, 2.0 p.p. higher than the LAC average and 1.0 p.p. above its pre-crisis level in 2019.
- The increase in the average tax-to-GDP ratio for Central America and Mexico over the period has followed a similar trend to the LAC average, amounting to 6.4 p.p. Between 1990 and 2022, the average tax-to-GDP ratio of this sub-region remained below the average for the LAC region; in 2022, it stood at 19.4%, 2.2 p.p. lower than the LAC average but 0.9 p.p. higher than its pre-crisis level (18.5% in 2019).
- The average tax-to-GDP ratio of the Caribbean increased by 3.4 p.p. between 1990 and 2022, and it has been consistently higher than the LAC average. After a sharp increase between 2017 and 2019, the Caribbean's tax revenue as a percentage of GDP declined strongly. The Caribbean is the only sub-region that has not recovered to its pre-pandemic level: the average tax-to-GDP ratio stood at 21.7% in 2022, 2.2 p.p. lower than in 2019.

Figure 1.8. Average tax-to-GDP ratios, LAC and sub-regions, 1990-2022

Percentage of GDP

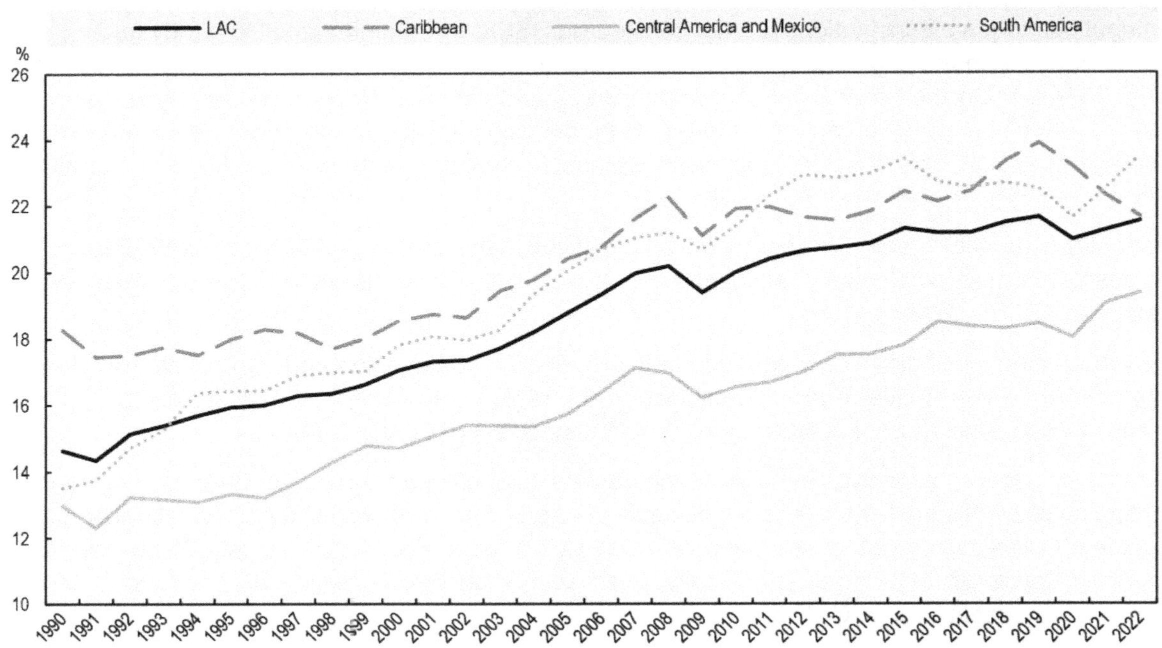

Note: The LAC average represents the unweighted average of 26 LAC countries included in this publication and excludes Cuba (up to 2020) and Venezuela due to data issues. The Caribbean includes eight countries (Antigua and Barbuda, Bahamas, Barbados, Belize, Guyana, Jamaica, Saint Lucia and Trinidad and Tobago), Central America and Mexico nine countries (Costa Rica, Cuba from 2021, Dominican Republic, El Salvador, Guatemala, Honduras, Mexico, Nicaragua and Panama) and South America nine countries (Argentina, Bolivia, Brazil, Chile, Colombia, Ecuador, Paraguay, Peru and Uruguay). The classification of countries into the different sub-regions follows ECLAC's classification and is based on the spoken language of countries. The Caribbean includes the English-speaking countries and Guyana while Central America and Mexico covers Spanish-speaking countries including Dominican Republic.
Source: Authors' calculations based on OECD et al. (2024[4]), Chapter 4.

StatLink https://stat.link/m63oi7

Evolution of revenue by tax type since 1990

Tax-to-GDP ratios in LAC countries increased in the early 1990s after a decade of macroeconomic instability. During the 1980s, many countries ran large fiscal imbalances and some resorted to alternative ways of financing expenditure (borrowing or printing money). This caused rapid inflation across the region, which eroded the value of tax revenue in real terms. Reforms in the 1990s focused on price stability, trade liberalisation and fiscal discipline. Most governments reduced spending and implemented policies to increase tax revenues; budget management and fiscal balances improved considerably. Policy makers implemented reforms to tax policy and administration to reinforce tax systems against inflationary episodes by shortening collection lags and indexing tax liabilities (ECLAC, 2018[24]).

The introduction of VAT has been the most significant tax reform across the LAC region of the past three decades. By the early 1990s, almost all countries were implementing a VAT system and reforms aimed to increase its rate, to widen its base and to improve collections. Several countries have moved towards single-rate VAT schemes (ECLAC, 2018[24]).

Countries in the LAC region have made significant efforts to modernise tax administration over the last two decades. New information technology systems have been implemented, tax collection systems became more efficient, and staff have gained expertise (IDB, 2013[25]). Tax reforms have included the introduction or development of simplified regimes for small taxpayers, the taxation of property based on presumed incomes and the expansion of taxation to labour and capital income, including dividends. Reforms have also included the establishment of minimum taxes, taxes on financial transactions and gradual reductions in the real income level taxed at the top marginal rate (ECLAC, 2013[26]; ECLAC, 2018[24]).

Figure 1.9. Revenue from selected taxes in the LAC region, 1990-2022

Percentage of GDP

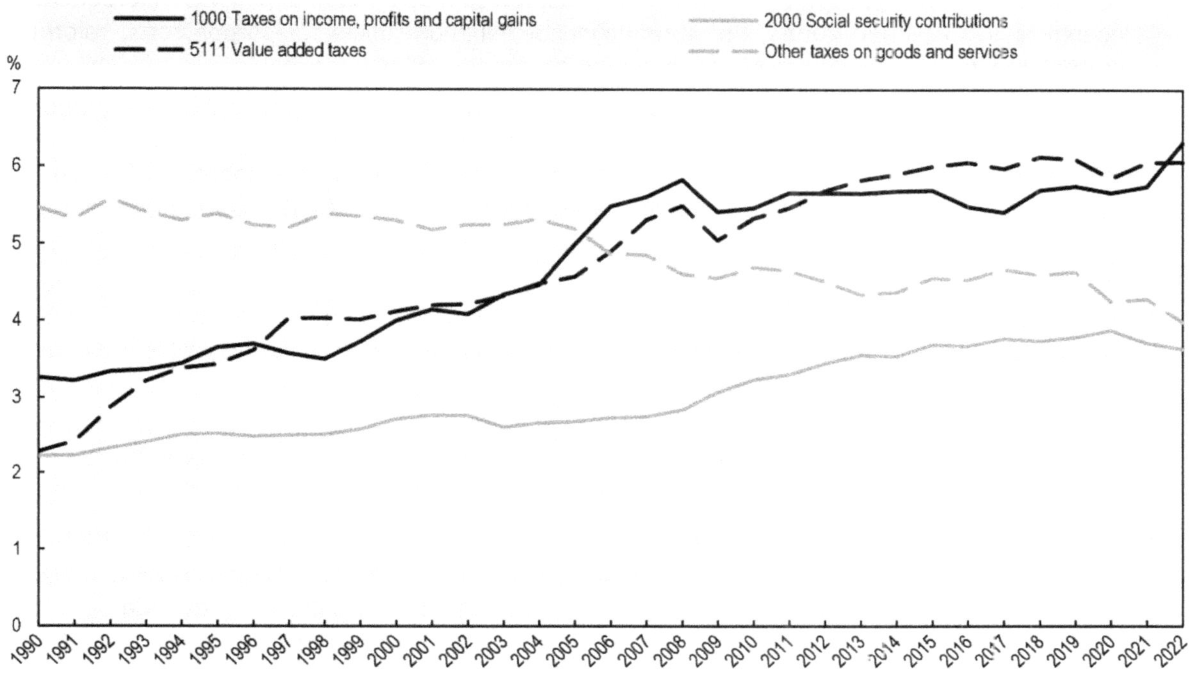

Note: The LAC average represents the unweighted average of 26 LAC countries included in this publication and excludes Cuba (up to 2020) and Venezuela due to data issues.
Source: Authors' calculations based on OECD et al. (2024[4]), Chapter 4.

StatLink https://stat.link/kn1b6p

The increase in the average tax-to-GDP ratio in the LAC region since 1990 has largely been driven by increases in revenue from VAT and from taxes on income and profits (FIT and CIT combined), which increased by 3.8 p.p. and 3.1 p.p. respectively between 1990 and 2022. In 2022, revenue from VAT amounted to 6.1% of GDP while revenue from taxes on income and profits amounted to 6.3% of GDP (Figure 1.9).

Between 1990 and 2022, revenue from OCT decreased as a percentage of GDP in the LAC region. This decline is associated with trade liberalisation, as a result of which LAC countries changed the way they tax imported and exported goods as well as specific goods and services. These changes included a reduction of import tariffs, narrowing the base of products and services subject to excises, and the elimination of taxes on exports. One exception is Argentina, where taxes on exports were re-established in 2002, partly abolished in 2015, then reintroduced in 2018.

Five distinct phases in the evolution of tax revenue in the LAC region can be distinguished:

- Between 1990 and 2002, VAT contributed more to the increase in tax revenue than taxes on income and profits (1.9% of GDP versus 0.8%). Over that period, five countries introduced VAT (Barbados, Belize, El Salvador, Jamaica and Paraguay). Several other countries increased standard VAT rates and undertook reforms to widen the tax base and improve revenue collection.
- Between 2002 and 2008, taxes on income and profits contributed more than VAT to the increase in the average tax-to-GDP ratio (the increases amounted to 1.7% and 1.3% of GDP respectively). The increase in revenue from income taxes was partly explained by the commodity price boom after 2003, which drove up CIT revenue from the natural resource sector (ECLAC, 2014[21]; Barreix, Benítez and Pecho, 2017[27]). In several countries, it was also a result of policies that reduced tax incentives in free-trade zones, the introduction of minimum taxes for corporations, reforms in international taxation and agreements between countries to fight tax evasion.
- Revenue from VAT and income taxes declined during the GFC. During the subsequent recovery, VAT revenue grew faster than income tax revenue on average across the region, exceeding them as a percentage of GDP in 2013. Commodity prices, contributed to a stagnation of income tax revenue between 2011 and 2015 and a decrease between 2015 and 2016. During this period, two more Caribbean countries introduced a VAT (Saint Lucia in 2012 and The Bahamas in 2015).
- Between 2016 and the start of the COVID-19 crisis in 2020, commodity prices recovered and income tax revenues rebounded. Between 2017 and 2018, revenues from income taxes recorded their largest yearly increase since 2011, at 0.3 p.p. on average, due to strong profits in the mining and oil and gas extraction sectors.
- In 2020, all main tax categories except for SSCs declined as a percentage of GDP due to the COVID-19 pandemic before increasing in 2021. In 2022, only CIT increased as a share of GDP relative to 2021 as explained earlier in this chapter.

Figure 1.11 shows the evolution of revenue from PIT, CIT and taxes on income in total since 2005. Over this period, CIT has remained the main share of income tax revenue in the LAC region, at around 60% on average. Although CIT revenue as a percentage of GDP has been more volatile than revenue from PIT, it has been the larger driver of growth in total revenue from income tax over time. Statutory CIT rates are relatively high in the LAC region and tax provisions are less generous than in other countries, resulting in higher effective average and marginal corporate tax rates in the LAC region (see Box 1.4).

Box 1.4. Corporate effective taxes rates in Latin America and the Caribbean

Tax rates on corporate profits in the LAC region are high by international standards and may jeopardise competitiveness and investments. This is a particular concern given the low level of private investment in LAC countries.

The perception that tax burdens on corporate profits are high in the LAC region is based on two factors. First, average CIT collections are relatively high; in 2021; they amounted to 3.4% of GDP versus 3.3% of GDP in OECD countries. Second, statutory CIT rates (STRs) are relatively high: while the average CIT rate is 23.6% in the OECD, it is 24.1% in the LAC region.

However, revenue levels and STRs do not show the whole picture of the tax system's impact on business investments. For instance, STRs do not consider tax provisions that affect the definition of corporate tax bases. These provisions include allowances for fiscal depreciation, deductions for interest payments, and equity financing. Because these provisions can significantly affect tax liabilities, they are key for the correct measurement of effective taxation across tax systems.

To better gauge the tax burdens on companies, (Hanappi et al., 2023[28]) calculated forward-looking effective tax rates (ETRs) for 21 LAC countries. Their methodology is based on the OECD's *Corporate Tax Statistics* (OECD, 2022[29]) and allows comparison across 77 jurisdictions. This methodology does not require information from tax returns since calculations are based on assumptions about the financial returns of hypothetical investment projects, to which existing tax laws are applied to determine the amount of tax owed. Two types of ETR are calculated: (i) the effective average tax rate (EATR), which measures the percentage of profits companies allocate to paying the CIT and (ii) the effective marginal tax rate (EMTR), which measures the extent to which taxes increase the marginal cost of capital (for more detail see (Hanappi et al., 2023[28])).

Results show that LAC countries have high average and marginal effective tax rates. In 2021, the average EATR in the 21 LAC countries was 23.9%, compared to 21.9% in OECD countries and 17.1% in the remaining countries analysed. In the case of the EMTR, the average rate was 13.8% in the LAC region, almost double the average of 7.6% in OECD countries and 7.8% in the remaining countries (Figure 1.10). At the country level, Argentina, Brazil, and Chile have the highest EATR of the 89 jurisdictions analysed. In the case of EMTR, Argentina, Bolivia, Chile, Jamaica and Peru appear in the top ten.

The high ETRs in LAC countries are mainly explained by the high statutory CIT rates. However, they are also due in part to ungenerous tax provisions. The average EATR in LAC countries is only 0.2 p.p. lower than statutory rates on average while in OECD countries it is 1.7 p.p. lower.

An example of ungenerous tax provisions is the treatment of software depreciation in several countries in the LAC region. While research has estimated that the annual economic depreciation rate of software is 40%, the Chilean legislation does not allow software to be depreciated while the depreciation rates in Argentina and Bolivia are very low (2% and 5%, respectively).

Figure 1.10. Statutory tax rates and effective tax rates, 2021

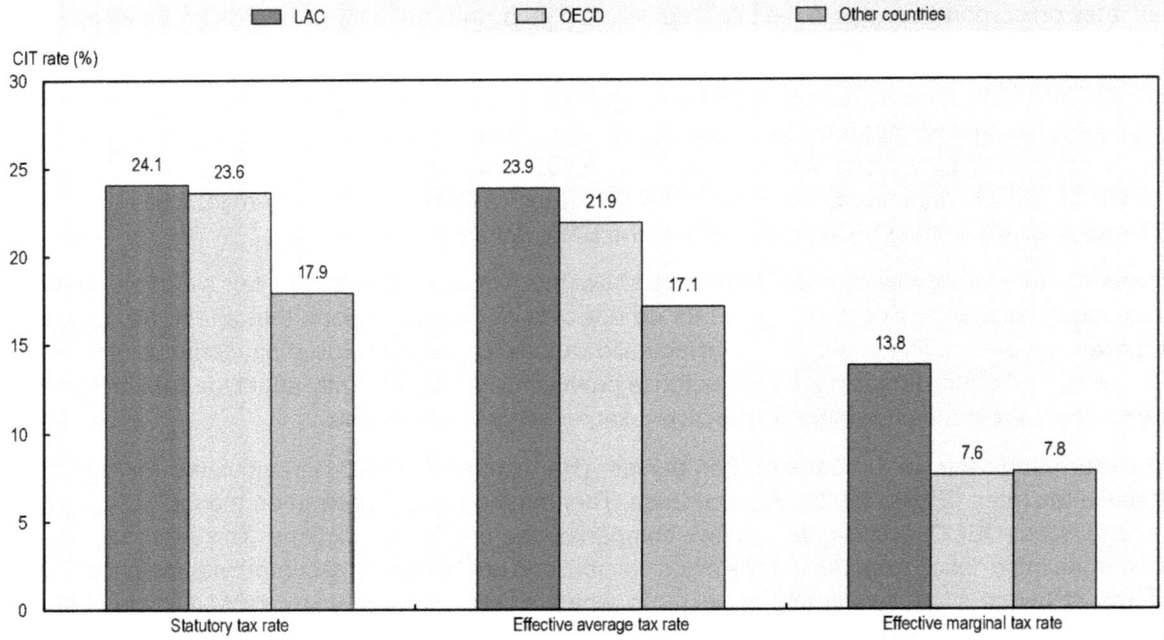

Source: (Hanappi et al., 2023[28])

StatLink https://stat.link/pc7uyl

Meanwhile, PIT revenue has steadily increased on average across the region and was more resilient than CIT revenue during the GFC and the COVID-19 crisis. In 2022, the LAC averages for CIT and PIT revenue stood at 3.9% and 2.0% of GDP, respectively.

There are notable differences between the three LAC sub-regions in the evolution of the main tax categories over the last two decades:

- In the Caribbean, VAT revenue as a percentage of GDP increased greatly on average as seven of the eight Caribbean countries included in this report[2] introduced a VAT system over the period, later than most countries in Central America and Mexico and in South America. VAT was the main driver behind the overall increase in the Caribbean's tax-to-GDP ratio over the period.
- In Central America and Mexico and in South America, taxes on income and profits contributed most to the increase in the overall tax-to-GDP ratio, followed by VAT. Revenue from taxes on income and profits were influenced by increases in mineral and oil prices between 2003 and 2010.

Figure 1.11. Revenue from taxes on income and profits, CIT and PIT in the LAC region, 2005-22

Percentage of GDP

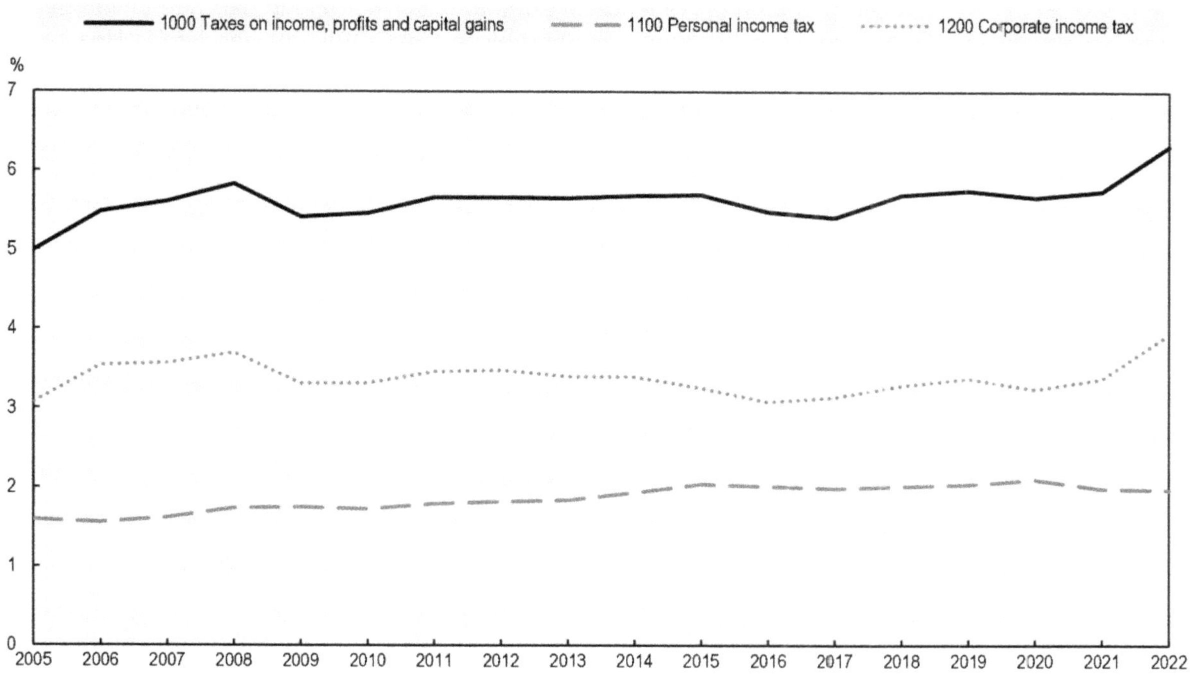

Note: The LAC averages exclude Cuba (up to 2020) and Venezuela due to data issues.; Ecuador is included in the LAC average for total income tax revenues but excluded from the LAC averages for PIT and CIT revenues as a percentage of GDP.
Source: OECD et al. (2024[4]), "Revenue Statistics in Latin America and the Caribbean: Comparative tables", *OECD Tax Statistics* (database), http://dx.doi.org/10.1787/data-00641-en.

StatLink https://stat.link/10wark

Tax structures in the LAC region

The tax structure (defined as the share of major tax types in total tax revenue) depicts the composition of tax revenues by different tax types. It is an important indicator for understanding the economic and social effects of tax systems in the LAC region.

Evolution of tax structures, 1990-2022

Taxes on goods and services generated the largest share of total tax revenue in the LAC region in 2022, representing about half of total taxation on average. During the last three decades, the average LAC mix has shifted towards VAT, taxes on income and profits, and SSCs while OCT have been less prominent.

- The share of VAT in total tax revenue was 28.3% in 2022, corresponding to an increase of 12.1 p.p. since 1990. The revenue share of other taxes on goods and services (including excises, customs and import duties) declined by 22.1 p.p. over the same period.
- The share of revenue from taxes on incomes and profits grew by 9.4 p.p. (from 20.3% to 29.8% of total tax revenues) between 1990 and 2022.
- The share of SSCs in total tax revenue increased by 2.7 p.p. from 1990 to 16.7% in 2022. Two (opposing) factors have influenced the trajectory of SSCs. While rising personal incomes have led

to higher collections, this was counter-balanced by the full or partial privatisation of social security that occurred in many countries, principally between the mid-1990s and 2010 (OECD et al., 2015[19]).

The share of PIT grew from 8.0% of total tax revenue in 2005 to 9.2% in 2022, in part due to increases in personal incomes across the region in the two decades before the COVID-19 pandemic. However, in comparison to OECD countries, the average share of PIT revenue remains low in LAC countries despite some countries implementing reforms to expand the tax base. After the GFC, several countries established flat rates on capital income that had previously been exempt and implemented progressive rates on labour income (ECLAC, 2014[21]). There are relatively few PIT payers in the LAC region, largely due to high levels of informality and the concentration of income earners at low-income levels: in 2013, only 10% of the population in Latin America were registered taxpayers (IDB, 2013[25]).

Figure 1.12. Average tax structure in the LAC region, 2005-22

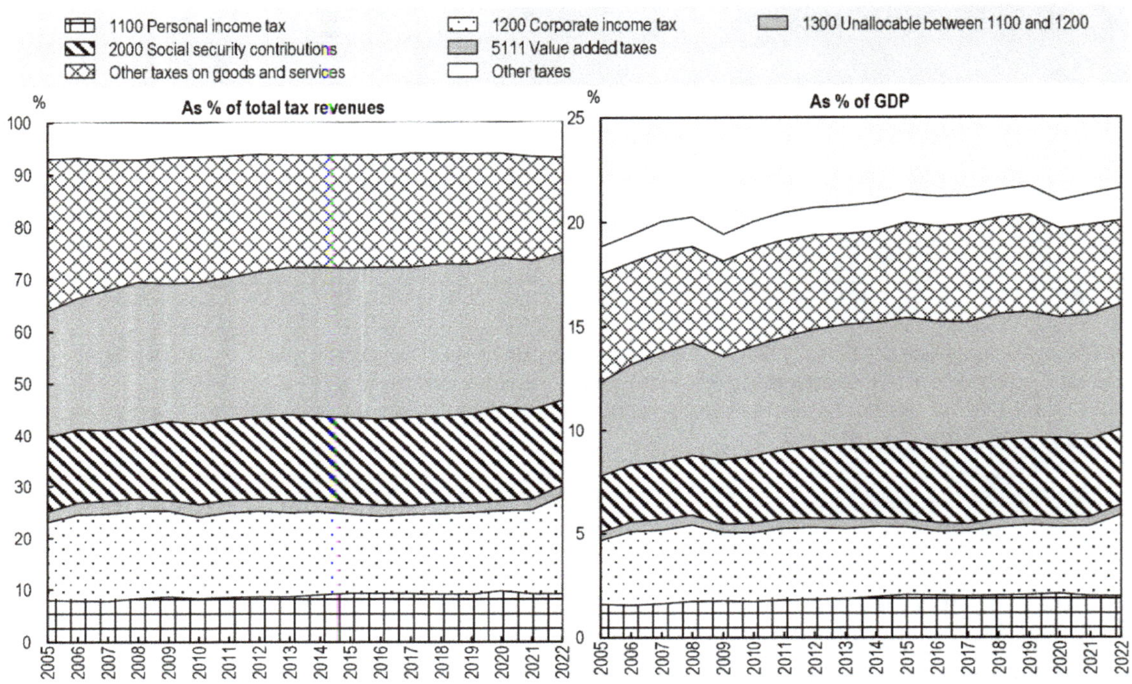

Note: The LAC average excludes Cuba (up to 2020) and Venezuela due to data issues. Ecuador is excluded from the LAC average for PIT and CIT revenues due to data quality issues.
Source: Authors' calculations based on OECD et al. (2024[4]), "Revenue Statistics in Latin America: Comparative tables", *OECD Tax Statistics* (database), http://dx.doi.org/10.1787/data-00641-en.

StatLink https://stat.link/3zje9y

Several other factors continue to limit PIT revenue, including a small tax base that is comprised primarily of wages (since tax privileges are often granted to returns on capital), high tax reliefs (such as personal deductions and income exemptions), high tax allowances, and high levels of evasion (Barreix, Benítez and Pecho, 2017[27]; ECLAC, 2014[21]; ECLAC, 2023[8]). (ECLAC, 2020[23]) finds that the evasion rates for PIT are high in selected LAC countries that conducted tax evasion studies, ranging from 18.7% in Mexico (2016 figure, equivalent to revenue losses of 0.8% of GDP) to 69.9% in Guatemala (2006 figure, equivalent to revenue losses of 0.5% of GDP). Evasion is more common among the self-employed than employees. A study for Mexico concluded that tax revenue losses as a percentage of GDP are nearly five times higher for individuals with business activities and almost seven times higher for persons with rental income than for wage earners. Similarly, in Costa Rica, the evasion rate for wage-earners and pensioners was only 3.5% in 2018, while the non-compliance rate for profit-making activities was 82.7% in 2018 and has been trending upward since 2015 (ECLAC, 2023[8])

The redistributive impact of PIT in Latin America is weak, achieving a reduction of just 2% in income inequality, which contrasts markedly with the countries of the European Union, where income taxes reduce inequality by 12% in 2014. The reduction in the Gini coefficient attributable to PIT in the LAC region ranged from 0.3% (Paraguay) to 5.9% (Mexico) in 2014 (OECD et al., 2018[30]). Many LAC countries often implement tax deferrals, reduced rates and exemptions, which typically have less redistributive impact than targeted tax reliefs. Deferrals postpone the deadline for filing and paying taxes but do not adjust tax calculations based on household income. PIT exemptions, on the other hand, might reduce revenue and decrease redistributive effectiveness. However, it is important to consider the region's heterogeneity, as removing many of these tax privileges or lowering their thresholds may enhance redistributive effectiveness at the expense of exacerbating distortions in allocative efficiency, which may influence taxpayers' decisions and behaviour (ECLAC, 2023[8])..

Enhancing the design of PIT has the potential to increase the progressivity of tax systems in the LAC region and to generate higher revenue. More progressive tax regimes in the region require more efficient tax administrations. It is essential that the design of PIT in each country, as well as potential reforms to enhance its effectiveness, achieves a balance between the principles of administrative simplicity, distributive equity and revenue sufficiency (ECLAC, 2023[8])..

The share of CIT in total tax revenue increased by 3.6 p.p. between 2005 and 2022, reaching 18.8%, mainly due to the significant increase in CIT revenue and decrease of OCT revenue between 2021 and 2022. CIT evasion is also a significant issue in the LAC region, with higher evasion rates than for PIT. ECLAC (2020[23]) states that "evasion rates for CIT range from 19.9% in Mexico to almost 80% in Guatemala". Revenue losses attributed to tax evasion are estimated to exceed 4% of GDP in the Dominican Republic, Guatemala, Peru and Panama.

For all three regions, the most significant share of revenue was derived from VAT. South America had the highest share of VAT revenue in 2022, at 30.8% on average. SSCs were lowest in the Caribbean in 2022, at 11.8% of total tax revenue on average. This was slightly less than half of the average for the other sub-regions (18.9% and 18.5% respectively in Central America and Mexico, and in South America). All three sub-regions generated higher revenue from CIT than from PIT.

Average tax structures in LAC and the OECD

Relative to the average for OECD countries, the average tax mix for the LAC region is characterised by low revenue from PIT and SSCs (Figure 1.13). LAC countries rely more on taxes on goods and services, which make up half of tax revenue on average, compared with around one-third in OECD economies on average. As a percentage of GDP, revenue from taxes on goods and services in the LAC region and in the OECD were similar in 2021, at 10.3% and 10.7% respectively.[3]

By contrast, the combined share of taxes on income and profits and SSCs as percentage of total tax revenue was much lower in the LAC region than in the OECD in 2021 (45.0% versus 60.7%, on average). As a percentage of GDP, these two categories amounted to 9.5% in the LAC region, less than half the OECD average (21.0%). The tendency towards private provision of social security in many LAC countries explains some of this difference.

On average, CIT generated 16.3% of total tax revenue in the LAC region, compared with 10.2% in the OECD (respectively 3.4% and 3.3% of GDP). The most striking difference relates to revenue from PIT, which contributed 23.7% of total tax revenues in the OECD on average in 2021 versus 9.2% of total tax revenue in the LAC region. PIT revenue amounted to 2.0% of GDP in the LAC region on average, compared with 8.3% for the OECD.

Figure 1.13. Average tax structure in the LAC and the OECD, 2021

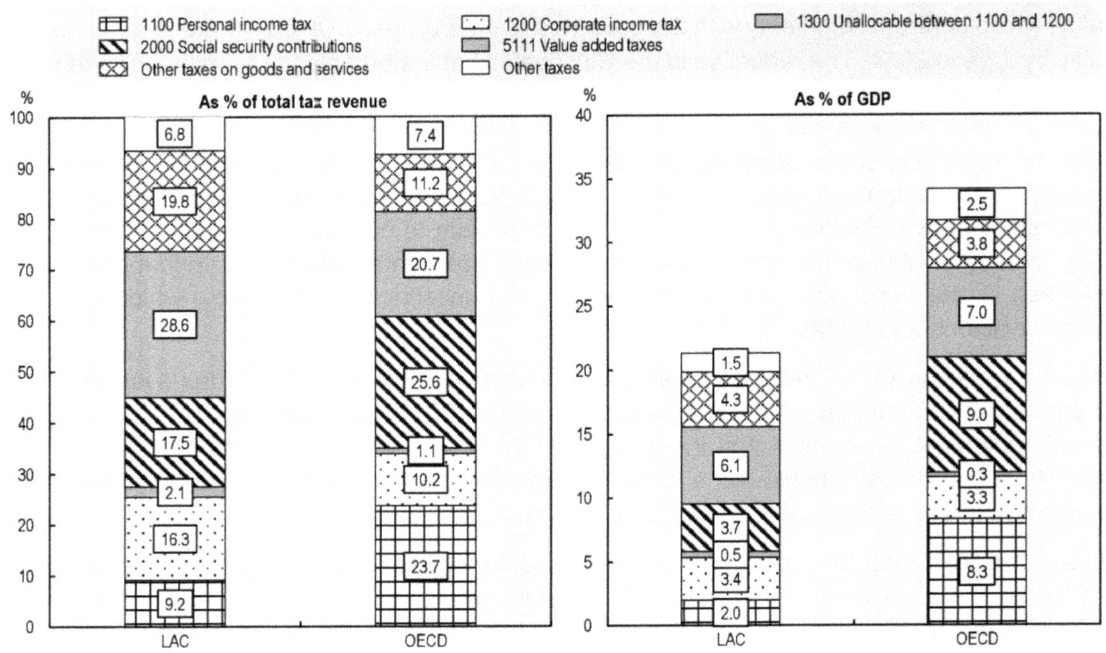

Note: The year of comparison is 2021 as the 2022 tax structure for the OECD average is not available. The LAC average excludes Venezuela due to data issues. Ecuador is excluded from the LAC average for PIT and CIT revenues due to data quality issues. The OECD average represents the unweighted average of the 38 OECD member countries. Chile, Colombia, Costa Rica and Mexico are also part of the OECD (38).

Source: Authors' calculations based on OECD et al. (2024[4]), "Revenue Statistics in Latin America: Comparative tables", *OECD Tax Statistics* (database), http://dx.doi.org/10.1787/data-00641-en.

StatLink https://stat.link/nxvr58

Taxes on immovable property and payroll (contained within the category "other taxes") are a less important source of revenue for the LAC region on average than in the OECD, although there are challenges with data availability for property taxes.

Tax structures in LAC countries

Taxes on goods and services were the main source of revenue for all LAC countries except Costa Rica, Cuba, Guyana, Mexico, Panama, and Trinidad and Tobago in 2022 (Figure 1.14). For Cuba, Guyana, Mexico and Trinidad and Tobago, taxes on income and profits accounted for the largest share, whereas SSCs were the most important source of tax revenue for Costa Rica and Panama.

In most of the countries where taxes on goods and services were the main source of revenue, VAT contributed a larger share than OCT. Seventeen countries recorded higher tax revenue from VAT, ranging from 21.0% of total tax revenue in Brazil to 46.8% in The Bahamas. In contrast, three countries (including two in the Caribbean) received a larger share of revenue from taxes on goods and services other than VAT. This group includes Argentina, which sourced 28.7% of total tax revenue from taxes on goods and services other than VAT: export taxes represented just under a quarter of this category and were equivalent to 2.1% of GDP, compared with less than 0.1% of GDP on average in the region.

Figure 1.14. Tax structures in LAC countries, 2022

Percentage of total tax revenue

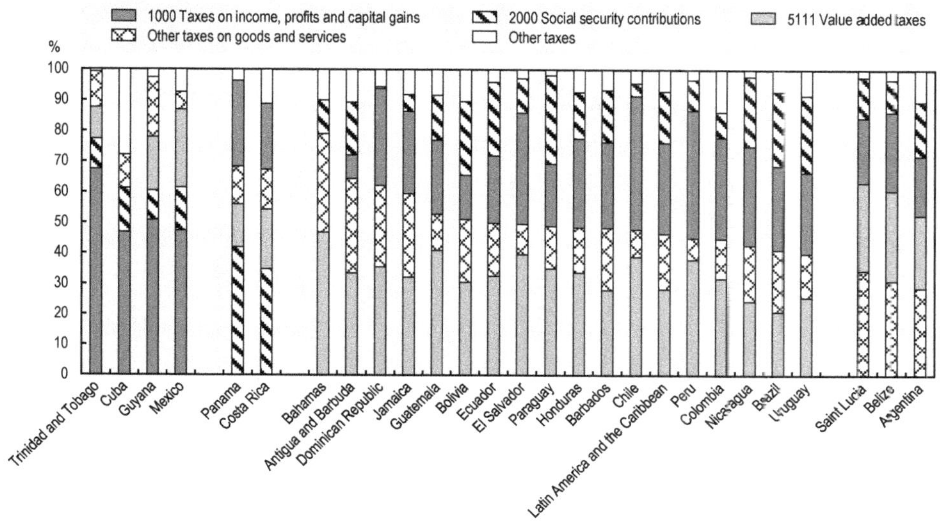

Note: Countries are grouped by the main share of tax revenues among 1000 taxes on income and profits, 2000 social security contributions, 5111 value added taxes and other taxes on goods and services. The Bahamas does not tax income. There is no VAT system in Cuba. The LAC average represents the unweighted average of 26 LAC countries included in this publication and excludes Venezuela due to data availability issues.
Source: Authors' calculations based on OECD et al. (2024[4]), Chapter 4.

StatLink https://stat.link/vbmfl5

In 2022, SSCs ranged from 0.6% of total tax revenue in the Dominican Republic to 42.0% in Panama. The level of this revenue reflects choices about how to finance social security (see Box 1.3): in countries with public or mixed social security schemes (including Argentina, Bolivia, Brazil, Costa Rica, Panama, Paraguay and Uruguay), SSCs accounted for over 17% of total tax revenue.

VAT revenue ratio

This section discusses the VAT revenue ratio (VRR) in LAC countries in 2022. The VRR "measures the difference between the VAT revenue collected and what would theoretically be raised if VAT was applied at the standard rate to the entire potential tax base in a "pure" VAT regime and all revenue was collected" (OECD, 2022[31]). The VRR is the ratio of the actual VAT revenues to the product of final consumption (net of VAT revenues) and the standard VAT rate. The calculation is shown below.

$$\frac{\text{VAT revenues}}{(\text{final consumption expenditure} - \text{VAT revenues}).\text{standard VAT rate}}$$

This indicator provides a sense of VAT revenue loss related to exemptions and reduced rates, fraud, evasion and tax planning as well as weaknesses in tax administrations. However, this indicator needs to be interpreted with reference to the underlying characteristics of the VAT system in each country, as a higher VRR could result from cascading effects (for example when exemption occurs early in the supply chain) or from a failure to refund VAT input credits. Other factors may also influence the ratio upwards or downwards, for example when the place of taxation rules for international trade diverge from the destination principle or when the tax on inbound digital supplies is not collected. It is also important to note that the interpretation of the VRR is also more difficult for countries relying significantly on tourism. These countries may record a high VRR due to methodological reasons: purchases by non-residents may not be included in final consumption expenditure (the denominator) whereas the VAT on these purchases is included in the overall VAT revenues (the numerator) (Keen, 2013[32]).

Table 1.3. VRR and VAT rates in LAC countries by sub-region, 2022

	VRR	VAT rate (%)
Central America and Mexico	**0.49**	**13.6**
Costa Rica	0.50	13.0
Dominican Republic	0.38	18.0
El Salvador	0.73	13.0
Guatemala	0.52	12.0
Honduras	0.52	15.0
Mexico	0.33	16.0
Nicaragua	0.52	15.0
Panama	0.41	7.0
South America	**0.60**	**16.8**
Argentina	0.47	21.0
Bolivia	0.70	13.0
Chile	0.71	19.0
Colombia	0.42	19.0
Ecuador	0.81	12.0
Paraguay	0.69	10.0
Peru	0.58	18.0
Uruguay	0.45	22.0
Caribbean	**0.64**	**13.6**
Antigua and Barbuda	0.71	15.0
Bahamas	1.26	10.0
Barbados	0.62	17.5
Belize	0.71	12.5
Guyana	0.22	14.0
Jamaica	0.73	15.0
Saint Lucia	0.59	12.5
Trinidad and Tobago	0.27	12.5
LAC average	**0.58**	**14.7**
OECD average (2020)	**0.56**	**19.1**

Note: Brazil, Cuba and Venezuela are excluded. Brazil operates a multiple-rate system with tax levied at different rates for each sub-national level. Cuba did not operate a VAT system in 2022. Venezuela's tax revenue data are not available.
Source: VAT rates are sourced from (OECD, 2022[31]), the final expenditure consumption figures from the WEO (IMF, 2023[5]) and VAT revenues from the country tables in OECD et al. (2024[4]), Chapter 5, (OECD, 2022[31]), for the OECD figures.

Table 1.3 presents the VRR for LAC countries and for the three sub-regions. The highest VRR is seen in The Bahamas and stands well above 1. This is a notable example of the impact of the methodology on the interpretation of the VRR as explained above. The high VRR in The Bahamas is due to the nominator being artificially high while the denominator does not correspond to the actual tax base. This is partly explained by the high share of revenue that the country receives from tourism driving up the VRR as tourism receipts are not accounted for in the final consumption expenditure in the denominator. Despite this caveat, it is important to note that The Bahamas introduced a VAT in 2015 following international good practice, including a broad-based VAT with a low standard rate (at 7.5%, increased to 12.0% in 2018), a limited number of exemptions and no reduced rates. These also contribute to the country's high VRR.

By contrast, the lowest VRRs were seen in Guyana and Trinidad and Tobago in the Caribbean and in the Dominican Republic and Mexico in Central America. Several factors contribute to the low VRR in Mexico, including the scope of VAT exemptions, the application of a domestic zero rate to numerous goods and services, as well as low compliance (OECD, 2022[31]); (OECD, 2018[33]). However, Mexico implemented a VAT reform in January 2014 including the replacement of some reduced and zero rates with the standard rate and the introduction of improved processes. The VRR in Mexico increased from 0.26 in 2013 to 0.29 in 2014. The VRR increased to 0.35 in 2020 as a result of the broadening of the VAT base for digital services in line with OECD recommendations (KPMG, 2019[34]), effective from June 2020.

Several factors may contribute to the low VRR in the Dominican Republic. The design of VAT in the country is one factor: the Dominican Republic has numerous VAT exemptions (Schlotterbeck, 2017[35]). Tax-exempt goods include educational materials, medicines, health services, financial services, utilities, renewable energy equipment and inland transportation services, while exempted services include education, cultural services and electricity (OECD, 2022[36]). VAT evasion is another important factor for the low VRR. ECLAC (2020[23]) calculates that VAT evasion in the Dominican Republic is among the highest in the LAC region at 43.8% (2017 figure), against an average of 30% in a sample of 12 countries.

VAT evasion remains an important challenge elsewhere in the LAC region. ECLAC (2020[23]) examined various studies on VAT evasion in 12 countries and observed that VAT non-compliance rates in the region ranged from 14.8% in Uruguay to 45.3% in Panama in 2016. Guatemala, the Dominican Republic and Panama recorded the largest increases (by 30% of more) in their VAT evasion rate since 2009.

Environmentally related tax revenues

Through the Paris Agreement of 2016, countries have committed to decarbonise their economies by the middle of the 21st Century, implying a shift away from fossil fuels as a source of energy. To reduce emissions and drive decarbonisation, an increasing number of countries are deploying environmentally related taxes and price-based policy instruments. By incorporating a price signal into consumer decisions, environmental taxation gives effect to the polluter-pays principle to favour greener over more polluting economic activities. Well-designed systems of environmental taxation can encourage businesses and households to consider the environmental costs of their behaviour.

An environmentally related tax is a tax whose base is a physical unit (or a proxy of a physical unit) of something that has a proven, specific negative impact on the environment regardless of whether the tax is intended to change behaviours or is levied for another purpose (OECD, 2005[37]).

Countries in the LAC region have generally been slow to implement environmentally related taxes. Although they have introduced fuel taxes (mainly for revenue collection rather than environmental purposes), many countries also provide subsidies for energy products (Lorenzo, 2016[38]) despite the strain these can put on national budgets to mitigate the impact of high and volatile fuel prices, control inflation, boost competitiveness and protect the poorest sections of the population. While energy support decreased between 2012 and 2019 by around 30%, it more than doubled in 2021 (OECD, 2023[39]).

However, revenue from energy taxes was greater than the cost of subsidies for five of the six LAC countries included in (OECD, 2021[40]) (Costa Rica, Dominican Republic, Guatemala, Jamaica and Uruguay, with the exception being Ecuador), representing on average a net positive impact on public finances in these six countries (roughly 0.6% of GDP in 2018 on average).

Beyond taxes on fuel and the registration or use of vehicles, environmental taxes are still underdeveloped across the LAC region. However, a few LAC countries have introduced green tax reforms in recent years. Argentina, Chile, Colombia, Mexico and Uruguay introduced carbon pricing policies through carbon taxes, primarily in the transport sector, although these remain limited and the effective carbon rates are not at a level that can reduce carbon emissions effectively (OECD, 2023[39]).

A detailed examination of country-specific taxes[4] reveals that environmentally related tax revenue (ERTR) in the LAC region in 2022 ranged from 0.1% of GDP in Belize to 1.7% in Dominican Republic (Figure 1.15). On average across 23 LAC countries in this report, ERTR amounted to 0.8%[5] of GDP in 2022, below the OECD average of 1.9% of GDP (estimated 2022 figure) (OECD, 2022[41]).

Figure 1.15. Environmentally related tax revenue in LAC countries by main tax base, 2022

Percentage of GDP

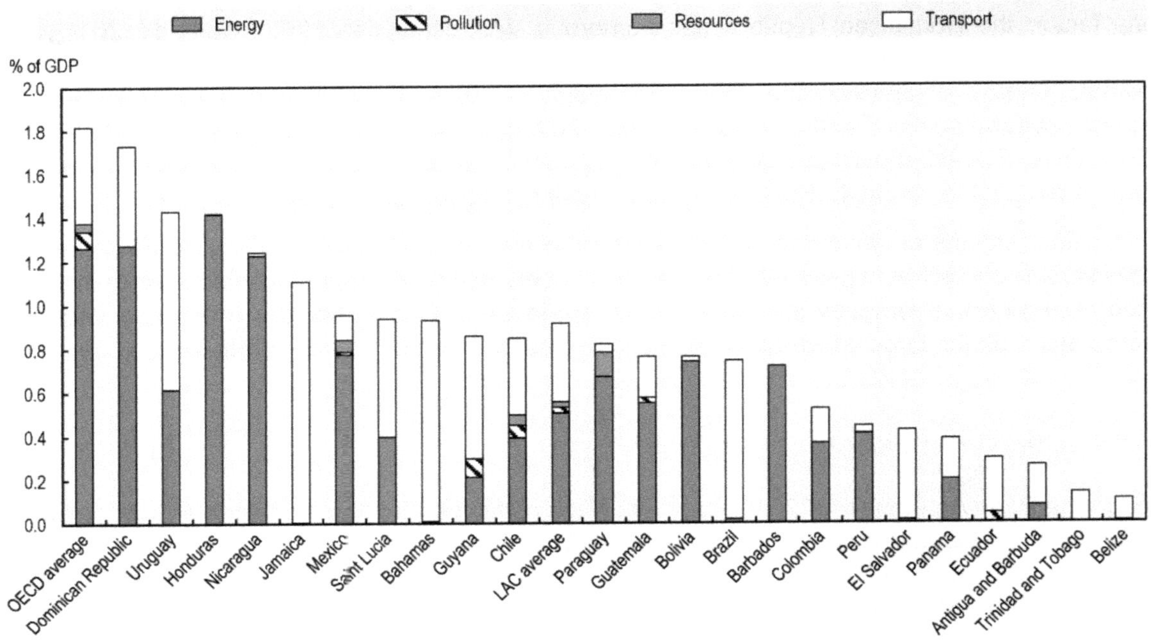

Note: The LAC average represents the unweighted average of 23 LAC countries included in this publication and excludes Argentina, Costa Rica, Cuba and Venezuela due to data issues. The figure does not include Jamaica's revenues from the special consumption tax on petroleum products (estimated to be more than 2.0% of GDP in 2018) (OECD, 2021[40]) as the data are not available. The OECD average represents the unweighted average of 37 OECD member countries excluding Costa Rica.

Source: *PINE* database for Chile, Colombia and Mexico, and author's calculations for other countries based on OECD et al. (2024[4]), Chapter 5.

StatLink https://stat.link/kpcjyq

In 2022, revenue from energy taxes (most commonly excises on diesel and petrol) generated the highest share of total ERTR in the LAC region. Revenue from energy taxes amounted to 0.5% of GDP on average, while revenue from motor vehicle and transport services amounted to 0.4% of GDP and represented most of the remainder. Revenue from tax levied on other environmentally related bases was negligible (i.e. < 1.5% of the total ERTR). ERTR was higher in the OECD than in the LAC region in 2022 across the different bases, notably for energy-related taxes that amounted to 1.3% of GDP (OECD, 2022[41]).

There were notable differences in the composition of ERTR across the LAC sub-regions in 2022, on average (Figure 1.16). Energy-related taxes accounted for the highest share of ERTR in Central America and Mexico (0.8% of GDP out of a total of 1.1%); energy- and transport-related taxes were similar in South America at 0.4% and 0.3% of GDP respectively in 2022, and transport-related taxes represented the highest share of ERTR in the Caribbean region at around 0.5% of GDP. Transport-related tax revenue for most Caribbean countries was mainly sourced from travel or departure taxes, an important source of revenue for tourism-reliant countries.

Between 2021 and 2022, average ERTRs in the LAC region declined by 0.1 p.p. due to a fall in energy-related tax revenue. This was also the case for all three sub-regions as well as for the OECD, which recorded a 0.2% average decline over the same period. The fall in energy-related tax revenue across the LAC region and sub-regions was associated with lower demand and energy tax reductions and suspensions (e.g. VAT or excise tax rate reduction or suspension) as an important component of support measures aiming to reduce the effective prices consumers pay. (see Box 1.3).

In most LAC countries, ERTR declined as a share of GDP (14 countries) or remained at the same level (8 countries) in 2022. Only three out of the 23 LAC countries with available data recorded increases in their ERTR. The changes in ERTR over the period ranged from a decrease of 1.8% of GDP in Guyana to an increase of 0.5% in The Bahamas.

Figure 1.16. Environmentally related tax revenue in the OECD, LAC and sub-regional averages by main tax base, 2022

Percentage of GDP

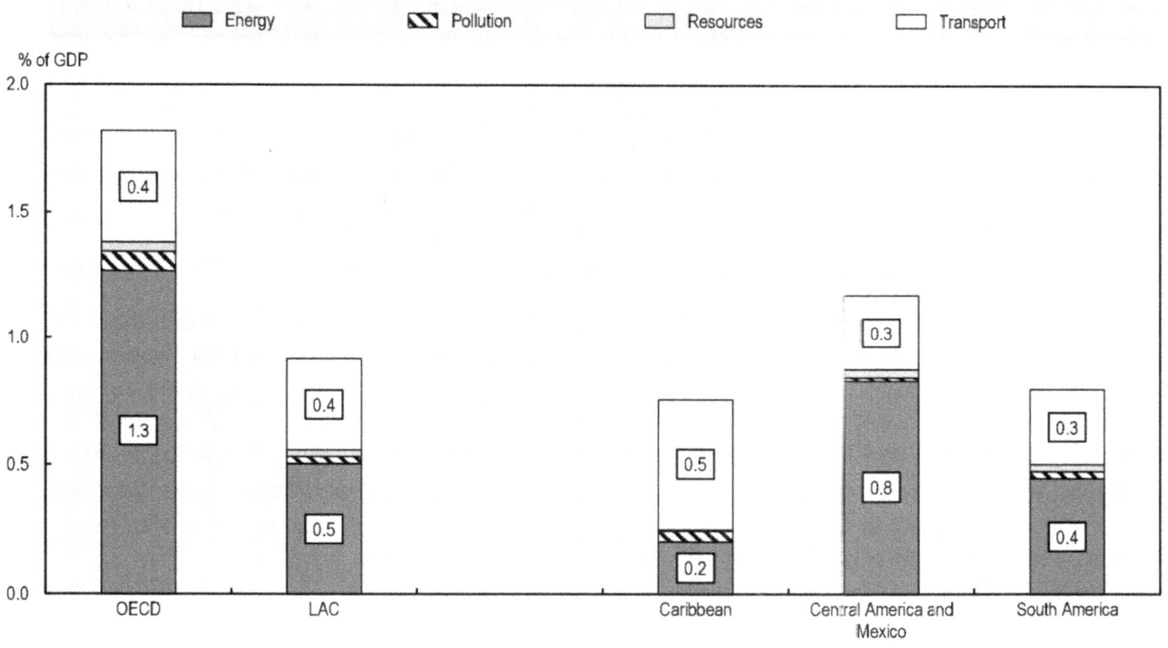

Note: The LAC average represents the unweighted average of 23 LAC countries included in this publication and excludes Argentina, Costa Rica, Cuba and Venezuela due to data issues. The OECD average represents the unweighted average of 37 OECD member countries excluding Costa Rica. As well as being part of the LAC region, Chile, Colombia and Mexico are also member countries of the OECD and thus are incorporated in both averages.
Source: *PINE* database for Chile, Colombia and Mexico, and authors' calculations for other countries based on OECD et al. (2024[4]), Chapter 5.

StatLink https://stat.link/0u3pm2

Taxes by level of government

In LAC countries, tax revenue is collected predominantly by central or federal entities. Sub-national public spending is financed through transfers from upper to lower levels of government to a greater extent than in OECD countries. Countries covered in this report exhibit varied structural configurations: Argentina, Brazil, Mexico and Venezuela have federal systems whereas the others are unitary states.

Where sub-national data for LAC countries is available, tax revenue collected by central government accounted for more than two-thirds of the total collections, whereas the corresponding figure for OECD countries was about 60% (2021 figure). Brazil is a notable exception: central government tax revenue amounted to 46.2% of tax collected in 2022 (Table 1.4).

There are two statistical issues to consider when comparing the attribution of revenue for LAC countries with that of OECD members. First, revenue of both groups have been attributed to different levels of government according to guidelines set out in the 2008 System of National Accounts (SNA).[6] The second issue is that some LAC countries lack tax revenue statistics at sub-national level.

For the 19 LAC countries in this report for which sub-national data is available, the share of sub-national tax revenue in total tax revenue was below 7.0% in 2022 except in Argentina, Brazil and Colombia. Federal systems tend to raise more substantial own revenue compared to unitary states. In Brazil, states and municipalities collect about a third of total tax revenue, indicating a significant degree of decentralisation of tax collection. A large part of the VAT (ICMS – *imposto sobre operações relativas à circulação de mercadorias e prestação de serviços de transporte interestadual e intermunicipal e de comunicação*) is collected at the state level.

Sub-national tax revenue in Argentina and Colombia accounts for more than 16% of total tax revenue. Argentina has a significant collection at state level, due in part to the provincial sales tax (*impuesto sobre los ingresos brutos*). As a percentage of GDP, sub-national tax revenue ranged from less than 0.1% in Guyana and Guatemala to 9.9% in Brazil in 2022 and the median value amounted to 0.4% of GDP. Low sub-national tax revenue across the LAC region reflects the fact that sub-national governments in LAC countries tend to have a relatively narrow range of taxes under their jurisdiction. The taxes most frequently assigned to sub-national entities are property taxes, motor-vehicle licenses, taxes on specific services and municipal fees. The revenue-generation potential of these instruments is limited relative to the tax bases under central jurisdiction, such as VAT and income taxes.

In 2022, all subnational tax revenue in Belize and Guatemala and Jamaica, and more than half of tax revenue collected at the sub-national level in Peru, Uruguay, Ecuador and Paraguay, was sourced from property taxes (Figure 1.17). All other countries in the region rely principally on taxes on goods and services. Mexico is the only country that also collected revenue from different tax bases. In 2022, nearly half of sub-national tax revenue in Mexico came from payroll taxes. In OECD countries, sub-national entities tend to have much broader potential tax bases. A substantial proportion of revenue collection by sub-national governments in OECD countries is generated by taxes on income and profits (representing more than a third of the total collected at sub-national level on average).

The COVID-19 crisis has highlighted the need for structural reforms to improve the collection and enhance the sources of revenue at sub-national level. Options for doing so include improvements in information and statistics regarding the revenue from these taxes, the administrative capacity to collect at the local level, effective co-ordination with national authorities, and promotion of sustainable sources of tax revenue at this level (Nieto-Parra and Orozco, 2020[42]).

Figure 1.17. Tax mix of sub-national tax revenue in LAC countries, 2022

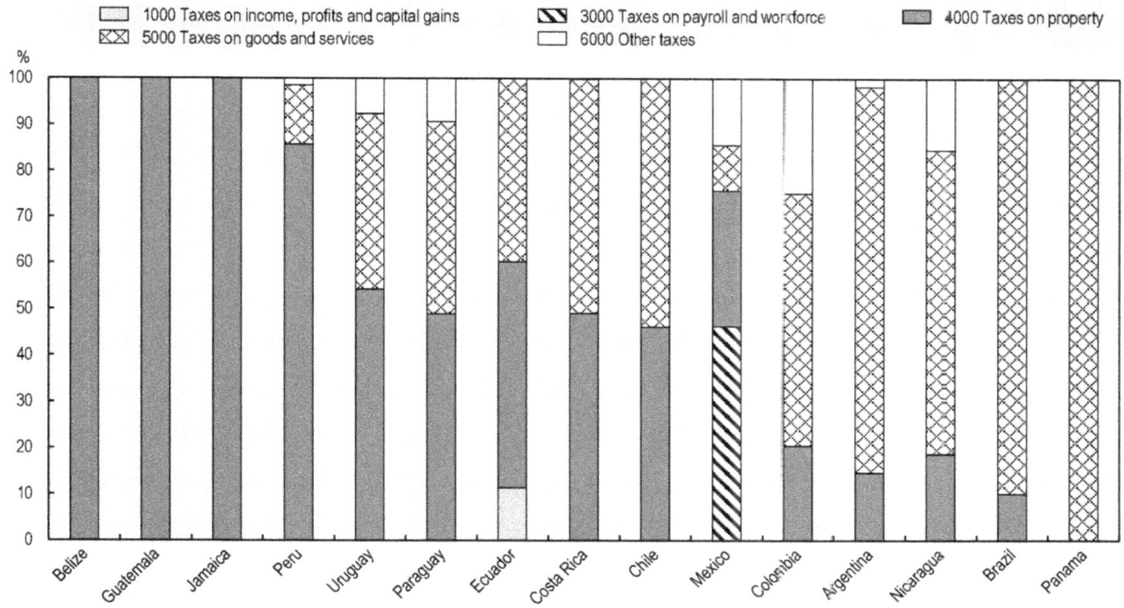

Note: Figures for Antigua and Barbuda, Bahamas, Barbados, Bolivia, Cuba, Dominican Republic, El Salvador, Guyana, Honduras, Saint Lucia, Trinidad and Tobago and Venezuela are excluded as either the sub-national tax revenue data or the breakdown of sub-national tax revenue data by the main type of tax category is not available. Figures exclude local government revenues for Argentina but include provincial revenues. Data for Ecuador, Nicaragua, Panama and Uruguay are estimated for 2022.
Source: Authors' calculations based on OECD et al. (2024[4]), Chapter 6.

StatLink https://stat.link/po53ih

Low tax revenue at the sub-national level in LAC countries may result from a lack of administrative and technical capacity. Property taxes require sophisticated systems and information, and collecting this revenue is expensive. Appropriate property registers are lacking in many countries; where they exist, they are rarely updated (Canavire-Bacarreza, Martínez-Vázquez and Sepúlveda, 2012[43]); (OECD et al., 2023[6]). As a result, tax authorities lack access to accurate valuations of lands and buildings; real estate registries are often reluctant to share this information. Property tax also suffers from a high level of informality: buildings are constructed without permits, properties are not registered and reported prices of some real estate transactions are falsified. As property tax is one of the most controversial taxes with citizens and has high political costs, politicians are often unwilling to invest sufficient resources to raise revenue via this instrument.

Table 1.4. Attribution of tax revenue to sub-sectors of general government in LAC countries

Percentage of total tax revenue

	Central government			State or regional government			Local government[1]			Social Security funds		
	1995	2000	2022	1995	2000	2022	1995	2000	2021	1995	2000	2022
Federal countries												
Argentina	59.0	66.4	65.1	17.5	17.8	17.1	..	..	..	23.4	15.8	17.7
Brazil	44.8	47.9	46.2	26.5	25.0	23.4	3.7	3.4	6.2	25.0	23.7	24.2
Mexico	73.9	78.3	79.5	2.8	2.7	4.5	1.5	1.0	1.8	21.8	18.0	14.1
Venezuela[3]	94.6	94.6	..	..	..	..	..	..	..	5.4	5.4	..
Regional countries												
Colombia[4]	63.2	68.7	75.2	5.5	5.6	4.8	8.6	9.4	11.7	22.7	16.3	8.3
Unitary countries												
Antigua and Barbuda[2]	100.0	100.0	82.8				..	..	..	..	..	17.2
Bahamas[2]	89.1	88.1	89.0				..	..	..	10.9	11.9	11.0
Barbados	85.6	84.4	83.0				..	..	..	14.4	15.6	17.0
Belize	93.2	93.5	88.8				0.5	0.7	0.5	6.3	5.8	10.7
Bolivia	94.3	86.4	71.5				5.7	6.3	4.4	..	7.3	24.1
Chile[3]	89.9	87.8	89.9				6.5	7.9	6.9	3.6	4.4	3.2
Costa Rica[3]	65.5	63.3	61.4				1.6	1.9	2.7	33.0	34.8	35.9
Cuba[5]	..	..	..				..	..	..	11.3	10.4	14.4
Dominican Republic	99.3	99.0	99.4				..	..	..	0.7	1.0	0.6
Ecuador[2]	70.5	87.7	73.3				4.0	1.6	2.7	25.5	10.7	24.0
El Salvador	80.9	80.5	86.9				..	..	1.9	19.1	19.5	11.2
Guatemala	83.6	83.6	84.5				0.6	0.9	0.9	15.8	15.5	14.7
Guyana	92.6	88.6	90.3				..	..	0.0	7.4	11.4	9.7
Honduras	86.1	85.3	81.2				4.4	5.2	3.6	9.5	9.4	15.2
Jamaica	100.0	99.3	93.2				..	0.7	1.3	..	..	5.5
Nicaragua[2]	80.4	72.5	71.3				4.6	9.5	5.9	15.0	18.0	22.8
Panama[2]	67.2	59.6	56.4				..	2.2	1.6	32.8	38.2	42.0
Paraguay	92.0	74.4	68.8				..	..	2.4	8.0	25.6	28.8
Peru	88.7	86.5	88.0				..	1.6	2.1	11.3	11.9	9.9
Saint Lucia[2]	100.0	90.0	86.7				..	..	..	..	10.0	13.3
Trinidad and Tobago	96.8	93.6	90.1				..	..	..	3.2	6.4	9.9
Uruguay[2]	61.7	63.6	69.2				8.8	8.9	5.6	29.5	27.5	25.2

1. The data exclude local government revenues for Antigua and Barbuda, Argentina (but include provincial revenues), The Bahamas, Barbados, Cuba, the Dominican Republic, Saint Lucia, Trinidad and Tobago and Venezuela as the data are not available. Local government revenue data have been available since 1991 for Nicaragua, since 1994 for Bolivia, since 1995 for Guatemala, since 1998 for Jamaica, since 1999 for Panama, since 2000 for Peru, since 2002 for El Salvador and Guyana, since 2006 for Paraguay and since 1990 for all other countries.
2. The data include the following estimations: Antigua and Barbuda (social security contributions for 2019-2022), Bahamas (social security contributions for 2021 and 2022), Ecuador (local tax revenues for 2021 and 2022), Nicaragua (local tax revenues for 2022), Panama (local tax revenues and social security contributions for 2022), Saint Lucia (social security contributions for 2021 and 2022) and Uruguay (local tax revenues for 2022). See the corresponding country tables for more information.
3. Some tax revenue data between 2014 and 2017 and all data from 2018 are not available. The breakdown by sub-sectors of general government is not available for those years.
4. Colombia is constitutionally a unitary country with high autonomy of its territorial entities.
5. Data for sub-sectors of general government in Cuba are only available between 2002 and 2012.
Source : OECD et al. (2024[4]), Table 4.11.

References

Amaglobeli, D. et al. (2023), *Policy Responses to High Energy and Food Prices*, https://doi.org/10.5089/9798400237768.001. [12]

Barreix, A., J. Benítez and M. Pecho (2017), "Revisiting personal income tax in Latin America: Evolution and impact", *OECD Development Centre Working Papers*, No. 338, OECD Publishing, Paris, https://doi.org/10.1787/16d42b4a-en. [27]

Canavire-Bacarreza, G., J. Martínez-Vázquez and C. Sepúlveda (2012), *Sub-national Revenue Mobilization in Peru, IDB Working Paper Series No. 299*, IDB, https://publications.iadb.org/en/sub-national-revenue-mobilization-peru. [43]

ECLAC (2023), *Economic Survey of Latin America and the Caribbean*, Economic Commission for Latin America and the Caribbean, https://repositorio.cepal.org/server/api/core/bitstreams/3e801708-1d17-4f7b-bb58-256903679cae/content. [11]

ECLAC (2023), *Fiscal Panorama of Latin America and the Caribbean 2023: fiscal policy for growth, redistribution and productive transformation*, Economic Commission for Latin America and the Caribbean, https://www.cepal.org/en/publications/48900-fiscal-panorama-latin-america-and-caribbean-2023-fiscal-policy-growth. [8]

ECLAC (2022), *Fiscal Panorama of Latin America and the Caribbean 2022*, Economic Commission for Latin America and the Caribbean, Santiago., https://www.cepal.org/en/publications/48015-fiscal-panorama-latin-america-and-caribbean-2022-fiscal-policy-challenges. [7]

ECLAC (2020), *Fiscal Panorama of Latin America and the Caribbean 2020: Fiscal policy amid the crisis arising from the coronavirus disease (COVID-19) pandemic*, Economic Commission for Latin America and the Caribbean, https://repositorio.cepal.org/items/a4a90b62-2e90-4eca-87ca-ce61fb15693f. [23]

ECLAC (2018), *The Fiscal Panorama of Latin America and the Caribbean*, United Nations, https://www.cepal.org/en/publications/43406-fiscal-panorama-latin-america-and-caribbean-2018-public-policy-challenges. [24]

ECLAC (2014), *Tax policy in Latin America: Assessment and guidelines for a second generation of reforms*, United Nations, https://repositorio.cepal.org/handle/11362/36806. [21]

ECLAC (2013), *Fiscal Panorama of Latin America and the Caribbean: Tax reform and renewal of the fiscal covenant*, United Nations, https://www.cepal.org/en/publications/3101-fiscal-panorama-latin-america-and-caribbean-2013-tax-reform-and-renewal-fiscal. [26]

Government of Belize (2022), *Government Mitigating Impacts of Fuel Prices*, Government of Belize, https://www.pressoffice.gov.bz/government-mitigating-impacts-of-fuel-prices/. [13]

Hanappi, T. et al. (2023), "Corporate Effective Tax Rates in Latin America and the Caribbean", *Technical Note No IDB-TN- 2782*, https://doi.org/10.18235/0005168. [28]

IDB (2013), *More than revenues, Taxation as a development tool*, Inter-American Development Bank, https://publications.iadb.org/en/publication/more-revenue-taxation-development-tool-executive-summary. [25]

IMF (2023), *World Economic Outlook Database, October 2023*, https://www.imf.org/en/Publications/WEO/weo-database/2023/October (accessed on 20 September 2021). [5]

IMF (2022), *Sixth Review under the Extended Arrangement under the Extended Fund Facility and Financing Assurances Review*, International Monetary Fund, https://www.finanzas.gob.ec/wp-content/uploads/downloads/2023/05/Staff-Report-diciembre-2022-ingles29052023.pdf. [9]

Keen, M. (2013), *The anatomy of VAT, WP/13/111*, IMF, https://www.imf.org/en/Publications/WP/Issues/2016/12/31/The-Anatomy-of-the-VAT-40543. [32]

KPMG (2019), *Mexico: Tax reform 2020, VAT on services provided from digital platforms*, https://home.kpmg/us/en/home/insights/2019/11/tnf-mexico-tax-reform-2020-vat-services-digital-platforms.html. [34]

Lorenzo, F. (2016), *Inventario de instrumentos fiscales verdes en América Latina*, CEPAL, https://agua.org.mx/biblioteca/inventario-instrumentos-fiscales-verdes-en-america-latina-experiencias-efectos-alcances/. [38]

Melguizo, A. et al. (2017), "No sympathy for the devil! Policy priorities to overcome the middle-income trap in Latin America", *OECD Development Centre Working Papers*, No. 340, OECD, https://doi.org/10.1787/26b78724-en. [16]

Ministry of Finance Trinidad and Tobago (2022), *Budget Statement 2023: Tenacity and Stability in the Face of Global Challenges*, Ministry of Finance Trinidad and Tobago, https://www.finance.gov.tt/wp-content/uploads/2022/09/Budget-Statement-2023-E-Version.pdf. [10]

Nieto-Parra, S. and R. Orozco (2020), *Potencializar los impuestos subnacionales en América Latina y el Caribe en tiempos del Covid-19 in Los desafíos de las finanzas intergubernamentales ante el Covid-19*, AIFIL - Asociación Iberoamericana de Financiación, https://www.aifil-jifl.org/wp-content/uploads/2020/11/AIFIL-2.11.pdf. [42]

OECD (2024), *OECD Tax Database*, OECD Publishing, Paris, https://www.oecd.org/tax/tax-policy/tax-database/. [14]

OECD (2023), *Environment at a Glance in Latin America and the Caribbean , Spotlight on Climate Change*, OECD Publishing, https://doi.org/10.1787/2431bd6c-en. [39]

OECD (2022), *Consumption Tax Trends 2022: VAT/GST and Excise, Core Design Features and Trends*, OECD Publishing, Paris, https://doi.org/10.1787/6525a942-en. [31]

OECD (2022), *Corporate Tax Statistics: Fourth Edition*, OECD Publishing, https://doi.org/10.1787/5c8d8887-en. [29]

OECD (2022), *Multi-dimensional Review of the Dominican Republic: Towards Greater Well-being for All, OECD Development Pathways*, OECD Publishing, Paris, https://doi.org/10.1787/560c12bf-en. [36]

OECD (2022), *PINE database*, OECD Publishing, Paris, http://www.oecd.org/environment/tools-evaluation/environmentaltaxation.htm. [41]

OECD (2022), *Tax Policy Reforms 2022*, OECD Publishing, Paris, https://doi.org/10.1787/067c593d-en. [15]

OECD (2021), *Environmental policy: Environmentally related tax revenue accounts, OECD Environment Statistics (database)*, https://stats.oecd.org/Index.aspx?DataSetCode=ERTR_ACC. [44]

OECD (2021), *Taxing Energy Use for Sustainable Development*, OECD Publishing, Paris, https://www.oecd.org/tax/tax-policy/taxing-energy-use-for-sustainable-development.htm. [40]

OECD (2020), "COVID-19 in Latin America and the Caribbean: Regional socio-economic implications and policy priorities", *OECD Policy Responses to Coronavirus (COVID-19)*, http://www.oecd.org/coronavirus/policy-responses/covid-19-in-latinamerica-and-the-caribbean-regional-socio-economic-implications-and-policy-priorities-93a64fde/. [22]

OECD (2019), *Tax Morale: What Drives People and Businesses to Pay Tax?*, OECD Publishing, Paris, https://doi.org/10.1787/f3d8ea10-en. [18]

OECD (2018), *Consumption Tax Trends 2018: VAT/GST and Excise Rates, Trends and Policy Issues*, OECD Publishing, Paris, https://doi.org/10.1787/ctt-2018-en. [33]

OECD (2014), *Development Co-operation Report 2014: Mobilising Resources for Sustainable Development*, OECD Publishing, Paris, https://doi.org/10.1787/dcr-2014-en. [17]

OECD (2005), *Glossary of statistical terms*, https://stats.oecd.org/glossary/detail.asp?ID=6437. [37]

OECD et al. (2024), *Revenue Statistics in Latin America and the Caribbean 2024*, OECD Publishing, Paris. [4]

OECD et al. (2023), *Latin American Economic Outlook 2023: Investing in Sustainable Development*, OECD Publishing, Paris, https://doi.org/10.1787/8c93ff6e-en. [1]

OECD et al. (2023), *Revenue Statistics in Latin America and the Caribbean*, OECD Publishing, Paris, https://doi.org/10.1787/a7640683-en. [6]

OECD et al. (2022), *Latin American Economic Outlook 2022: Towards a Green and Just Transition*, OECD Publishing, Paris, https://doi.org/10.1787/3d5554fc-en. [2]

OECD et al. (2021), *Latin American Economic Outlook 2021: Working Together for a Better Recovery*, OECD Publishing, Paris, https://doi.org/10.1787/5fedabe5-en. [3]

OECD et al. (2018), *Revenue Statistics in Latin America and the Caribbean*, OECD Publishing, Paris, https://doi.org/10.1787/rev_lat_car-2018-en-fr. [30]

OECD et al. (2015), *Revenue Statistics in Latin America and the Caribbean 2015*, OECD Publishing, Paris, https://doi.org/10.1787/rev_lat-2015-en-fr. [19]

OECD/IDB/The World Bank (2014), *Pensions at a Glance: Latin America and the Caribbean*, OECD Publishing, Paris, https://doi.org/10.1787/pension_glance-2014-en. [20]

Schlotterbeck, S. (2017), *Tax Administration Reforms in the Caribbean, "Challenges, Achievements, and Next Steps".* [35]

Notes

[1] The OECD figure is provisional and is based on preliminary data provided for the year 2022. The data need to be interpreted with caution as they are subject to revisions in future years that can affect the magnitude, and less commonly, the direction, of change between the last two years of data.

[2] VAT was introduced in 1991 in Jamaica, 1997 in Barbados, 2006 in Belize (the General Sales Tax), 2007 in Guyana and Antigua and Barbuda, 2012 in Saint Lucia and in 2014 in the Bahamas.

[3] The year of comparison is 2021 as the average tax structure for OECD countries in 2022 is not available at the time of writing.

[4] Although environmentally related tax revenues are not separately identified in the standard OECD classification of tax revenues, they can be identified through the detailed list of specific taxes included for most countries within this overarching classification. It is on this basis that they are included in the OECD Policy Instruments for the Environment (PINE) database (OECD, 2022[41]). In 2020, the OECD started the collection of Environmentally Related Tax Revenue (ERTR) accounts in line with the System of Environmental and Economic Accounting and ERTR accounts are disaggregated by industries and households (OECD, 2021[44]).

[5] Both LAC and OECD figures here refer to unweighted averages comprising 26 countries for the LAC region and 38 countries for the OECD.

[6] This means that revenues are generally attributed to the level of government that exercises the authority to impose the tax or has the final discretion to set and vary the tax rate. This has implications for situations where one level of government collects tax revenues and transfers them in whole or in part to other levels. Regional examples of this type of mechanism are the Co-participation Law in Argentina, federal participations in Mexico (mandated in the Fiscal Co-ordination Law) and participation funds in Brazil (defined in Article 159 of the Constitution).

2 Fiscal revenues from non-renewable natural resources in Latin America and the Caribbean

Principal findings

Hydrocarbon revenues surged in 2022 in the context of elevated market volatility

International oil and gas prices surged in the first half of 2022 due to Russia's invasion of Ukraine and constrained global supply. While oil prices gave ground in the second half of the year as macroeconomic concerns weighed on market sentiment, natural gas prices remained exceptionally volatile. Rising hydrocarbon output in the region led hydrocarbon revenues to register 4.4% of GDP (compared to 2.6% of GDP in 2021), a significant upswing.

Mining revenues rose marginally in 2022 amidst weakening prices and lower production volumes.

After a short-lived jump after Russia's invasion of Ukraine, prices for many metals and minerals fell for the year. Demand in China was buffeted by consecutive COVID-19 lockdowns, weakening residential construction, and reduced steel production. However, prices for coal and lithium continued to rise strongly. Fiscal revenues from mining rose to 0.75% of GDP (up from 0.67% of GDP in 2021), driven by strong outturns in Chile (where lithium revenues compensated for a fall in copper receipts) and Colombia.

Market uncertainty and macroeconomic headwinds impacted fiscal revenues from non-renewable natural resources in Latin America and the Caribbean during 2023.

Global energy markets remained volatile in 2023, reflecting shifts in market sentiment, normalisation of natural gas prices in Europe, and disparate trends in the supply and demand of hydrocarbons. While the overall trend in prices remained down, higher than expected oil demand in the third quarter sparked a rally that was given further impetus by the escalation of the conflict between Israel and Hamas after the October 7th attacks. Metals and minerals prices largely fell for the year, but some rebounded in the second half due to rising demand in China.

Hydrocarbon revenues in the region dipped to an estimated 3.9% of GDP (compared to 4.4% of GDP in 2022). Lower prices dragged down payments of royalties and other State participations in the commercial value of production, which represent the primary fiscal instruments applied to the sector. Mining revenues are estimated to have contracted sharply, falling to 0.5% of GDP in 2023 (compared with 0.8% of GDP in 2022). Volatile CIT receipts were the principal factor behind this decline.

Hydrocarbon revenues surged in 2022 in the context of elevated market volatility

Global energy markets were marked by significant volatility in 2022. Prices for oil and natural gas surged in the first half of the year due to Russia's invasion of Ukraine in February 2022 and the subsequent application of economic sanctions on the Russian Federation by the European Union and the United States. In March, benchmark prices leapt for most energy products, including month-on-month increases of 56% for natural gas in Europe (or 592% year-on-year) and 21% for Brent crude oil (or 77% year-on-year). Prices remained high for the remainder of the first half of the year because of additional policy measures, constrained production (especially in OPEC+ countries) and a reordering of energy trade. Members of the European Union adopted a plan to reduce natural gas imports from the Russian Federation by two-thirds by the end of 2023. Additionally, in March, the United States banned imports of Russian oil, liquified natural gas (LNG), and coal.

Trends in energy prices largely decoupled in the second half of the year. Natural gas prices were highly volatile; in Europe, prices reached an all-time high of USD 70 per million British thermal units (MMBtu) in August due to large European purchases of LNG in global markets and the Russian Federation's cut in supply to some European countries. However, prices subsequently trended lower as gas inventories in Europe filled ahead of schedule and industrial and residential demand declined. By December, the price of natural gas in Europe was down 49% from its high in August and down 5% from a year prior. In contrast, oil prices slid as markets priced in the impact of higher crude oil production, increasingly restrictive monetary policy and slowing global growth. The spot price of Brent in December was 33% below its peak in June but 9% over the price at the end of 2021. Despite its weak second half performance, the average annual price of Brent was up 41.7% for the year.

Latin America and the Caribbean (LAC) experienced a strong increase in hydrocarbon production and exports in 2022. The region produced 7.9 million barrels per day, up 7.6% from the previous year but still well below the high of 9.6 million barrels per day in 2014 (Table 2.1). Production in Brazil reached an all-time high during the year and crude oil output in Mexico hit its highest level since 2018. Oil output continued to ramp up in Guyana as an additional floating production storage and offloading unit, the Liza Unity, entered operation (Bank of Guyana, 2023[1]). Sizeable increases in production were also seen in Argentina – especially from the Vaca Muerte shale formation – and in the Bolivarian Republic of Venezuela. The rise in crude oil exports was largely driven by Brazil, Colombia and Guyana.

Natural gas production also increased in 2022, although the trend was not generalised across the region. In Argentina, natural gas output rose 7%, reflecting strong production in the Vaca Muerta shale gas field. Exports from Argentina, largely to Chile, also grew strongly. Trinidad and Tobago also experienced a rise in production (marking a modest rebound after contracting sharply in 2020 and 2021) and a significant increase in exports. Peru experienced a similar dynamic, with higher exports due to a base effect; the Melchorita natural gas liquefaction plant temporarily closed during the months of May, July and August 2021 (Banco Central de Reserva del Perú, 2023[2]). In the Plurinational State of Bolivia, production continued to trend lower as existing fields are depleted. Export volumes also decreased due to lower demand in Argentina and Brazil.

Table 2.1. Latin America and the Caribbean and selected country groupings: Crude oil and natural gas production and exports, 2021-2022

Thousand barrels daily, billion standard cubic metres and percentages

Selected country groupings and countries	Crude oil (thousand barrels daily)						Dry natural gas (billion standard cubic meters)					
	Production			Exports			Production			Exports		
	2021	2022	%	2021	2022	%	2021	2022	%	2021	2022	%
Latin America and the Caribbean	7301	7858	7.6	3829	4072	6.3	178	183	2.6	27	30	11.3
Argentina	508	583	14.8	...	...	...	40	43	7.1	1	3	290.5
Bolivia	31	28	-10.9	...	...	...	15	14	-9.5	12	10	-15.4
Brazil	2905	3022	4.0	1292	1346	4.2	24	23	-5.5	...	...	...
Colombia	736	754	2.4	422	487	15.4	1	1	0.0	...	...	...
Ecuador	473	481	1.7	316	313	-0.8	11	11	-1.2	...	...	...
Guatemala	7	7	-1.8	...	...	...	0	0	...	...	...	...
Guyana	117	290	147.7	42	101	139.4	...	...	...	...	...	...
Mexico	1780	1843	3.6	1091	1012	-7.3	30	31	5.7	...	...	...
Peru	38	41	5.6	...	...	...	12	12	1.5	4	5	22.5
Trinidad and Tobago	60	58	-2.4	61	54	-11.9	26	27	4.1	9	11	15.7
Venezuela	595	704	18.3	448	438	-2.2	16	18	11	...	...	...
Other LAC	51	49	-4.5	156	320	105.1	2	2	0.0	...	...	...
Total World	77 214	80 833	4.7	40 794	43 477	6.6	4 083	4 108	0.6	1 286	1 288	0.1
OPEC	27 190	29 556	8.7	19 656	21 389	8.8	640	649	1.4	110	103	-5.9
Saudi Arabia	9 313	10 644	14.3	6 227	7 364	18.2	116	122	5.4	...	...	...
Non-OPEC	50 025	51 277	2.5	21 138	22 088	4.5	3 443	3 459	0.5	1 177	1 185	0.7
Russian Federation	10 112	10 314	2.0	4 510	4 780	6.0	702	618	-11.9	251	176	-29.8
United States	11 268	11 911	5.7	2 963	3 604	21.6	978	1 029	5.3	188	195	3.8

Source: Economic Commission for Latin America and the Caribbean (ECLAC), based on data from the U.S. Energy Information Administration (EIA) and Annual Statistical Bulletin 2023, Organization of the Petroleum Exporting Countries (OPEC).

Against this backdrop, hydrocarbon revenues in the LAC region registered a marked increase in 2022. Total fiscal revenues from oil and gas exploration and production – upstream activities – reached USD 115.5 billion for the year, roughly double the 2021 level of USD 58.4 billion (Table 2.2). Relative to GDP, revenues reached an average of 4.4% of GDP (compared with 2.6% of GDP in 2021), bolstered by an exceptionally strong increase in Trinidad and Tobago (+6.9 percentage points of GDP year-on-year). Non-tax revenues, principally related to royalties and other related payments associated with the commercial value of production, reached 3.5% of GDP (compared to 2.3% of GDP in 2021) with significant increases in most countries, especially in Guyana. Tax revenues also registered significant dynamism, especially in Trinidad and Tobago.

Table 2.2. Latin America and the Caribbean (10 countries): General government fiscal revenues from oil and gas exploration and production, by type of revenue, 2021-2022

Percent of GDP, percentage points of GDP and percentages

Country	Billions of US dollars			Percentage of GDP								
	Total revenues			Total revenues			Tax revenues			Non-tax revenues		
	2021	2022	2022/2021 (%)	2021	2022	2022/2021 (p.p. of GDP)	2021	2022	2022/2021 (p.p. of GDP)	2021	2022	2022/2021 (p.p. of GDP)
Argentina	2.2	3.4	55	0.4	0.5	0.1	0.05	0.12	0.1	0.4	0.4	0.0
Bolivia (Plur. State of)	1.3	1.7	30	3.2	3.8	0.6	0.1	0.1	0.0	3.1	3.7	0.6
Brazil	21.4	50.0	134	1.3	2.6	1.3	0.18	0.73	0.5	1.1	1.9	0.8
Colombia	3.5	9.4	172	1.1	2.7	1.7	0.4	0.6	0.2	0.7	2.1	1.4
Ecuador	8.7	11.2	29	8.2	9.8	1.6	...	...	...	8.2	9.8	1.6
Guatemala	0.04	0.06	44	0.05	0.06	0.01	0.02	0.02	-0.003	0.03	0.04	0.02
Guyana	0.4	1.4	245	5.3	9.7	4.4	...	...	...	5.3	9.7	4.4
Mexico	18.3	32.2	75	1.4	2.2	0.8	0.03	0.04	0.01	1.4	2.2	0.8
Peru	1.6	2.9	82	0.7	1.2	0.5	0.2	0.4	0.3	0.5	0.8	0.2
Trinidad and Tobago	1.0	3.2	216	4.4	11.3	6.9	2.6	7.2	4.7	1.8	4.0	2.2
LAC	58.4	115.5	98	2.6	4.4	1.8	0.4	0.9	0.6	2.3	3.5	1.2

Note: Revenue-to-GDP ratios for Latin America and the Caribbean correspond to a simple average of the countries included in the sample. Figures may not sum due to rounding. Data for Mexico correspond to federal government oil revenue; they exclude own revenues of Pemex, the State-owned oil and gas producer. Data for Ecuador correspond to oil revenues of the non-financial public sector derived from exports of crude oil. Data for Guyana refer to revenues deposited in the Natural Resource Fund.

Source: Economic Commission for Latin America and the Caribbean (ECLAC), based on data from ECLAC's Fiscal Revenues from Non-Renewable Natural Resources in Latin America and the Caribbean database.

Hydrocarbon tax revenues were buoyed by a dramatic increase in CIT payments during 2022. Compared with 2021, CIT receipts more than doubled in US dollar terms for several countries in the region (Figure 2.1). Higher production and favourable price dynamics improved profitability and led to greater advance tax payments for fiscal year 2022. Operating income at Ecopetrol rose significantly in US dollar terms (+79%) (Ecopetrol, 2023[3]). Likewise, operating income at Petrobras rose 52% in US dollar terms, building on a 274% increase in 2021 (Petrobras, 2022[4]; Petrobras, 2023[5]). Strong profits in 2021 also led to an increase in payments for annual tax filings made in 2022, as estimated tax payments paid during fiscal year 2021 fell short of year-end tax liabilities.

Figure 2.1. Latin America and the Caribbean (5 countries): Year-on-year variation in general government CIT receipts from oil and gas exploration and production, 2021-2022

Percentage points of GDP and percentages based on US dollars

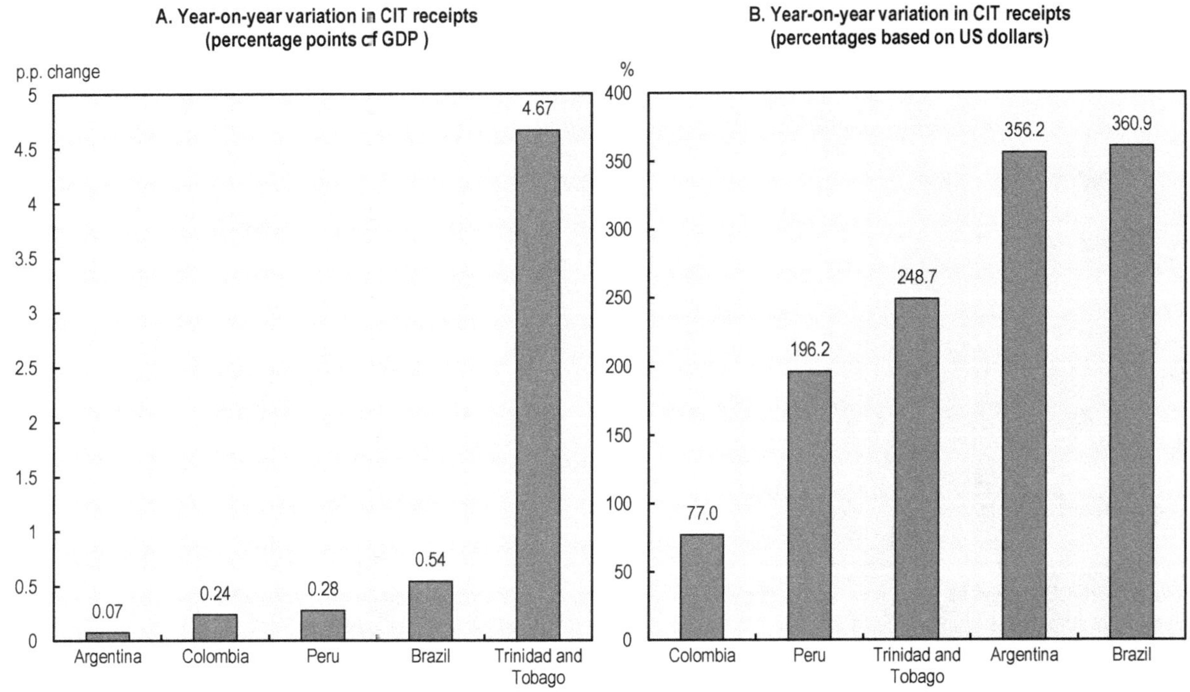

Note: Data for Mexico correspond to federal government oil revenue, they exclude own revenues of Pemex, the State-owned oil and gas producer.

Source: Economic Commission for Latin America and the Caribbean (ECLAC), based on data from ECLAC's Fiscal Revenues from Non-Renewable Natural Resources in Latin America and the Caribbean database.

StatLink https://stat.link/xpqldi

Non-tax hydrocarbon revenues, which make up the bulk of oil and gas revenues in most countries, also grew strongly. Payments of royalties and other participations in the commercial value of production surged in US dollar terms, and in some countries exceeded the increase in the annual average spot price of Brent (Figure 2.2).

This dynamic was particularly apparent in Guyana and Trinidad and Tobago. In Guyana, oil output continues to expand rapidly; the principal driver of higher revenues was production as new fields are being brought online. Higher hydrocarbon production was also a determining factor of strong revenue growth for Brazil, Mexico and Peru. In Colombia, the strong outturn also reflected a more than tripling of the payments for the government's participation in production, which is determined by the price of Western Texas Intermediate and thresholds specified in the contracts with producers (ANH, 2023[6]). In contrast to other countries, the impulse to royalties in Trinidad and Tobago was purely from prices as hydrocarbon production largely slipped during the year.

Figure 2.2. Latin America and the Caribbean (10 countries): Year-on-year variation in general government non-tax revenues from oil and gas exploration and production, 2021-2022

Percentage points of GDP and percentages based on US dollars

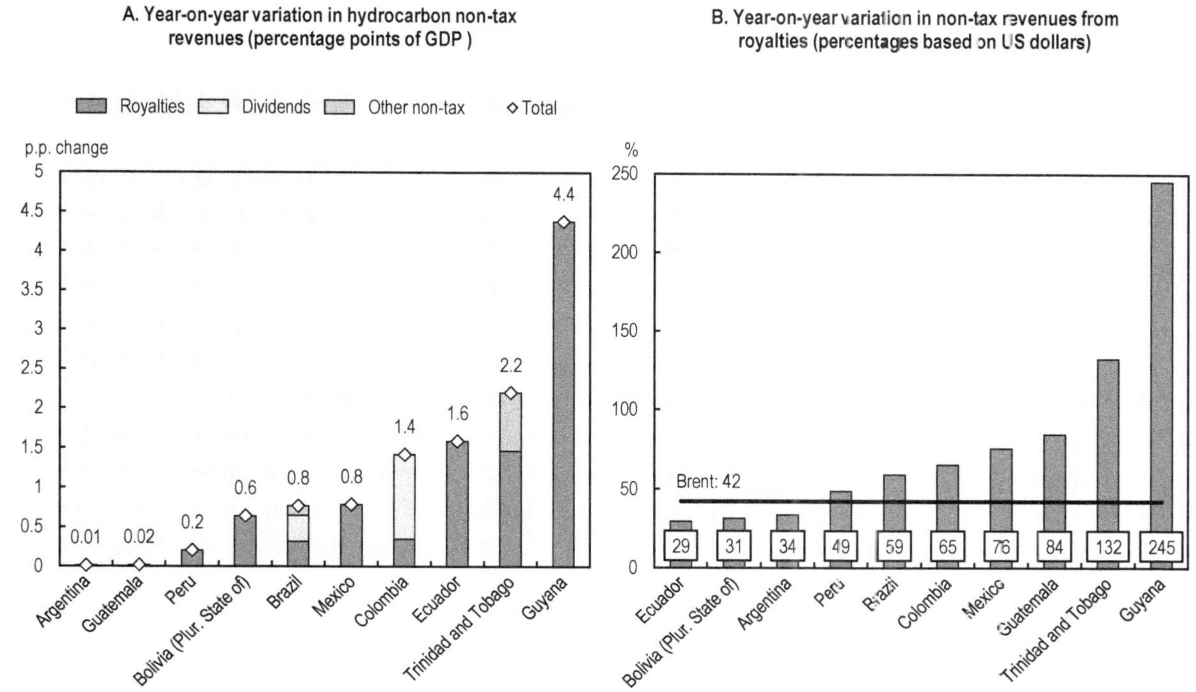

Note: Data for Mexico correspond to federal government oil revenue, they exclude own revenues of Pemex, the State-owned oil and gas producer. Data for Ecuador correspond to oil revenues of the non-financial public sector derived from exports of crude oil. Data for Guyana refers to revenues deposited in the Natural Resource Fund.

Source: Economic Commission for Latin America and the Caribbean (ECLAC), based on data from ECLAC's Fiscal Revenues from Non-Renewable Natural Resources in Latin America and the Caribbean database.

StatLink https://stat.link/6cyame

Other non-tax revenues were also significant in some countries. In Brazil, dividend payments by Petrobras to the federal government reached 0.6% of GDP (compared with 0.2% of GDP in 2021). This was complemented by an additional 0.1% of GDP in signing bonuses from the second transfer-of-rights production sharing auction that was held in December 2021 (Tesouro Nacional, 2023[7]). In Colombia, dividend payments by Ecopetrol to the Treasury reached 1.1% of GDP, compared with less than 0.1% of GDP in 2021, reflecting high profits during the previous year and the issuance of an extraordinary dividend paid in June (Ecopetrol, 2023[3]; Ministerio de Hacienda y Crédito Público de Colombia, 2023[8]). In the case of Trinidad and Tobago, the country received extraordinary payments, equivalent to 0.9% of GDP, within the framework of an agreement between the country and major producers, such as British Petroleum (BP) and Royal Dutch Shell, to settle past obligations (Central Bank of Trinidad and Tobago, 2023[9]).

Mining revenues rose modestly in 2022 amidst weakening prices and lower production volumes

Markets for metals and minerals in 2022 were buffeted by the war in Ukraine and rising uncertainty about global economic conditions. During the first half of the year, prices for many metals and minerals continued their upwards momentum, building on the sharp increase experienced in 2021 as economic activity rebounded. However, this rally was cut short as industrial production slowed and market participants became increasingly wary of the deterioration of global macroeconomic fundamentals. Markets were significantly impacted by COVID-19 lockdowns in China, which disrupted domestic industrial production, as well as the downturn in the real estate market. Prices for most industrial metals and minerals ended the year in negative territory (Figure 2.3). While prices for iron ore fell (-25%) they experienced a high level of volatility during the year, reaching a high in March as a response to the invasion of Ukraine – one of the largest exporters of the mineral – before sliding as residential construction and steel production declined in China.

Figure 2.3. Year-on-year variation of international spot prices for selected minerals and metals, 2021-2022

Percentage

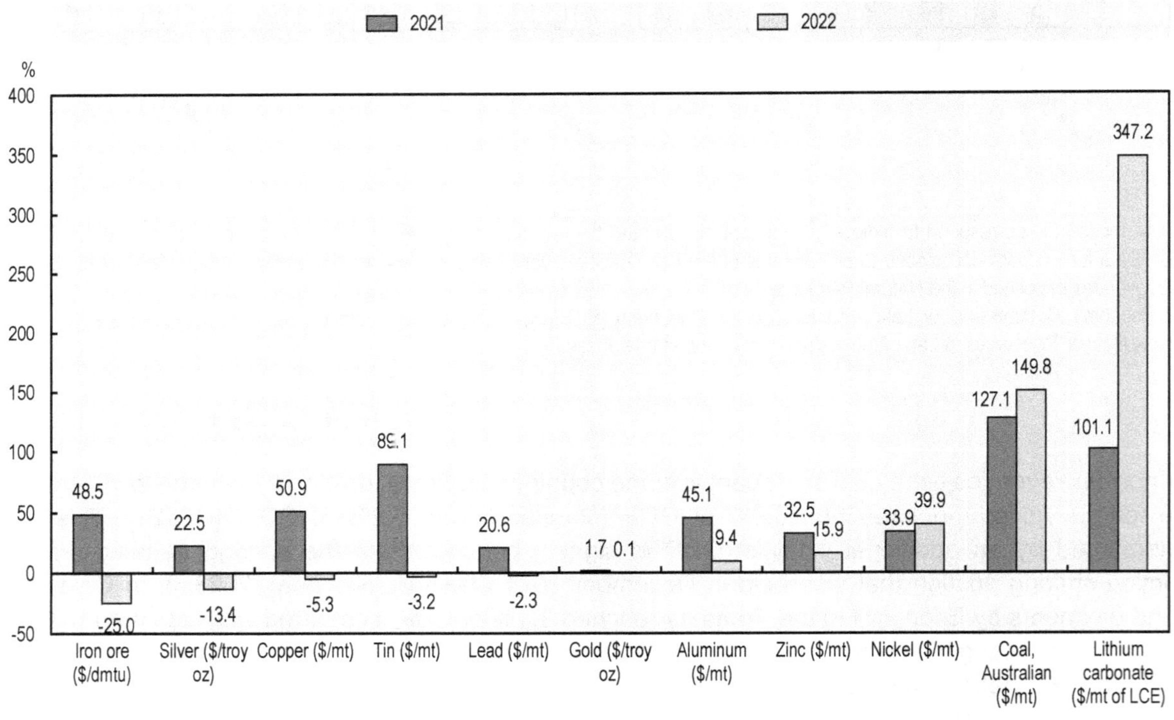

Source: Economic Commission for Latin America and the Caribbean (ECLAC), based on World Bank Commodity Price Data (The Pink Sheet), World Bank, and Ministerio de Economía de la Argentina.

StatLink https://stat.link/xrlvp2

However, market dynamics also drove prices up for some metals and minerals during the year. The surge in natural gas prices, which was further fueled by the war in Ukraine and the subsequent economic sanctions imposed on the Russian Federation, prompted coal prices to more than double. Spot prices for

Australian coal peaked at a record high of USD 431 per metric ton in September before trending lower in the fourth quarter of the year. Prices for nickel also posted continued strength mainly due to lower supply caused by disruptions in production in the Russian Federation and higher demand as traders made large purchases to cover short positions (LME, 2023[10]). Strong lithium demand for battery production and tight supply gave rise to a quadrupling in prices.

Mineral output in Latin America and the Caribbean generally trended lower in 2022 (Table 2.3). Copper production in Chile, the world's largest producer, contracted 5.2%, driven in large part by a 10.4% decline in output at Codelco because of lower ore grades and the depletion of existing mines (Codelco, 2023[11]). In contrast, production of copper expanded in Peru largely due to the initiation of production at the Quellaveco mine and increased output at the Cerro Verde mine, which compensated for lower production at other mines due to social conflicts (Banco Central de Reserva del Perú, 2023[2]).

Production of other industrial metals such as zinc, lead and tin also declined in most countries. Iron ore output also contracted, largely due to disruptions to production in Brazil caused by heavy rainfall (Vale, 2023[12]). Silver output contracted significantly among the largest producers, particularly in Mexico and Peru. Gold production also fell, but higher output in Mexico and the Plurinational State of Bolivia partially offset the decline.

Table 2.3. Latin America and the Caribbean (11 countries): Mine production, by country and product, 2021-2022

Thousands of metric tons and percentages

Metals and minerales	Year and percentage change	Price	Production in thousands of metric tons unless otherwise specified											
			LAC-11	Argentina	Bolivia	Brazil	Chile	Colombia	Dominican Republic	Ecuador	Jamaica	Mexico	Nicaragua	Peru
Copper	2021	6 174	9 584		3	1 153	5 625		5			473		2 326
	2022	9 317	9 295		4	1 024	5 330		5			486		2 445
	% variation	50.9	-3.0			-11.1	-5.2					2.8		5.1
Zinc	2021	2 266	2 854		500	426						395		1 533
	2022	3 003	2 626		518	418						319		1 370
	% variation	32.5	-8.0		3.8	-1.9						-19.1		-10.7
Lead	2021	1 825	540		93							182		264
	2022	2 200	488		90							143		255
	% variation	20.6	-9.6		-3.4							-21.7		-3.4
Tin	2021	17 125	65		20	18								27
	2022	32 384	59		18	13								28
	% variation	89.1	-8.6		-10.7	-25.9								4.6
Nickel	2021	13 787	408			342		38	28					
	2022	18 465	432			361		42	29					
	% variation	33.9	5.7			5.4		9.2	5.0					
Iron ore	2021	109	442 892			423 185		750				6 807		12 149

	2022	162	423 259			403 025		497				6 800		12 937
	% variation	48.5	-4.4			-4.8		-33.7				-0.1		6.5
Coal	2021	61	65 460					60 747				4 569		145
	2022	138	67 696					62 872				4 633		192
	% variation	127.1	3.4					3.5				1.4		
Bauxite / alumina	2021	1 704	39 386			33 365			72		5 950			
	2022	2 473	36 711			31 608			104		4 999			
	% variation	45.1	-6.8			-5.3			45.6		-16.0			
Lithium	2021	1 770	36	6		2	28							
	2022	1 800	47	6		2	39							
	% variation	1.7	32.3	6.9		29.4	37.8							
Gold (metric tons)	2021	1 770	480	35	46	82	34	55	25	13		81	11	97
	2022	1 800	475	35	53	77	31	49	22	15		83	11	97
	% variation	1.7	-1.0	0.0	16.8	-6.2	-9.6	-10.9	-12.4	19.8		3.1	5.7	-0.8
Silver (metric tons)	2021	21	11 141	824	1 292		1 383	27	80	2		4 176	23	3 334
	2022	25	10 199	551	1 219		1 274	34	73	2		3 941	22	3 083
	% variation	22.5	-8.5	-33.2	-5.7		-7.9	26.5	-7.9	-10.8		-5.6	-6.5	-7.5

Source: Economic Commission for Latin America and the Caribbean (ECLAC), on the basis of Instituto Nacional de Estadísticas del Estado Plurinacional de Bolivia; Agência Nacional de Mineração do Brasil; Comisión Chilena de Cobre (Cochilco); Agencia Nacional de Minería de Colombia; Oficina Nacional de Estadística de la República Dominicana; Banco Central del Ecuador; Instituto Nacional de Estadística y Geografía de México; Banco Central de Nicaragua, Instituto Nacional de Estadística e Informática de Perú; Energy Institute; and, United States Geological Survey, Mineral Commodities Summaries: Bauxite and Alumina, 2024.

A defining feature of metals and minerals production in the region for 2022 was the solid growth in lithium output. Argentina, Brazil, and Chile accounted for 36% of global lithium production during the year and an estimated 53% of reserves (Energy Institute, 2023[13]). However, among these countries, only Chile currently stands out as a major producer, representing 30% of global output alone. Lithium output in Chile was propelled in 2022 by a 50% increase in production capacity by SQM, the country's principal producer (SQM, 2023[14]). Production in Argentina is also ramping up, with six projects under construction in 2022 and a large number under consideration[1]. In contrast, lithium carbonate output in the Plurinational State of Bolivia remains limited, despite having potentially the largest reserves of lithium in the world (Ministerio de Minería y Metalurgia de Bolivia, 2023[15]; USGS, 2024[16]).

Despite the softening of international prices and generally lower production levels, fiscal revenues from mining rose in the LAC region in 2022. Total mining revenues reached USD 30.4 billion (up 11% from the 2021 level of USD 27.4 billion) (Table 2.4). However, this increase was largely due to the exceptional outturn in Colombia, which was bolstered by high coal prices and rising production. In relative terms, mining revenues averaged 0.75% of GDP (up from 0.67% of GDP in 2021). Mining tax revenues remained dominant, averaging 0.47% of GDP (compared to 0.42% of GDP in 2021) propelled by increases in Colombia, Peru and the Plurinational State of Bolivia. Non-tax revenues, largely payments of royalties tied to the commercial value of production, were impacted by price and production dynamics in some countries. However, the regional average benefitted from a surge in lithium payments in Chile and greater coal royalties in Colombia.

Table 2.4. Latin America and the Caribbean (12 countries): General government revenues from mining, 2021-2022

Billions of US dollars, percentage, percentage of GDP and percentage points of GDP

Country	Billions of US dollars			Percentage of GDP								
	Total revenues			Total revenues			Tax revenues			Non-tax revenues		
	2021	2022	2022/2021 (%)	2021	2022	2022/2021 (p.p. of GDP)	2021	2022	2022/2021 (p.p. of GDP)	2021	2022	2022/2021 (p.p. of GDP)
Argentina	0.3	0.3	-4	0.05	0.04	-0.01	0.04	0.03	-0.01	0.02	0.01	0.00
Bolivia	0.4	0.6	53	0.90	1.27	0.37	0.28	0.69	0.41	0.62	0.58	-0.04
Brazil	8.0	7.7	-3	0.48	0.40	-0.08	0.36	0.30	-0.05	0.13	0.10	-0.03
Chile	9.5	9.8	3	3.01	3.25	0.24	1.85	1.79	-0.06	1.16	1.47	0.31
Colombia	1.0	2.9	206	0.30	0.85	0.55	0.09	0.30	0.21	0.21	0.54	0.33
Ecuador	0.1	0.4	190	0.12	0.33	0.21	0.07	0.17	0.10	0.05	0.16	0.11
Guatemala	0.03	0.03	1	0.03	0.03	0.00	0.02	0.02	-0.001	0.006	0.005	0.00
Jamaica	0.02	0.01	-34	0.14	0.08	-0.06	0.00	0.00	0.000	0.14	0.08	-0.06
Mexico	3.8	4.2	13	0.29	0.29	0.00	0.29	0.29	0.002	...	...	...
Nicaragua	0.1	0.1	13	0.57	0.58	0.01	0.40	0.42	0.02	0.17	0.17	0.00
Peru	3.8	4.3	13	1.66	1.74	0.08	1.23	1.48	0.25	0.43	0.26	-0.17
Dominican Republic	0.5	0.2	-65	0.54	0.15	-0.38	0.43	0.15	-0.28	0.11	0.01	-0.10
LAC	27.4	30.4	11	0.67	0.75	0.08	0.42	0.47	0.05	0.25	0.28	0.03

Note: Revenue-to-GDP ratios for Latin America and the Caribbean corresponds to a simple average of the countries included in the sample. Figures may not sum due to rounding. In the case of Chile, lithium revenues refer to property rents received by the central government from the participation of the State in lithium sales as established in contracts with SQM Salar S.A. and Albemarle Ltda.
Source: Economic Commission for Latin America and the Caribbean (ECLAC), based on data from ECLAC's Fiscal Revenues from Non-Renewable Natural Resources in Latin America and the Caribbean database.

The regional increase in tax revenues was driven by higher CIT payments in Colombia, Ecuador, Peru and the Plurinational State of Bolivia (Figure 2.4). The increase in the Plurinational State of Bolivia reflected large annual tax filing payments as profits in the sector rose sharply in 2021 due to surging prices for tin and zinc. Minera San Cristóbal, the principal private zinc mining company in the country, registered its highest profits since 2017 in 2021, a marked improvement over the financial loss reported in 2020 (Minera San Cristóbal, 2023[17]). Payments for annual tax filings also boosted CIT receipts in Peru, especially in the first half of the year. Income tax payments in 2022 for the annual tax filing season for fiscal year 2021 reached an all-time high in the country, with the mining sector representing 43% of the total[2]. However, CIT revenues from the sector for the year rose less dramatically, due largely to the high base of comparison with the 4th quarter of 2021, when mining companies made substantial extraordinary payments to address outstanding tax liabilities (Ministerio de Economía y Finanzas del Perú, 2023[18]). In Colombia, there was a similar uptick in CIT receipts for the annual tax campaign, reflecting both higher profits from the dramatic increase in the price of coal as well as advance payments for fiscal year 2022.

Figure 2.4. Latin America and the Caribbean (11 countries): Year-on-year variation in general government CIT receipts from mining, 2021-2022

Percentage points of GDP and percentages based on US dollars

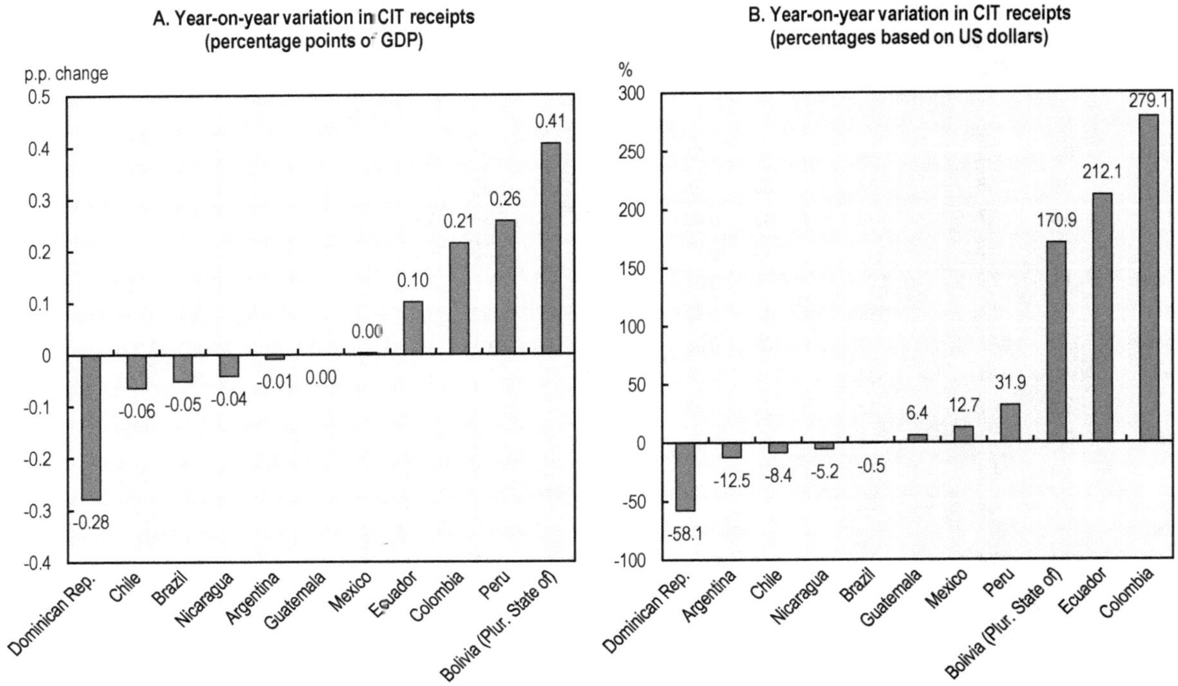

Source: Economic Commission for Latin America and the Caribbean (ECLAC), based on data from ECLAC's Fiscal Revenues from Non-Renewable Natural Resources in Latin America and the Caribbean database.

StatLink https://stat.link/q17286

Non-tax revenues from mining in 2022 were impacted by weakening prices and, in some cases, lower production (Figure 2.5). In Brazil, payments of the federal royalty as well as state-level payments based on the commercial value of production dipped as iron ore prices fell over the year. Likewise, royalty receipts in Peru slipped, but this was also influenced by extraordinary payments in 2021 to liquidate outstanding liabilities by two major mining companies. While price and production influenced royalty payments, declines in some countries were the result of one-off events. In the Dominican Republic, receipts were impacted by prepayments made by Barrick Gold for the years 2021-2023 during 2020 to support COVID-19 relief efforts in the country[3]. Payments of the bauxite levy in Jamaica declined due to a major fire that led to the closure of the Jamalco alumina refinery in August 2021 (Ministry of Finance and the Public Service of Jamaica, 2023[19]). Limited production commenced in August 2022 with the intention to reach regular levels by the end of 2023.

Figure 2.5. Latin America and the Caribbean (11 countries): Year-on-year variation in general government mining non-tax revenues, 2021-2022

Percentage points of GDP and percentages based on US dollars

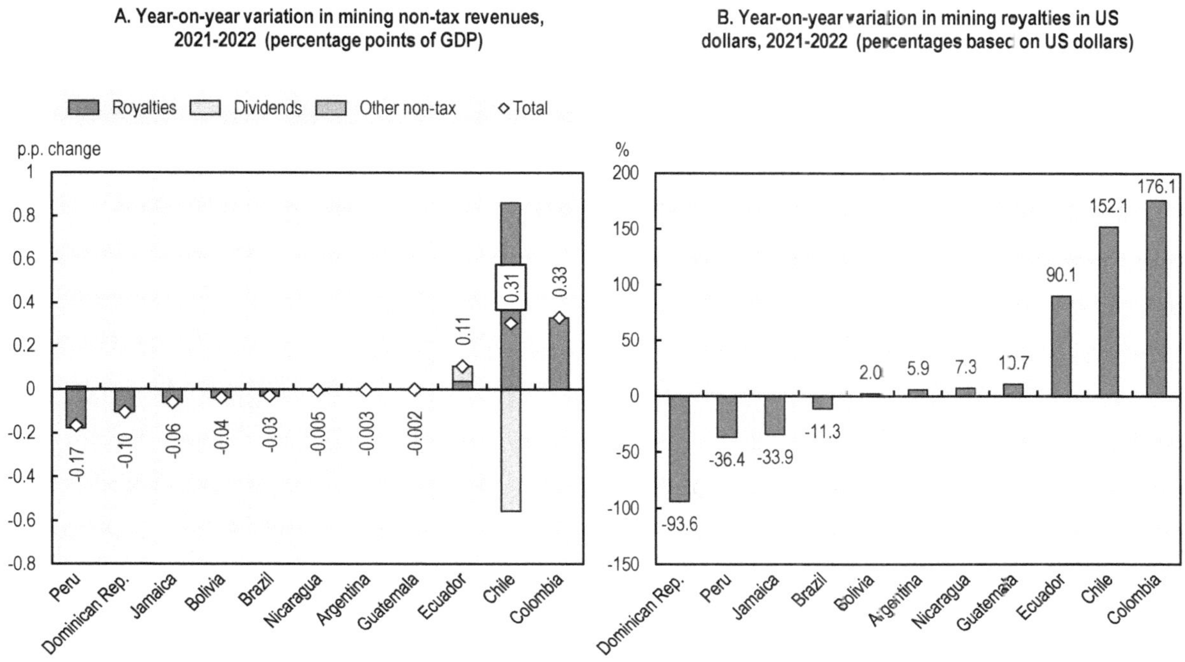

Source: Economic Commission for Latin America and the Caribbean (ECLAC), based on data from ECLAC's Fiscal Revenues from Non-Renewable Natural Resources in Latin America and the Caribbean database.

StatLink https://stat.link/3cahmy

In contrast, non-tax revenues rose strongly in Chile, Colombia and Ecuador in 2022. In Chile, the year-on-year increase was the result of the interplay between falling copper-related revenues and a dramatic upswing in lithium-related payments to the central government. Falling copper prices led to lower receipts of the special contribution paid by Codelco on the USD value of its exports[4]. Additionally, payments of dividends by Codelco to the Treasury fell sharply to 0.1% of GDP (compared with 0.6% of GDP in 2021) (Codelco, 2023[20]). However, these losses were more than compensated by the State's participation in the sales of lithium products by SQM Salar S.A. and Albemarle Limitada, which generated revenues equivalent to 1% of GDP (DIPRES, 2023[21]). In Colombia, royalties associated with coal mining continued to expand significantly in line with the strong growth in prices and an uptick in production. Higher gold production and exports in Ecuador drove royalty payments higher. This was complemented by profit-sharing payments made by mining concessionaires to the Treasury that were equivalent to 0.1% of GDP.

Uncertainty and price volatility strongly impacted fiscal revenues from non-renewable natural resources in the LAC region during 2023

Increasing uncertainty about macroeconomic trends in a high interest rate environment weighed on energy markets during early 2023. Industrial production in advanced economies slowed sharply and even contracted in some European countries, particularly Germany. Economic output also proved sluggish in China; growth in the second quarter significantly undershot market expectations. Against this backdrop, prices in June for Brent and Western Texas Intermediate declined 38% and 39% year-on-year, respectively, while spot prices for natural gas in Europe contracted sharply (-69%) (Figure 2.6).

Figure 2.6. International spot prices for selected energy commodities, January 2021 – December 2023

US dollars per barrel and US dollars per million BTUs

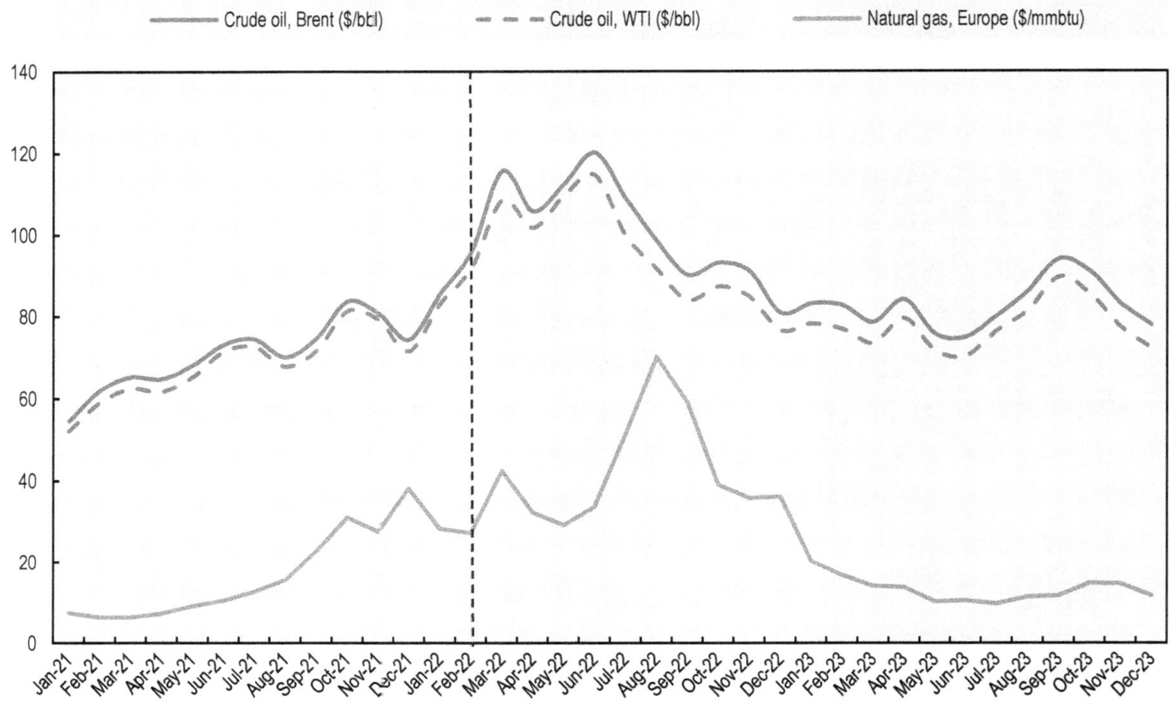

Source: Economic Commission for Latin America and the Caribbean (ECLAC), based on World Bank Commodity Price Data [online] https://www.worldbank.org/en/research/commodity-markets.

StatLink https://stat.link/nygx02

Price dynamics during the first half of the year were also shaped by persistent oversupply conditions. Although consumption rebounded strongly, production continued to outpace demand. In response to this situation, several members of the Organization of Petroleum Exporting Countries and allied countries (OPEC+) announced voluntary production cuts of 1.66 million barrels per day between May and the end of the year[5]. In July, Saudi Arabia announced an additional voluntary cut of 1 million barrels per day; the Russian Federation also committed to a reduction in its oil exports.

Global oil markets exhibited significant volatility in the second half of 2023. Economic activity in the United States surpassed expectations during the third quarter. Likewise, consumption in China rose sharply, propelled by a large increase in petrochemical output and a rebound in transportation after lifting COVID-19 restrictions in 2022. Oil prices rallied in the third quarter reflecting changing market sentiment; Brent reached USD 94 per barrel in September, compared to USD 74.89 in June (+26%). However, these gains were largely reversed by year's end as production in the United States and Brazil reached record levels and production in the Islamic Republic of Iran hit a five-year high (IEA, 2023[22]).

The escalation of the conflict between Israel and Hamas after the 7 October attacks intensified uncertainty in global markets in the fourth quarter of the year. While international oil prices continued to trend lower, natural gas prices in Europe increased. Natural gas prices on the continent were significantly impacted by the shutdown of a coastal gas field in Israel and an explosion of pipeline infrastructure in the Baltic Sea (World Bank, 2023[23]). Disruptions to tanker traffic in the Red Sea also exerted pressure on oil prices, but this proved to be transitory and was offset by slowing global oil demand and increased output in the fourth quarter of the year.

Hydrocarbon revenues in the LAC region fell in 2023 in line with market conditions. General government revenues from oil and gas exploration and production activities averaged an estimated 3.9% in 2023 (down from 4.4% of GDP in 2022) (Figure 2.7). Non-tax revenues from royalties and other participations in the commercial value of production, which make up the bulk of revenues in the region, declined in most countries due to the fall in oil prices. In Brazil, record production attenuated the fall in payments of royalties and special participations but could not offset the halving of dividends paid by Petrobras to the federal government. While oil output increased in Mexico, revenues in national currency tumbled due to the appreciation of the Mexican peso and the deferral to 2024 of Pemex's profit-sharing duty payments for the months of October and November.[6]

Figure 2.7. Latin America and the Caribbean (10 countries): General government revenues from oil and gas exploration and production, 2013 – 2023

Percentage of GDP

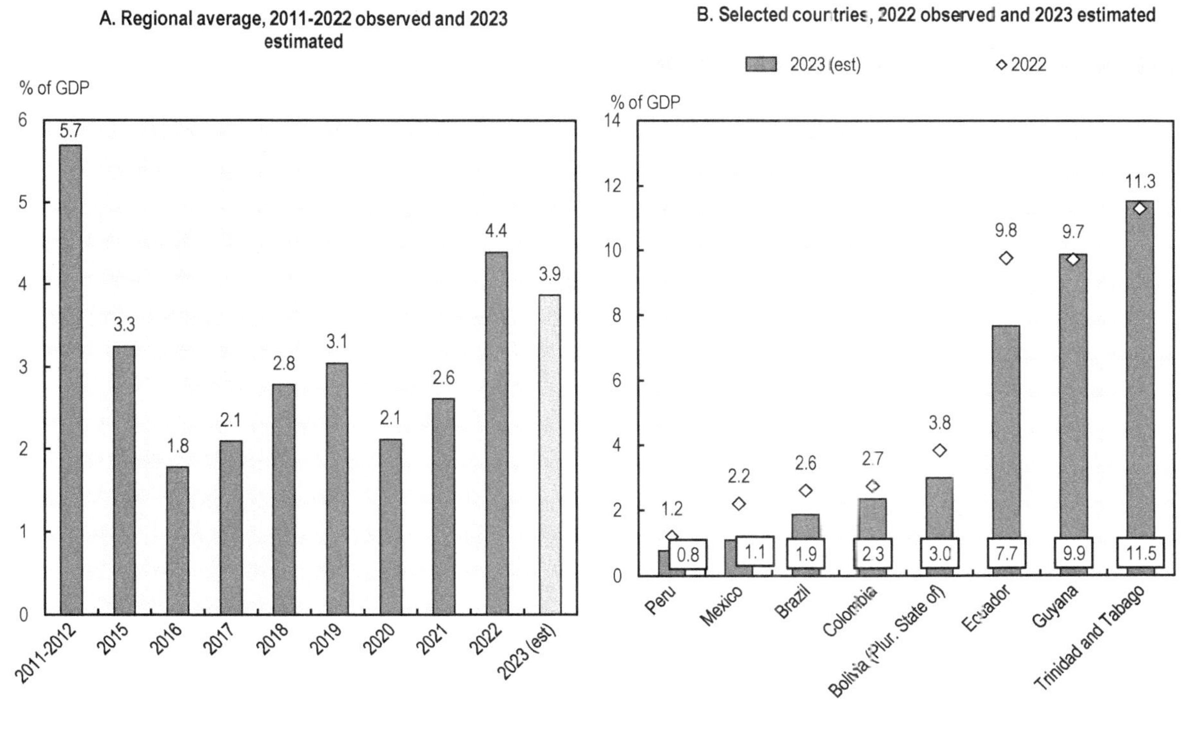

Note: 10 countries include Argentina, Bolivia (Plurinational State of), Brazil, Colombia, Ecuador, Guatemala, Guyana, Mexico, Peru, and Trinidad and Tobago. Data for Mexico correspond to federal government oil revenue, they exclude own revenues of Pemex the State-owned oil and gas producer. In Ecuador to oil revenues of the non-financial public sector derived from exports of crude oil. In Guyana to revenues deposited in the Natural Resource Fund. Regional average refers to simple average. Figures for 2023 are based on official sources, forecasts and estimates based on the 2023 annual variation in representative products applied to revenues in 2022.
Source: Economic Commission for Latin America and the Caribbean (ECLAC), based on data from ECLAC's Fiscal Revenues from Non-Renewable Natural Resources in Latin America and the Caribbean database.

StatLink https://stat.link/oem8xs

Lower production of oil and gas aggravated the impact of lower prices on non-tax revenues in some countries. A marginal reduction in oil output in Ecuador combined with the decline in the export price led to a sharp contraction in oil revenues as a share of GDP; being a dollarised economy, these price shocks are not buffered by movements in the exchange rate (Ministerio de Economía y Finanzas del Ecuador, 2024[24]). Although production of crude oil contracted significantly in Trinidad and Tobago, royalty revenue surged, in part due to production-sharing contract payments related to the previous year, when prices were high. In the Plurinational State of Bolivia, hydrocarbon revenues fell due to the progressive depletion of existing fields reducing natural gas production and declining demand lowering exports to Brazil (Banco Central de Bolivia, 2023[25]).

Hydrocarbon tax revenues generally trended lower in 2023 as the decline in international prices impacted profit margins. CIT receipts contracted in Brazil and Peru because of lower payments from annual tax declarations for fiscal year 2022 and a decline in estimated tax payments for fiscal year 2023 (Receita Federal, 2024[26]; Ministerio de Economía y Finanzas del Perú, 2024[27]). A similar dynamic occurred in Trinidad and Tobago, where CIT payments, which constitute a significant share of total revenues from oil, contracted sharply as price swings impacted profit margins. In contrast, CIT receipts in Colombia were robust in the face of lower prices due in large part to the structural tax reform approved in late 2022[7]. Most notably, the reform set the CIT rate to 35% and included several provisions specifically targeting the oil and gas sector. Hydrocarbon producers must now pay a CIT surcharge that ranges from 5 percentage points to 15 percentage points depending on the price level. Royalty payments are also no longer deductible from the CIT[8].

The factors that roiled energy markets in 2023 also affected global markets for minerals and metals. The deceleration of industrial production in advanced economies and weak residential construction in China prompted a significant correction in the prices of a wide range of minerals and metals during the first half of the year (Figure 2.8). However, prices rebounded in the second half of the year.

Imports of copper concentrates and refined copper in China grew strongly, supported by rising investments in the country's electricity sector, supporting a recovery in copper prices. Iron ore prices also recovered because year-end steel production caps in China, which reduced output in prior years, were not enforced. Gold prices also rallied in part due to the escalation of the conflict between Israel and Hamas after the 7 October attacks. In contrast, prices for thermal coal fell markedly because higher supply from Australia and Indonesia outpaced demand growth. Lithium prices, which surged in 2022, plummeted due to oversupply in the market.

Figure 2.8. Year-on-year variation of international spot prices for selected minerals and metals, 2022-2023

Percentage

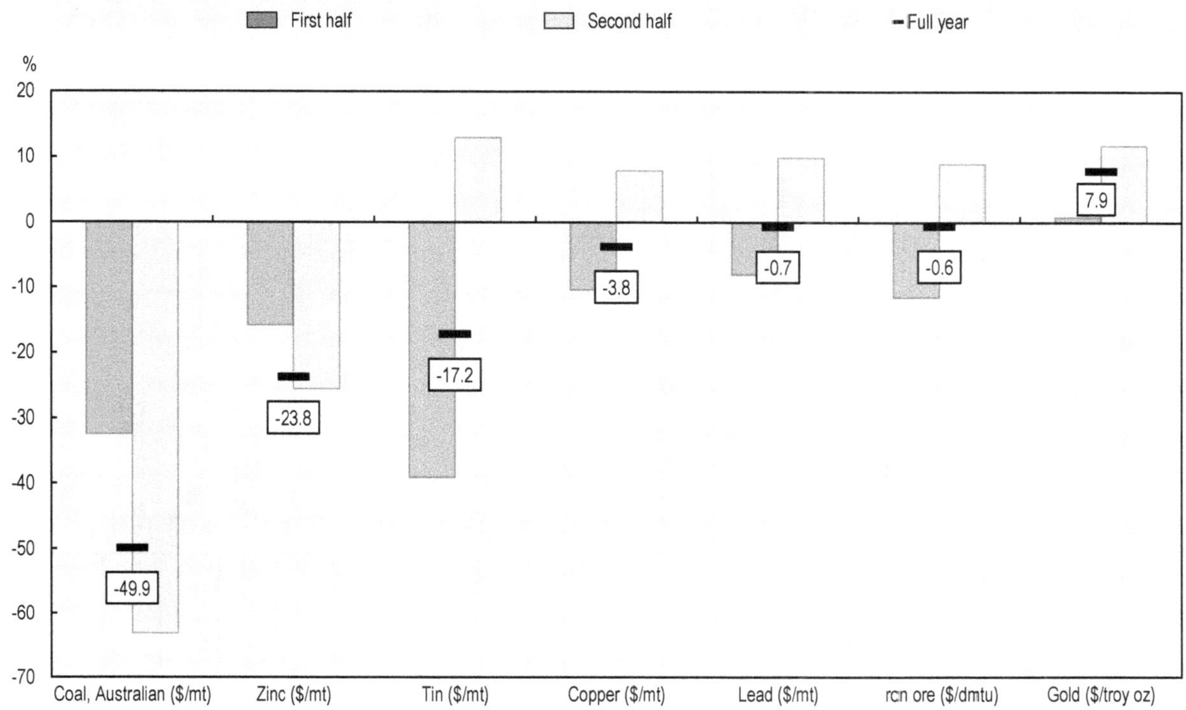

Source: Economic Commission for Latin America and the Caribbean (ECLAC), based on World Bank Commodity Price Data [online] https://www.worldbank.org/en/research/commodity-markets.

StatLink https://stat.link/5mdip9

Fiscal revenues from mining in Latin America and the Caribbean were affected by trends in global markets and domestic production. Mining revenues are estimated to have fallen to 0.53% of GDP (compared to a high of 0.75% of GDP in 2022) (Figure 2.9). Lower prices dragged down non-tax revenues from royalties tied to the commercial value of production in most countries. However, lithium payments in Chile remained strong despite the decline in prices. The principal driver of lower mining revenues was a collapse in CIT payments in Brazil, Chile and Peru. Advance CIT payments made in 2022 were higher than year-end tax liabilities in some cases, leading to a significant decline in annual tax payments made in 2023 (DIPRES, 2024[28]; Receita Federal, 2024[26]). Advance tax payments in 2023 were lower as taxpayers made use of 2022 overpayments to cover their estimated liabilities (Ministerio de Economía y Finanzas del Perú, 2024[27]).

Figure 2.9. Latin America and the Caribbean (12 countries): General government fiscal revenues from mining, 2011-2023

Percentage of GDP

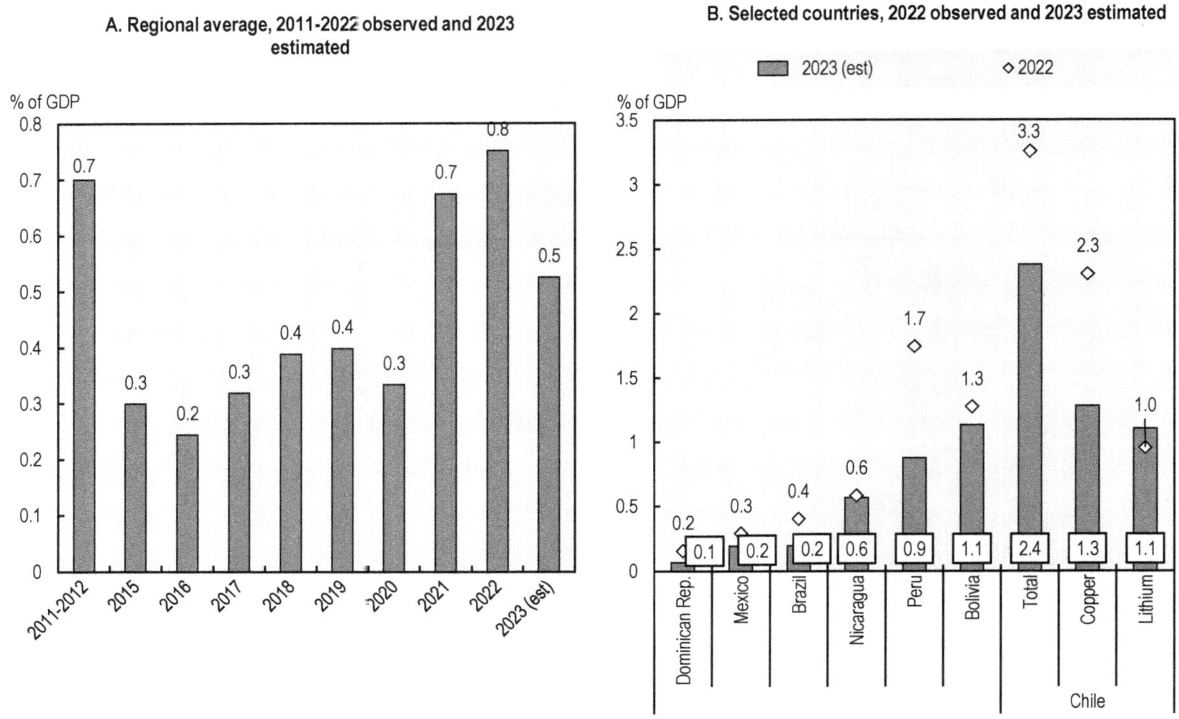

Note: 12 countries include Argentina, Bolivia (Plurinational State of), Brazil, Chile, Colombia, Dominican Republic, Ecuador, Guatemala, Jamaica, Mexico, Nicaragua, and Peru. In the case of Chile, lithium revenues refer to property rents received by the central government from the participation of the State in lithium sales as established in contracts with SQM Salar S.A. and Albemarle Ltda. Regional average refers to simple average. Figures for 2023 are based on official sources, forecasts and estimates based on the 2023 annual variation in representative products applied to revenues in 2022.

Source: Economic Commission for Latin America and the Caribbean (ECLAC), based on data from ECLAC's Fiscal Revenues from Non-Renewable Natural Resources in Latin America and the Caribbean database.

StatLink https://stat.link/ezlok4

References

ANH (2023), *Informe de Gestión 2022*, Agencia Nacional de Hidrocarburos de Colombia, https://www.anh.gov.co/documents/21271/Informe_de_gesti%C3%B3n_2022.pdf. [6]

Banco Central de Bolivia (2023), *Memoria 2022*, Banco Central de Bolivia, https://www.bcb.gob.bo/webdocs/publicacionesbcb/2023/05/28/CAP%201.pdf. [25]

Banco Central de Reserva del Perú (2023), *Memoria 2022*, Banco Central de Reserva del Perú, https://www.bcrp.gob.pe/publicaciones/memoria-anual/memoria-2022.html. [2]

Bank of Guyana (2023), *Annual Report 2022*, Bank of Guyana, https://bankofguyana.org.gy/bog/images/research/Reports/ANNREP2022.pdf. [1]

Central Bank of Trinidad and Tobago (2023), *Annual Economic Survey 2022*, Central Bank of Trinidad and Tobago, https://www.central-bank.org.tt/sites/default/files/page-file-uploads/annual-economic-survey-2022-20230515.pdf. [9]

Codelco (2023), *Consolidated Financial Statements (December 31, 2022)*, Corporación Nacional del Cobre de Chile, https://www.codelco.com/sites/site/docs/20221206/20221206195727/eeff_31_12_2022_codelco_ingles.pdf. [20]

Codelco (2023), *Memoria Integrada 2022*, Corporación Nacional del Cobre de Chile, https://www.codelco.com/sites/site/docs/20230607/20230607094540/m22_eng__1_.pdf. [11]

DIPRES (2024), *Informe de ejecución del gobierno central: cuarto trimester 2023*, Dirección de Presupuestos de Chile, https://www.dipres.gob.cl/598/articles-309977_doc_pdf_Presentacion_IT.pdf. [28]

DIPRES (2023), *Informe de finanzas públicas: cuarto trimester 2022*, Dirección de Presupuestos de Chile, https://www.dipres.gob.cl/598/articles-306313_Informe_PDF.pdf. [21]

Ecopetrol (2023), *Form 20-F 2022, U.S. Securities and Exchange Commission*, https://www.sec.gov/ixviewer/ix.html?doc=/Archives/edgar/data/1444406/000140578230000400/ec-20221231x20f.htm. [3]

Energy Institute (2023), *Statistical Review of World Energy 2023*, https://www.energyinst.org/__data/assets/pdf_file/0004/1055542/EI_Stat_Review_PDF_single_3.pdf. [13]

IEA (2023), *Oil Market Report – December 2023*, International Energy Agency, https://www.iea.org/reports/oil-market-report-december-2023. [22]

LME (2023), *Independent Review of Events in the Nickel Market in March 2022*, London Metal Exchange, https://www.lme.com/-/media/Files/Trading/New-initiatives/Nickel-independent-review/Independent-Review-of-Events-in-the-Nickel-Market-in-March-2022---Final-Report.pdf. [10]

Minera San Cristóbal (2023), *Sustainability Report 2022*, https://www.minerasancristobal.com/reportedesostenibilidad/pdfs/Sustainability%20Report%20MSC%202022.pdf?v=21. [17]

Ministerio de Economía y Finanzas del Ecuador (2024), *Informe de ejecución del Presupuesto General del Estado, correspondiente a los períodos octubre-diciembre 2023 y enero-diciembre 2023*, https://www.finanzas.gob.ec/wp-content/uploads/downloads/2024/02/Informe_ejecucion_PGE_ene_dic_4to-trim_2023_vf-1.pdf. [24]

Ministerio de Economía y Finanzas del Perú (2024), *Report fiscal trimestral: seguimiento de las reglas macrofiscales cuarto trimestre 2023*, https://cdn.www.gob.pe/uploads/document/file/5782584/5135441-informe-trimestral-de-reglas-fiscales-4t2023.pdf?v=1706667603. [27]

Ministerio de Economía y Finanzas del Perú (2023), *Report fiscal trimestral: seguimiento de las reglas macrofiscales cuarto trimestre 2022*, https://cdn.www.gob.pe/uploads/document/file/4081096/Informe_Trimestral_de_Reglas_Fiscales_IV_Trim2022.pdf.pdf?v=1675185187. [18]

Ministerio de Hacienda y Crédito Público de Colombia (2024), *Plan Financiero 2024*, https://www.minhacienda.gov.co/webcenter/ShowProperty?nodeId=%2FConexionContent%2FWCC_CLUSTER-238250%2F%2FidcPrimaryFile&revision=latestreleased. [29]

Ministerio de Hacienda y Crédito Público de Colombia (2023), *Cierre fiscal: gobierno nacional central 2022*, https://www.minhacienda.gov.co/webcenter/ShowProperty?nodeId=%2FConexionContent%2FWCC_CLUSTER-214767%2F%2FidcPrimaryFile&revision=latestreleased. [8]

Ministerio de Minería y Metalurgia de Bolivia (2023), *Anuario Estadístico y Situación del la Minería 2022*, https://mineria.gob.bo/revista/pdf/20230322-15-01-44.pdf. [15]

Ministry of Finance and the Public Service of Jamaica (2023), *Opening Budget Presentation 2023*, https://www.mof.gov.jm/wp-content/uploads/HMFPS-BUDGET-PRESENTATION-Edited-Final-1-5.pdf. [19]

Petrobras (2023), *Annual report and Form 20-F 2022*, https://api.mziq.com/mzfilemanager/v2/d/25fdf098-34f5-4608-b7fa-17d60b2de47d/23f48cb9-9972-be78-2996-b3a79b5c351c?origin=1. [5]

Petrobras (2022), *Annual report and Form 20-F 2021*, https://api.mziq.com/mzfilemanager/v2/d/25fdf098-34f5-4608-b7fa-17d60b2de47d/2741b9b8-e6d8-4d84-0458-43d96f085287?origin=1. [4]

Receita Federal (2024), *Análise da Arrecadação das Receitas Federais – Dezembro de 2023*, https://www.gov.br/receitafederal/pt-br/centrais-de-conteudo/publicacoes/relatorios/arrecadacao-federal/2023/analise-mensal-dez-2023.pdf. [26]

SQM (2023), *Form 20-F 2022*, Sociedad Química y Minera de Chile, https://s25.q4cdn.com/757756353/files/doc_financials/2022/ar/20f-2022_final.pdf. [14]

Tesouro Nacional (2023), *Resultado do Tesouro Nacional: Dezembro 2022*, Secretaria do Tesouro Nacional Brasil, https://sisweb.tesouro.gov.br/apex/f?p=2501:9::::9:P9_ID_PUBLICACAO:46073. [7]

USGS (2024), *Mineral Commodity Summaries: Lithium, January 2024*, United States Geological Survey, https://pubs.usgs.gov/periodicals/mcs2024/mcs2024-lithium.pdf. [16]

Vale (2023), *Vale's production and sales in 4Q22 and 2022*, https://api.mziq.com/mzfilemanager/v2/d/53207d1c-63b4-48f1-96b7-19869fae19fe/3273bd23-534d-9b9f-8bc3-3d0643bae6ee?origin=1. [12]

World Bank (2023), *Commodity Markets Outlook: October 2023*, World Bank, Washington, D.C., https://openknowledge.worldbank.org/server/api/core/bitstreams/27189ca2-d947-4ca2-8e3f-a36b3b5bf4ba/content. [23]

Notes

[1] Ministerio de Desarrollo Productivo de Argentina, Tablero global del litio, https://www.argentina.gob.ar/economia/mineria/siacam/tablero-global-del-litio.

[2] Sunat, "Campaña de renta alcanza recaudación histórica de más de s/ 13 mil millones", https://www.sunat.gob.pe/salaprensa/2022/abril/NotaPrensaN0272022.doc.

[3] Barrick Gold, "El pago de impuestos y regalías de $108 millones de Pueblo Viejo lleva las contribuciones al Gobierno a más de $385 millones en 2020", https://www.barrick.com/Spanish/noticias/news-details/2020/El-pago-de-impuestos-y-regalas-de-108-millones-de-Pueblo-Viejo-lleva-las-contribuciones-al-Gobierno-a-ms-de-385-millones-en-2020/default.aspx.

[4] Law 13.196 establishes that Codelco will remit 10% of the USD value of the exports of copper and associated by-products to the treasury.

[5] Organization of the Petroleum Exporting Countries (OPEC), press release, "48th Meeting of the Joint Ministerial Monitoring Committee", 3 April 2023, https://www.opec.org/opec_web/en/press_room/7120.htm.

[6] Diario Official de la Federación, "Décima resolución de modificaciones a la resolución miscelánea fiscal para 2023", 28 December 2023 https://www.dof.gob.mx/nota_detalle.php?codigo=5712946&fecha=28/12/2023#gsc.tab=0.

[7] Ley 2277 de 2022, "por medio de la cual se adopta una reforma tributaria para la igualdad y la justicia social y se dictan otras disposiciones", https://www.funcionpublica.gov.co/eva/gestornormativo/norma.php?i=199883.

[8] In November 2023 the Colombian Supreme Court ruled against the non-deducibility of royalties (decision C-489 of 2023). However, advanced payments for fiscal year 2023 were already made during the year based on the non-deducibility of royalties. The Ministry of Finance projects that taxpayers will claim these overpayments on their tax filings in 2024, depressing income tax revenues for that year (Ministerio de Hacienda y Crédito Público de Colombia, 2024[29]).

3 Equivalent fiscal pressure in Latin America and the Caribbean (1990-2021): Updating the enlarged map of the region's fiscal revenues

Introduction to Equivalent Fiscal Pressure (EFP)

The tax burden is a crucial variable for public policies, defined as the amount of financial resources – as a percentage of the gross domestic product (GDP) – that a country raises through taxes and contributions to public social security arrangements to finance public spending. However, other sources of public revenues and alternative configurations of the basic functions of the State exist in different countries, which could affect the comparability of tax burden indicators.

For example, the availability of natural resources – whether renewable or non-renewable – may allow governments to supplement public finances by raising revenues through non-tax instruments such as royalties or dividends and interests, revenues not computed in the tax burden ratio. This is the case for certain hydrocarbon and mineral resources, of great relevance in several Latin American and Caribbean (LAC) countries, as well as the management of other infrastructure, such as the the Transoceanic Canal in Panama or the hydroelectric power stations of Itaipú and Yacyretá in Paraguay.

In a similar vein, in the areas of health and social security, some countries implement private schemes of individual capitalisation – of a mandatory nature, established in legislation – that replace, complement or compete with the public social security system. These private social security contributions, although not included in public financing and administered by private entities, are part of the overall amount of resources that are compulsory and collectively mobilised; their consideration allows for more homogeneous comparisons between countries.

In order to take into account these alternative ways to finance public spending, this chapter discusses the concept of 'Equivalent Fiscal Pressure' (EFP), which includes two additional sources of revenue beyond those traditionally considered (tax revenues including public social security contributions [SSCs]), which also represent a fiscal effort required from taxpayers when they are mandatory: contributions to a private social security system (pensions and health) and non-tax revenues (dividends, royalties, among others) from the exploitation of natural resources. .

Consideration of all these additional components (when official data are available) helps nourish and enrich analyses of fiscal conditions in LAC countries. However, the EFP indicator does not invalidate or contradict conventional measures of public financing. Rather, the aim is to expand the possibilities for regional and international comparison and to provide new elements that are, at least for the specific context in LAC, crucial to a broad and comprehensive perspective of these issues[1].

Evolution of Equivalent Fiscal Pressure in the LAC region

The analysis in this chapter, as well as regional and sub-regional averages cited herein, refer to 25 of the 27 countries for which data appears in this publication, and does not include Cuba and Venezuela[2]. The revenue indicators are not directly comparable with the results shown in Chapter 1, as it is based on data available prior to the publication of this report.

The tax-to-GDP ratio (which includes tax revenues and public SSCs) for the LAC countries considered in this chapter stood at 21.9% of GDP in 2021 (Figure 3.1). The additional revenues accounted for using the EFP methodology increase this ratio by 1.7% of GDP, bringing the total to 23.6% of GDP.

On average across the LAC region, social security contributions to private systems amounted to 0.9% of GDP in 2021, a value that has increased by 0.6 percentage points (p.p.) since 1990 and that has been stable over the five years up to and including 2021. Meanwhile, non-tax public revenues from natural resources amounted to 0.8% of GDP in 2021, a contraction of 0.3 p.p. since 1990, with an even greater decline relative to the figures recorded for such revenues in 2008 and 2013 (1.5% of GDP)

Figure 3.1. Equivalent Fiscal Pressure in Latin America and the Caribbean, 1990-2021

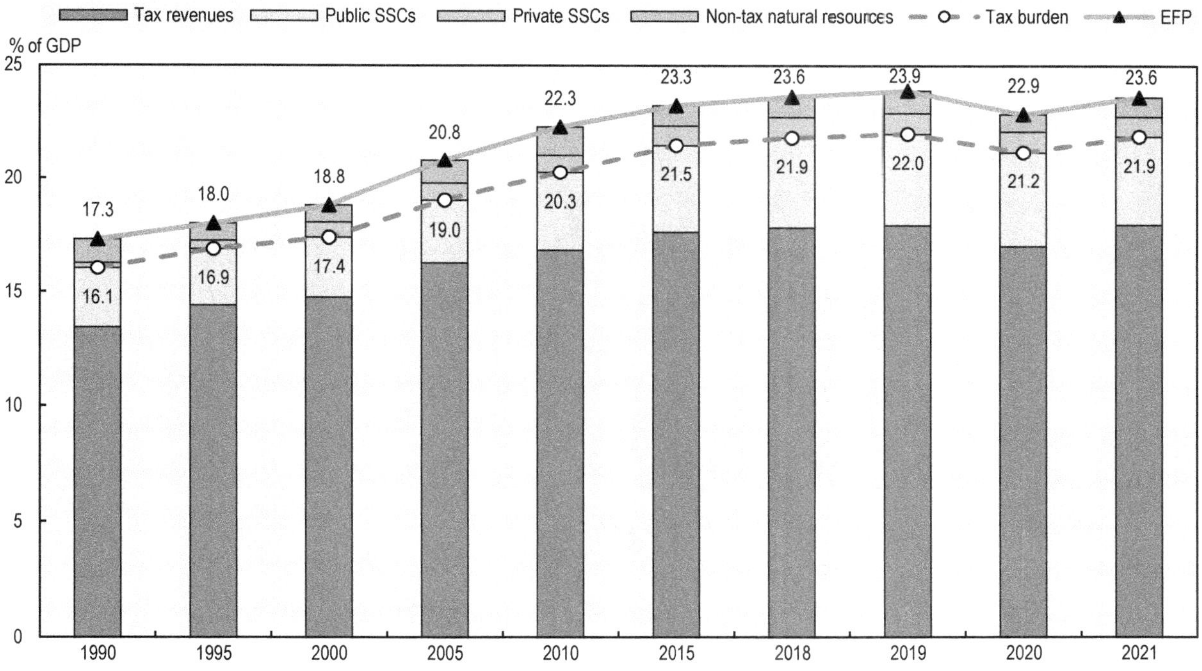

Note: Data refers to the simple average of the 25 LAC countries included in this publication excluding Cuba and Venezuela due to data issues.
Source: Prepared by the authors based on data in (IDB-CIAT, 2023[1]).

StatLink https://stat.link/24wik0

As regards the composition of EFP, the share of tax revenue (including public social security contributions) has remained relatively stable since 1990. In 2021, it accounted for 92.8% of total EFP; excluding public SSCs, this proportion has fluctuated around 75% throughout the period. Private SSCs have increased their share since their implementation in several countries across the region in the 1990s, and in 2021 they accounted for 3.7% of the LAC region's EFP. The share of non-tax revenues from natural resources was 3.6% of the EFP in 2021 but has been more volatile within the structure of the EFP over time.

Evolution of EFP by country

Individual countries in the LAC region show a high degree of heterogeneity in terms of the evolution and level of tax revenues and EFP (Figure 3.2). Although tax revenues have increased in all the countries analysed between 1990 and 2021 with the exceptions of Panama and Trinidad and Tobago, the magnitude of the change has been very uneven, with particularly large increases in Argentina (+13.7 p.p.), Bolivia (+13.0 p.p.), Ecuador (+12.1 p.p.) and El Salvador (+11.7 p.p.).

Similar trends can be noted with respect to EFP levels. With the exception of Panama and Trinidad and Tobago (where EFP fell by 2.4 p.p. and 2.5 p.p., respectively, between 1990 and 2021), all countries in the region show an increase in this indicator. The increases of Argentina (+16.2 p.p.), El Salvador (+15.3 p.p.), Ecuador (+13.0 p.p.), Bolivia (+12.5 p.p.), Dominican Republic (+10.2 p.p.) and Colombia (+9.8 p.p.) stand out.

Figure 3.2. Tax Burden and Equivalent Fiscal Pressure, Latin American and Caribbean (1990 and 2021)

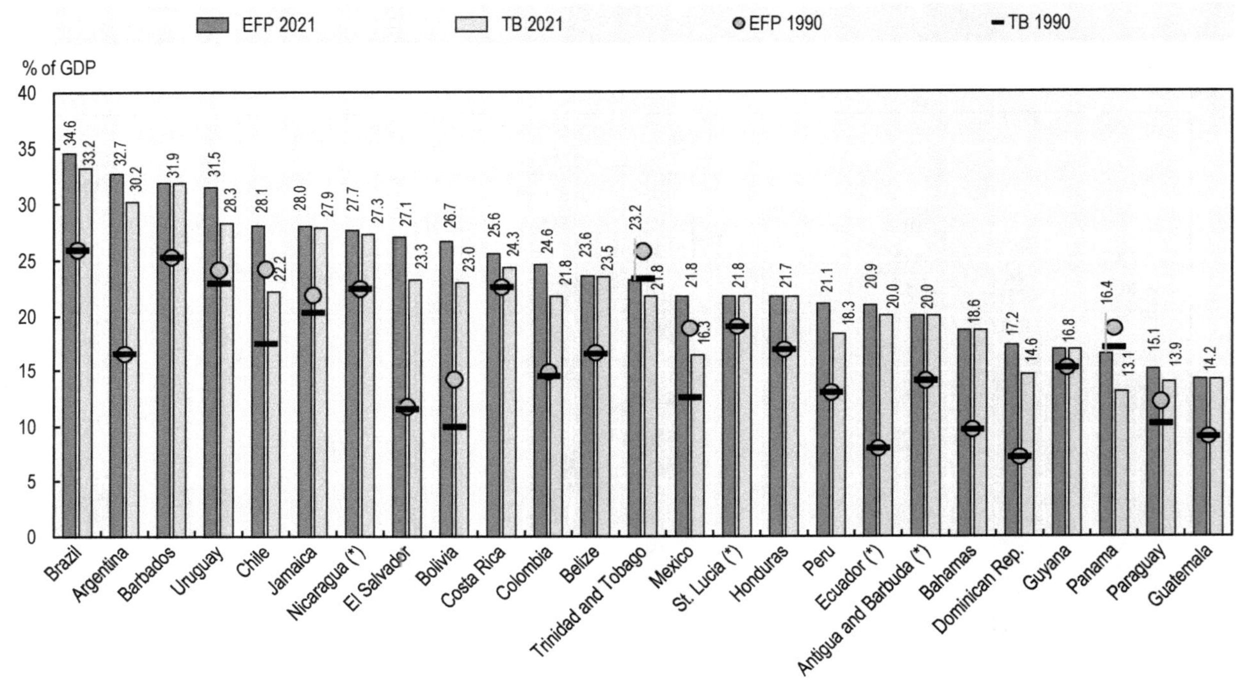

Note: Countries were ordered from highest to lowest according to the level of the Equivalent Fiscal Pressure (EFP) in 2021. For countries marked with an asterisk (*) there is no data for 1990. In these cases, both for tax revenues and EFP, the first year with available information was used as a reference, namely: 1991 in Antigua and Barbuda and Nicaragua; 1992 in Saint. Lucia; and 1993 in Ecuador. This figure does not present the cases of Cuba (according to official figures, in 1990, the EFP stood at 29.1% of GDP and in 2021 it was 17.7%) or Venezuela (due to lack of official information from 2016 to date), although the figures collected can be consulted in the updated EFP database (see the Statistical annex at the end of this chapter).

Source: Prepared by the authors with data from the Equivalent Fiscal Pressure for Latin America and the Caribbean 1990-2021 (IDB-CIAT, 2023[1]).

StatLink https://stat.link/34jlmt

Figure 3.2 ranks countries according to the level of their EFP in 2021. This ranking differs from when countries are ordered according to the level of tax revenues, due to significant gaps between the respective indicators for some countries in particular, as can be appreciated in Figure 3.3.

Figure 3.3. Non-tax revenues from natural resources and private SSCs components of Equivalent Fiscal Pressure, Latin American and Caribbean Countries, 2021

As percentage of GDP (left axis) and percentage of total tax revenues (right axis)

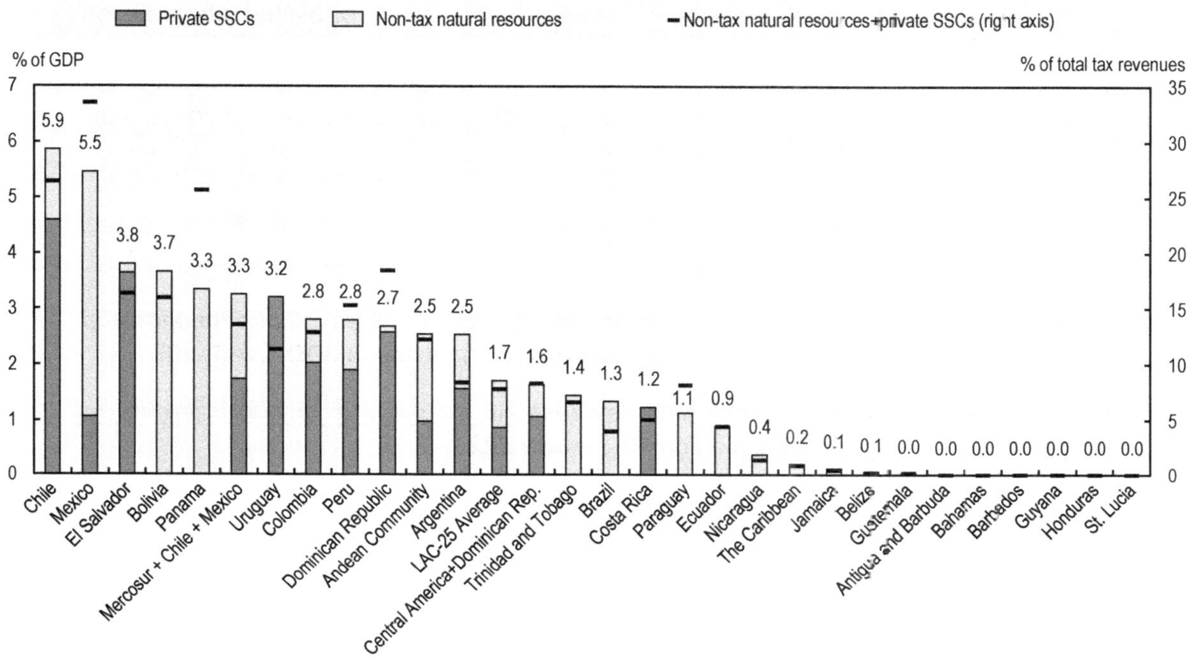

Source: Prepared by the authors with data from the Equivalent Fiscal Pressure for Latin America and the Caribbean 1990-2021 (IDB-CIAT, 2023[1]).

StatLink https://stat.link/n4zlt5

In two countries, mandatory private social security contributions and non-tax revenues from natural resources (which are included in the EFP indicator but not in the tax-to-GDP ratio) amounted to more than 5% of GDP in 2021: Chile (5.9% of GDP) and Mexico (5.5% of GDP). In four countries, they amounted to more than 3% of GDP (El Salvador, Bolivia, Panama and Uruguay); and in another four countries more than 2% of GDP (Colombia, Peru, Dominican Republic and Argentina). In contrast, there is a set of countries (mostly in the Caribbean) where these revenues are practically nil.

In relative terms as regards the tax-to-GDP ratio, considering compulsory private SSCs and non-tax natural resources substantially changes the picture for comparision among countries. Most notably, the EFP is 33.5% higher than the tax-to-GDP ratio in Mexico, 26.4% higher in Chile and 25.6% higher in Panama.

By subsets of countries, considering EFP instead of the tax-to-GDP ratio significantly increases the average for Mercosur+Chile+Mexico (+3.3% of GDP and 13.6% more resources) while the figures for other sub-regions remain practically unchanged (notably among Caribbean countries). The average EFP for all LAC countries considered is 1.7 p.p. of GDP higher than the tax-to-GDP ratio (or 7.8% higher).

The balance between the additional contribution of compulsory private SSCs and non-tax natural resources also varies among countries. Private SSCs account for the bulk of the additional resources in Chile, El Salvador, Uruguay, Dominican Republic and Costa Rica, while non-tax revenues from natural resources do so in Mexico, Bolivia, Panama, Trinidad and Tobago, Brazil, Paraguay, Ecuador and Nicaragua.[3]

Final Comments

Countries' different approaches to designing and structuring public spending and, in particular, how these approaches are financed, can lead in some specific cases to misleading or biased interpretations of the indicators and ratios generally used to evaluate their dimensions and economic effects. EFP aims to complement the benchmark tax-to-GDP ratio for countries that adopt significantly different options, as is the case of LAC countries, to raising public revenues from natural resources (tax or non-tax instruments) or to collecting compulsory contributions to social security systems (public and private schemes).

References

Barreix, A. et al. (2013), *Putting Pressure: Estimating the real fiscal burden in Latin America and the Caribbean. Concept, development and international comparison*, s. IDB, CIAT, IEF. [2]

IDB-CIAT (2023), *IDB-CIAT Revenue Collection database*, https://www.ciat.org/idb-ciat-revenue-collection-database/?lang=en (accessed on 16 January 2024). [1]

Morán, D. and M. Solera (2023), *Equivalent Fiscal Pressure in Latin America and the Caribbean (1990-2021)*, IDB and CIAT, https://biblioteca.ciat.org/opac/book/5852. [3]

OECD et al. (2020), *Revenue Statistics in Latin America and the Caribbean 2020*, OECD Publishing, Paris, https://doi.org/10.1787/68739b9b-en-es. [4]

Annex 3.A. Statistical annex

Annex Table 3.A.1. Structure of the Equivalent Fiscal Pressure (by main tax type) in Latin American and Caribbean countries, 2021

Individual data, as a percentage of GDP

Country	ISO Code	Income Tax				Public SSCs	Property	Goods and services				Other taxes	Tax Revenue (TR)	Private SSCs	Non tax Natural Resources	Total EFP
		Personal	Corporate	Non classifiable	Total IT			General		Excise	International Trade					
								VAT	Other							
Antigua and Barbuda	ATG	0.0	2.1	0.0	2.1	3.3	0.6	6.1	1.9	3.5	2.4	0.1	20.0	0.0	0.0	20.0
Argentina	ARG	2.2	2.5	0.4	5.1	5.1	1.3	7.0	3.8	3.5	3.1	1.3	30.2	1.6	1.0	32.7
Bahamas	BHS	0.0	0.0	0.0	0.0	2.2	1.5	7.5	0.0	2.6	2.9	1.9	18.6	0.0	0.0	18.6
Barbados	BRB	3.8	4.4	0.6	8.8	5.8	2.0	8.7	0.0	4.2	2.2	0.1	31.9	0.0	0.0	31.9
Belize	BLZ	2.2	2.9	0.0	5.1	2.4	0.2	6.6	0.0	5.1	4.1	0.1	23.5	0.0	0.1	23.6
Bolivia	BOL	0.2	2.6	0.0	2.8	6.0	0.1	6.9	1.8	1.9	1.1	2.4	23.0	0.0	3.7	26.7
Brazil	BRA	2.9	3.6	1.3	7.8	7.7	1.6	7.4	4.9	1.5	0.7	1.6	33.2	0.0	1.3	34.6
Chile	CHL	2.4	3.8	2.3	8.5	1.2	0.8	9.5	0.0	1.5	0.2	0.5	22.2	4.6	1.3	28.1
Colombia	COL	1.3	4.5	0.3	6.1	4.6	1.0	5.9	0.9	1.7	0.4	1.1	21.8	2.0	0.8	24.6
Costa Rica	CRI	1.6	3.1	0.5	5.2	9.9	1.1	5.1	0.4	2.2	0.5	0.0	24.3	1.2	0.0	25.6
Dominican Rep.	DOM	1.3	2.8	1.0	5.1	0.1	0.6	4.8	0.0	3.2	0.8	0.1	14.6	2.6	0.1	17.2
Ecuador	ECU	0.1	0.6	3.2	3.9	5.0	0.6	6.2	0.0	2.1	1.1	1.0	20.0	0.0	0.9	20.9
El Salvador	SLV	3.0	3.5	1.1	7.6	2.8	0.1	9.7	0.0	1.7	1.0	0.3	23.3	3.6	0.2	27.1
Guatemala	GTM	0.7	2.8	0.8	4.3	2.2	0.3	5.6	0.0	1.1	0.5	0.3	14.2	0.0	0.0	14.2
Guyana	GUY	2.6	4.5	0.3	7.4	1.6	0.3	2.9	0.0	2.8	1.5	0.4	16.8	0.0	0.0	16.8
Honduras	HND	2.1	3.1	0.0	5.1	3.5	0.2	7.2	0.0	4.0	0.8	0.9	21.7	0.0	0.0	21.7
Jamaica	JAM	3.5	3.1	2.4	9.0	1.4	0.4	8.8	0.0	3.8	2.9	1.5	27.9	0.0	0.1	28.0
Mexico	MEX	3.6	3.4	0.2	7.2	1.8	0.0	4.3	0.0	1.6	0.3	1.2	16.3	1.1	4.4	21.8
Nicaragua	NIC	1.6	6.7	0.0	8.3	6.5	0.3	6.7	0.9	3.5	0.7	0.4	27.3	0.0	0.4	27.7

Panama	PAN	1.7	0.9	0.5	3.1	5.6	0.5	1.8	0.0	0.8	0.4	0.8	13.1	0.0	3.3	16.4
Paraguay	PRY	0.1	2.4	0.0	2.6	3.8	0.2	5.1	0.1	1.1	0.9	0.2	13.9	0.0	1.1	15.1
Peru	PER	1.5	4.7	0.8	7.0	1.9	0.4	7.2	0.0	1.1	0.0	0.8	18.3	1.9	0.9	21.1
St. Lucia	LCA	2.7	1.8	0.3	4.8	2.4	0.2	6.4	0.0	3.5	4.3	0.1	21.8	0.0	0.0	21.8
Trinidad and Tobago	TTO	3.6	7.1	0.0	10.8	2.8	0.0	5.2	0.5	0.8	1.4	0.2	21.8	0.0	1.4	23.2
Uruguay	URY	3.7	2.4	0.3	6.4	8.9	1.9	7.9	0.0	2.5	1.1	-0.3	28.3	3.2	0.0	31.5
Mercosur + Chile + Mexico		2.5	3.0	0.8	6.3	4.7	1.0	6.8	1.5	1.9	1.1	0.7	24.0	1.7	1.5	27.3
Andean Community		0.8	3.1	1.1	5.0	4.4	0.5	6.5	0.7	1.7	0.7	1.3	20.8	1.0	1.6	23.3
Central America and Dominican Rep.		1.7	3.3	0.6	5.5	4.4	0.4	5.8	0.2	2.1	0.7	0.4	19.8	1.1	0.6	21.4
Caribbean		2.3	3.3	0.5	6.0	2.7	0.6	6.5	0.3	3.3	2.7	0.6	22.8	0.0	0.2	23.0
Average LAC-25		1.9	3.2	0.7	5.8	3.9	0.6	6.4	0.6	2.5	1.4	0.7	21.9	0.9	0.8	23.6
Cuba	CUB	1.4	6.8	0.0	8.2	4.4	0.0	0.0	1.2	0.8	0.0	3.2	17.7	0.0	0.0	17.7

Note: "Other taxes" includes payroll taxes, taxes on financial transactions, taxes and simplified non-classifiable regimes, among others.
Source: Prepared by the authors with data from the Equivalent Fiscal Pressure for Latin America and the Caribbean 1990-2021 (IDB-CIAT, 2023[1]).

Annex Table 3.A.2. Structure of the Equivalent Fiscal Pressure (by main tax type) in Latin American and Caribbean countries, 2021

Individual data, as a percentage of total EFP

Country	ISO Code	Income Tax				Public SSCs	Property	Goods and services				Other taxes	Tax Revenue (TR)	Private SSCs	Non tax Natural Resources	Total EFP
		Personal	Corporate	Non classifiable	Total IT			General		Excise	International Trade					
								VAT	Other							
Antigua and Barbuda	ATG	0.0	10.4	0.0	10.4	16.5	3.0	30.4	9.3	17.7	12.2	0.5	100.0	0.0	0.0	100.0
Argentina	ARG	6.6	7.6	1.3	15.5	15.7	3.9	21.4	11.8	10.6	9.6	3.9	92.3	4.8	3.0	100.0
Bahamas	BHS	0.0	0.0	0.0	0.0	12.0	7.8	40.4	0.0	14.0	15.7	10.0	100.0	0.0	0.0	100.0
Barbados	BRB	11.9	13.9	1.9	27.7	18.4	6.3	27.3	0.0	13.1	6.8	0.4	100.0	0.0	0.0	100.0
Belize	BLZ	9.2	12.5	0.0	21.6	10.0	0.7	27.8	0.0	21.7	17.3	0.6	99.8	0.0	0.2	100.0
Bolivia	BOL	0.6	9.7	0.0	10.3	22.6	0.3	25.8	6.8	7.2	4.0	9.1	86.2	0.0	13.8	100.0
Brazil	BRA	8.5	10.5	3.7	22.7	22.3	4.7	21.4	14.1	4.3	2.0	4.7	96.1	0.0	3.9	100.0
Chile	CHL	8.6	13.5	8.2	30.3	4.2	2.9	33.8	0.0	5.4	0.7	1.8	79.1	16.4	4.5	100.0
Colombia	COL	5.3	18.5	1.2	25.0	18.9	4.1	23.8	3.6	7.1	1.4	4.7	88.6	8.2	3.2	100.0
Costa Rica	CRI	6.2	12.0	1.9	20.1	38.7	4.4	19.9	1.4	8.7	1.9	0.1	95.2	4.8	0.0	100.0
Dominican Rep.	DOM	7.4	16.2	5.7	29.4	0.4	3.2	28.1	0.0	18.5	4.6	0.3	84.4	14.9	0.6	100.0
Ecuador	ECU	0.6	2.9	15.3	18.8	23.9	3.1	29.6	0.0	10.2	5.4	4.7	95.7	0.0	4.3	100.0
El Salvador	SLV	11.1	12.9	4.0	28.1	10.5	0.5	35.7	0.0	6.3	3.7	1.1	86.0	13.5	0.6	100.0
Guatemala	GTM	5.1	19.6	5.7	30.4	15.2	2.0	39.2	0.0	7.5	3.7	1.8	99.8	0.0	0.2	100.0
Guyana	GUY	15.2	26.9	1.9	43.9	9.5	1.8	17.1	0.0	16.4	9.1	2.2	100.0	0.0	0.0	100.0
Honduras	HND	9.6	14.1	0.0	23.7	16.2	0.7	33.2	0.0	18.5	3.6	4.2	100.0	0.0	0.0	100.0
Jamaica	JAM	12.6	11.1	8.5	32.2	5.1	1.5	31.4	0.0	13.7	10.2	5.4	99.6	0.0	0.4	100.0
Mexico	MEX	16.4	15.8	1.0	33.2	8.2	0.0	19.6	0.0	7.2	1.3	5.4	74.9	4.9	20.2	100.0
Nicaragua	NIC	5.7	24.2	0.0	29.9	23.5	1.3	24.2	3.2	12.8	2.4	1.3	98.6	0.0	1.4	100.0
Panama	PAN	10.6	5.6	3.0	19.2	34.2	3.1	10.8	0.0	4.9	2.7	4.6	79.6	0.0	20.4	100.0
Paraguay	PRY	0.9	16.1	0.0	17.0	25.2	1.6	33.6	0.6	7.4	5.9	1.1	92.5	0.0	7.5	100.0
Peru	PER	7.0	22.5	3.7	33.2	8.9	1.8	34.0	0.0	5.1	0.2	3.7	86.7	9.0	4.3	100.0
St. Lucia	LCA	12.5	8.1	1.5	22.1	10.9	0.8	29.6	0.0	16.3	19.6	0.7	100.0	0.0	0.0	100.0
Trinidad and Tobago	TTO	15.6	30.7	0.0	46.4	12.2	0.0	22.4	2.4	3.5	6.2	0.8	93.8	0.0	6.2	100.0

Uruguay	URY	11.7	7.5	1.0	20.3	28.1	5.9	25.0	0.0	7.8	3.6	-1.0	89.8	10.2	0.0	100.0
Mercosur + Chile + Mexico		9.1	11.1	2.8	23.0	17.4	3.5	25.1	5.4	7.1	3.9	2.7	88.1	6.4	5.6	100.0
Andean Community		3.3	13.4	4.6	21.3	18.8	2.3	28.0	2.9	7.4	2.8	5.7	89.1	4.2	6.7	100.0
Central America and Dominican Rep.		8.0	15.2	2.6	25.8	20.4	2.1	27.2	0.8	11.0	3.1	1.8	92.3	5.0	2.7	100.0
Caribbean		10.0	14.1	2.0	26.1	11.9	2.8	28.4	1.3	14.4	11.8	2.4	99.1	0.0	0.9	100.0
Average LAC-25		8.2	13.5	2.8	24.4	16.7	2.7	27.1	2.6	10.4	6.0	2.9	92.8	3.7	3.6	100.0
Cuba	CUB	7.6	38.5	0.0	46.2	25.0	0.0	0.0	6.7	4.2	0.0	17.9	100.0	0.0	0.0	100.0

Note: "Other taxes" includes payroll taxes, taxes on financial transactions, taxes and simplified non-classifiable regimes, among others.
Source: Prepared by the authors with data from the Equivalent Fiscal Pressure for Latin America and the Caribbean 1990-2021 (IDB-CIAT, 2023[1]).

Notes

[1] For more detail about the methodological basis of the EFP and previous analysis of the figures available during the last decade, refer to the IDB-CIAT Revenue Collection database webpage (https://www.ciat.org/idb-ciat-revenue-collection-database/?lang=en) and (Barreix et al., 2013[2]). The figures used in this chapter are based on Morán and Solera (2023). The chapter updates previous analysis of EFP, prior to the COVID-19 pandemic, contained in the 2020 edition of this report (OECD et al., 2020[4]).

[2] In the case of Cuba, a recent monetary reform and the inflation triggered by the COVID-19 pandemic led to a sharp increase in nominal GDP between 2020 and 2021 (a more than five-fold increase in nominal terms) and created a sructural break in the country's tax level and structure. This resulted in an unprecedented drop in EFP from 37 5% percent of GDP in 2020 to 17.7% of GDP in 2021, which is mainly explained by the drop in the sales tax rate and the reclassification of extraordinary revenues as non-taxable. In a medium-term analysis, this would undoubtedly introduce an artificial bias in the averages calculated for the region as a whole. In the case of Venezuela, no official data are available since 2016. However, figures compiled at the individual level are included (in Cuba until 2021 and in Venezuela until 2015), which are made available to interested users in the EFP online database. There is also no official statistical information available for certain countries in particular years, namely: Antigua and Barbuda (1990), Ecuador (1990-92), Nicaragua (1990) and Saint Lucia (1990-91).

[3] Detailed figures can be found in the statistical annex at the end of the chapter while methodology and sources of information may be consulted in (Morán and Solera, 2023[3]).

4 Tax levels and tax structures, 1990-2022

In all of the following tables a (..) indicates not available. The main series in this volume cover the years 1990 to 2022.

Figures referring to 1991-99, 2001-04, 2006-09, 2011-16 in Tables 4.1 to 4.2 and Tables 4.15 to 4.17, figures relating to 1991-99, 2001-09 and 2011-20 in Tables 4.5 to 4.10 and figures relating to 1990-94, 1996-99 and 2001-21 in Tables 4.11 to 4.13 have been omitted because of lack of space. Complete series are, however, available on line at www.latameconomy.org and in the database OECD (2024), "Revenue Statistics in Latin America and the Caribbean: Comparative tables", *OECD Tax Statistics,* http://dx.doi.org/10.1787/data-00641-en.

Table 4.1. Total tax revenue as % of GDP, 1990-2022

	1990	2000	2005	2010	2017	2018	2019	2020	2021	2022
Antigua and Barbuda[1]	..	12.0	15.4	21.3	19.6	19.0	18.0	19.8	20.1	19.1
Argentina	13.3	19.2	24.5	29.1	30.0	28.5	28.5	29.7	29.0	29.6
Bahamas[1]	9.7	12.2	11.2	12.7	17.3	16.9	19.1	18.4	18.0	19.6
Barbados	25.3	30.9	31.3	30.0	32.7	33.3	32.3	33.4	31.9	30.5
Belize	15.9	14.1	16.6	21.0	23.0	24.1	24.7	21.4	21.6	22.1
Bolivia	6.5	17.6	20.0	22.9	25.9	25.0	24.7	22.2	22.6	23.7
Brazil	27.8	29.4	32.7	31.7	31.7	32.0	31.9	30.5	32.5	33.3
Chile	16.8	18.7	20.8	19.7	20.2	21.3	21.0	19.3	22.2	23.9
Colombia	11.3	15.7	18.3	18.1	19.0	19.3	19.7	18.8	19.2	19.7
Costa Rica	22.4	21.1	21.8	22.1	23.0	23.2	23.4	22.6	25.0	25.5
Cuba[2]	31.9	37.2	41.1	37.2	42.4	42.3	42.1	37.5	17.7	18.3
Dominican Republic	8.3	12.1	13.8	12.2	13.1	13.1	13.4	12.5	14.5	13.9
Ecuador[1]	7.1	11.6	13.8	16.8	20.2	21.1	19.9	18.7	19.4	20.9
El Salvador	11.3	14.2	17.0	18.7	21.0	21.3	21.0	21.7	22.8	22.9
Guatemala	7.9	11.7	13.1	12.5	13.2	13.2	13.0	12.4	14.1	14.4
Guyana	15.2	15.7	17.6	16.0	19.5	22.2	23.2	21.3	16.8	10.6
Honduras	12.4	17.2	17.9	18.2	21.7	21.9	21.5	19.2	21.2	21.4
Jamaica	20.3	22.2	23.3	24.9	27.3	27.7	28.6	27.7	27.9	29.3
Mexico	12.1	11.5	11.4	12.8	16.1	16.1	16.3	17.7	17.3	16.9
Nicaragua[1]	..	14.3	17.4	19.3	23.8	23.2	25.5	25.4	27.0	27.8
Panama[1]	16.6	15.5	13.6	16.4	15.1	14.3	13.5	12.7	12.0	13.1
Paraguay	8.5	11.6	10.7	12.1	14.0	13.9	13.9	13.5	13.9	14.7
Peru	12.0	15.2	16.6	17.8	15.3	16.5	16.7	15.3	18.1	19.2
Saint Lucia[1]	..	19.3	19.4	20.6	20.4	20.7	20.8	21.3	19.8	18.4
Trinidad and Tobago	23.3	21.9	28.3	28.7	19.7	22.8	24.3	22.1	22.4	23.7
Uruguay[1]	18.3	21.3	22.9	24.2	26.5	26.7	26.2	26.6	25.6	26.6
Venezuela[3]	21.2	13.5	15.9	11.8	..	..	..	..	..	..
Unweighted average										
LAC[4]	**14.6**	**17.1**	**18.8**	**20.0**	**21.2**	**21.5**	**21.6**	**21.0**	**21.3**	**21.5**
OECD[5]	**30.8**	**32.9**	**32.6**	**31.5**	**33.3**	**33.5**	**33.4**	**33.6**	**34.2**	**34.0**

.. Not available

Note: The figures exclude local government revenues for Antigua and Barbuda, Argentina (but include provincial revenues), the Bahamas, Barbados, Cuba (except for 2002-2012), the Dominican Republic, Saint Lucia, Trinidad and Tobago and Venezuela as the data are not available. Local government revenue data have been available since 1991 for Nicaragua, since 1994 for Bolivia, since 1995 for Guatemala, since 1996 for Jamaica, since 1999 for Panama, since 2000 for Peru, since 2002 for El Salvador and Guyana, since 2006 for Paraguay and since 1990 for all other countries.

1. The data include the following estimations: Antigua and Barbuda (social security contributions for 2019-2022), the Bahamas (social security contributions for 2021 and 2022), Ecuador (local tax revenues for 2021 and 2022), Nicaragua (local tax revenues for 2022), Panama (local tax revenues and social security contributions for 2022), Saint Lucia (social security contributions for 2021 and 2022) and Uruguay (local tax revenues for 2022). See the corresponding country tables for more information.
2. Figures in and after 2021 are not comparable to data in previous years due to large changes as a result of Cuba's currency reform.
3. Some tax revenue data are not available between 2014 and 2017 and therefore total figures have not been included. Data for 2018 and subsequent years are not available.
4. Represents the group of 26 Latin American and Caribbean countries included in this publication and excludes Cuba (up to 2020) and Venezuela due to data issues. Chile, Colombia, Costa Rica and Mexico are also part of the OECD (38) group.
5. Calculated by applying the unweighted average percentage change for 2022 in the 36 countries providing data for that year to the overall average tax to GDP ratio in 2021.

Table 4.2. Total tax revenue in millions of USD at market exchange rates, 1990-2022

	1990	2000	2005	2010	2017	2018	2019	2020	2021	2022
Antigua and Barbuda[1]	..	99	158	244	287	305	304	271	295	336
Argentina	20 952	61 084	48 885	123 456	193 442	149 532	127 342	114 585	141 542	186 877
Bahamas[1]	505	965	1 060	1 277	2 118	2 120	2 486	2 076	1 831	2 425
Barbados	513	946	1 225	1 368	1 640	1 717	1 721	1 491	1 621	1 822
Belize	89	159	247	370	527	565	577	467	564	673
Bolivia	317	1 478	1 910	4 527	9 777	10 136	10 173	8 176	9 213	10 498
Brazil	133 077	192 661	291 327	700 962	654 769	613 148	598 172	449 511	536 248	638 812
Chile	5 829	14 650	25 487	42 836	55 902	62 806	58 332	49 029	70 363	72 000
Colombia	5 136	14 657	26 583	51 824	59 207	64 358	63 721	50 780	61 288	67 788
Costa Rica	1 285	3 182	4 363	8 397	13 903	14 449	15 086	14 086	16 125	17 504
Cuba[2]	6 870	11 367	17 528	23 949	41 022	42 307	43 504	40 263	4 022	2 577
Dominican Republic	664	2 951	4 946	6 600	10 509	11 237	11 935	9 854	13 683	15 868
Ecuador[1]	1 078	2 125	5 724	11 693	21 036	22 656	21 501	18 543	20 647	24 070
El Salvador	543	1 669	2 497	3 447	5 234	5 545	5 640	5 404	6 708	7 430
Guatemala	593	2 129	3 560	5 153	9 481	9 643	10 018	9 652	12 166	13 673
Guyana	104	234	302	549	927	1 061	1 200	1 168	1 355	1 556
Honduras	515	1 233	1 751	2 887	5 009	5 274	5 386	4 543	5 998	6 743
Jamaica	1 027	1 998	2 617	3 286	4 026	4 338	4 514	3 842	4 093	4 982
Mexico	35 908	81 160	99 772	135 866	186 897	198 032	207 926	193 857	220 159	240 116
Nicaragua[1]	..	733	1 097	1 693	3 288	3 025	3 244	3 223	3 824	4 353
Panama[1]	948	1 942	2 257	4 815	9 366	9 631	9 382	7 240	8 106	10 038
Paraguay	494	1 029	1 146	3 286	5 469	5 575	5 289	4 791	5 544	6 124
Peru	3 389	7 674	12 338	26 478	33 099	37 473	38 777	31 635	41 038	46 947
Saint Lucia[1]	..	178	227	307	410	429	437	342	388	430
Trinidad and Tobago	1 158	1 746	4 414	6 261	4 617	5 449	5 686	4 630	5 142	6 749
Uruguay[1]	2 051	5 303	4 351	10 618	17 275	17 404	16 273	14 288	15 725	18 905
Venezuela[3]	10 259	12 758	23 076	38 220	..	..	..	..	..	..

.. Not available

Note: The figures exclude local government revenues for Antigua and Barbuda, Argentina (but include provincial revenues), the Bahamas, Barbados, Cuba (except for 2002-2012), the Dominican Republic, Saint Lucia, Trinidad and Tobago and Venezuela as the data are not available. Local government revenue data have been available since 1991 for Nicaragua, since 1994 for Bolivia, since 1995 for Guatemala, since 1998 for Jamaica, since 1999 for Panama, since 2000 for Peru, since 2002 for El Salvador and Guyana, since 2006 for Paraguay and since 1990 for all other countries.

1. The data include the following estimations: Antigua and Barbuda (social security contributions for 2019-2022), the Bahamas (social security contributions for 2021 and 2022), Ecuador (local tax revenues for 2021 and 2022), Nicaragua (local tax revenues for 2022), Panama (local tax revenues and social security contributions for 2022), Saint Lucia (social security contributions for 2021 and 2022) and Uruguay (local tax revenues for 2022). See the corresponding country tables for more information.
2. Figures in 2021 and thereafter are not comparable to data in previous years due to large changes as a result of Cuba's currency reform.
3. Some tax revenue data are not available between 2014 and 2017 and therefore total figures have not been included. Data for 2018 and subsequent years are not available.

Table 4.3. Tax revenue of main headings as % of GDP, 2022

	1000 Income & profits	2000 Social security	3000 Payroll	4000 Property	5000 Goods and services	6000 Others
Antigua and Barbuda[1]	1.5	3.3	0.0	2.0	12.3	0.0
Argentina	5.7	5.3	0.0	2.9	15.6	0.2
Bahamas[1]	0.0	2.2	0.0	1.9	15.5	0.0
Barbados	8.6	5.2	0.0	2.0	14.7	0.0
Belize	5.7	2.4	0.0	0.7	13.4	0.0
Bolivia	3.4	5.7	0.0	0.3	12.1	2.2
Brazil	9.2	8.1	0.5	1.6	13.7	0.2
Chile	10.5	1.0	0.0	1.2	11.5	-0.2
Colombia	6.6	1.6	0.3	1.5	8.8	0.9
Costa Rica	5.5	8.9	1.4	0.5	8.3	0.9
Cuba	8.6	2.6	1.0	0.0	2.0	4.1
Dominican Republic	4.4	0.1	0.1	0.7	8.7	0.0
Ecuador[1]	4.6	5.0	0.0	0.9	10.4	0.0
El Salvador	8.3	2.6	0.1	0.2	11.3	0.3
Guatemala	3.5	2.1	0.2	0.2	7.6	0.8
Guyana	5.4	1.0	0.0	0.2	3.9	0.1
Honduras	6.2	3.3	0.2	0.6	10.4	0.8
Jamaica	7.9	1.6	1.5	0.8	17.4	0.1
Mexico	8.0	2.4	0.5	0.3	5.3	0.4
Nicaragua[1]	9.0	6.3	0.0	0.3	11.9	0.3
Panama[1]	3.7	5.5	0.2	0.3	3.5	0.0
Paraguay	3.0	4.2	0.0	0.2	7.2	0.1
Peru	8.0	1.9	0.0	0.4	8.6	0.2
Saint Lucia[1]	3.9	2.4	0.0	0.4	11.6	0.0
Trinidad and Tobago	16.0	2.4	0.0	0.2	5.2	0.0
Uruguay[1]	7.1	6.7	0.0	2.0	10.6	0.2
Venezuela[2]	..	..	..	..	..	..
Unweighted average						
LAC[3]	**6.3**	**3.6**	**0.2**	**0.9**	**10.1**	**0.4**
OECD[4]	**12.0**	**9.0**	**0.5**	**1.9**	**10.7**	**0.1**

.. Not available

Note: The figures exclude local government revenues for Antigua and Barbuda, Argentina (but include provincial revenues), the Bahamas, Barbados, Cuba (except for 2002-2012), the Dominican Republic, Saint Lucia, Trinidad and Tobago and Venezuela as the data are not available. Local government revenue data have been available since 1991 for Nicaragua, since 1994 for Bolivia, since 1995 for Guatemala, since 1998 for Jamaica, since 1999 for Panama, since 2000 for Peru, since 2002 for El Salvador and Guyana, since 2006 for Paraguay and since 1990 for all other countries.

1. The data include the following estimations: Antigua and Barbuda (social security contributions for 2019-2022), the Bahamas (social security contributions for 2021 and 2022), Ecuador (local tax revenues for 2021 and 2022), Nicaragua (local tax revenues for 2022), Panama (local tax revenues and social security contributions for 2022), Saint Lucia (social security contributions for 2021 and 2022) and Uruguay (local tax revenues for 2022). See the corresponding country tables for more information.
2. Data for 2018 and subsequent years are not available.
3. Represents the group of 26 Latin American and Caribbean countries included in this publication and excludes Cuba (up to 2020) and Venezuela due to data issues. Chile, Colombia, Costa Rica and Mexico are also part of the OECD (38) group.
4. Represents the unweighted average for OECD member countries. Data for 2021 are used as data for 2022 were not available at the time of publication..

Table 4.4. Tax revenue of main headings as % of total tax revenue, 2022

	1000 Income & profits	2000 Social security	3000 Payroll	4000 Property	5000 Goods and services	6000 Others
Antigua and Barbuda[1]	7.8	17.2	0.0	10.6	64.4	0.0
Argentina	19.4	17.7	0.0	9.8	52.6	0.5
Bahamas[1]	0.0	11.0	0.0	9.9	79.1	0.0
Barbados	28.1	17.0	0.0	6.5	48.3	0.0
Belize	25.6	10.7	0.0	3.1	60.6	0.0
Bolivia	14.4	24.1	0.0	1.1	51.1	9.3
Brazil	27.6	24.2	1.6	4.9	41.1	0.6
Chile	43.7	4.1	0.0	5.1	47.8	-0.8
Colombia	33.2	8.3	1.5	7.8	44.8	4.4
Costa Rica	21.5	34.8	5.7	2.0	32.6	3.5
Cuba	46.8	14.4	5.4	0.0	10.9	22.5
Dominican Republic	31.7	0.6	0.4	5.2	62.2	0.0
Ecuador[1]	22.1	24.0	0.0	4.1	49.8	0.0
El Salvador	36.4	11.2	0.6	0.8	49.6	1.4
Guatemala	24.2	14.7	1.0	1.5	52.8	5.8
Guyana	50.8	9.7	0.0	2.0	36.9	0.6
Honduras	29.1	15.2	0.7	2.9	48.5	3.6
Jamaica	26.9	5.5	5.0	2.7	59.5	0.3
Mexico	47.3	14.1	2.9	1.9	31.1	2.7
Nicaragua[1]	32.5	22.8	0.0	1.2	42.7	0.9
Panama[1]	28.0	42.0	1.3	2.1	26.4	0.3
Paraguay	20.4	28.8	0.0	1.2	48.9	0.7
Peru	41.9	9.9	0.1	2.0	44.9	1.2
Saint Lucia[1]	21.2	13.3	0.0	2.3	63.2	0.0
Trinidad and Tobago	67.4	9.9	0.0	0.8	21.8	0.0
Uruguay[1]	26.6	25.2	0.0	7.7	39.9	0.6
Venezuela[2]	..	..	..	..	..	..
Unweighted average						
LAC[3]	**29.8**	**16.7**	**1.0**	**3.8**	**46.5**	**2.2**
OECD[4]	**35.1**	**25.6**	**1.3**	**5.6**	**31.9**	**0.4**

.. Not available

Note: The figures exclude local government revenues for Antigua and Barbuda, Argentina (but include provincial revenues), the Bahamas, Barbados, Cuba (except for 2002-2012), the Dominican Republic, Saint Lucia, Trinidad and Tobago and Venezuela as the data are not available. Local government revenue data have been available since 1991 for Nicaragua, since 1994 for Bolivia, since 1995 for Guatemala, since 1998 for Jamaica, since 1999 for Panama, since 2000 for Peru, since 2002 for El Salvador and Guyana, since 2006 for Paraguay and since 1990 for all other countries.

1. The data include the following estimations: Antigua and Barbuda (social security contributions for 2019-2022), the Bahamas (social security contributions for 2021 and 2022), Ecuador (local tax revenues for 2021 and 2022), Nicaragua (local tax revenues for 2022), Panama (local tax revenues and social security contributions for 2022), Saint Lucia (social security contributions for 2021 and 2022) and Uruguay (local tax revenues for 2022). See the corresponding country tables for more information.
2. Data for 2018 and subsequent years are not available.
3. Represents the group of 26 Latin American and Caribbean countries included in this publication and excludes Cuba (up to 2020) and Venezuela due to data issues. Chile, Colombia, Costa Rica and Mexico are also part of the OECD (38) group.
4. Represents the unweighted average for OECD member countries. Data for 2021 are used as data for 2022 were not available at the time of publication.

Table 4.5. Taxes on income and profits (1000) as % of GDP and as % of total tax revenue

	% of GDP					% of total tax revenue				
	1990	2000	2010	2021	2022	1990	2000	2010	2021	2022
Antigua and Barbuda	..	1.7	3.0	2.1	1.5	..	14.0	14.0	10.5	7.8
Argentina	0.7	3.6	4.7	5.1	5.7	5.3	18.5	16.2	17.5	19.4
Bahamas	0.0	0.0	0.0	0.0	0.0	0.0	0.0	0.0	0.0	0.0
Barbados	6.1	9.8	8.4	8.8	8.6	24.3	31.7	28.0	27.7	28.1
Belize	3.3	3.4	7.1	4.3	5.7	20.9	23.9	33.6	19.8	25.6
Bolivia	0.4	2.3	4.6	2.7	3.4	6.7	13.2	20.0	12.1	14.4
Brazil	5.1	5.7	6.7	7.8	9.2	18.3	19.5	21.0	24.1	27.6
Chile	3.9	4.4	7.5	8.5	10.5	23.2	23.3	38.1	38.3	43.7
Colombia	3.4	3.6	4.8	6.1	6.6	29.9	23.2	26.6	31.9	33.2
Costa Rica	2.3	2.8	3.8	5.1	5.5	10.0	13.2	17.1	20.6	21.5
Cuba[1]	0.1	6.0	5.6	8.2	8.6	0.2	16.1	15.0	46.2	46.8
Dominican Republic	2.1	2.7	2.7	4.9	4.4	25.7	22.0	21.7	33.7	31.7
Ecuador	0.9	1.5	4.2	4.2	4.6	12.9	12.6	25.0	21.5	22.1
El Salvador	2.0	3.6	5.4	7.7	8.3	17.6	25.7	23.9	33.7	36.4
Guatemala	1.5	2.3	2.3	3.5	3.5	19.2	19.9	13.6	24.7	24.2
Guyana	5.1	5.9	5.7	7.4	5.4	33.5	37.8	35.4	43.9	50.8
Honduras	2.5	2.7	4.4	5.1	6.2	20.3	15.9	24.3	24.3	29.1
Jamaica	9.5	9.0	9.2	7.6	7.9	47.0	40.4	36.9	27.1	26.9
Mexico	4.1	4.1	5.1	7.4	8.0	34.0	36.0	39.8	42.7	47.3
Nicaragua	..	1.8	4.5	8.2	9.0	..	12.3	23.1	30.3	32.5
Panama	3.8	3.9	4.5	3.0	3.7	22.9	25.0	27.4	24.6	28.0
Paraguay	1.0	1.5	1.6	2.6	3.0	12.1	13.1	13.4	18.4	20.4
Peru	0.7	2.9	6.5	7.0	8.0	5.8	19.0	36.5	38.4	41.9
Saint Lucia	..	5.5	5.6	4.3	3.9	..	28.6	27.1	21.9	21.2
Trinidad and Tobago	12.3	12.4	19.6	11.1	16.0	52.7	56.8	68.5	49.5	67.4
Uruguay	0.9	2.9	4.8	6.7	7.1	4.7	13.6	20.0	26.1	26.6
Venezuela[2]	17.7	5.8	3.6	..	..	83.7	43.2	30.7	..	..
Unweighted average										
LAC[3]	**3.3**	**4.0**	**5.5**	**5.7**	**6.3**	**20.3**	**22.4**	**26.4**	**27.3**	**29.8**
OECD[4]	**11.5**	**11.4**	**10.2**	**12.0**	**..**	**36.2**	**33.9**	**32.2**	**35.1**	**..**

.. Not available

Note: The figures exclude local government revenues for Antigua and Barbuda, Argentina (but include provincial revenues), the Bahamas, Barbados, Cuba (except for 2002-2012), the Dominican Republic, Saint Lucia, Trinidad and Tobago and Venezuela as the data are not available. Local government revenue data have been available since 1991 for Nicaragua, since 1994 for Bolivia, since 1995 for Guatemala, since 1998 for Jamaica, since 1999 for Panama, since 2000 for Peru, since 2002 for El Salvador and Guyana, since 2006 for Paraguay and since 1990 for all other countries.

1. Figures in 2021 and thereafter are not comparable to data in previous years due to large changes as a result of Cuba's currency reform.
2. Some tax revenue data between 2014 and 2017 are not available. In those years data as % of total tax revenue cannot be calculated. Data for 2018 and subsequent years are not available.
3. Represents the group of 26 Latin American and Caribbean countries included in this publication and excludes Cuba (up to 2020) and Venezuela due to data issues. Chile, Colombia, Costa Rica and Mexico are also part of the OECD (38) group.
4. Represents the unweighted average for OECD member countries.

Table 4.6. Social security contributions (2000) as % of GDP and as % of total tax revenue

	% of GDP					% of total tax revenue				
	1990	2000	2010	2021	2022	1990	2000	2010	2021	2022
Antigua and Barbuda[1]	..	..	2.7	3.3	3.3	..	..	12.6	16.4	17.2
Argentina	3.4	3.0	6.2	5.2	5.3	25.3	15.8	21.2	17.8	17.7
Bahamas[1]	1.3	1.5	1.7	2.2	2.2	13.2	11.9	13.1	12.0	11.0
Barbados	3.3	4.8	6.2	5.9	5.2	13.1	15.6	20.6	18.4	17.0
Belize	0.9	0.8	1.7	2.2	2.4	5.7	5.8	8.2	10.4	10.7
Bolivia	0.0	1.3	3.8	6.0	5.7	0.0	7.3	16.7	26.6	24.1
Brazil	6.8	7.0	8.1	7.8	8.1	24.3	23.7	25.7	24.0	24.2
Chile	1.5	1.4	1.3	1.2	1.0	9.0	7.3	6.8	5.3	4.1
Colombia	0.9	2.6	2.1	1.9	1.6	7.9	16.3	11.7	10.0	8.3
Costa Rica	6.5	6.4	7.3	9.0	8.9	28.9	30.4	33.1	36.0	34.8
Cuba[2]	3.5	3.9	4.6	4.4	2.6	11.0	10.4	12.4	25.0	14.4
Dominican Republic	0.1	0.1	0.1	0.1	0.1	0.8	1.0	0.8	0.4	0.6
Ecuador	1.6	1.2	3.7	5.0	5.0	22.5	10.7	21.7	25.7	24.0
El Salvador	2.2	2.8	2.5	2.6	2.6	19.2	19.5	13.6	11.5	11.2
Guatemala	1.3	1.8	1.9	2.2	2.1	16.5	15.5	15.2	15.2	14.7
Guyana	0.6	1.8	1.4	1.6	1.0	3.7	11.4	9.0	9.5	9.7
Honduras	1.0	1.6	2.9	3.5	3.3	8.5	9.4	15.9	16.5	15.2
Jamaica	..	..	0.7	1.4	1.6	..	..	2.9	5.1	5.5
Mexico	2.0	2.1	2.1	2.4	2.4	16.8	18.0	16.2	13.7	14.1
Nicaragua	..	2.6	4.3	6.4	6.3	..	18.0	22.4	23.8	22.8
Panama[1]	5.7	5.9	5.6	5.3	5.5	34.2	38.2	34.0	44.0	42.0
Paraguay	0.4	3.0	2.8	3.8	4.2	4.8	25.6	22.7	27.5	28.8
Peru	0.9	1.8	1.9	1.9	1.9	7.8	11.9	10.6	10.3	9.9
Saint Lucia[1]	..	1.9	2.3	2.4	2.4	..	10.0	11.1	12.0	13.3
Trinidad and Tobago	0.9	1.4	1.9	2.9	2.4	3.7	6.4	6.7	13.0	9.9
Uruguay[3]	5.5	5.9	5.6	6.2	6.7	29.9	27.5	23.4	24.2	25.2
Venezuela[4]	1.0	0.7	1.0	..	..	4.9	5.4	8.1	..	..
Unweighted average										
LAC[5]	**2.2**	**2.7**	**3.2**	**3.7**	**3.6**	**14.1**	**15.5**	**15.8**	**17.5**	**16.7**
OECD[6]	**7.1**	**8.4**	**8.6**	**9.0**	..	**21.8**	**24.9**	**26.6**	**25.6**	..

.. Not available

Note: The figures exclude local government revenues for Antigua and Barbuda, Argentina (but include provincial revenues), the Bahamas, Barbados, Cuba (except for 2002-2012), the Dominican Republic, Saint Lucia, Trinidad and Tobago and Venezuela as the data are not available. Local government revenue data have been available since 1991 for Nicaragua, since 1994 for Bolivia, since 1995 for Guatemala, since 1998 for Jamaica, since 1999 for Panama, since 2000 for Peru, since 2002 for El Salvador and Guyana, since 2006 for Paraguay and since 1990 for all other countries.

1. Revenues from social security contributions are estimated in the following countries: Antigua and Barbuda (2019-2022), the Bahamas (2021 and 2022), Panama (2022) and Saint Lucia (2021 and 2022).
2. Figures in 2021 and thereafter are not comparable to data in previous years due to large changes as a result of Cuba's currency reform.
3. Figures for 1990-98 are estimated by the Direction General of Taxes as the methodology they use to calculate social security contributions was not employed until 1999.
4. Some tax revenue data between 2014 and 2017 are not available. In those years data as % of total tax revenue cannot be calculated. Data for 2018 and subsequent years are not available.
5. Represents the group of 26 Latin American and Caribbean countries included in this publication and excludes Cuba (up to 2020) and Venezuela due to data issues. Chile, Colombia, Costa Rica and Mexico are also part of the OECD (38) group.
6. Represents the unweighted average for OECD member countries.

Table 4.7. Taxes on payroll (3000) as % of GDP and as % of total tax revenue

	% of GDP					% of total tax revenue				
	1990	2000	2010	2021	2022	1990	2000	2010	2021	2022
Antigua and Barbuda	..	0.0	0.0	0.0	0.0	..	0.0	0.0	0.0	0.0
Argentina	0.0	0.0	0.0	0.0	0.0	0.0	0.0	0.0	0.0	0.0
Bahamas	0.0	0.0	0.0	0.0	0.0	0.0	0.0	0.0	0.0	0.0
Barbados	0.0	0.0	0.0	0.0	0.0	0.0	0.0	0.0	0.0	0.0
Belize	0.0	0.0	0.0	0.0	0.0	0.0	0.0	0.0	0.0	0.0
Bolivia	0.0	0.0	0.0	0.0	0.0	0.0	0.0	0.0	0.0	0.0
Brazil	0.4	0.5	0.5	0.5	0.5	1.6	1.5	1.7	1.6	1.6
Chile	0.0	0.0	0.0	0.0	0.0	0.0	0.0	0.0	0.0	0.0
Colombia	0.0	0.7	0.7	0.3	0.3	0.0	4.2	4.1	1.7	1.5
Costa Rica	1.4	1.3	1.3	1.4	1.4	6.4	6.3	5.9	5.7	5.7
Cuba[1]	0.0	3.2	6.9	1.1	1.0	0.0	8.5	18.4	6.2	5.4
Dominican Republic	0.0	0.0	0.1	0.1	0.1	0.0	0.0	0.6	0.5	0.4
Ecuador	0.0	0.0	0.0	0.0	0.0	0.0	0.0	0.0	0.0	0.0
El Salvador	0.0	0.0	0.1	0.1	0.1	0.0	0.0	0.6	0.6	0.6
Guatemala	0.0	0.0	0.1	0.2	0.2	0.0	0.0	1.1	1.1	1.0
Guyana	0.0	0.0	0.0	0.0	0.0	0.0	0.0	0.0	0.0	0.0
Honduras	0.0	0.0	0.2	0.2	0.2	0.0	0.0	0.9	0.7	0.7
Jamaica	0.8	1.0	1.1	1.5	1.5	3.9	4.4	4.5	5.2	5.0
Mexico	0.2	0.2	0.3	0.5	0.5	1.8	1.5	2.2	2.6	2.9
Nicaragua	..	0.0	0.0	0.0	0.0	..	0.0	0.0	0.0	0.0
Panama	0.0	0.3	0.2	0.2	0.2	0.0	1.9	1.2	1.4	1.3
Paraguay	0.0	0.0	0.0	0.0	0.0	0.0	0.0	0.0	0.0	0.0
Peru	0.0	0.7	0.0	0.0	0.0	0.0	4.4	0.1	0.1	0.1
Saint Lucia	..	0.0	0.0	0.0	0.0	..	0.0	0.0	0.0	0.0
Trinidad and Tobago	0.0	0.0	0.0	0.0	0.0	0.0	0.0	0.0	0.0	0.0
Uruguay	0.0	0.0	0.0	0.0	0.0	0.0	0.0	0.0	0.0	0.0
Venezuela[2]	0.0	0.0	0.0	..	..	0.0	0.0	0.0	..	..
Unweighted average										
LAC[3]	**0.1**	**0.2**	**0.2**	**0.2**	**0.2**	**0.6**	**1.0**	**0.9**	**1.1**	**1.0**
OECD[4]	**0.4**	**0.4**	**0.4**	**0.5**	**..**	**1.2**	**1.2**	**1.2**	**1.3**	**..**

.. Not available

Note: The figures exclude local government revenues for Antigua and Barbuda, Argentina (but include provincial revenues), the Bahamas, Barbados, Cuba (except for 2002-2012), the Dominican Republic, Saint Lucia, Trinidad and Tobago and Venezuela as the data are not available. Local government revenue data have been available since 1991 for Nicaragua, since 1994 for Bolivia, since 1995 for Guatemala, since 1998 for Jamaica, since 1999 for Panama, since 2000 for Peru, since 2002 for El Salvador and Guyana, since 2006 for Paraguay and since 1990 for all other countries.

1. Figures in 2021 and thereafter are not comparable to data in previous years due to large changes as a result of Cuba's currency reform.
2. Some tax revenue data between 2014 and 2017 are not available. In those years data as % of total tax revenue cannot be calculated. Data for 2018 and subsequent years are not available.
3. Represents the group of 26 Latin American and Caribbean countries included in this publication and excludes Cuba (up to 2020) and Venezuela due to data issues. Chile, Colombia, Costa Rica and Mexico are also part of the OECD (38) group.
4. Represents the unweighted average for OECD member countries.

Table 4.8. Taxes on property (4000) as % of GDP and as % of total tax revenue

	% of GDP					% of total tax revenue				
	1990	2000	2010	2021	2022	1990	2000	2010	2021	2022
Antigua and Barbuda	..	0.6	1.6	2.3	2.0	..	4.9	7.5	11.6	10.6
Argentina	1.5	1.2	2.6	3.1	2.9	11.4	6.3	9.0	10.5	9.8
Bahamas	1.1	2.6	2.7	2.0	1.9	11.2	21.6	21.1	11.1	9.9
Barbados	3.6	1.8	1.4	2.2	2.0	14.4	5.7	4.8	6.7	6.5
Belize	3.1	0.6	0.6	1.2	0.7	19.2	4.2	3.1	5.6	3.1
Bolivia	0.0	0.0	0.3	0.3	0.3	0.1	0.0	1.2	1.2	1.1
Brazil	1.6	2.0	1.4	1.6	1.6	5.9	6.7	4.3	4.9	4.9
Chile	1.0	1.3	0.8	1.1	1.2	6.2	7.0	4.1	4.9	5.1
Colombia	0.2	1.0	1.6	1.7	1.5	2.2	6.6	8.7	8.7	7.8
Costa Rica	0.3	0.2	0.3	0.5	0.5	1.3	0.9	1.5	2.1	2.0
Cuba	0.0	0.0	0.0	0.0	0.0	0.0	0.0	0.0	0.0	0.0
Dominican Republic	0.1	0.2	0.6	0.8	0.7	1.2	1.3	5.1	5.9	5.2
Ecuador	0.1	0.1	0.2	0.3	0.9	1.5	0.8	1.4	1.7	4.1
El Salvador	0.5	0.1	0.1	0.2	0.2	4.8	0.7	0.6	0.7	0.8
Guatemala	0.4	0.2	0.4	0.2	0.2	5.6	2.1	2.9	1.5	1.5
Guyana	0.2	0.3	0.3	0.3	0.2	1.0	1.6	1.8	2.0	2.0
Honduras	0.1	0.3	0.3	0.6	0.6	0.7	1.5	1.8	2.8	2.9
Jamaica	2.5	1.1	0.9	0.8	0.8	12.5	4.9	3.5	2.9	2.7
Mexico	0.2	0.2	0.3	0.4	0.3	1.9	1.8	2.3	2.0	1.9
Nicaragua	..	0.0	0.2	0.4	0.3	..	0.1	1.2	1.3	1.2
Panama	0.6	0.3	0.5	0.3	0.3	3.4	2.2	2.9	2.2	2.1
Paraguay	0.2	0.2	0.2	0.2	0.2	2.8	2.0	1.8	1.3	1.2
Peru	1.6	0.2	0.5	0.4	0.4	13.6	1.2	3.0	2.1	2.0
Saint Lucia	..	0.4	0.5	0.6	0.4	..	2.2	2.3	3.0	2.3
Trinidad and Tobago	0.4	0.3	0.1	0.2	0.2	1.8	1.6	0.5	0.8	0.8
Uruguay	1.6	1.8	2.2	2.0	2.0	8.9	8.6	8.9	7.6	7.7
Venezuela[1]	0.1	0.5	0.0	..	..	0.3	3.7	0.2	..	..
Unweighted average										
LAC[2]	**1.0**	**0.7**	**0.8**	**0.9**	**0.9**	**6.0**	**3.9**	**4.2**	**4.0**	**3.8**
OECD[3]	**1.7**	**1.7**	**1.6**	**1.9**	..	**5.5**	**5.3**	**5.4**	**5.6**	..

.. Not available

Note: The figures exclude local government revenues for Antigua and Barbuda, Argentina (but include provincial revenues), the Bahamas, Barbados, Cuba (except for 2002-2012), the Dominican Republic, Saint Lucia, Trinidad and Tobago and Venezuela as the data are not available. Local government revenue data have been available since 1991 for Nicaragua, since 1994 for Bolivia, since 1995 for Guatemala, since 1998 for Jamaica, since 1999 for Panama, since 2000 for Peru, since 2002 for El Salvador and Guyana, since 2006 for Paraguay and since 1990 for all other countries.

1. Some tax revenue data between 2014 and 2017 are not available. In those years data as % of total tax revenue cannot be calculated. Data for 2018 and subsequent years are not available.
2. Represents the group of 26 Latin American and Caribbean countries included in this publication and excludes Cuba (up to 2020) and Venezuela due to data issues. Chile, Colombia, Costa Rica and Mexico are also part of the OECD (38) group.
3. Represents the unweighted average for OECD member countries.

Table 4.9. Taxes on goods and services (5000) as % of GDP and as % of total tax revenue

	% of GDP					% of total tax revenue				
	1990	2000	2010	2021	2022	1990	2000	2010	2021	2022
Antigua and Barbuda	..	9.7	14.0	12.3	12.3	..	61.1	65.9	61.5	64.4
Argentina	7.3	10.9	15.2	15.6	15.6	55.2	56.5	52.4	53.6	52.6
Bahamas	7.4	7.9	7.8	13.8	15.5	76.4	64.3	61.1	76.9	79.1
Barbados	12.2	14.5	14.0	15.1	14.7	48.2	47.0	46.6	47.2	48.3
Belize	8.6	9.3	11.6	13.8	13.4	54.1	66.1	55.2	64.2	60.6
Bolivia	5.9	12.8	12.9	11.5	12.1	90.2	72.7	56.4	50.9	51.1
Brazil	13.5	14.1	15.0	14.7	13.7	48.7	48.0	47.2	45.3	41.1
Chile	10.6	11.9	10.1	11.8	11.5	62.9	63.8	51.2	53.1	47.8
Colombia	6.1	7.3	8.2	8.3	8.8	53.8	46.3	45.1	43.3	44.8
Costa Rica	10.2	9.9	8.9	8.7	8.3	45.5	46.7	40.3	34.8	32.6
Cuba[1]	27.7	22.0	19.1	1.9	2.0	86.9	59.2	51.3	11.0	10.9
Dominican Republic	5.8	9.1	8.8	8.6	8.7	69.8	74.7	71.9	59.5	62.2
Ecuador	4.5	8.8	8.7	9.9	10.4	63.0	75.7	51.9	50.9	49.8
El Salvador	5.4	7.7	10.2	11.9	11.3	47.7	54.1	54.5	52.1	49.6
Guatemala	4.6	7.3	7.0	7.3	7.6	58.7	62.4	56.0	51.7	52.8
Guyana	6.4	7.6	8.5	7.4	3.9	42.0	48.6	53.0	43.9	36.9
Honduras	8.2	11.7	9.7	11.1	10.4	66.2	68.0	53.1	52.3	48.5
Jamaica	7.4	11.1	13.0	16.5	17.4	36.4	50.1	52.1	59.3	59.5
Mexico	5.3	4.8	4.9	6.4	5.3	44.0	41.7	38.0	37.0	31.1
Nicaragua	..	8.6	10.1	11.8	11.9	..	60.0	52.4	43.6	42.7
Panama	6.1	4.9	5.5	3.3	3.5	36.8	31.3	33.7	27.4	26.4
Paraguay	6.1	6.7	7.3	7.2	7.2	72.1	58.0	60.5	52.1	48.9
Peru	8.5	9.2	8.6	8.5	8.6	71.4	60.8	48.6	46.7	44.9
Saint Lucia	..	11.4	12.3	12.5	11.6	..	59.1	59.5	63.2	63.2
Trinidad and Tobago	9.7	7.7	7.0	8.2	5.2	41.7	35.2	24.3	36.7	21.8
Uruguay	10.4	10.7	11.4	10.6	10.6	56.6	50.1	47.1	41.5	39.9
Venezuela[2]	2.4	6.4	7.2	..	..	11.1	47.7	61.1	..	..
Unweighted average										
LAC[3]	**7.7**	**9.4**	**10.0**	**10.3**	**10.1**	**56.4**	**56.9**	**51.1**	**48.4**	**46.5**
OECD[4]	**9.9**	**10.8**	**10.5**	**10.7**	**..**	**33.7**	**33.9**	**34.0**	**31.9**	**..**

.. Not available

Note: The figures exclude local government revenues for Antigua and Barbuda, Argentina (but include provincial revenues), the Bahamas, Barbados, Cuba (except for 2002-2012), the Dominican Republic, Saint Lucia, Trinidad and Tobago and Venezuela as the data are not available. Local government revenue data have been available since 1991 for Nicaragua, since 1994 for Bolivia, since 1995 for Guatemala, since 1998 for Jamaica, since 1999 for Panama, since 2000 for Peru, since 2002 for El Salvador and Guyana, since 2006 for Paraguay and since 1990 for all other countries.

1. Figures in 2021 and thereafter are not comparable to data in previous years due to large changes as a result of Cuba's currency reform.
2. Some tax revenue data between 2014 and 2017 are not available. In those years data as % of total tax revenue cannot be calculated. Data for 2018 and subsequent years are not available.
3. Represents the group of 26 Latin American and Caribbean countries included in this publication and excludes Cuba (up to 2020) and Venezuela due to data issues. Chile, Colombia, Costa Rica and Mexico are also part of the OECD (38) group.
4. Represents the unweighted average for OECD member countries.

Table 4.10. Value added taxes (5111) as % of GDP and as % of total tax revenue

	% of GDP					% of total tax revenue				
	1990	2000	2010	2021	2022	1990	2000	2010	2021	2022
Antigua and Barbuda	..	..	5.8	6.1	6.4	..	..	27.2	30.3	33.5
Argentina	2.1	6.0	7.0	7.0	7.1	15.6	31.1	24.1	24.1	23.9
Bahamas	0.0	0.0	0.0	7.3	9.2	0.0	0.0	0.0	40.4	46.8
Barbados	0.0	8.0	8.4	8.7	8.6	0.0	26.0	28.1	27.3	28.1
Belize	0.0	0.0	5.7	5.9	6.5	0.0	0.0	26.9	27.1	29.5
Bolivia	2.8	5.7	7.4	6.9	7.2	43.0	32.2	32.5	30.4	30.6
Brazil	8.0	6.9	6.9	7.3	7.0	28.7	23.3	21.7	22.5	21.0
Chile	6.3	7.8	7.6	9.5	9.3	37.4	41.8	38.5	42.6	39.0
Colombia	2.6	4.3	5.3	5.9	6.3	22.6	27.6	29.3	30.5	31.8
Costa Rica	4.1	4.8	4.6	5.1	5.0	18.1	22.8	21.0	20.4	19.4
Cuba	0.0	0.0	0.0	0.0	0.0	0.0	0.0	0.0	0.0	0.0
Dominican Republic	1.3	2.5	4.1	4.8	5.0	15.1	20.8	33.5	33.4	35.6
Ecuador	2.0	5.0	5.4	6.2	6.8	28.0	43.5	32.1	31.9	32.6
El Salvador	0.0	6.1	7.8	9.4	9.1	0.0	42.8	41.6	41.3	39.6
Guatemala	2.3	4.4	5.1	5.6	5.9	28.8	37.9	40.9	39.3	41.0
Guyana	0.0	0.0	3.9	2.9	1.9	0.0	0.0	24.2	17.1	17.5
Honduras	2.0	4.8	5.4	7.2	7.2	16.2	28.1	29.4	34.0	33.8
Jamaica	0.8	5.7	7.1	8.8	9.4	3.8	25.5	28.7	31.6	32.1
Mexico	3.2	2.8	3.8	4.4	4.3	26.1	24.7	29.4	25.2	25.4
Nicaragua	..	4.5	5.5	6.6	6.8	..	31.5	28.6	24.5	24.4
Panama	1.4	0.6	2.6	1.7	1.8	8.5	3.6	15.9	14.2	14.0
Paraguay	0.0	3.7	4.6	5.1	5.1	0.0	32.1	38.3	36.5	35.0
Peru	2.1	5.5	6.9	7.2	7.3	17.1	36.0	38.9	39.4	38.0
Saint Lucia	..	0.0	0.0	5.8	5.3	..	0.0	0.0	29.2	28.9
Trinidad and Tobago	4.4	3.8	4.4	5.3	2.4	18.8	17.3	15.2	23.9	10.2
Uruguay	5.0	6.0	7.9	6.9	6.8	27.5	28.0	32.8	27.0	25.6
Venezuela[1]	0.0	4.1	5.5	..	..	0.0	30.2	46.7	..	..
Unweighted average										
LAC[2]	**2.3**	**4.1**	**5.3**	**6.1**	**6.1**	**16.2**	**24.0**	**27.2**	**28.6**	**28.3**
OECD[3]	**5.1**	**6.3**	**6.4**	**7.0**	**..**	**17.0**	**19.6**	**20.5**	**20.7**	**..**

.. Not available

Note: The figures exclude local government revenues for Antigua and Barbuda, Argentina (but include provincial revenues), the Bahamas, Barbados, Cuba (except for 2002-2012), the Dominican Republic, Saint Lucia, Trinidad and Tobago and Venezuela as the data are not available. Local government revenue data have been available since 1991 for Nicaragua, since 1994 for Bolivia, since 1995 for Guatemala, since 1998 for Jamaica, since 1999 for Panama, since 2000 for Peru, since 2002 for El Salvador and Guyana, since 2006 for Paraguay and since 1990 for all other countries.

1. Some tax revenue data between 2014 and 2017 are not available. In those years data as % of total tax revenue cannot be calculated. Data for 2018 and subsequent years are not available.
2. Represents the group of 26 Latin American and Caribbean countries included in this publication and excludes Cuba (up to 2020) and Venezuela due to data issues. Chile, Colombia, Costa Rica and Mexico are also part of the OECD (38) group.
3. Represents the unweighted average for OECD member countries.

Table 4.11. Tax revenues of sub-sectors of general government as % of total tax revenue

	Central government			State or regional government			Local government			Social Security Funds		
	1995	2000	2022	1995	2000	2022	1995	2000	2022	1995	2000	2022
Federal countries												
Argentina	59.0	66.4	65.1	17.5	17.8	17.1	..	..	..	23.4	15.8	17.7
Brazil	44.8	47.9	46.2	26.5	25.0	23.4	3.7	3.4	6.2	25.0	23.7	24.2
Mexico	73.9	78.3	79.5	2.8	2.7	4.5	1.5	1.0	1.8	21.8	18.0	14.1
Venezuela[1]	94.6	94.6	..	..	..	..	..	..	..	5.4	5.4	..
Regional country												
Colombia	63.2	68.7	75.2	5.5	5.6	4.8	8.6	9.4	11.7	22.7	16.3	8.3
Unitary countries												
Antigua and Barbuda	100.0	100.0	82.8	..	..	..	..	..	..	..	..	17.2
Bahamas	89.1	88.1	89.0	..	..	..	..	..	..	10.9	11.9	11.0
Barbados	85.6	84.4	83.0	..	..	..	..	..	..	14.4	15.6	17.0
Belize	93.2	93.5	88.8	..	..	..	0.5	0.7	0.5	6.3	5.8	10.7
Bolivia	94.3	86.4	71.5	..	..	..	5.7	6.3	4.4	..	7.3	24.1
Chile	89.9	87.8	89.9	..	..	..	6.5	7.9	6.9	3.6	4.4	3.2
Costa Rica	65.5	63.3	61.4	..	..	..	1.6	1.9	2.7	33.0	34.8	35.9
Cuba[2]	..	..	..	..	..	..	..	..	..	11.3	10.4	14.4
Dominican Republic	99.3	99.0	99.4	..	..	..	..	..	..	0.7	1.0	0.6
Ecuador[3]	70.5	87.7	73.3	..	..	..	4.0	1.6	2.7	25.5	10.7	24.0
El Salvador	80.9	80.5	86.9	..	..	..	..	..	1.9	19.1	19.5	11.2
Guatemala	83.6	83.6	84.5	..	..	..	0.6	0.9	0.9	15.8	15.5	14.7
Guyana	92.6	88.6	90.3	..	..	..	..	..	0.0	7.4	11.4	9.7
Honduras	86.1	85.3	81.2	..	..	..	4.4	5.2	3.6	9.5	9.4	15.2
Jamaica	100.0	99.3	93.2	..	..	..	..	0.7	1.3	..	..	5.5
Nicaragua[3]	80.4	72.5	71.3	..	..	..	4.6	9.5	5.9	15.0	18.0	22.8
Panama[3]	67.2	59.6	56.4	..	..	..	..	2.2	1.6	32.8	38.2	42.0
Paraguay	92.0	74.4	68.8	..	..	..	..	..	2.4	8.0	25.6	28.8
Peru	88.7	86.5	88.0	..	..	..	..	1.6	2.1	11.3	11.9	9.9
Saint Lucia	100.0	90.0	86.7	..	..	..	..	..	..	..	10.0	13.3
Trinidad and Tobago	96.8	93.6	90.1	..	..	..	..	..	..	3.2	6.4	9.9
Uruguay[3]	61.7	63.6	69.2	..	..	..	8.8	8.9	5.6	29.5	27.5	25.2

.. Not available

Note: The figures exclude local government revenues for Antigua and Barbuda, Argentina (but include provincial revenues), the Bahamas, Barbados, Cuba (except for 2002-2012), the Dominican Republic, Saint Lucia, Trinidad and Tobago and Venezuela as the data are not available. Local government revenue data have been available since 1991 for Nicaragua, since 1994 for Bolivia, since 1995 for Guatemala, since 1998 for Jamaica, since 1999 for Panama, since 2000 for Peru, since 2002 for El Salvador and Guyana, since 2006 for Paraguay and since 1990 for all other countries.

1. Some tax revenue data between 2014 and 2017 and data for 2018 and subsequent years are not available. The breakdown by sub-sectors of general government is not available for those years.
2. Figures in 2021 and thereafter are not comparable to data in previous years due to large changes as a result of Cuba's currency reform.
3. Revenues from local government are estimated in the following countries: Ecuador (2021 and 2022), Nicaragua (2022), Panama (2022) and Uruguay (2022). See the corresponding country tables for more information.

Table 4.12. Main central government taxes as % of total tax revenues of central government, 2022

	1000 Income & profits	2000 Social security	3000 Payroll	4000 Property	5000 Goods and services	6000 Others
Federal countries						
Argentina	29.7	0.0	0.0	11.2	58.7	0.4
Brazil	59.8	0.0	3.6	4.0	31.4	1.3
Mexico	59.5	0.0	0.0	0.0	38.3	2.2
Venezuela	..	..	..	..	..	..
Regional country						
Colombia	44.2	0.0	2.0	5.8	47.6	0.4
Unitary countries						
Antigua and Barbuda	9.4	0.0	0.0	12.8	77.8	0.0
Bahamas	0.0	0.0	0.0	11.2	88.8	0.0
Barbados	33.8	0.0	0.0	7.9	58.3	0.0
Belize	28.9	0.0	0.0	3.0	68.2	0.0
Bolivia	20.2	0.0	0.0	1.5	71.5	6.8
Chile	48.6	1.0	0.0	2.2	49.1	-0.9
Costa Rica	35.1	7.4	0.0	1.0	50.8	5.7
Cuba	..	..	..	..	..	..
Dominican Republic	31.8	0.0	0.4	5.2	62.5	0.0
Ecuador	29.7	0.0	0.0	3.8	66.5	0.0
El Salvador	41.9	0.0	0.6	0.7	56.7	0.0
Guatemala	28.7	0.0	1.2	0.7	62.6	6.9
Guyana	56.3	0.0	0.0	2.2	40.9	0.6
Honduras	35.8	0.0	0.9	3.6	59.7	0.0
Jamaica	28.9	0.0	5.3	1.6	63.9	0.4
Nicaragua	45.5	0.0	0.0	0.1	54.4	0.0
Panama	49.6	0.0	2.3	3.7	44.0	0.5
Paraguay	29.7	0.0	0.0	0.0	69.6	0.7
Peru	47.6	0.0	0.1	0.2	50.8	1.3
Saint Lucia	24.4	0.0	0.0	2.6	72.9	0.0
Trinidad and Tobago	74.9	0.0	0.0	0.9	24.2	0.0
Uruguay	38.5	0.0	0.0	6.7	54.6	0.2

.. Not available
Note: Excluding social security contributions collected by social security funds.

Table 4.13. Main state government taxes as % of total tax revenues of state government, 2022

	1000 Income & profits	2000 Social security	3000 Payroll	4000 Property	5000 Goods and services	6000 Others
Federal countries						
Argentina	0.0	0.0	0.0	14.7	83.6	1.7
Brazil	0.0	0.0	0.0	1.9	98.1	0.0
Mexico	0.0	0.0	64.5	15.3	13.5	6.6
Venezuela	..	..	..	..	..	..
Regional country						
Colombia	0.0	0.0	0.0	0.0	70.7	29.3
Unitary countries						
Antigua and Barbuda	..	..	..	..	..	..
Bahamas	..	..	..	..	..	..
Barbados	..	..	..	..	..	..
Belize	..	..	..	..	..	..
Bolivia	..	..	..	..	..	..
Chile	..	..	..	..	..	..
Costa Rica	..	..	..	..	..	..
Cuba	..	..	..	..	..	..
Dominican Republic	..	..	..	..	..	..
Ecuador	..	..	..	..	..	..
El Salvador	..	..	..	..	..	..
Guatemala	..	..	..	..	..	..
Guyana	..	..	..	..	..	..
Honduras	..	..	..	..	..	..
Jamaica	..	..	..	..	..	..
Nicaragua	..	..	..	..	..	..
Panama	..	..	..	..	..	..
Paraguay	..	..	..	..	..	..
Peru	..	..	..	..	..	..
Saint Lucia	..	..	..	..	..	..
Trinidad and Tobago	..	..	..	..	..	..
Uruguay	..	..	..	..	..	..

.. Not available

Table 4.14. Main local government taxes as % of total tax revenues of local government, 2022

	1000 Income & profits	2000 Social security	3000 Payroll	4000 Property	5000 Goods and services	6000 Others
Federal countries						
Argentina	..	..	..	..	..	..
Brazil	0.0	0.0	0.0	41.1	58.7	0.2
Mexico	0.0	0.0	0.0	65.3	1.0	33.7
Venezuela	..	..	..	..	..	..
Regional country						
Colombia	0.0	0.0	0.0	28.9	48.1	22.9
Unitary countries						
Antigua and Barbuda	..	..	..	..	..	..
Bahamas	..	..	..	..	..	..
Barbados	..	..	..	..	..	..
Belize	0.0	0.0	0.0	100.0	0.0	0.0
Bolivia	0.0	0.0	0.0	0.0	0.0	100.0
Chile	0.0	0.0	0.0	46.1	53.9	0.0
Costa Rica	0.0	0.0	0.0	49.1	50.9	0.1
Cuba	..	..	..	..	..	..
Dominican Republic	..	..	..	..	..	..
Ecuador	11.3	0.0	0.0	48.9	39.8	0.0
El Salvador	0.0	0.0	0.0	7.8	14.7	77.5
Guatemala	0.0	0.0	0.0	100.0	0.0	0.0
Guyana	0.0	0.0	0.0	0.0	0.0	100.0
Honduras	0.0	0.0	0.0	0.0	0.0	100.0
Jamaica	0.0	0.0	0.0	100.0	0.0	0.0
Nicaragua	0.0	0.0	0.0	18.7	65.8	15.4
Panama	0.0	0.0	0.0	0.0	100.0	0.0
Paraguay	0.0	0.0	0.0	49.0	41.7	9.3
Peru	0.0	0.0	0.0	85.7	12.8	1.5
Saint Lucia	..	..	..	..	..	..
Trinidad and Tobago	..	..	..	..	..	..
Uruguay	0.0	0.0	0.0	54.3	38.1	7.6

.. Not available

Table 4.15. Gross domestic product for tax reporting years at market prices, in millions of national currency

		1990	2000	2005	2010	2017	2018	2019	2020	2021	2022
Antigua and Barbuda	XCD	1 241	2 231	2 762	3 101	3 964	4 336	4 556	3 700	3 972	4 746
Argentina	ARS	77 060	317 759	582 538	1 661 721	10 660 228	14 744 811	21 558 444	27 209 814	46 346 227	82 436 434
Bahamas	BSD	5 218	7 880	9 446	10 039	12 243	12 541	13 024	11 270	10 170	12 370
Barbados	BBD	4 059	6 116	7 838	9 124	10 021	10 308	10 654	8 921	10 166	11 943
Belize	BZD	1 124	2 256	2 983	3 518	4 587	4 681	4 665	4 366	5 230	6 087
Bolivia	BOB	15 443	51 928	77 024	137 876	259 185	278 388	282 587	253 112	279 206	304 097
Brazil	BRL	12	1 199 092	2 170 585	3 885 847	6 585 479	7 004 141	7 389 131	7 609 597	8 898 727	9 915 316
Chile	CLP	10 594 797	42 215 030	68 467 940	110 777 867	179 314 910	189 434 867	195 752 228	201 428 894	240 371 473	262 593 356
Colombia	COP	22 731 433	195 108 574	337 958 000	544 060 000	920 471 000	987 791 000	1 060 068 000	997 742 000	1 192 586 000	1 463 873 100
Costa Rica	CRC	525 310	4 627 051	9 577 022	19 802 011	34 343 647	36 014 719	37 832 150	36 495 246	40 112 925	44 251 690
Cuba	CUP	19 645	30 565	42 644	64 328	96 851	100 050	103 428	107 352	545 218	633 442
Dominican Republic	DOP	77 344	393 303	1 083 445	1 983 202	3 802 656	4 235 847	4 562 235	4 456 657	5 392 714	6 260 564
Ecuador	USD	15 232	18 319	41 507	69 555	104 296	107 562	108 108	99 291	106 166	115 049
El Salvador	USD	4 818	11 785	14 698	18 448	24 979	26 021	26 881	24 930	29 451	32 489
Guatemala	GTQ	33 613	140 702	207 729	333 093	526 507	551 368	593 972	600 089	665 568	736 109
Guyana	GYD	34 523	273 054	342 157	699 064	980 498	994 472	1 078 729	1 140 757	1 676 624	3 068 784
Honduras	HNL	17 141	106 654	183 747	299 286	543 403	575 285	614 918	585 734	684 204	776 636
Jamaica	JMD	38 145	395 009	700 275	1 152 780	1 895 025	2 027 251	2 110 433	1 966 928	2 210 219	2 623 255
Mexico	MXN	843 623	6 693 683	9 562 648	13 366 377	21 934 168	23 524 390	24 445 735	23 430 377	25 803 508	28 463 841
Nicaragua	NIO	519	64 812	105 777	187 053	414 279	410 988	420 614	435 395	497 524	562 208
Panama	PAB	5 723	12 502	16 638	29 440	62 203	67 294	69 722	57 087	67 407	76 523
Paraguay	PYG	7 147 738	30 874 088	66 335 828	129 092 883	219 122 277	230 576 477	236 681 497	239 914 729	270 633 896	291 336 457
Peru	PEN	5 322	175 862	244 652	420 906	703 501	745 710	775 571	720 778	877 822	939 444
Saint Lucia	XCD	1 587	2 489	3 154	4 021	5 439	5 593	5 677	4 332	5 295	6 317
Trinidad and Tobago	TTD	21 105	50 098	97 612	138 557	157 931	161 436	157 875	141 395	155 360	192 660
Uruguay	UYU	13 103	301 275	463 684	881 592	1 864 140	2 003 380	2 187 545	2 254 724	2 674 703	2 930 192
Venezuela	VES	0	1	3	10	2 009	..	..	..	..	..

.. Not available

Source: OECD National Accounts data for Chile, Colombia, Costa Rica and Mexico, the *World Economic Outlook* (IMF) for Barbados, Belize, Saint Lucia, Trinidad & Tobago and Uruguay, and official National Accounts data for Bolivia, Brazil, Ecuador, Paraguay, Peru and Venezuela. For Antigua and Barbuda, Argentina, the Bahamas, Dominican Republic, El Salvador, Guatemala, Guyana, Honduras, Jamaica, Nicaragua and Panama, official national sources were used where available, together with data from the IMF. For Cuba, figures since 1996 have come from Oficina Nacional de Estadística e Información (ONEI), while data before 1996 come from ECLAC/CEPAL. For Bahamas, Barbados, Belize, Saint Lucia and Trinidad and Tobago, GDP figures are reported on a fiscal year basis. For Jamaica, GDP for 1990-2003 are reported on a fiscal year basis, while for other years they are reported on a calendar year basis.

Table 4.16. Gross domestic product for tax reporting years at market prices, in millions of USD

	1990	2000	2005	2010	2017	2018	2019	2020	2021	2022
Antigua and Barbuda	459	826	1 023	1 149	1 468	1 606	1 687	1 370	1 472	1 758
Argentina	158 024	317 759	199 273	424 729	643 861	524 431	446 762	385 219	487 377	630 606
Bahamas	5 218	7 880	9 446	10 039	12 243	12 541	13 024	11 270	10 170	12 370
Barbados	2 030	3 058	3 919	4 562	5 011	5 154	5 327	4 461	5 083	5 972
Belize	562	1 128	1 491	1 759	2 293	2 340	2 332	2 183	2 615	3 043
Bolivia	4 868	8 385	9 573	19 786	37 782	40 581	41 193	36 897	40 701	44 329
Brazil	478 052	655 453	891 633	2 208 704	2 063 519	1 916 934	1 873 286	1 476 092	1 649 626	1 920 023
Chile	34 748	78 265	122 329	217 219	276 432	295 118	278 331	254 421	316 353	300 707
Colombia	45 258	93 461	145 588	286 379	311 888	334 063	323 087	269 980	318 505	343 744
Costa Rica	5 736	15 054	20 040	37 943	60 487	62 397	64 448	62 419	64 558	68 632
Cuba	21 541	30 565	42 644	64 328	96 851	100 050	103 428	107 352	22 717	14 064
Dominican Republic	7 995	24 306	35 948	53 921	80 082	85 630	89 032	78 923	94 458	113 873
Ecuador	15 232	18 319	41 507	69 555	104 296	107 562	108 108	99 291	106 166	115 049
El Salvador	4 818	11 785	14 698	18 448	24 979	26 021	26 881	24 930	29 451	32 489
Guatemala	7 535	18 124	27 203	41 327	71 624	73 331	77 156	77 714	86 041	95 004
Guyana	685	1 497	1 712	3 432	4 748	4 788	5 174	5 471	8 042	14 718
Honduras	4 169	7 187	9 757	15 839	23 136	24 068	25 091	23 662	28 291	31 523
Jamaica	5 058	8 997	11 233	13 193	14 755	15 648	15 808	13 885	14 674	17 003
Mexico	296 972	708 096	878 139	1 058 146	1 162 291	1 226 624	1 272 106	1 094 833	1 275 927	1 418 556
Nicaragua	519	5 109	6 321	8 759	13 786	13 025	12 713	12 682	14 145	15 671
Panama	5 723	12 502	16 638	29 440	62 203	67 294	69 722	57 087	67 407	76 523
Paraguay	5 812	8 856	10 738	27 129	38 997	40 225	37 925	35 432	39 951	41 722
Peru	28 326	50 414	74 232	148 991	215 740	226 858	232 419	206 199	226 231	245 008
Saint Lucia	588	922	1 168	1 489	2 014	2 071	2 103	1 604	1 961	2 340
Trinidad and Tobago	4 966	7 986	15 573	21 841	23 399	23 894	23 367	20 945	22 993	28 516
Uruguay	11 204	24 892	18 986	43 967	65 068	65 229	62 056	53 664	61 413	71 177
Venezuela	48 391	94 665	145 343	323 200	143 834	..	..	..	..	..

.. Not available

Source: The figures are derived by dividing the GDP data in Table 4.15 by the exchange rate in Table 4.17.

Table 4.17. Exchange rates used, national currency per US dollar at market exchange rates

		1990	2000	2005	2010	2017	2018	2019	2020	2021	2022
Antigua and Barbuda	XCD	2.704	2.701	2.700	2.699	2.700	2.700	2.701	2.701	2.699	2.700
Argentina	ARS	0.488	1.000	2.923	3.912	16.557	28.116	48.255	70.635	95.093	130.726
Bahamas	BSD	1.000	1.000	1.000	1.000	1.000	1.000	1.000	1.000	1.000	1.000
Barbados	BBD	2.000	2.000	2.000	2.000	2.000	2.000	2.000	2.000	2.000	2.000
Belize	BZD	2.000	2.000	2.000	2.000	2.000	2.000	2.000	2.000	2.000	2.000
Bolivia	BOB	3.172	6.193	8.046	6.968	6.860	6.860	6.860	6.860	6.860	6.860
Brazil	BRL	0.000	1.829	2.434	1.759	3.191	3.654	3.944	5.155	5.394	5.164
Chile	CLP	304.903	539.388	559.705	509.982	648.677	641.896	703.308	791.715	759.820	873.254
Colombia	COP	502.259	2 087.587	2 321.331	1 899.793	2 951.288	2 956.897	3 281.065	3 695.612	3 744.319	4 258.609
Costa Rica	CRC	91.579	307.357	477.895	521.889	567.781	577.188	587.023	584.680	621.350	644.765
Cuba	CUP	0.912	1.000	1.000	1.000	1.000	1.000	1.000	1.000	24.000	45.040
Dominican Republic	DOP	9.674	16.181	30.139	36.780	47.485	49.467	51.243	56.468	57.091	54.978
Ecuador	USD	1.000	1.000	1.000	1.000	1.000	1.000	1.000	1.000	1.000	1.000
El Salvador	USD	1.000	1.000	1.000	1.000	1.000	1.000	1.000	1.000	1.000	1.000
Guatemala	GTQ	4.461	7.763	7.636	8.060	7.351	7.519	7.698	7.722	7.735	7.748
Guyana	GYD	50.399	182.401	199.858	203.670	206.508	207.701	208.490	208.510	208.489	208.505
Honduras	HNL	4.112	14.840	18.832	18.896	23.487	23.902	24.508	24.754	24.185	24.637
Jamaica	JMD	7.541	43.907	62.341	87.378	128.433	129.553	133.504	141.658	150.621	154.282
Mexico	MXN	2.841	9.453	10.890	12.632	18.871	19.178	19.217	21.401	20.223	20.065
Nicaragua	NIO	1.000	12.686	16.734	21.356	30.051	31.554	33.085	34.332	35.173	35.876
Panama	PAB	1.000	1.000	1.000	1.000	1.000	1.000	1.000	1.000	1.000	1.000
Paraguay	PYG	1 229.845	3 486.234	6 177.671	4 758.483	5 618.952	5 732.168	6 240.778	6 771.131	6 774.146	6 982.802
Peru	PEN	0.188	3.488	3.296	2.825	3.261	3.287	3.337	3.496	3.880	3.834
Saint Lucia	XCD	2.700	2.700	2.700	2.700	2.700	2.700	2.700	2.700	2.700	2.700
Trinidad and Tobago	TTD	4.250	6.273	6.268	6.344	6.749	6.756	6.756	6.751	6.757	6.756
Uruguay	UYU	1.169	12.103	24.422	20.051	28.649	30.713	35.251	42.016	43.553	41.168
Venezuela	VES	0.000	0.000	0.000	0.000	0.014	..	..	..	..	..

.. Not available

Note: Annual average market exchange rates.

Source: *World Economic Outlook* (IMF), October 2023.

5 Country tables, 1990-2022 – Tax revenues

In all of the following tables a ("..") indicates not available. The main series in this volume cover the years 1990 to 2022.

Figures referring to 1991-99, 2001-04, 2006-09 and 2011-16 in Tables 5.1 to 5.27 have been omitted because of lack of space. Complete series are, however, available on line at http://dx.doi.org/10.1787/data-00641-en.

Table 5.1. Antigua and Barbuda

Details of tax revenue

Million XCD

	1990	2000	2005	2010	2017	2013	2019	2020	2021	2022
Total tax revenue	..	**268**	**426**	**660**	**776**	**823**	**822**	**732**	**797**	**908**
1000 Taxes on income, profits and capital gains	..	**38**	**62**	**92**	**74**	**78**	**79**	**87**	**83**	**71**
1100 Taxes of individuals	..	0	23	33	2	0	1	0	0	0
1110 On income and profits	..	0	23	33	2	0	1	0	0	0
1120 On capital gains	..	..	..	..	..	..	..	..	..	..
1200 Corporate	..	37	38	59	72	78	79	87	83	71
1210 On profits	..	37	38	59	72	78	79	87	83	71
1220 On capital gains of corporates	..	..	..	..	..	..	..	..	..	..
1300 Unallocable between 1100 and 1200	..	0	0	0	0	0	0	0	0	0
2000 Social security contributions (SSC)	..	..	..	**83**	**140**	**143**	**150**	**122**	**131**	**156**
2100 Employees SSC	..	..	..	..	..	..	..	..	..	..
2110 On a payroll basis	..	..	..	..	..	..	..	..	..	..
2120 On an income tax basis	..	..	..	..	..	..	..	..	..	..
2200 Employers	..	..	..	..	..	..	..	..	..	..
2210 On a payroll	..	..	..	..	..	..	..	..	..	..
2220 On an income tax basis	..	..	..	..	..	..	..	..	..	..
2300 Self-employed or non-employed	..	..	..	..	..	..	..	..	..	..
2310 On a payroll basis	..	..	..	..	..	..	..	..	..	..
2320 On an income tax basis	..	..	..	..	..	..	..	..	..	..
2400 Unallocable between 2100, 2200 and 2300	..	..	..	83	140	143	150	122	131	156
2410 On a payroll basis	..	..	..	83	140	143	150	122	131	156
2420 On an income tax basis	..	..	..	0	0	0	0	0	0	0
3000 Taxes on payroll and workforce	..	**0**	**0**	**0**	**0**	**0**	**0**	**0**	**0**	**0**
4000 Taxes on property	..	**13**	**36**	**49**	**70**	**62**	**72**	**56**	**93**	**96**
4100 Recurrent taxes on immovable property	..	0	0	18	20	21	29	18	24	32
4110 Households	..	..	..	18	20	21	29	18	24	32
Property tax	..	..	..	18	19	20	24	18	23	30
Land tax	..	..	..	0	2	[illegible]	2	0	0	2
Non-Citizens Undeveloped Land Tax	..	..	..	0	0	0	3	0	0	1
4120 Others	..	..	..	0	0	0	0	0	0	0
4200 Recurrent taxes on net wealth	..	0	0	0	0	0	0	0	0	0
4210 Individual	..	..	..	..	..	..	..	..	..	..
4220 Corporate	..	..	..	..	..	..	..	..	..	..
4300 Estate, inheritance and gift taxes	..	0	0	0	0	0	0	0	0	0
4310 Estate and inheritance taxes	..	..	..	..	..	..	..	..	..	..
4320 Gift taxes	..	..	..	..	..	..	..	..	..	..
4400 Taxes on financial and capital transactions	..	13	36	32	50	41	43	38	69	64
Stamp duties	..	13	36	31	50	41	43	38	69	64
Other taxes on transactions	..	0	0	0	0	0	0	0	0	0
4500 Non-recurrent taxes	..	0	0	0	0	0	0	0	0	0
4510 On net wealth	..	..	..	..	..	..	..	..	..	..
4520 Other non-recurrent taxes	..	..	..	..	..	..	..	..	..	..
4600 Other recurrent taxes on property	..	0	0	0	0	0	0	0	0	0
5000 Taxes on goods and services	..	**217**	**328**	**435**	**492**	**539**	**521**	**467**	**490**	**585**
5100 Taxes on production, sale, transfer, etc	..	217	328	429	489	535	517	464	487	581
5110 General taxes	..	0	0	179	312	362	333	273	315	396
5111 Value added taxes	..	..	..	179	237	278	253	207	242	305
5112 Sales tax	..	..	..	0	75	84	80	66	74	91
5113 Other	..	..	..	0	0	0	0	0	0	0
5120 Taxes on specific goods and services	..	217	328	250	177	173	185	191	171	186
5121 Excises	..	72	111	34	68	56	67	83	52	39
Consumption duties	..	72	103	31	64	53	64	79	48	35
Environmental tax	..	0	8	3	3	3	3	4	5	4
5122 Profits of fiscal monopolies	..	0	0	0	0	0	0	0	0	0
5123 Customs and import duties	..	83	137	96	93	101	102	86	97	113
Import duties	..	57	71	79	88	97	93	82	93	110
Throughput Levy on Fuel Products	..	0	0	12	5	4	4	4	4	4
Other customs charges	..	26	66	5	0	0	0	0	0	0
5124 Taxes on exports	..	0	0	0	0	0	0	0	0	0
5125 Taxes on investment goods	..	0	0	0	0	0	0	0	0	0
5126 Taxes on specific services	..	53	78	54	17	16	15	22	22	33
Travel tax	..	4	5	4	6	7	7	3	3	7
Insurance levy	..	0	0	4	7	5	5	7	8	6
Money transfer levy	..	0	1	1	2	2	1	1	1	1
Other taxes on hospitality, transport and telecommunication services	..	49	73	44	2	2	2	11	9	20
5127 Other taxes on internat. trade and transactions	..	9	1	66	0	0	0	0	0	0
5128 Other taxes	..	0	0	0	0	0	0	0	0	0

	1990	2000	2005	2010	2017	2018	2019	2020	2021	2022
5130 Unallocable between 5110 and 5120	..	0	0	0	0	0	0	0	0	0
5200 Taxes on use of goods and perform activities	..	0	0	6	3	3	4	3	3	4
5210 Recurrent taxes	..	..	..	6	3	3	4	3	3	4
5211 Paid by households: motor vehicles	..	..	..	0	0	0	0	0	0	0
5212 Paid by others: motor vehicles	..	..	..	3	2	2	2	2	2	2
5213 Paid in respect of other goods	..	..	..	2	1	1	2	1	1	2
5220 Non-recurrent taxes	..	..	..	0	0	0	0	0	0	0
5300 Unallocable between 5100 and 5200	..	0	0	0	0	0	0	0	1	0
6000 Other taxes	**..**	**0**	**0**	**0**	**0**	**0**	**0**	**0**	**0**	**0**
6100 Paid solely by business	..	..	..	..	..	..	..	..	..	..
6200 Other	..	..	..	..	..	..	..	..	..	..

.. Not available

Note: Year ending 31st December.

The data are on a cash basis.

The figures do not include local tax revenues because data are not available.

Heading 2000: Social security contributions for 2019-22 are estimated.

Heading 5112: The Revenue Recovery Charge, levied on all goods imported into or manufactured in Antigua and Barbuda, is classified under this heading according to the OECD classification described in the Interpretative Guide.

Heading 5121: The environmental tax, levied on specific goods imported into or manufactured in Antigua and Barbuda, is classified under this heading according to the OECD classification described in the Interpretative Guide.

Heading 5126: This heading includes tourism accommodation introduced in 2021.

Source: Ministry of Finance; Corporate Governance and Social Security Board.

Table 5.2. Argentina

Details of tax revenue

Million ARS

	1990	2000	2005	2010	2017	2018	2019	2020	2021	2022
Total tax revenue	**10 217**	**61 084**	**142 906**	**483 014**	**3 202 762**	**4 204 218**	**6 144 864**	**8 093 674**	**13 459 652**	**24 429 642**
1000 Taxes on income, profits and capital gains	**542**	**11 303**	**29 203**	**78 427**	**559 755**	**746 994**	**1 102 982**	**1 470 348**	**2 351 998**	**4 727 878**
1100 Of individuals	141	3 937	8 192	23 980	236 284	297 200	433 621	634 425	1 004 641	2 083 662
1110 On income and profits	130	3 854	8 151	23 858	234 117	294 320	429 882	632 276	999 346	2 071 777
1120 On capital gains	11	82	41	122	2 167	2 880	3 739	2 150	5 295	11 886
1200 Corporate	357	6 575	19 602	50 664	297 111	401 270	589 993	756 440	1 151 704	2 398 339
1210 On profits	357	6 575	19 602	50 664	297 111	401 270	589 993	756 440	1 151 704	2 398 339
Corporate income taxes	198	5 956	18 494	49 012	294 546	399 210	587 272	755 545	1 151 650	2 397 764
Tax on assets	160	19	5	4	5	5	5	2	3	9
Tax on assumed minimum income	0	600	1 102	1 648	2 560	2 055	2 716	893	51	565
1220 On capital gains of corporates	..	..	..	..	..	..	..	..	..	..
1300 Unallocable between 1100 and 1200	43	792	1 409	3 783	26 360	48 524	79 367	79 483	195 653	245 876
Non resident taxpayers	11	792	1 409	3 783	26 360	48 524	79 367	79 483	195 653	245 876
Other	33	0	0	0	0	0	0	0	0	0
2000 Social security contributions	**2 583**	**9 670**	**17 400**	**102 460**	**733 527**	**914 436**	**1 225 664**	**1 543 052**	**2 398 126**	**4 331 972**
2100 Employees	..	2 486	3 690	37 990	288 985	364 291	481 007	625 400	967 274	1 719 052
2110 On a payroll basis	..	2 486	3 690	37 990	288 985	364 291	481 007	625 400	967 274	1 719 052
2120 On an income tax basis	..	0	0	0	0	0	0	0	0	0
2200 Employers	..	6 069	12 557	54 713	413 212	512 615	699 601	864 329	1 356 354	2 492 899
2210 On a payroll basis	..	6 069	12 557	54 713	413 212	512 615	699 601	864 329	1 356 354	2 492 899
2220 On an income tax basis	..	0	0	0	0	0	0	0	0	0
2300 Self-employed or non-employed	98	1 115	1 153	9 757	31 330	37 529	45 056	57 323	74 498	120 021
2310 On a payroll basis	98	1 115	1 153	9 757	31 330	37 529	45 056	57 323	74 498	120 021
2320 On an income tax basis	0	0	0	0	0	0	0	0	0	0
2400 Unallocable between 2100, 2200 and 2300	2 485	0	0	0	0	0	0	0	0	0
2410 On a payroll basis	2 485	..	..	..	..	..	..	..	..	..
2420 On an income tax basis	0	..	..	..	..	..	..	..	..	..
3000 Taxes on payroll and workforce	**0**	**0**	**0**	**0**	**0**	**0**	**0**	**0**	**0**	**0**
4000 Taxes on property	**1 164**	**3 867**	**15 997**	**43 538**	**303 382**	**395 484**	**562 785**	**883 844**	**1 417 635**	**2 401 021**
4100 Recurrent taxes on immovable property	419	1 809	2 837	5 035	44 236	66 035	87 589	113 268	170 405	262 053
4110 Households	0	0	0	0	0	0	0	0	0	0
4120 Others	419	1 809	2 837	5 035	44 236	66 035	87 589	113 268	170 405	262 053
4200 Recurrent taxes on net wealth	246	1 084	1 867	5 248	22 786	15 296	32 383	209 929	283 469	428 916
4210 Individual	3	1 024	1 813	5 147	22 165	14 517	31 184	207 382	278 770	421 969
Personal assets	0	1 024	1 813	5 147	22 165	14 517	31 184	207 382	278 770	421 969
Recurrent taxes on net wealth	3	0	0	0	0	0	0	0	0	0
4220 Corporate	242	60	55	101	621	778	1 199	2 547	4 699	6 947
4300 Estate, inheritance and gift taxes	0	0	0	0	0	0	0	0	0	0
4310 Estate and inheritance taxes	..	..	..	..	..	..	..	..	..	..
4320 Gift taxes	..	..	..	..	..	..	..	..	..	..
4400 Taxes on financial and capital transactions	459	904	11 272	33 252	236 360	314 153	442 812	560 648	963 760	1 710 052
Immovable property transfers	0	54	116	539	4 091	5 935	5 575	4 958	9 796	14 368
Movable property transfers	44	0	0	0	0	0	0	0	0	0
Bank accounts' credits and debits	205	0	9 434	26 885	172 838	234 300	349 559	452 459	750 414	1 343 374
Stamp taxes	211	850	1 722	5 829	59 431	73 918	87 678	103 231	203 551	352 310
4500 Non-recurrent taxes	40	70	21	3	0	0	0	0	0	0
4510 On net wealth	0	0	0	0	..	..	..	..	..	..
4520 Other non-recurrent taxes	40	70	21	3	..	..	..	..	..	..
4600 Other recurrent taxes on property	0	0	0	0	0	0	0	0	0	0
5000 Taxes on goods and services	**5 636**	**34 539**	**77 959**	**253 092**	**1 531 220**	**2 119 852**	**3 209 278**	**4 131 958**	**7 210 692**	**12 838 534**
5100 Taxes on production, sale, transfer, etc	5 462	34 288	78 555	252 550	1 520 300	2 112 824	3 181 178	4 088 803	7 154 673	12 758 527
5110 General taxes	2 384	25 123	51 467	167 534	1 188 317	1 671 105	2 317 817	2 957 036	5 022 050	9 143 893
5111 Value added taxes	1 594	19 009	36 853	116 386	765 336	1 104 580	1 532 597	1 905 385	3 243 608	5 831 330
5112 Sales tax	0	0	0	0	0	0	0	0	0	0
5113 Other	791	6 114	14 613	51 148	422 981	566 524	785 220	1 051 651	1 778 442	3 312 564
5120 Taxes on specific goods and services	3 077	9 166	27 088	85 016	331 983	441 719	863 362	1 131 767	2 132 623	3 614 634
5121 Excises	1 866	5 850	10 609	26 208	182 818	204 903	282 001	394 311	665 896	931 669
Alcoholic beverages	25	36	73	238	1 591	2 186	4 571	5 779	10 862	22 140
Non alcoholic beverages	25	90	189	501	3 136	3 700	6 415	8 520	15 274	28 044
Beers	0	50	131	212	2 811	4 626	1 695	15 523	27 401	43 535
Tobacco products	425	1 875	3 460	6 884	60 249	67 264	90 857	132 703	188 239	275 753
Liquid fuels and gas	1 073	3 478	6 017	15 269	102 846	116 409	161 666	195 659	356 273	431 487
Electricity	72	205	283	591	1 768	2 171	7 818	7 139	13 507	19 294
Motor vehicles	59	20	0	27	476	342	242	3 616	10 156	39 383
Other	189	96	456	2 485	9 942	8 202	8 736	25 372	44 185	72 033
5122 Profits of fiscal monopolies	0	0	0	0	0	0	0	0	0	0

	1990	2000	2005	2010	2017	2018	2019	2020	2021	2022
5123 Customs and import duties	219	1 976	3 877	11 428	70 635	107 178	163 076	199 737	371 011	639 130
Import duties	166	1 938	3 780	11 183	69 259	104 991	132 405	164 888	305 698	531 892
Import fees	53	38	96	246	1 376	2 187	30 671	34 848	65 312	107 238
5124 Taxes on exports	724	32	12 323	45 547	66 121	114 160	398 312	387 643	963 117	1 649 418
5125 Taxes on investment goods	0	0	0	0	0	0	0	0	0	0
5126 Taxes on specific services	163	1 233	150	1 429	7 792	9 389	10 692	11 683	16 556	23 919
Insurance services	42	194	8	21	167	198	289	376	590	930
Financial services	32	855	2	0	0	0	0	0	0	0
Telephone services	82	33	110	936	4 061	4 722	4 312	4 497	5 910	7 498
Other specific services	7	151	31	472	3 564	4 469	6 090	6 809	10 055	15 491
5127 Other taxes on internat. trade and transactions	98	74	129	404	4 616	6 089	9 281	138 394	116 043	370 498
5128 Other taxes	8	0	0	0	0	0	0	0	0	0
5130 Unallocable between 5110 and 5120	0	0	0	0	0	0	0	0	0	0
5200 Taxes on use of goods and perform activities	177	833	1 289	3 598	35 873	41 628	57 370	75 337	121 969	189 977
5210 Recurrent taxes	177	833	1 289	3 598	35 873	41 628	57 370	75 337	121 969	189 977
5211 Paid by households: motor vehicles	177	833	1 289	3 598	35 873	41 628	57 370	75 337	121 969	189 977
5212 Paid by others: motor vehicles	0	0	0	0	0	0	0	0	0	0
5213 Paid in respect of other goods	0	0	0	0	0	0	0	0	0	0
5220 Non-recurrent taxes	0	0	0	0	0	0	0	0	0	0
5300 Unallocable between 5100 and 5200	-3	-583	-1 885	-3 056	-24 953	-34 600	-29 270	-32 182	-65 950	-109 970
6000 Other taxes	**292**	**1 704**	**2 347**	**5 497**	**74 878**	**27 452**	**44 156**	**59 470**	**81 201**	**130 238**
6100 Paid solely by business	0	354	757	2 093	10 544	16 052	20 635	29 169	31 500	39 721
Simplified system for small taxpayers	..	354	757	2 093	10 544	16 052	20 635	29 169	31 500	39 721
6200 Other	292	1 351	1 590	3 404	64 334	11 399	23 521	30 301	49 702	90 517
Tax debt payments	135	24	112	293	46 131	-8 646	-1 070	6 215	5 262	18 284
Special payments	79	6	1	0	0	0	0	0	0	0
Other national level	0	12	7	0	0	0	0	0	0	0
Other provincial level	78	1 309	1 469	3 110	18 202	20 045	24 591	24 086	44 440	72 233

.. Not available

Note: Year ending 31st December.

The data are on a cash basis.

The figures exclude local government tax revenues as the data are not available (but include provincial revenues).

Heading 2000: The figures may be under-estimated as they exclude certain types of social security contributions for which data are not readily available.

Heading 5212: In ECLAC data, property tax on motor vehicles is classified in category 4000.

Heading 5300: The figures are negative as they represent general reimbursements of exports and specific taxes on goods and services.

Heading 6200: The tax debt payments from 2016 include revenue following the implementation of a new voluntary disclosure regime in July 2016 (Law 27260).

Source: Subsecretaría de Ingresos Públicos, Dirección Nacional de Investigaciones y Análisis Fiscal, Ministerio de Hacienda (Undersecretary of Public Revenue, National Direction of Research and Fiscal Analysis, Ministry of Finance).

Table 5.3. Bahamas

Details of tax revenue

Million BSD

	1990	2000	2005	2010	2017	2018	2019	2020	2021	2022
Total tax revenue	**505**	**965**	**1 060**	**1 277**	**2 118**	**2 120**	**2 486**	**2 076**	**1 831**	**2 425**
1000 Taxes on income, profits and capital gains	**0**	**0**	**0**	**0**	**0**	**0**	**0**	**0**	**0**	**0**
1100 Of individuals	0	0	0	0	0	0	0	0	0	0
1110 On income and profits	..	..	..	..	..	..	..	..	..	..
1120 On capital gains	..	..	..	..	..	..	..	..	..	..
1200 Corporate	0	0	0	0	0	0	0	0	0	0
1210 On profits	..	..	..	..	..	..	..	..	..	..
1220 On capital gains of corporates	..	..	..	..	..	..	..	..	..	..
1300 Unallocable between 1100 and 1200	0	0	0	0	0	0	0	0	0	0
2000 Social security contributions	**66**	**115**	**136**	**167**	**277**	**284**	**287**	**226**	**219**	**267**
2100 Employees	..	..	..	60	110	111	115	..	..	..
2110 On a payroll basis	..	..	..	..	..	..	..	..	..	..
2120 On an income tax basis	..	..	..	..	..	..	..	..	..	..
2200 Employers	..	..	..	104	161	166	166	..	..	..
2210 On a payroll basis	..	..	..	..	..	..	..	..	..	..
2220 On an income tax basis	..	..	..	..	..	..	..	..	..	..
2300 Self-employed or non-employed	..	..	..	3	7	8	7	..	..	..
2310 On a payroll basis	..	..	..	..	..	..	..	..	..	..
2320 On an income tax basis	..	..	..	..	..	..	..	..	..	..
2400 Unallocable between 2100, 2200 and 2300	66	115	136	0	-1	-1	-1	226	219	267
2410 On a payroll basis	..	..	..	..	..	..	..	..	..	..
2420 On an income tax basis	..	..	..	..	..	..	..	..	..	..
3000 Taxes on payroll and workforce	**0**	**0**	**0**	**0**	**0**	**0**	**0**	**0**	**0**	**0**
4000 Taxes on property	**56**	**208**	**302**	**269**	**233**	**237**	**345**	**174**	**203**	**241**
4100 Recurrent taxes on immovable property	19	32	54	92	121	124	109	100	143	147
4110 Households	0	0	0	0	0	0	0	0	0	0
4120 Others	19	32	54	92	121	124	109	100	143	147
4200 Recurrent taxes on net wealth	0	0	0	0	0	0	0	0	0	0
4210 Individual	..	..	..	..	..	..	..	..	..	..
4220 Corporate	..	..	..	..	..	..	..	..	..	..
4300 Estate, inheritance and gift taxes	0	0	0	0	0	0	0	0	0	0
4310 Estate and inheritance taxes	..	..	..	..	..	..	..	..	..	..
4320 Gift taxes	..	..	..	..	..	..	..	..	..	..
4400 Taxes on financial and capital transactions	37	176	248	177	112	114	235	74	60	94
Stamp Tax from Imports	0	102	112	15	0	0	0	0	0	0
Stamp Tax from Exports	0	0	0	0	0	0	0	0	0	0
All Other Stamp Tax	37	74	135	162	112	114	235	74	60	94
4500 Non-recurrent taxes	0	0	0	0	0	0	0	0	0	0
4510 On net wealth	..	..	..	..	..	..	..	..	..	..
4520 Other non-recurrent taxes	..	..	..	..	..	..	..	..	..	..
4600 Other recurrent taxes on property	0	0	0	0	0	0	0	0	0	0
5000 Taxes on goods and services	**386**	**620**	**623**	**780**	**1 608**	**1 598**	**1 854**	**1 676**	**1 408**	**1 917**
5100 Taxes on production, sale, transfer, etc	354	552	545	657	1 386	1 407	1 623	1 524	1 253	1 745
5110 General taxes	0	0	0	0	638	681	897	876	740	1 136
5111 Value added taxes	0	0	0	0	638	681	897	876	740	1 136
5112 Sales tax	..	..	..	..	0	0	0	0	0	0
5113 Other	..	..	..	..	0	0	0	0	0	0
5120 Taxes on specific goods and services	354	552	545	657	747	726	727	649	513	609
5121 Excises	0	0	0	188	289	257	242	206	176	47
Fuel surcharges	..	..	..	..	1	1	1	1	1	1
Other excises	..	..	..	..	287	255	241	205	175	45
5122 Profits of fiscal monopolies	0	0	0	0	0	0	0	0	0	0
5123 Customs and import duties	289	435	413	348	286	270	284	224	192	249
5124 Taxes on exports	6	13	13	14	9	18	13	53	96	177
5125 Taxes on investment goods	0	0	0	0	0	0	0	0	0	0
5126 Taxes on specific services	59	104	119	106	163	130	187	165	49	137
Departure tax	27	64	69	70	135	143	147	125	11	85
Gaming tax	27	20	25	10	27	37	40	40	38	51
Hotel occupancy tax	5	20	25	25	1	0	0	0	0	1
5127 Other taxes on internat. trade and transactions	0	0	0	0	0	0	0	0	0	0
5128 Other taxes	0	0	0	0	0	0	0	0	0	0
5130 Unallocable between 5110 and 5120	0	0	0	0	0	0	0	0	0	0
5200 Taxes on use of goods and perform activities	32	69	78	123	222	192	231	152	155	172
5210 Recurrent taxes	32	69	78	123	222	192	231	152	155	172
Motor vehicle tax	10	14	18	21	30	37	35	31	32	34
5211 Paid by households: motor vehicles	..	..	..	..	..	..	..	..	..	..
5212 Paid by others: motor vehicles	..	..	..	..	..	..	..	..	..	..

	1990	2000	2005	2010	2017	2018	2019	2020	2021	2022
5213 Paid in respect of other goods	22	55	61	102	193	155	195	122	123	138
Company fees and registration	0	5	5	5	0	0	0	0	0	0
International business companies	0	17	15	19	0	0	0	0	0	0
Others	22	33	40	78	193	155	195	122	123	138
5220 Non-recurrent taxes	0	0	0	0	0	0	0	0	0	0
5300 Unallocable between 5100 and 5200	0	0	0	0	0	0	0	0	0	0
6000 Other taxes	**-4**	**21**	**-1**	**60**	**0**	**0**	**0**	**0**	**0**	**0**
6100 Paid solely by business	0	0	0	0	..	..	..	..	..	..
6200 Other	-4	21	-1	60	..	..	..	..	..	..
Incentive acts and other refunds	-8	14	-15	11	..	..	..	..	..	..
Other taxes	4	7	15	49	..	..	..	..	..	..

.. Not available

Note: Fiscal year ending on 30th June. For example, the data for 2022 represent July 2021 to June 2022.

The data are on a cash basis.

The figures exclude local government tax revenues as the data are not available. Central government tax revenue data are preliminary for 2020-22.

Heading 2000: The data are estimated for 2021 and 2022.

Heading 2400: This heading includes refunds of social security contributions as reported by the National Insurance Board (NIB) before 2020.

Heading 4400: This heading includes all stamp taxes.

Heading 5111: A value added tax was enforced on 1st January 2015.

Source: The Central Bank of The Bahamas; Ministry of Finance of The Bahamas; National Insurance Board of The Bahamas; Centro Interamericano de Administraciones Tributarias (Inter-American Center of Tax Administrations).

Table 5.4. Barbados

Details of tax revenue

Million BBD

	1990	2000	2005	2010	2017	2018	2019	2020	2021	2022
Total tax revenue	**1 026**	**1 892**	**2 450**	**2 736**	**3 280**	**3 434**	**3 442**	**2 982**	**3 241**	**3 643**
1000 Taxes on income, profits and capital gains	**250**	**599**	**722**	**766**	**783**	**921**	**823**	**976**	**897**	**1 023**
1100 Of individuals	140	293	306	395	463	482	455	308	385	393
1110 On income and profits	140	293	306	395	463	482	455	308	385	393
Personal income tax	140	293	306	395	463	482	455	308	385	393
Consolidation tax	0	0	0	0	0	0	0	0	0	0
1120 On capital gains	..	..	..	..	..	..	..	..	..	..
1200 Corporate	95	269	360	294	275	355	309	613	451	549
1210 On profits	95	269	360	294	275	355	309	613	451	549
1220 On capital gains of corporates	..	..	..	..	..	..	..	..	..	..
1300 Unallocable between 1100 and 1200	15	37	56	76	45	83	59	55	61	81
2000 Social security contributions	**134**	**295**	**408**	**565**	**624**	**621**	**671**	**595**	**595**	**621**
2100 Employees	..	..	..	..	..	..	..	..	..	..
2110 On a payroll basis	..	..	..	..	..	..	..	..	..	..
2120 On an income tax basis	..	..	..	..	..	..	..	..	..	..
2200 Employers	..	..	..	..	..	..	..	..	..	..
2210 On a payroll basis	..	..	..	..	..	..	..	..	..	..
2220 On an income tax basis	..	..	..	..	..	..	..	..	..	..
2300 Self-employed or non-employed	..	..	..	..	..	..	..	..	..	..
2310 On a payroll basis	..	..	..	..	..	..	..	..	..	..
2320 On an income tax basis	..	..	..	..	..	..	..	..	..	..
2400 Unallocable between 2100, 2200 and 2300	134	295	408	565	624	621	671	595	595	621
2410 On a payroll basis	..	..	..	..	..	..	..	..	..	..
2420 On an income tax basis	..	..	..	..	..	..	..	..	..	..
3000 Taxes on payroll and workforce	**0**	**0**	**0**	**0**	**0**	**0**	**0**	**0**	**0**	**0**
4000 Taxes on property	**147**	**108**	**159**	**130**	**148**	**172**	**226**	**189**	**219**	**239**
4100 Recurrent taxes on immovable property	46	95	137	118	138	161	215	182	205	217
Property tax	46	95	137	118	138	161	215	182	205	217
Municipal solid waste tax	0	0	0	0	0	0	0	0	0	0
4110 Households	..	..	..	..	..	..	..	..	..	..
4120 Others	..	..	..	..	..	..	..	..	..	..
4200 Recurrent taxes on net wealth	0	0	0	0	0	0	0	0	0	0
4210 Individual	..	..	..	..	..	..	..	..	..	..
4220 Corporate	..	..	..	..	..	..	..	..	..	..
4300 Estate, inheritance and gift taxes	0	0	0	0	0	0	0	0	0	0
4310 Estate and inheritance taxes	..	..	..	..	..	..	..	..	..	..
4320 Gift taxes	..	..	..	..	..	..	..	..	..	..
4400 Taxes on financial and capital transactions	101	13	22	12	11	11	11	8	13	22
Stamp duties	101	13	22	12	11	11	11	8	13	22
4500 Non-recurrent taxes	0	0	0	0	0	0	0	0	0	0
4510 On net wealth	..	..	..	..	..	..	..	..	..	..
4520 Other non-recurrent taxes	..	..	..	..	..	..	..	..	..	..
4600 Other recurrent taxes on property	0	0	0	0	0	0	0	0	0	0
5000 Taxes on goods and services	**495**	**889**	**1 161**	**1 276**	**1 726**	**1 719**	**1 723**	**1 223**	**1 531**	**1 761**
5100 Taxes on production, sale, transfer, etc	424	788	1 035	1 105	1 610	1 599	1 607	1 171	1 459	1 686
5110 General taxes	197	492	683	768	1 039	990	967	706	885	1 023
5111 Value added taxes	0	492	683	768	887	941	967	706	885	1 023
5112 Sales tax	197	0	0	0	152	49	0	0	0	0
Social responsibility levy	0	0	..	..	152	49	0	..	..	..
Consumption tax	197	0	..	..	0	0	0	..	..	..
5113 Other	0	0	0	0	0	0	0	0	0	0
5120 Taxes on specific goods and services	227	296	353	337	570	608	640	465	575	663
5121 Excises	91	175	172	146	303	271	251	154	212	247
Excises	0	160	172	146	303	271	251	154	212	247
Levies	91	15	0	0	0	0	0	0	0	0
5122 Profits of fiscal monopolies	0	0	0	0	0	0	0	0	0	0
5123 Customs and import duties	118	121	180	191	219	282	314	256	291	323
Import duties	118	121	180	191	219	214	232	192	221	242
Fuel tax	0	0	0	0	0	69	82	64	70	81
5124 Taxes on exports	0	0	0	0	0	0	0	0	0	0
5125 Taxes on investment goods	0	0	0	0	0	0	0	0	0	0
5126 Taxes on specific services	17	1	0	0	49	55	76	55	71	93
Hotel and restaurant tax	17	1	..	..	0	0	0	0	0	0
Banks and other asset tax	0	0	..	..	49	45	47	46	46	53
Room rate levy	0	0	..	..	0	10	28	10	25	40
5127 Other taxes on internat. trade and transactions	0	0	0	0	0	0	0	0	0	0
5128 Other taxes	0	0	0	0	0	0	0	0	0	0
5130 Unallocable between 5110 and 5120	0	0	0	0	0	0	0	0	0	0

	1990	2000	2005	2010	2017	2018	2019	2020	2021	2022
5200 Taxes on use of goods and perform activities	71	101	126	171	116	121	115	52	72	75
5210 Recurrent taxes	71	101	126	171	116	121	115	52	72	75
5211 Paid by households: motor vehicles	0	0	0	0	0	0	0	0	0	0
5212 Paid by others: motor vehicles	0	0	0	0	0	0	0	0	0	0
5213 Paid in respect of other goods	71	101	126	171	116	121	115	52	72	75
5220 Non-recurrent taxes	0	0	0	0	0	0	0	0	0	0
5300 Unallocable between 5100 and 5200	0	0	0	0	0	0	0	0	0	0
6000 Other taxes	**0**	**0**	**0**	**0**	**0**	**0**	**0**	**0**	**0**	**0**
6100 Paid solely by business	..	..	..	..	..	..	..	..	..	..
6200 Other	..	..	..	..	..	..	..	..	..	..

.. Not available

Note: Year ending 31st March, except for social security contributions which use calendar year. For example, the data for 2022 represent April 2022 to March 2023.

The data are on a cash basis, except for social security contributions which are on an accrual basis.

The figures exclude local government tax revenues as the data are not available.

Heading 1300: This heading includes withholding taxes levied on both individuals and corporate entities.

Heading 2000: Social security contributions refer to contribution income of National Insurance Scheme. The values for 2021 and 2022 are government projections under the best estimate scenario in the 17th Actuarial Review of the National Insurance Fund.

Heading 5213: This heading includes miscellaneous indirect taxes levied on a recurrent basis such as revenues from various licences.

Source: The Central Bank of Barbados; National Insurance Board of Barbados.

Table 5.5. Belize

Details of tax revenue

Million BZD

	1990	2000	2005	2010	2017	2018	2019	2020	2021	2022
Total tax revenue	**178**	**318**	**495**	**740**	**1 054**	**1 129**	**1 153**	**935**	**1 128**	**1 346**
1000 Taxes on income, profits and capital gains	**37**	**76**	**129**	**248**	**269**	**286**	**291**	**237**	**224**	**345**
1100 Of individuals	21	19	35	52	93	101	105	92	78	121
1110 On income and profits	21	19	35	52	93	101	105	92	78	121
Income tax (PAYE)	20	19	35	52	93	101	105	92	78	121
Income tax on individuals	1	0	0	0	0	0	0	0	0	0
1120 On capital gains	..	..	..	..	..	..	..	..	..	..
1200 Corporate	12	51	90	189	166	173	174	134	126	211
Income tax (companies)	12	1	0	51	0	3	3	1	0	6
Income tax (business tax)	0	51	90	138	166	170	171	133	126	205
Income tax (supplemental petroleum tax)	0	0	0	0	0	0	0	0	0	0
1210 On profits	..	..	..	..	..	..	..	..	..	..
1220 On capital gains of corporates	..	..	..	..	..	..	..	..	..	..
1300 Unallocable between 1100 and 1200	4	6	4	7	10	12	12	11	20	13
Income tax (arrears)	4	3	1	1	2	3	2	2	2	1
Income tax (withholding)	0	3	2	6	8	10	10	9	18	12
2000 Social security contributions	**10**	**18**	**50**	**60**	**83**	**87**	**100**	**110**	**117**	**144**
2100 Employees	..	..	..	..	..	..	..	..	..	..
2110 On a payroll basis	..	..	..	..	..	..	..	..	..	..
2120 On an income tax basis	..	..	..	..	..	..	..	..	..	..
2200 Employers	..	..	..	..	..	..	..	..	..	..
2210 On a payroll basis	..	..	..	..	..	..	..	..	..	..
2220 On an income tax basis	..	..	..	..	..	..	..	..	..	..
2300 Self-employed or non-employed	..	..	..	..	..	..	..	..	..	..
2310 On a payroll basis	..	..	..	..	..	..	..	..	..	..
2320 On an income tax basis	..	..	..	..	..	..	..	..	..	..
2400 Unallocable between 2100, 2200 and 2300	10	18	50	60	83	87	100	110	117	144
2410 On a payroll basis	..	..	..	..	..	..	..	..	..	..
2420 On an income tax basis	..	..	..	..	..	..	..	..	..	..
3000 Taxes on payroll and workforce	**0**	**0**	**0**	**0**	**0**	**0**	**0**	**0**	**0**	**0**
4000 Taxes on property	**34**	**13**	**27**	**23**	**32**	**49**	**39**	**34**	**63**	**42**
4100 Recurrent taxes on immovable property	1	2	6	7	6	6	7	7	9	6
4110 Households	1	2	6	7	6	6	7	7	9	6
4120 Others	0	0	0	0	0	0	0	0	0	0
4200 Recurrent taxes on net wealth	0	0	0	0	0	0	0	0	0	0
4210 Individual	..	..	..	..	..	..	..	..	..	..
4220 Corporate	..	..	..	..	..	..	..	..	..	..
4300 Estate, inheritance and gift taxes	0	0	0	0	0	0	0	0	0	0
4310 Estate and inheritance taxes	..	0	0	0	0	0	0	0	0	0
4320 Gift taxes	..	0	0	0	0	0	0	0	0	0
4400 Taxes on financial and capital transactions	33	11	22	16	26	44	32	27	54	35
Stamp duties on customs	28	0	0	0	0	0	0	0	0	0
Stamp duties (other departments)	5	11	22	16	26	44	14	3	8	3
Stamp duties (land transactions)	0	0	0	0	0	0	18	24	46	32
4500 Non-recurrent taxes	0	0	0	0	0	0	0	0	0	0
4510 On net wealth	..	..	..	..	..	..	..	..	..	..
4520 Other non-recurrent taxes	..	..	..	..	..	..	..	..	..	..
4600 Other recurrent taxes on property	0	0	0	0	0	0	0	0	0	0
5000 Taxes on goods and services	**97**	**211**	**288**	**409**	**670**	**707**	**723**	**553**	**724**	**815**
5100 Taxes on production, sale, transfer, etc.	94	207	282	400	662	696	712	546	715	806
5110 General taxes	0	82	131	199	292	317	323	244	306	397
5111 Value added taxes	0	0	0	199	292	317	323	244	306	397
5112 Sales tax	..	82	131	0	0	0	0	0	0	0
5113 Other	..	0	0	0	0	0	0	0	0	0
5120 Taxes on specific goods and services	94	125	151	200	369	379	389	302	409	409
5121 Excises	35	47	57	31	187	193	194	155	192	156
Revenue replacement duty	18	39	57	7	1	1	1	1	1	1
Excise duties	17	8	0	22	186	191	192	151	191	155
Excise on locally refined petroleum products	0	0	0	0	0	1	0	3	0	0
Excise on locally extracted crude oil	0	0	0	1	1	1	1	0	0	0
5122 Profits of fiscal monopolies	0	0	0	0	0	0	0	0	0	0
5123 Customs and import duties	50	64	80	144	139	139	137	105	159	189
Import duties	50	64	80	123	98	98	95	71	109	128
Environmental tax	0	0	0	21	40	41	42	34	49	61
Imports into EPZs	0	0	0	0	0	0	0	0	0	0
5124 Taxes on exports	0	0	0	0	0	0	0	2	0	0
5125 Taxes on investment goods	0	0	0	0	0	0	0	0	0	0
5126 Taxes on specific services	0	0	0	0	0	0	0	0	1	0

	1990	2000	2005	2010	2017	2018	2019	2020	2021	2022
5127 Other taxes on internat. trade and transactions	8	14	15	25	43	47	59	40	57	64
Goods in transit - administration charge	3	1	1	1	1	1	1	1	1	1
Goods in transit - social fee	0	5	4	8	17	23	22	17	23	26
Taxes on foreign currency transactions	6	8	9	16	25	23	35	21	33	37
5128 Other taxes	0	0	0	0	0	0	0	0	0	0
5130 Unallocable between 5110 and 5120	0	0	0	0	0	0	0	0	0	0
5200 Taxes on use of goods and perform activities	3	4	6	9	9	11	11	7	9	9
5210 Recurrent taxes	3	4	6	9	9	11	11	7	9	9
5211 Paid by households: motor vehicles	2	3	5	3	5	5	5	5	6	6
5212 Paid by others: motor vehicles	0	0	0	0	0	0	0	0	0	0
5213 Paid in respect of other goods	1	1	1	6	4	6	5	2	3	4
5220 Non-recurrent taxes	0	0	0	0	0	0	0	0	0	0
5300 Unallocable between 5100 and 5200	0	0	0	0	0	0	0	0	0	0
6000 Other taxes	**0**	**0**	**0**	**0**	**0**	**0**	**0**	**0**	**0**	**0**
6100 Paid solely by business	..	..	..	..	..	..	..	..	..	..
6200 Other	..	..	..	..	..	..	..	..	..	..

.. Not available

Note: Year ending 31st March. For example, the data for 2022 represent April 2022 to March 2023.

The data are on a cash basis.

The tax revenue data for 2022 represent the government revised estimates for the 2022/23 fiscal year reported in the Approved Estimates of Revenue and Expenditure for Fiscal Year 2023/24.

Heading 2000: Social security contributions refer to total contributions to the Social Security Fund excluding government contributions to the National Health Insurance (NHI) fund. The government contributions are government subsidies to the social security system and hence are not considered as tax revenues according to the OECD classification described in the Interpretative Guide.

Heading 4400: This heading includes all stamp duties.

Source: Ministry of Finance of Belize; Social Security Board Belize.

Table 5.6. Bolivia

Details of tax revenue

Million BOB

	1990	2000	2005	2010	2017	2018	2019	2020	2021	2022
Total tax revenue	**1 005**	**9 151**	**15 370**	**31 549**	**67 072**	**69 535**	**69 785**	**56 088**	**63 203**	**72 013**
1000 Taxes on income, profits and capital gains	**68**	**1 209**	**2 383**	**6 294**	**10 152**	**10 591**	**11 356**	**7 402**	**7 644**	**10 397**
1100 Of individuals	68	214	214	263	502	525	518	470	457	502
1110 On income and profits	68	214	214	263	502	525	518	470	457	502
Value added supplementary scheme	62	161	187	237	441	475	464	426	423	476
Fiscal notes on value added supplementary scheme	6	52	27	26	61	50	53	44	33	25
1120 On capital gains	..	..	..	..	..	..	..	..	..	..
1200 Corporate	0	995	2 169	6 031	9 650	10 066	10 838	6 931	7 187	9 896
1210 On profits	..	995	2 169	6 031	9 650	10 066	10 838	6 931	7 187	9 896
Corporate tax	..	804	1 872	5 089	8 655	9 165	9 724	6 465	6 986	9 209
Fiscal notes on corporate tax	..	191	297	942	995	901	1 115	467	201	686
1220 On capital gains of corporates	..	..	..	..	..	..	..	..	..	..
1300 Unallocable between 1100 and 1200	0	0	0	0	0	0	0	0	0	0
2000 Social security contributions	**0**	**666**	**936**	**5 265**	**15 915**	**16 767**	**17 500**	**16 494**	**16 814**	**17 351**
2100 Employees	..	..	..	..	..	..	..	..	..	..
2110 On a payroll basis	..	..	..	..	..	..	..	..	..	..
2120 On an income tax basis	..	..	..	..	..	..	..	..	..	..
2200 Employers	..	..	..	..	..	..	..	..	..	..
2210 On a payroll basis	..	..	..	..	..	..	..	..	..	..
2220 On an income tax basis	..	..	..	..	..	..	..	..	..	..
2300 Self-employed or non-employed	..	..	..	..	..	..	..	..	..	..
2310 On a payroll basis	..	..	..	..	..	..	..	..	..	..
2320 On an income tax basis	..	..	..	..	..	..	..	..	..	..
2400 Unallocable between 2100, 2200 and 2300	..	666	936	5 265	15 915	16 767	17 500	16 494	16 814	17 351
2410 On a payroll basis	..	666	936	5 265	15 915	16 767	17 500	16 494	16 814	17 351
2420 On an income tax basis	..	0	0	0	0	0	0	0	0	0
3000 Taxes on payroll and workforce	**0**	**0**	**0**	**0**	**0**	**0**	**0**	**0**	**0**	**0**
4000 Taxes on property	**1**	**3**	**640**	**367**	**492**	**543**	**522**	**421**	**743**	**767**
4100 Recurrent taxes on immovable property	0	0	0	0	0	0	0	0	0	0
4110 Households	..	..	..	..	..	..	..	..	..	..
4120 Others	..	..	..	..	..	..	..	..	..	..
4200 Recurrent taxes on net wealth	0	0	0	0	0	0	0	0	241	205
4210 Individual	..	..	..	..	..	..	..	..	241	205
4220 Corporate	..	..	..	..	..	..	..	..	0	0
4300 Estate, inheritance and gift taxes	1	3	7	20	1	0	0	0	0	0
4310 Estate and inheritance taxes	1	3	7	20	1	0	0	..	..	..
4320 Gift taxes	0	0	0	0	0	0	0	..	..	..
4400 Taxes on financial and capital transactions	0	0	633	347	491	543	522	421	502	561
4500 Non-recurrent taxes	0	0	0	0	0	0	0	0	0	0
4510 On net wealth	..	..	..	..	..	..	..	..	..	..
4520 Other non-recurrent taxes	..	..	..	..	..	..	..	..	..	..
4600 Other recurrent taxes on property	0	0	0	0	0	0	0	0	0	0
5000 Taxes on goods and services	**907**	**6 656**	**10 457**	**17 791**	**34 022**	**35 215**	**34 187**	**25 866**	**32 190**	**36 806**
5100 Taxes on production, sale, transfer, etc.	907	6 656	10 457	17 791	34 022	35 215	34 187	25 866	32 190	36 806
5110 General taxes	584	3 953	7 018	12 541	24 591	25 615	25 405	19 124	24 307	27 953
5111 Value added taxes	432	2 949	5 314	10 259	20 199	20 977	20 391	15 146	19 237	22 027
VAT (internal market)	178	1 204	1 937	4 100	9 910	10 155	10 000	7 692	9 452	9 608
VAT (imports)	178	1 445	2 637	5 193	9 154	9 387	8 594	6 522	7 950	8 983
VAT fiscal notes (internal market)	56	223	584	581	439	411	271	336	417	659
VAT fiscal notes (imports)	20	76	156	385	696	1 024	1 526	596	1 418	2 776
5112 Sales tax	0	0	0	0	0	0	0	0	0	0
5113 Other	151	1 005	1 704	2 282	4 392	4 638	5 014	3 978	5 070	5 926
Transactions tax	136	943	1 455	2 174	4 323	4 547	4 652	3 446	4 309	4 804
Fiscal note on transactions tax	15	62	250	107	69	92	362	531	761	1 122
5120 Taxes on specific goods and services	324	2 702	3 439	5 250	9 430	9 600	8 782	6 742	7 883	8 853
5121 Excises	118	2 047	2 604	3 658	6 032	6 191	5 187	4 563	4 820	4 807
Excises (internal market)	61	244	209	933	1 450	1 649	1 456	1 225	1 359	1 234
Excises (Imports)	22	298	208	379	953	1 091	785	561	699	803
Special tax on hydrocarbons and derivatives	0	1 348	1 529	1 070	3 105	3 076	1 911	1 697	1 977	800
Fiscal notes on excises	35	118	309	155	442	272	442	315	328	571
Fiscal notes on special tax on hydrocarb. and deriv.	0	40	350	1 121	82	103	594	765	456	1 400
5122 Profits of fiscal monopolies	0	0	0	0	0	0	0	0	0	0
5123 Customs and import duties	204	640	803	1 545	3 198	3 185	3 373	2 091	3 004	3 934
Customs and import duties	163	616	777	1 504	3 043	2 937	2 973	1 998	2 567	2 936
Fiscal notes on customs and import duties	41	24	26	41	155	248	399	93	437	999
5124 Taxes on exports	0	0	0	0	0	0	0	0	0	0
5125 Taxes on investment goods	0	0	0	0	0	0	0	0	0	0

	1990	2000	2005	2010	2017	2018	2019	2020	2021	2022
5126 Taxes on specific services	2	15	32	47	200	224	218	89	60	112
Air departure tax	2	15	32	47	122	128	130	42	30	69
Tax on gambling	0	0	0	0	78	96	88	47	30	42
5127 Other taxes on internat. trade and transactions	0	0	0	0	0	0	0	0	0	0
5128 Other taxes	0	0	0	0	0	0	0	0	0	0
5130 Unallocable between 5110 and 5120	0	0	0	0	0	0	0	0	0	0
5200 Taxes on use of goods and perform activities	0	0	0	0	0	0	0	0	0	0
5210 Recurrent taxes	..	..	..	..	..	..	..	..	..	..
5211 Paid by households: motor vehicles	..	..	..	..	..	..	..	..	..	..
5212 Paid by others: motor vehicles	..	..	..	..	..	..	..	..	..	..
5213 Paid in respect of other goods	..	..	..	..	..	..	..	..	..	..
5220 Non-recurrent taxes	..	..	..	..	..	..	..	..	..	..
5300 Unallocable between 5100 and 5200	0	0	0	0	0	0	0	0	0	0
6000 Other taxes	**30**	**617**	**954**	**1 832**	**6 491**	**6 419**	**6 220**	**5 905**	**5 812**	**6 692**
6100 Paid solely by business	4	6	4	12	30	33	36	25	29	30
Simplified tax regime	3	6	4	12	30	33	36	25	29	30
Integrated tax system	1	0	0	0	0	0	0	0	0	0
6200 Other	26	611	949	1 819	6 461	6 386	6 184	5 880	5 783	6 662
Municipal taxes	0	575	762	1 381	3 737	3 561	3 203	2 715	2 815	3 166
Other taxes	20	35	178	422	2 685	2 784	2 866	3 107	2 923	3 442
Fiscal notes on other taxes	3	0	5	3	8	9	88	32	11	21
Unified agricultural regime	2	1	5	14	31	32	28	27	34	33

.. Not available

Note: Year ending 31st December.

The data are on a cash basis.

The figures exclude local government tax revenues for the period 1990-1993 as the data are not available. Central government tax revenue data are preliminary for 2021 and 2022. Local government tax revenue data and social security contributions are preliminary for 2020-2022.

Heading 1210: Corporate tax under heading 1210 includes revenues from IUE (corporate tax), IUE-RE (corporate tax remittances) and IUM (mining profits). Fiscal notes on corporate tax include fiscal notes on IUE and IUM.

Heading 2000: The figures include social security contributions to Bolivia's pension system and healthcare related funds. Contributions to the pension system between 1997 and 2009 are excluded because Bolivia's pension system was private during this period.

Heading 4210: This heading includes the tax on large fortunes (IGF). This tax is levied on net wealth of natural persons and was introduced in 2020.

Heading 5113: This heading includes IT (transactions tax), its fiscal notes as well as the Special Integrated System of Transition for Entrepreneurs (SIETE-RG).

Heading 5127: This heading includes IVME (tax on the sales of foreign currency).

Heading 6200: Other taxes include revenues from "conceptos varios" (miscellaneous concepts), programa transitorio (transitional programme) and otros ingresos en efectivo (other cash revenue). Fiscal notes on other taxes include fiscal notes on "conceptos varios".

Source: Ministerio de Economía y Finanzas Públicas de Bolivia (Ministry of Economy and Public Finance of Bolivia); Servicio de Impuestos Nacionales (National Tax Service); Aduana Nacional de Bolivia (National Customs of Bolivia); Caja Nacional de Salud (National Health Fund).

Table 5.7. Brazil

Details of tax revenue

Million BRL

	1990	2000	2005	2010	2017	2018	2019	2020	2021	2022
Total tax revenue	**3**	**352 456**	**709 203**	**1 233 226**	**2 089 618**	**2 240 335**	**2 359 475**	**2 317 334**	**2 892 731**	**3 298 931**
1000 Taxes on income, profits and capital gains	**1**	**68 667**	**149 063**	**258 738**	**458 646**	**490 734**	**537 894**	**525 627**	**698 098**	**910 191**
1100 Of individuals	0	3 406	46 766	87 828	177 710	196 255	221 730	225 912	262 008	303 290
1110 On income and profits	0	3 406	46 766	87 828	177 710	196 255	221 730	225 912	262 008	303 290
Withholding income tax (IRRF)	0	0	39 870	71 579	147 206	163 742	184 030	186 211	208 219	248 230
Other personal income taxes	0	3 406	6 896	16 248	30 504	32 513	37 700	39 701	53 788	55 059
1120 On capital gains	..	..	..	..	..	..	..	..	..	..
1200 Corporate	0	25 430	72 455	128 255	184 501	194 814	207 505	200 032	322 527	437 358
1210 On profits	0	25 430	72 455	128 255	184 501	194 814	207 505	200 032	322 527	437 358
Corporate income tax	0	16 680	47 455	82 474	113 815	119 063	127 130	122 679	210 058	281 264
Social contribution on net profits (CSLL)	0	8 750	25 001	45 780	70 686	75 751	80 374	77 352	112 469	156 093
1220 On capital gains of corporates	..	..	..	..	..	..	..	..	..	..
1300 Unallocable between 1100 and 1200	0	39 831	29 842	42 656	96 434	99 666	108 659	99 684	113 564	169 543
Withholding tax on non-resident income (remittances abroad)	..	..	6 183	11 537	27 270	35 33[illegible]	39 293	39 602	44 400	55 497
Withholding tax on capital income	..	..	19 976	24 887	59 470	53 585	57 184	48 346	55 576	97 047
Withholding tax on other income	..	..	3 682	6 232	9 694	10 749	12 182	11 736	13 588	17 000
2000 Social security contributions	**1**	**83 469**	**168 298**	**316 530**	**565 982**	**584 640**	**616 961**	**610 312**	**694 877**	**798 214**
2100 Employees	..	..	39 070	75 509	131 697	139 610	147 749	151 462	182 011	..
2110 On a payroll basis	..	..	39 070	75 509	131 697	139 610	147 749	151 462	182 011	..
2120 On an income tax basis	..	..	0	0	0	0	0	0	0	..
2200 Employers	0	18 709	128 843	240 280	414 399	429 833	457 463	447 791	499 361	156 298
2210 On a payroll basis	0	18 709	128 843	240 280	414 399	429 833	457 463	447 791	499 361	156 298
2220 On an income tax basis	0	0	0	0	0	0	0	0	0	0
2300 Self-employed or non-employed	..	..	..	..	..	..	..	..	..	..
2310 On a payroll basis	..	..	..	..	..	..	..	..	..	..
2320 On an income tax basis	..	..	..	..	..	..	..	..	..	..
2400 Unallocable between 2100, 2200 and 2300	1	64 760	385	741	19 885	15 192	11 749	11 059	13 505	641 917
2410 On a payroll basis	1	64 760	385	741	19 885	15 192	11 749	11 059	13 505	641 917
2420 On an income tax basis	0	0	0	0	0	0	0	0	0	0
3000 Taxes on payroll and workforce	**0**	**5 437**	**10 417**	**21 348**	**39 824**	**42 223**	**42 907**	**40 397**	**47 320**	**54 297**
Payroll-based contribution to education	0	2 791	5 762	11 049	20 010	21 979	21 977	21 086	23 833	27 024
"S" System contributions	0	2 646	4 470	9 925	19 075	19 820	20 549	18 970	23 103	27 273
Other payroll taxes	0	0	185	374	739	423	381	340	384	0
4000 Taxes on property	**0**	**23 524**	**49 011**	**53 495**	**93 013**	**101 560**	**112 641**	**92 120**	**141 844**	**160 045**
4100 Recurrent taxes on immovable property	0	4 753	11 026	18 367	40 864	46 187	50 386	47 830	59 286	66 922
Tax on rural land property (ITR)	0	234	273	485	1 273	1 4[illegible]9	1 630	1 761	2 167	2 594
Tax on urban land property (IPTU)	0	4 519	10 753	17 882	39 591	44 769	48 756	46 069	57 119	64 328
4110 Households	..	..	..	..	..	..	..	..	..	..
4120 Others	..	..	..	..	..	..	..	..	..	..
4200 Recurrent taxes on net wealth	0	0	0	0	0	0	0	0	0	0
4210 Individual	..	..	..	..	..	..	..	..	..	..
4220 Corporate	..	..	..	..	..	..	..	..	..	..
4300 Estate, inheritance and gift taxes	0	329	816	2 518	7 178	7 330	8 582	8 521	12 330	12 874
4310 Estate and inheritance taxes	..	..	..	..	..	..	..	..	..	..
4320 Gift taxes	..	..	..	..	..	..	..	..	..	..
4400 Taxes on financial and capital transactions	0	18 442	37 169	32 610	44 971	48 042	53 673	35 769	70 228	80 249
Tax on financial operations (IOF)	0	3 096	5 966	26 571	34 660	36 615	40 945	21 949	49 024	58 989
Tax on real estate property transfers (ITBI)	0	950	2 201	6 050	10 288	11 424	12 762	13 820	21 227	21 260
Other	0	14 396	29 001	-12	23	3	-34	-1	-23	0
4500 Non-recurrent taxes	0	0	0	0	0	0	0	0	0	0
4510 On net wealth	..	..	..	..	..	..	..	..	..	..
4520 Other non-recurrent taxes	..	..	..	..	..	..	..	..	..	..
4600 Other recurrent taxes on property	0	0	0	0	0	0	0	0	0	0
5000 Taxes on goods and services	**2**	**169 181**	**331 732**	**582 636**	**931 290**	**1 020 915**	**1 049 071**	**1 048 885**	**1 310 448**	**1 356 614**
5100 Taxes on production, sale, transfer, etc	2	163 887	319 213	555 871	883 276	968 526	997 208	994 090	1 244 306	1 292 683
5110 General taxes	1	136 743	277 011	484 000	785 204	854 955	881 936	872 412	1 088 855	1 152 337
5111 Value added taxes	1	82 279	153 976	268 117	443 775	479 310	507 053	522 690	652 284	692 147
Tax on the circulation of goods and services (ICMS)	1	82 279	153 976	268 117	443 775	479 310	507 053	522 690	652 284	692 147
5112 Sales tax	0	0	0	0	0	0	0	0	0	0
5113 Other	0	54 464	123 035	215 883	341 429	375 644	374 883	349 722	436 572	460 191
Contribution to COFINS	0	38 707	86 678	140 939	221 670	244 287	237 372	218 602	269 705	271 903
Contribution to PIS	0	8 339	18 478	30 714	49 380	54 461	51 390	46 626	57 614	58 408
Contribution to PASEP	0	1 312	2 863	9 880	11 395	12 063	12 626	14 686	16 871	20 022
Tax on general services (ISS)	0	6 106	14 817	33 696	58 062	63 792	72 428	68 688	90 900	109 858
Others	0	0	201	656	922	1 038	1 067	1 119	1 483	0
5120 Taxes on specific goods and services	0	27 144	42 202	71 870	98 072	113 571	115 272	121 678	155 451	140 346

	1990	2000	2005	2010	2017	2018	2019	2020	2021	2022
5121 Excises	0	18 699	31 760	48 254	60 864	67 121	65 626	68 467	84 242	73 386
Vehicles	..	..	3 744	5 787	4 467	5 713	5 639	3 446	3 447	4 048
Beverages	..	..	2 359	2 431	2 944	2 768	3 641	2 985	2 687	2 513
Tobacco	..	..	2 300	3 704	5 210	5 208	5 559	5 975	5 577	6 732
Fuels	..	..	7 681	7 759	5 821	3 928	2 776	1 986	1 924	1 660
Other excises	..	..	15 676	28 573	42 422	49 504	48 011	54 075	70 607	58 433
5122 Profits of fiscal monopolies	0	0	0	0	0	0	0	0	0	0
5123 Customs and import duties	0	8 445	8 895	21 072	32 284	40 575	42 842	45 671	61 876	58 981
5124 Taxes on exports	0	0	48	47	66	129	91	51	160	53
5125 Taxes on investment goods	0	0	0	0	40	26	26	24	20	0
5126 Taxes on specific services	0	0	867	1 286	1 807	1 623	1 561	1 565	1 568	0
Contribution on revenues of telecom companies	..	..	795	1 186	1 610	1 440	1 392	1 357	1 340	..
Contribution on billing of IT companies	..	..	71	100	196	182	168	208	228	..
Other taxes on specific services	..	..	1	1	1	1	1	0	1	..
5127 Other taxes on internat. trade and transactions	0	0	633	1 212	3 011	4 097	5 127	5 900	7 585	7 925
CIDE on remittances abroad	..	..	633	1 212	3 011	4 097	5 127	5 900	7 585	7 925
5128 Other taxes	0	0	0	0	0	0	0	0	0	0
5130 Unallocable between 5110 and 5120	0	0	0	0	0	0	0	0	0	0
5200 Taxes on use of goods and perform activities	0	5 294	12 519	26 765	48 014	52 389	51 862	54 795	66 142	63 931
5210 Recurrent taxes	0	5 294	11 535	24 417	45 152	48 668	48 632	49 587	53 070	63 931
5211 Paid by households: motor vehicles	0	5 294	11 401	24 197	43 737	45 432	47 169	48 351	51 775	63 931
Motor vehicle property tax (IPVA)	0	5 294	10 406	21 367	40 436	43 120	46 141	48 178	51 762	63 928
Contributions to DPVAT	0	0	995	2 830	3 302	2 312	1 027	173	13	3
5212 Paid by others: motor vehicles	0	0	0	0	0	0	0	0	0	0
5213 Paid in respect of other goods	0	0	134	220	1 415	3 235	1 463	1 235	1 296	0
CONDECINE	..	..	36	49	1 133	1 084	1 061	885	974	..
Others	..	..	98	170	281	2 151	402	350	321	..
5220 Non-recurrent taxes	0	0	984	2 349	2 862	3 722	3 231	5 208	13 072	0
AFRMM	..	..	984	2 349	2 862	3 722	3 231	5 208	13 072	..
5300 Unallocable between 5100 and 5200	0	0	0	0	0	0	0	0	0	0
6000 Other taxes	**0**	**2 178**	**682**	**480**	**864**	**263**	**1**	**-7**	**144**	**19 569**
6100 Paid solely by business	0	0	0	0	0	0	0	0	0	0
6200 Other	0	2 178	682	480	864	263	1	-7	144	19 569

.. Not available

Note: Year ending 31st December.

The data are on a cash basis.

Data in 2021 have been updated with detailed information from Carga Tributária no Brasil by the Secretaria da Receita Federal do Brasil. Data for 2022 are sourced from latest reports of Secretaria do Tesouro Nacional and may be adjusted next year.

Heading 2000: Social security contributions include contributions to the General Social Security Regime (RGPS), contributions to the Own Social Security Schemes (RPPS), contributions to the Severance Indemnity Fund (FGTS) and contributions to the health fund for military police and fire department.

Heading 4400: This heading includes the tax on real estate property transfers (ITBI) levied by the central and state governments.

Heading 5113: Contributions to PASEP are included in contributions to PIS before 2000 as they cannot be distinguished.

Heading 5123: This heading includes tax on exports before 2002.

Source: Secretaria da Receita Federal do Brasil, Ministério da Economia (Special Department of Federal Revenue of Brazil under Ministry of Economy); Secretaria do Tesouro Nacional, Ministério da Economia (National Treasury Secretariat under Ministry of Economy).

Table 5.8. Chile

Details of tax revenue

Million CLP

	1990	2000	2005	2010	2017	2018	2019	2020	2021	2022
Total tax revenue	**1 777 218**	**7 901 998**	**14 265 265**	**21 845 693**	**36 262 036**	**40 314 703**	**41 025 508**	**38 817 226**	**53 463 333**	**62 874 428**
1000 Taxes on income, profits and capital gains	**412 974**	**1 841 630**	**5 171 293**	**8 329 060**	**12 516 154**	**14 418 859**	**14 283 183**	**12 540 342**	**20 456 920**	**27 491 879**
1100 Of individuals	99 154	604 100	738 620	1 492 837	3 500 023	2 701 416	2 937 532	3 976 009	5 780 432	6 626 617
Second category tax	65 552	490 980	700 150	1 449 099	2 585 694	2 848 205	3 015 794	3 051 177	3 442 651	3 914 343
Global complementary tax	33 603	113 120	38 470	43 738	50 495	-146 789	-78 261	132 551	620 904	1 087 034
Others	0	0	0	0	863 834	0	0	792 281	1 716 877	1 625 240
1110 On income and profits	..	..	..	..	..	..	..	..	..	..
1120 On capital gains	..	..	..	..	..	..	..	..	..	..
1200 Corporate	219 586	882 896	3 155 480	4 448 745	7 658 420	8 920 497	9 597 472	9 429 787	9 145 873	14 900 568
First category tax	200 891	815 747	3 040 875	3 913 870	7 049 471	7 836 379	8 880 080	8 745 612	8 360 928	13 034 540
Surtax on state owned enterprises	16 074	47 634	78 267	194 203	193 058	184 442	122 054	203 416	249 073	475 034
Mining tax	0	0	0	298 558	101 970	184 382	277 861	267 544	393 548	1 223 807
Other	2 621	19 516	36 338	42 114	313 921	715 293	317 477	213 216	142 323	167 188
1210 On profits	..	..	..	..	..	..	..	..	..	..
1220 On capital gains of corporates	..	..	..	..	..	..	..	..	..	..
1300 Unallocable between 1100 and 1200	94 233	354 634	1 277 193	2 387 478	1 357 711	2 796 947	1 748 179	-865 454	5 530 616	5 964 694
Additional tax	59 082	350 301	799 648	1 414 057	1 453 577	2 127 948	1 902 585	2 063 149	2 534 906	2 731 170
Other	35 151	4 332	477 545	973 421	-95 865	668 998	-154 406	-2 928 603	2 995 710	3 233 524
2000 Social security contributions	**159 559**	**576 758**	**931 717**	**1 493 987**	**2 627 558**	**2 786 173**	**2 994 906**	**3 104 866**	**2 815 090**	**2 585 421**
2100 Employees	154 021	553 937	893 821	1 433 159	2 553 916	2 703 261	2 894 725	2 994 036	2 686 021	2 435 398
2110 On a payroll basis	154 021	553 937	893 821	1 433 159	2 553 916	2 703 261	2 894 725	2 994 036	2 686 021	2 435 398
2120 On an income tax basis	0	0	0	0	0	0	0	0	0	0
2200 Employers	5 538	22 821	37 896	60 828	73 643	82 912	100 181	110 830	129 068	150 023
2210 On a payroll basis	5 538	22 821	37 896	60 828	73 643	82 912	100 181	110 830	129 068	150 023
2220 On an income tax basis	0	0	0	0	0	0	0	0	0	0
2300 Self-employed or non-employed	0	0	0	0	0	0	0	0	0	0
2310 On a payroll basis	..	..	..	..	..	..	..	..	..	..
2320 On an income tax basis	..	..	..	..	..	..	..	..	..	..
2400 Unallocable between 2100, 2200 and 2300	0	0	0	0	0	0	0	0	0	0
2410 On a payroll basis	..	..	..	..	..	..	..	..	..	..
2420 On an income tax basis	..	..	..	..	..	..	..	..	..	..
3000 Taxes on payroll and workforce	**0**	**0**	**0**	**0**	**0**	**0**	**0**	**0**	**0**	**0**
4000 Taxes on property	**109 319**	**554 037**	**901 776**	**898 607**	**1 969 157**	**2 086 866**	**2 242 561**	**2 071 921**	**2 606 922**	**3 205 276**
4100 Recurrent taxes on immovable property	59 968	302 244	416 565	662 368	1 248 136	1 373 495	1 507 182	1 562 317	1 724 276	2 023 347
4110 Households	..	..	..	..	..	..	..	..	..	..
4120 Others	..	..	..	..	..	..	..	..	..	..
4200 Recurrent taxes on net wealth	0	0	0	0	0	0	0	0	0	0
4210 Individual	..	..	..	..	..	..	..	..	..	..
4220 Corporate	..	..	..	..	..	..	..	..	..	..
4300 Estate, inheritance and gift taxes	3 444	10 906	23 184	39 338	202 376	125 649	62 824	155 433	291 830	416 219
4310 Estate and inheritance taxes	..	..	..	..	..	..	..	..	..	..
4320 Gift taxes	..	..	..	..	..	..	..	..	..	..
4400 Taxes on financial and capital transactions	45 907	240 886	462 027	196 901	518 645	587 721	672 555	354 171	590 816	765 709
4500 Non-recurrent taxes	0	0	0	0	0	0	0	0	0	0
4510 On net wealth	..	..	..	..	..	..	..	..	..	..
4520 Other non-recurrent taxes	..	..	..	..	..	..	..	..	..	..
4600 Other recurrent taxes on property	0	0	0	0	0	0	0	0	0	0
5000 Taxes on goods and services	**1 118 722**	**5 041 769**	**7 346 434**	**11 185 156**	**19 863 420**	**21 470 498**	**21 755 381**	**21 275 113**	**28 369 986**	**30 077 786**
5100 Taxes on production, sale, transfer, etc	1 074 009	4 789 827	6 952 092	10 532 904	18 599 503	19 953 036	20 167 012	19 614 250	26 629 396	28 078 581
5110 General taxes	664 421	3 306 350	5 391 285	8 399 926	15 069 540	16 211 646	16 348 944	15 963 032	22 785 935	24 515 246
5111 Value added taxes	664 421	3 306 350	5 391 285	8 399 926	15 069 540	16 211 646	16 348 944	15 963 032	22 785 935	24 515 246
5112 Sales tax	0	0	0	0	0	0	0	0	0	0
5113 Other	0	0	0	0	0	0	0	0	0	0
5120 Taxes on specific goods and services	409 588	1 483 477	1 560 807	2 132 978	3 529 963	3 741 389	3 818 068	3 651 218	3 843 461	3 563 334
5121 Excises	166 050	816 160	1 107 703	1 561 205	2 682 659	2 796 033	2 862 327	2 300 245	2 800 387	2 333 121
Cigarettes and tobacco	60 604	283 275	382 690	647 637	978 696	981 456	973 335	1 021 917	1 201 968	1 171 382
Gasoline and diesel	105 445	532 885	724 803	913 568	1 629 561	1 727 392	1 811 132	1 799 846	1 507 872	1 028 982
Oil stabilisation fund	0	0	210	0	0	0	0	0	0	1 547
Fisheries Law Extraction Rights	0	0	0	0	11 749	19 623	17 662	33 104	8 967	21 566
Additional tax on new motor vehicles	0	0	0	0	62 654	67 561	60 197	45 379	81 579	109 645
5122 Profits of fiscal monopolies	0	0	0	0	0	0	0	0	0	0
5123 Customs and import duties	222 486	548 571	286 044	267 331	321 156	347 555	331 846	294 204	468 128	555 863
5124 Taxes on exports	0	0	0	0	0	0	0	0	0	0
5125 Taxes on investment goods	0	0	0	0	0	0	0	0	0	0
5126 Taxes on specific services	21 052	118 746	167 060	304 442	526 147	597 802	623 895	456 768	574 947	674 351
5127 Other taxes on internat. trade and transactions	0	0	0	0	0	0	0	0	0	0
5128 Other taxes	0	0	0	0	0	0	0	0	0	0

	1990	2000	2005	2010	2017	2018	2019	2020	2021	2022
5130 Unallocable between 5110 and 5120	0	0	0	0	0	0	0	0	0	0
5200 Taxes on use of goods and perform activities	44 714	251 942	394 343	652 252	1 263 917	1 517 462	1 588 369	1 660 863	1 740 590	1 999 206
5210 Recurrent taxes	44 714	251 942	394 343	652 252	1 263 917	1 402 110	1 461 686	1 503 269	1 617 710	1 852 752
Motor vehicles	24 469	93 880	139 174	218 219	482 916	539 918	592 327	585 116	671 258	819 509
5211 Paid by households: motor vehicles	0	0	0	0	0	0	0	0	0	0
5212 Paid by others: motor vehicles	0	0	0	0	0	0	0	0	0	0
5213 Paid in respect of other goods	20 245	158 062	255 169	434 033	781 001	862 192	869 359	918 153	946 452	1 033 244
Municipal permits	18 401	136 138	234 460	396 944	727 246	806 734	813 159	862 199	885 324	966 478
Mining patents	3 374	34 730	20 094	36 213	52 254	53 854	54 696	54 932	59 801	65 122
Other	-1 530	-12 806	615	876	1 501	1 604	1 504	1 023	1 327	1 643
5220 Non-recurrent taxes	0	0	0	0	0	115 352	126 683	157 594	122 880	146 453
Tax on polluting fixed sources	..	..	..	..	..	115 352	126 683	157 594	122 880	146 453
5300 Unallocable between 5100 and 5200	0	0	0	0	0	0	0	0	0	0
6000 Other taxes	**23 356**	**-112 195**	**-85 954**	**-61 117**	**-714 253**	**-447 692**	**-250 523**	**-175 017**	**-785 585**	**-485 934**
6100 Paid solely by business	0	0	0	0	0	0	0	0	0	0
6200 Other	-23 356	-112 195	-85 954	-61 117	-714 253	-447 692	-250 523	-175 017	-785 585	-485 934

.. Not available

Note: Year ending 31st December.

The data are on a cash basis.

Heading 5121: In ECLAC data, figures from the Oil Prices Stabilisation Fund (FEPP) are considered as non-tax revenues.

Source: Servicio de Impuestos Internos (Chile's Tax Service).

Table 5.9. Colombia

Details of tax revenue

Million COP

	1990	2000	2005	2010	2017	2018	2019	2020	2021	2022
Total tax revenue	**2 579 426**	**30 598 630**	**61 707 388**	**98 455 335**	**174 735 823**	**190 299 911**	**209 071 314**	**187 664 589**	**229 480 845**	**288 683 841**
1000 Taxes on income, profits and capital gains	**771 694**	**7 103 525**	**17 348 618**	**26 218 852**	**57 615 236**	**64 043 928**	**67 519 599**	**61 812 525**	**73 222 876**	**95 891 679**
1100 Of individuals	47 210	1 499 345	3 594 441	5 192 384	10 402 187	12 265 425	14 244 001	14 327 856	15 758 043	18 984 236
1110 On income and profits	47 210	1 499 345	3 594 441	5 192 384	10 402 187	12 265 425	14 244 001	14 327 856	15 758 043	18 984 236
Income tax	47 210	1 499 345	3 594 441	5 192 384	10 402 187	12 265 425	14 237 452	14 292 259	15 687 699	18 850 046
Simple tax regime	0	0	0	0	0	0	6 549	35 598	70 344	134 190
1120 On capital gains	..	..	..	..	..	..	..	..	..	..
1200 Corporate	359 758	5 119 828	13 044 361	20 405 209	44 976 298	48 643 747	50 284 832	43 259 798	54 418 742	72 985 286
1210 On profits	359 758	5 119 828	13 044 361	20 405 209	44 976 298	48 643 747	50 284 832	43 259 798	54 418 742	72 985 286
Income tax	359 758	5 119 828	13 044 361	20 405 209	40 130 108	48 511 024	50 168 966	43 133 458	54 225 235	72 613 526
Pro Equity Income Tax - CREE	0	0	0	0	4 846 190	132 723	99 798	39 871	28 428	56 854
Simple tax regime	0	0	0	0	0	0	16 068	86 469	165 079	314 907
1220 On capital gains of corporates	..	..	..	..	..	..	..	..	..	..
1300 Unallocable between 1100 and 1200	364 726	484 352	709 816	621 258	2 236 750	3 134 756	2 990 766	4 224 870	3 046 091	3 922 156
Income tax	364 726	484 352	709 816	621 258	2 236 750	3 134 756	2 990 766	4 224 870	3 046 091	3 922 156
Pro Equity Income Tax - CREE	0	0	0	0	0	0	0	0	0	0
2000 Social security contributions	**203 596**	**4 989 000**	**7 845 000**	**11 478 085**	**13 351 711**	**18 192 049**	**19 875 398**	**18 615 408**	**22 844 403**	**23 907 649**
2100 Employees	..	..	..	..	..	..	..	..	..	..
2110 On a payroll basis	..	..	..	..	..	..	..	..	..	..
2120 On an income tax basis	..	..	..	..	..	..	..	..	..	..
2200 Employers	..	..	..	..	..	..	..	..	..	..
2210 On a payroll basis	..	..	..	..	..	..	..	..	..	..
2220 On an income tax basis	..	..	..	..	..	..	..	..	..	..
2300 Self-employed or non-employed	..	..	..	..	..	..	..	..	..	..
2310 On a payroll basis	..	..	..	..	..	..	..	..	..	..
2320 On an income tax basis	..	..	..	..	..	..	..	..	..	..
2400 Unallocable between 2100, 2200 and 2300	203 596	4 989 000	7 845 000	11 478 085	13 351 711	18 192 049	19 875 398	18 615 408	22 844 403	23 907 649
2410 On a payroll basis	203 596	4 989 000	7 845 000	11 478 085	13 351 711	18 192 049	19 875 398	18 615 408	22 844 403	23 907 649
2420 On an income tax basis	0	0	0	0	0	0	0	0	0	0
3000 Taxes on payroll and workforce	**0**	**1 286 803**	**2 179 842**	**4 022 503**	**3 200 238**	**3 461 352**	**3 604 071**	**3 670 490**	**3 927 070**	**4 421 997**
4000 Taxes on property	**56 160**	**2 027 654**	**4 838 158**	**8 535 238**	**17 950 494**	**15 265 472**	**18 984 414**	**18 167 358**	**20 048 796**	**22 382 815**
4100 Recurrent taxes on immovable property	56 160	991 070	1 974 213	3 338 935	7 310 244	7 981 989	8 743 115	9 109 598	9 039 961	9 794 710
4110 Households	0	0	0	0	0	0	0	0	0	0
4120 Others	56 160	991 070	1 974 213	3 338 935	7 310 244	7 981 989	8 743 115	9 109 598	9 039 961	9 794 710
4200 Recurrent taxes on net wealth	0	0	462 720	1 970 530	3 868 595	467 925	923 255	957 137	1 032 058	73 113
4210 Individual	..	..	..	..	..	..	..	..	..	..
4220 Corporate	..	..	..	..	..	..	..	..	..	..
4300 Estate, inheritance and gift taxes	0	0	0	0	0	0	0	0	0	0
4310 Estate and inheritance taxes	..	..	..	..	..	..	..	..	..	..
4320 Gift taxes	..	..	..	..	..	..	..	..	..	..
4400 Taxes on financial and capital transactions	0	1 036 584	2 401 226	3 225 773	6 771 655	6 815 558	8 190 516	7 476 295	9 831 204	12 281 751
4500 Non-recurrent taxes	0	0	0	0	0	0	1 127 528	624 327	145 573	233 241
4510 On net wealth	..	..	..	..	..	..	0	0	0	0
4520 Other non-recurrent taxes	..	..	..	..	..	..	1 127 528	624 327	145 573	233 241
4600 Other recurrent taxes on property	0	0	0	0	0	0	0	0	0	0
5000 Taxes on goods and services	**1 388 653**	**14 180 450**	**27 649 152**	**44 411 642**	**75 381 123**	**81 408 789**	**89 797 927**	**77 752 543**	**99 265 361**	**129 336 095**
5100 Taxes on production, sale, transfer, etc	1 388 653	14 048 655	27 370 638	44 038 074	74 003 567	79 935 336	88 064 087	75 960 351	97 222 272	127 050 537
5110 General taxes	672 368	9 585 866	19 934 400	33 333 802	58 565 799	64 316 019	71 235 138	62 863 653	80 101 256	105 105 388
5111 Value added taxes	583 078	8 445 776	17 427 948	28 811 682	50 619 849	55 879 110	61 936 282	53 912 648	69 883 378	91 744 973
5112 Sales tax	89 290	1 140 090	2 506 452	4 522 121	7 945 950	8 436 909	9 298 856	8 954 004	10 217 878	13 360 416
Industry and commerce tax (State)	89 290	1 140 090	2 506 452	4 522 121	7 945 950	8 436 909	9 298 856	8 954 004	10 217 878	13 360 416
5113 Other	0	0	0	0	0	0	0	0	0	0
5120 Taxes on specific goods and services	716 285	4 462 789	7 436 239	10 704 271	15 437 768	15 619 317	13 828 948	13 093 698	17 121 016	21 945 149

	1990	2000	2005	2010	2017	2018	2019	2020	2021	2022
5121 Excises	404 699	2 718 692	4 613 718	6 052 273	11 616 844	12 061 132	12 995 955	10 159 930	12 906 426	15 686 603
Oil	141 270	833 004	1 143 308	1 418 766	1 352 793	1 517 546	1 585 141	1 205 806	1 732 540	1 650 801
Tobacco (State)	52 898	213 412	287 379	390 472	887 534	1 145 879	1 278 561	1 239 269	1 451 431	1 638 694
Beer (State)	85 722	471 135	867 569	1 432 453	2 572 771	2 637 674	2 611 466	2 243 811	2 723 800	3 049 682
Liquors (State)	124 808	520 394	811 377	929 328	1 907 802	1 800 605	2 146 818	1 675 472	2 503 248	3 060 330
Restaurant, vehicles sale and mobile telephony	0	0	0	0	1 948 718	2 047 419	2 208 669	1 226 863	1 279 312	2 528 842
Carbon	0	0	0	0	474 596	288 373	436 914	281 911	330 567	361 899
Plastic bags	0	0	0	0	6 546	28 099	37 331	43 777	48 079	49 697
Medicinal cannabis	0	0	0	0	10	3	145	972	993	921
Diesel surcharge	0	85 716	251 542	500 405	546 243	579 613	599 600	505 000	570 600	655 000
Petrol surcharge	0	595 031	1 252 543	1 380 848	1 919 830	2 015 922	2 091 310	1 737 050	2 265 855	2 690 737
5122 Profits of fiscal monopolies	0	0	0	0	0	0	0	0	0	0
5123 Customs and import duties	311 586	1 744 097	2 822 520	4 651 999	3 820 924	3 558 185	3 832 994	2 933 768	4 214 590	6 258 546
Custom duties	180 989	1 744 097	2 822 520	4 651 999	3 820 924	3 558 185	3 832 994	2 933 768	4 214 590	6 258 546
Imports surcharge	130 597	0	0	0	0	0	0	0	0	0
5124 Taxes on exports	0	0	0	0	0	0	0	0	0	0
5125 Taxes on investment goods	0	0	0	0	0	0	0	0	0	0
5126 Taxes on specific services	0	0	0	0	0	0	0	0	0	0
5127 Other taxes on internat. trade and transactions	0	0	0	0	0	0	0	0	0	0
5128 Other taxes	0	0	0	0	0	0	0	0	0	0
5130 Unallocable between 5110 and 5120	0	0	0	0	0	0	0	0	0	0
5200 Taxes on use of goods and perform activities	0	131 795	278 514	373 568	1 377 556	1 473 453	1 733 840	1 792 192	2 043 090	2 285 557
5210 Recurrent taxes	..	131 795	278 514	373 568	1 377 556	1 473 453	1 733 840	1 792 192	2 043 090	2 285 557
5211 Paid by households: motor vehicles	..	131 795	278 514	373 568	1 377 556	1 473 453	1 733 840	1 792 192	2 043 090	2 285 557
Tax on motor vehicle ownership	..	131 795	278 514	373 568	1 377 556	1 473 453	1 733 840	1 792 192	2 043 090	2 285 557
5212 Paid by others: motor vehicles	..	..	..	..	..	..	..	..	..	..
5213 Paid in respect of other goods	..	..	..	..	..	..	..	..	..	..
5220 Non-recurrent taxes	..	..	..	..	..	..	..	..	..	..
5300 Unallocable between 5100 and 5200	0	0	0	0	0	0	0	0	0	0
6000 Other taxes	**159 323**	**1 011 197**	**1 846 617**	**3 789 014**	**7 237 021**	**7 928 320**	**9 289 906**	**7 646 264**	**10 172 339**	**12 743 607**
6100 Paid solely by business	0	0	0	0	0	0	0	0	0	0
6200 Other	159 323	1 011 197	1 846 617	3 789 014	7 237 021	7 928 320	9 289 906	7 646 264	10 172 339	12 743 607
Stamp tax	0	401 497	633 586	357 160	75 493	79 868	85 799	41 373	83 115	134 457
Other	78 306	79 287	48 498	126 602	403 473	461 160	533 852	245 541	423 822	788 653
Other (sub-national)	81 017	530 413	1 164 533	3 305 252	6 758 055	7 387 293	8 670 255	7 359 350	9 665 402	11 820 497

.. Not available

Note: Year ending 31st December.

The data are on a cash basis.

Includes the reported consolidated revenues of the territorial entities (departments and municipalities).

Heading 1000: The income tax figures in 2022 under headings 1100, 1200 and 1300 are estimated.

Heading 2000: Before 2013, social security contributions did not include all the contributions entering FOSYGA (Solidarity and Guarantee Fund). Only the portion of the contributions used to finance the subsidised regime (up to 1.5 pp of the 12.5% of the monthly wage paid by employers and employees as an obligatory health contribution) was included. The part of the contributions entering FOSYGA to finance the contributory regime was classified in the social security sector as "other incomes". From 2013 onwards, all of the health contributions entering FOSYGA are classified as social security contributions. The portion of the contributions not entering FOSYGA that is both collected and spent by the health insurers – EPS – is not part of the fiscal accounts.

Source: Dirección de Impuestos y Aduanas Nacionales de Colombia, Ministerio de Hacienda y Crédito Público y Banco Central de Colombia (National Tax and Customs Administration, Ministry of Finance and Public Credit and Central Bank of Colombia).

Table 5.10. Costa Rica

Details of tax revenue

Million CRC

	1990	2000	2005	2010	2017	2018	2019	2020	2021	2022
Total tax revenue	**117 711**	**978 114**	**2 084 914**	**4 382 367**	**7 893 642**	**8 339 991**	**8 855 885**	**8 235 528**	**10 019 264**	**11 285 967**
1000 Taxes on income, profits and capital gains	**11 820**	**128 805**	**324 224**	**748 093**	**1 562 063**	**1 699 258**	**1 854 866**	**1 651 249**	**2 063 810**	**2 430 200**
1100 Of individuals	..	..	16 438	202 849	446 519	483 645	540 954	556 084	622 772	691 305
1110 On income and profits	..	..	16 438	202 849	446 519	483 645	535 412	554 486	618 550	682 875
1120 On capital gains	..	..	0	0	0	0	5 542	1 598	4 222	8 430
1200 Corporate	..	..	288 355	450 312	843 879	915 284	1 058 086	692 551	970 546	1 188 835
1210 On profits	..	..	288 355	450 312	843 879	915 284	955 908	685 470	952 951	1 162 697
1220 On capital gains of corporates	..	..	0	0	0	0	102 177	7 081	17 595	26 138
1300 Unallocable between 1100 and 1200	11 820	128 805	19 430	94 932	271 664	300 330	255 827	402 613	470 492	550 059
2000 Social security contributions	**33 990**	**297 069**	**617 683**	**1 450 531**	**2 640 785**	**2 859 467**	**3 026 691**	**2 971 589**	**3 605 731**	**3 925 692**
2100 Employees	..	..	..	..	..	..	..	..	..	..
2110 On a payroll basis	..	..	..	..	..	..	..	..	..	..
2120 On an income tax basis	..	..	..	..	..	..	..	..	..	..
2200 Employers	3 447	37 313	84 988	207 206	361 161	368 865	381 940	387 340	389 183	412 852
Government contributions	3 447	37 313	84 988	207 206	361 161	368 865	381 940	387 340	389 183	412 852
2210 On a payroll basis	..	..	..	..	..	..	..	..	..	..
2220 On an income tax basis	..	..	..	..	..	..	..	..	..	..
2300 Self-employed or non-employed	..	..	..	..	..	..	..	..	..	..
2310 On a payroll basis	..	..	..	..	..	..	..	..	..	..
2320 On an income tax basis	..	..	..	..	..	..	..	..	..	..
2400 Unallocable between 2100, 2200 and 2300	30 543	259 756	532 695	1 243 325	2 279 624	2 490 602	2 644 751	2 583 749	3 216 548	3 512 840
Contributions by employees and non-government employers	30 543	249 182	497 341	1 139 265	1 971 472	2 157 256	2 274 644	2 212 249	2 447 640	2 697 026
Contributions for the special regimes	0	10 574	35 354	104 060	237 004	247 939	292 634	292 072	299 713	300 083
2410 On a payroll basis	..	..	..	..	..	..	..	..	..	..
2420 On an income tax basis	..	..	..	..	..	..	..	..	..	..
3000 Taxes on payroll and workforce	**7 575**	**61 796**	**115 730**	**260 664**	**471 206**	**498 577**	**522 529**	**537 654**	**569 339**	**639 737**
Contributions by non-government employers	7 484	59 129	112 082	248 259	453 128	478 523	501 734	515 624	546 262	616 504
Contributions by government employers	91	2 666	3 648	12 405	18 078	20 054	20 795	22 030	23 077	23 233
4000 Taxes on property	**1 566**	**8 396**	**25 110**	**63 706**	**145 955**	**149 310**	**167 952**	**162 950**	**208 531**	**220 741**
4100 Recurrent taxes on immovable property	1 200	5 390	14 264	48 963	107 156	113 586	125 398	127 625	150 279	154 930
Land tax	0	0	0	0	0	0	0	0	0	0
Additional land tax	0	0	0	0	0	0	0	0	0	0
Tax on sumptuary constructions	0	0	0	0	0	0	0	0	0	0
Immovable property tax	0	0	0	3 527	4 255	4 468	4 699	4 655	5 108	5 206
Municipal immovable property tax	1 200	5 390	14 264	45 436	102 901	109 119	120 698	122 970	145 171	149 724
4110 Households	..	..	..	..	..	..	..	..	..	..
4120 Others	..	..	..	..	..	..	..	..	..	..
4200 Recurrent taxes on net wealth	0	0	0	0	0	0	0	0	0	0
4210 Individual	..	..	..	..	..	..	..	..	..	..
4220 Corporate	..	..	..	..	..	..	..	..	..	..
4300 Estate, inheritance and gift taxes	0	0	0	0	0	0	0	0	0	0
4310 Estate and inheritance taxes	..	..	..	..	..	..	..	..	..	..
4320 Gift taxes	..	..	..	..	..	..	..	..	..	..
4400 Taxes on financial and capital transactions	366	3 007	10 846	14 743	38 799	35 724	42 554	35 300	58 206	65 802
4500 Non-recurrent taxes	0	0	0	0	0	0	0	24	46	8
4510 On net wealth	..	..	..	..	..	..	..	0	0	0
4520 Other non-recurrent taxes	..	..	..	..	..	..	..	24	46	8
4600 Other recurrent taxes on property	0	0	0	0	0	0	0	0	0	0
5000 Taxes on goods and services	**53 509**	**456 851**	**944 623**	**1 766 914**	**2 875 333**	**2 918 471**	**3 031 941**	**2 745 118**	**3 488 535**	**3 674 723**
5100 Taxes on production, sale, transfer, etc	49 867	425 713	884 453	1 600 302	2 575 411	2 608 864	2 756 759	2 500 510	3 150 398	3 330 772
5110 General taxes	21 326	222 775	485 168	920 298	1 466 986	1 513 677	1 662 503	1 649 531	2 065 623	2 217 743
5111 Value added taxes	21 326	222 775	485 168	920 298	1 453 348	1 487 620	1 634 986	1 623 695	2 039 997	2 193 160
5112 Sales tax	0	0	0	0	0	0	0	0	0	0
5113 Other	0	0	0	0	13 638	26 057	27 517	25 836	25 626	24 583
5120 Taxes on specific goods and services	28 541	202 939	399 286	680 004	1 108 425	1 095 187	1 094 256	850 979	1 084 775	1 113 029
5121 Excises	11 096	157 204	296 222	523 617	870 225	858 424	864 985	688 784	863 133	883 105
Fuels and energy	0	0	172 028	320 638	510 260	517 666	552 017	436 384	522 063	530 195
Alcoholic beverages	0	8 229	20 219	28 035	43 176	45 610	43 849	44 373	53 118	55 539
Non alcoholic beverages	0	0	12 491	26 566	39 781	40 182	41 247	38 510	43 234	49 556
Soaps	0	0	573	1 317	2 332	2 712	3 020	3 052	3 200	2 810
Cement	0	0	0	227	311	289	216	123	0	5 358
Tobacco	0	0	0	0	30 590	30 766	27 185	23 896	27 019	22 336
Abolished specific taxes on production and consumption	0	0	0	0	0	0	0	0	0	0
Other specific taxes on consumption	11 096	148 975	90 913	146 834	243 775	221 200	197 452	142 447	214 499	217 311
5122 Profits of fiscal monopolies	0	0	0	0	0	0	0	0	0	0

	1990	2000	2005	2010	2017	2018	2019	2020	2021	2022
5123 Customs and import duties	15 052	40 485	82 446	126 134	179 188	175 368	164 224	133 733	177 948	164 137
Import duties	13 977	32 336	66 598	103 851	152 756	149 017	140 919	114 777	152 133	137 668
Custom duties	1 075	8 149	15 848	22 284	26 432	26 351	23 305	18 956	25 815	26 469
Import duties on animals	0	0	0	0	0	0	0	0	0	0
5124 Taxes on exports	2 113	2 238	969	3 973	5 638	5 468	5 412	5 471	6 274	4 842
Export duties	2 113	2 088	830	3 816	3 673	3 594	3 502	3 777	4 064	3 100
Export duties Law 133	0	0	0	0	0	0	0	0	0	0
Export duties Law 5519	0	0	0	0	0	0	0	0	0	0
Tax on banana exports	0	150	139	157	199	193	184	199	203	150
Export duties on ground transportation	0	0	0	0	1 766	1 682	1 726	1 494	2 007	1 593
5125 Taxes on investment goods	0	0	0	0	0	0	0	0	0	0
5126 Taxes on specific services	280	2 929	19 555	24 767	48 290	50 554	54 556	18 463	31 742	55 167
Casinos and gambling	0	225	519	445	891	1 060	1 241	378	431	455
Port cargo movements	0	6	13	0	0	0	0	0	0	0
Overseas departure tax	0	0	19 022	24 322	47 399	49 494	53 315	18 085	31 311	54 711
10% on public shows	0	0	0	0	0	0	0	0	0	0
Pro-national airport's stamp tax	0	0	0	0	0	0	0	0	0	0
Stamp tax on the use of borders and ports	280	2 697	0	0	0	0	0	0	0	0
5127 Other taxes on internat. trade and transactions	0	83	94	1 513	3 695	3 785	3 841	3 304	3 916	3 919
5128 Other taxes	0	0	0	0	1 389	1 589	1 238	1 225	1 761	1 860
5130 Unallocable between 5110 and 5120	0	0	0	0	0	0	0	0	0	0
5200 Taxes on use of goods and perform activities	3 642	31 138	60 170	166 612	299 922	309 607	325 182	244 608	338 138	343 951
5210 Recurrent taxes	3 642	31 138	60 170	166 612	299 922	309 607	325 182	244 608	338 138	343 951
5211 Paid by households: motor vehicles	0	0	0	0	0	0	0	0	0	0
5212 Paid by others: motor vehicles	1 425	15 374	30 918	94 102	164 034	171 523	181 198	108 198	183 368	186 226
Property tax on vehicles, aircraft and boats	1 425	15 374	30 918	94 102	164 034	171 523	181 198	108 198	183 368	186 226
5213 Paid in respect of other goods	2 217	15 763	29 252	72 510	135 888	138 084	143 984	136 410	154 769	157 725
Local taxes	1 262	11 898	27 411	68 808	130 639	132 514	137 979	130 332	147 349	151 320
Hunting and fishing licences	0	0	0	0	0	0	0	0	0	0
Spirits licence	0	0	0	0	0	0	0	0	0	0
Revenue stamps	955	3 866	1 841	3 702	5 249	5 571	6 004	6 078	7 421	6 405
Sport stamp tax	0	0	0	0	0	0	0	0	0	0
5220 Non-recurrent taxes	0	0	0	0	0	0	0	0	0	0
5300 Unallocable between 5100 and 5200	0	0	0	0	0	0	0	0	0	0
6000 Other taxes	**9 251**	**25 198**	**57 545**	**92 460**	**198 300**	**214 908**	**201 906**	**166 969**	**83 319**	**394 874**
6100 Paid solely by business	0	0	0	0	0	0	0	0	0	0
6200 Other	9 251	25 198	57 545	92 460	198 300	214 908	201 906	166 969	83 319	394 874
Transfers of vehicles, aircraft and boats	497	2 530	6 357	12 311	21 872	22 265	23 223	22 593	28 064	27 597
Tax revenue from decentralised units	2 764	15 048	11 985	29 969	68 127	63 329	67 968	60 054	0	0
Other taxes	5 990	7 620	39 203	50 180	108 181	129 268	110 654	84 266	55 122	367 079

.. Not available

Note: Year ending 31st December.

The data are on a cash basis.

Heading 2000: The data include social security contributions paid by the governments for their employees as well as the contributions for special regimes (teachers and magistrates). In ECLAC data, social security contributions also include INA (National Institute of Apprenticeship), IMAS (Joint Social Aid Institute) and FODESAF (Social Development and Family Allowances Fund).

Heading 3000: In Costa Rica and for ECLAC, social security contributions from decentralised institutions are classified under heading 2000.

Heading 5212: In ECLAC data, tax on ownership of vehicles, aircraft and boats is classified in category 4000.

Heading 6200: The figures include the tax revenue of decentralised bodies (other than social security contributions). The tax revenue of decentralised bodies is classified under central government. In Costa Rica this revenue is classified under a separate unit (decentralised) considered to be separate from the central government.

In ECLAC data, the tax on the transfer of used vehicles Law No. 7088 of 30/11/87 is classified as a property tax.

Source: Secretaría Técnica de la Autoridad Presupuestaria, Ministerio de Finanzas y Contraloría General de la República (Technical Secretary of the Budgeting Authority, Ministry of Finance and National General Comptroller).

Table 5.11. Cuba

Details of tax revenue

Million CUP

	1990	2000	2005	2010	2017	2018	2019	2020	2021	2022
Total tax revenue	**6 265**	**11 367**	**17 528**	**23 949**	**41 021**	**42 307**	**43 504**	**40 263**	**96 521**	**116 046**
1000 Taxes on income, profits and capital gains	**14**	**1 826**	**2 451**	**3 603**	**9 931**	**11 094**	**12 257**	**11 383**	**44 545**	**54 354**
1100 Of individuals	14	291	326	554	3 279	4 002	4 762	4 586	7 383	7 501
1110 On income and profits	..	..	..	..	..	..	..	..	..	..
1120 On capital gains	..	..	..	..	..	..	..	..	..	..
1200 Corporate	0	1 535	2 126	3 049	6 651	7 092	7 495	6 796	37 162	46 853
1210 On profits	..	..	..	..	..	..	..	..	..	..
1220 On capital gains of corporates	..	..	..	..	..	..	..	..	..	..
1300 Unallocable between 1100 and 1200	0	0	0	0	0	0	0	0	0	0
2000 Social security contributions	**691**	**1 181**	**1 778**	**2 974**	**5 108**	**5 206**	**5 727**	**6 433**	**24 155**	**16 727**
2100 Employees	..	..	..	..	..	..	..	..	..	..
2110 On a payroll basis	..	..	..	..	..	..	..	..	..	..
2120 On an income tax basis	..	..	..	..	..	..	..	..	..	..
2200 Employers	..	..	..	..	..	..	..	..	..	..
2210 On a payroll basis	..	..	..	..	..	..	..	..	..	..
2220 On an income tax basis	..	..	..	..	..	..	..	..	..	..
2300 Self-employed or non-employed	..	..	..	..	..	..	..	..	..	..
2310 On a payroll basis	..	..	..	..	..	..	..	..	..	..
2320 On an income tax basis	..	..	..	..	..	..	..	..	..	..
2400 Unallocable between 2100, 2200 and 2300	691	1 181	1 778	2 974	5 108	5 206	5 727	6 433	24 155	16 727
2410 On a payroll basis	691	1 181	1 778	2 974	5 108	5 206	5 727	6 433	24 155	16 727
2420 On an income tax basis	0	0	0	0	0	0	0	0	0	0
3000 Taxes on payroll and workforce	**0**	**970**	**2 962**	**4 414**	**1 385**	**1 273**	**1 415**	**1 605**	**5 947**	**6 239**
4000 Taxes on property	**0**	**0**	**0**	**0**	**0**	**0**	**0**	**0**	**0**	**0**
4100 Recurrent taxes on immovable property	..	..	..	..	..	..	..	..	..	..
4110 Households	..	..	..	..	..	..	..	..	..	..
4120 Others	..	..	..	..	..	..	..	..	..	..
4200 Recurrent taxes on net wealth	..	..	..	..	..	..	..	..	..	..
4210 Individual	..	..	..	..	..	..	..	..	..	..
4220 Corporate	..	..	..	..	..	..	..	..	..	..
4300 Estate, inheritance and gift taxes	..	..	..	..	..	..	..	..	..	..
4310 Estate and inheritance taxes	..	..	..	..	..	..	..	..	..	..
4320 Gift taxes	..	..	..	..	..	..	..	..	..	..
4400 Taxes on financial and capital transactions	..	..	..	..	..	..	..	..	..	..
4500 Non-recurrent taxes	..	..	..	..	..	..	..	..	..	..
4510 On net wealth	..	..	..	..	..	..	..	..	..	..
4520 Other non-recurrent taxes	..	..	..	..	..	..	..	..	..	..
4600 Other recurrent taxes on property	..	..	..	..	..	..	..	..	..	..
5000 Taxes on goods and services	**5 443**	**6 732**	**9 844**	**12 283**	**22 055**	**21 969**	**20 995**	**18 673**	**10 582**	**12 657**
5100 Taxes on production, sale, transfer, etc	5 443	6 732	9 844	12 283	22 055	21 969	20 995	18 673	10 582	12 657
5110 General taxes	5 017	6 131	9 036	10 525	17 961	17 623	16 619	14 498	6 489	8 029
5111 Value added taxes	0	0	0	0	0	0	0	0	0	0
5112 Sales tax	5 017	6 131	9 036	10 525	17 961	17 623	16 619	14 498	6 489	8 029
5113 Other	0	0	0	0	0	0	0	0	0	0
5120 Taxes on specific goods and services	426	602	808	1 758	4 094	4 346	4 376	4 175	4 093	4 628
5121 Excises	..	..	..	..	..	..	..	..	..	..
5122 Profits of fiscal monopolies	..	..	..	..	..	..	..	..	..	..
5123 Customs and import duties	..	..	..	..	..	..	..	..	..	..
5124 Taxes on exports	..	..	..	..	..	..	..	..	..	..
5125 Taxes on investment goods	..	..	..	..	..	..	..	..	..	..
5126 Taxes on specific services	..	..	..	..	..	..	..	..	..	..
5127 Other taxes on internat. trade and transactions	..	..	..	..	..	..	..	..	..	..
5128 Other taxes	..	..	..	..	..	..	..	..	..	..
5130 Unallocable between 5110 and 5120	0	0	0	0	0	0	0	0	0	0
5200 Taxes on use of goods and perform activities	0	0	0	0	0	0	0	0	0	0
5210 Recurrent taxes	..	..	..	..	..	..	..	..	..	..
5211 Paid by households: motor vehicles	..	..	..	..	..	..	..	..	..	..
5212 Paid by others: motor vehicles	..	..	..	..	..	..	..	..	..	..
5213 Paid in respect of other goods	..	..	..	..	..	..	..	..	..	..
5220 Non-recurrent taxes	..	..	..	..	..	..	..	..	..	..
5300 Unallocable between 5100 and 5200	0	0	0	0	0	0	0	0	0	0
6000 Other taxes	**117**	**657**	**493**	**675**	**2 543**	**2 766**	**3 110**	**2 169**	**11 293**	**26 069**
6100 Paid solely by business	..	..	..	..	..	..	..	..	..	..
6200 Other	..	..	..	..	..	..	..	..	..	..

.. Not available

Note: Year ending 31st December.
The data are on a cash basis.
The figures for the sub-categories under the heading 5120 are not available.
Central and local government tax revenues are only available between 2002 and 2012.
Figures in 2021 and thereafter are not comparable to data in previous years due to large adjustments as a result of Cuba's currency reform.

Source: Ministerio de Finanzas y Precios de la República de Cuba (Ministry of Finance and Prices of the Republic of Cuba); Oficina Nacional de Estadísticas de Cuba (National Statistics Office of Cuba); Comisión Económica para América Latina y el Caribe (United Nations Economic Commission for Latin America and the Caribbean).

Table 5.12. Dominican Republic

Details of tax revenue

Million DOP

	1990	2000	2005	2010	2017	2018	2019	2020	2021	2022
Total tax revenue	**6 420**	**47 753**	**149 063**	**242 756**	**499 036**	**555 857**	**611 573**	**556 425**	**781 183**	**872 424**
1000 Taxes on income, profits and capital gains	**1 650**	**10 517**	**29 374**	**52 653**	**153 034**	**168 485**	**191 771**	**187 108**	**263 082**	**276 183**
1100 Of individuals	..	4 088	7 588	17 088	43 553	51 425	59 448	58 747	69 026	87 200
1110 On income and profits	..	4 070	7 509	16 901	43 097	51 031	58 842	58 355	68 593	86 504
1120 On capital gains	..	18	79	187	456	394	606	392	433	696
1200 Corporate	..	4 605	16 147	21 325	82 785	87 822	95 928	90 340	150 695	140 603
1210 On profits	..	4 605	16 147	21 325	82 785	87 822	95 928	90 340	150 695	140 603
1220 On capital gains of corporates	..	..	..	..	..	..	..	..	..	..
1300 Unallocable between 1100 and 1200	1 650	1 824	5 639	14 241	26 696	29 238	36 395	38 021	43 361	48 380
2000 Social security contributions	**53**	**490**	**35**	**1 845**	**2 635**	**2 514**	**2 553**	**2 661**	**3 420**	**4 923**
2100 Employees	..	..	..	1 720	1 535	..	..	..	..	..
2110 On a payroll basis	..	..	..	..	..	..	..	..	..	..
2120 On an income tax basis	..	..	..	..	..	..	..	..	..	..
2200 Employers	..	..	..	125	1 099	..	..	..	..	..
2210 On a payroll basis	..	..	..	..	..	..	..	..	..	..
2220 On an income tax basis	..	..	..	..	..	..	..	..	..	..
2300 Self-employed or non-employed	..	..	..	0	0	..	..	..	..	..
2310 On a payroll basis	..	..	..	..	..	..	..	..	..	..
2320 On an income tax basis	..	..	..	..	..	..	..	..	..	..
2400 Unallocable between 2100, 2200 and 2300	53	490	35	0	0	2 514	2 553	2 661	3 420	4 923
2410 On a payroll basis	53	490	35	..	..	2 514	2 553	2 661	3 420	4 923
2420 On an income tax basis	0	0	0	..	..	0	0	0	0	0
3000 Taxes on payroll and workforce	**0**	**0**	**671**	**1 385**	**2 912**	**3 282**	**3 502**	**3 141**	**3 810**	**3 811**
4000 Taxes on property	**74**	**644**	**6 622**	**12 416**	**21 502**	**23 955**	**27 374**	**24 367**	**45 798**	**45 061**
4100 Recurrent taxes on immovable property	9	115	1 710	555	2 166	2 527	2 904	2 857	4 171	4 438
4110 Households	9	115	1 710	555	2 166	2 527	2 904	2 857	4 171	4 438
4120 Others	0	0	0	0	0	0	0	0	0	0
4200 Recurrent taxes on net wealth	0	0	0	2 449	4 112	4 609	5 155	4 522	8 396	8 615
Tax on assets	..	..	..	2 449	4 112	4 609	5 155	4 522	8 396	8 615
4210 Individual	..	..	..	..	..	..	..	..	..	..
4220 Corporate	..	..	..	..	..	..	..	..	..	..
4300 Estate, inheritance and gift taxes	11	96	84	231	455	526	715	522	1 308	1 389
4310 Estate and inheritance taxes	..	..	..	..	..	..	..	..	..	..
4320 Gift taxes	..	..	..	..	..	..	..	..	..	..
4400 Taxes on financial and capital transactions	40	377	4 716	8 658	13 995	15 675	17 594	15 635	30 206	28 611
Tax on checks	0	0	3 133	4 262	7 117	8 139	8 646	8 644	11 231	13 547
Real estate operations	22	217	1 413	3 864	5 802	6 320	7 526	5 910	17 068	13 015
Tax on the transfer of immovable property	18	160	170	533	1 076	1 215	1 422	1 080	1 907	2 048
4500 Non-recurrent taxes	3	32	89	488	711	553	931	779	1 642	1 929
4510 On net wealth	3	32	89	488	711	553	931	779	1 642	1 929
4520 Other non-recurrent taxes	0	0	0	0	0	0	0	0	0	0
4600 Other recurrent taxes on property	11	25	24	35	62	66	75	52	76	81
5000 Taxes on goods and services	**4 484**	**35 672**	**110 758**	**174 457**	**318 953**	**357 620**	**386 372**	**339 147**	**465 072**	**542 443**
5100 Taxes on production, sale, transfer, etc	4 418	34 962	109 050	167 983	305 698	343 479	369 238	327 400	444 248	519 450
5110 General taxes	970	9 912	40 983	81 226	169 629	194 725	214 324	194 408	261 207	310 788
5111 Value added taxes	970	9 912	40 983	81 226	169 629	194 725	214 324	194 408	261 207	310 788
5112 Sales tax	0	0	0	0	0	0	0	0	0	0
5113 Other	0	0	0	0	0	0	0	0	0	0
5120 Taxes on specific goods and services	3 449	25 051	68 067	86 757	136 070	148 754	154 914	132 993	183 041	208 662
5121 Excises	495	6 320	26 923	55 224	88 455	95 912	100 396	85 534	117 330	130 628
Alcoholic beverages	251	2 455	8 142	15 054	25 694	28 882	30 610	29 336	39 822	42 492
Tobacco products	102	469	2 879	4 529	5 120	4 355	3 923	3 507	3 747	3 310
Petroleum products	89	3 143	14 712	34 598	53 074	57 053	60 828	47 854	67 823	78 575
Other excises	52	252	1 190	1 043	4 567	5 622	5 035	4 836	5 938	6 252
5122 Profits of fiscal monopolies	0	0	0	0	0	0	0	0	0	0
5123 Customs and import duties	1 548	13 459	14 400	19 455	28 703	32 096	32 478	29 630	42 638	50 635
Import duties	615	13 456	14 394	19 455	27 276	30 931	32 478	29 630	42 638	50 635
Others	933	3	6	0	1 426	1 165	0	0	0	0
5124 Taxes on exports	6	4	46	146	0	0	0	0	0	0
5125 Taxes on investment goods	0	0	0	0	0	0	0	0	0	0

	1990	2000	2005	2010	2017	2018	2019	2020	2021	2022
5126 Taxes on specific services	364	1 662	5 681	11 553	18 531	20 311	21 529	17 618	22 727	26 993
Telecommunications	85	5	3 193	4 886	6 782	7 146	7 313	7 494	8 117	8 716
Insurance premiums	33	584	0	3 088	5 236	5 976	6 782	7 128	8 560	9 567
Departure tax	204	809	2 413	3 428	6 252	6 933	7 180	2 894	5 870	8 428
Hotels	22	191	0	0	0	0	0	0	0	0
Casinos	16	59	73	151	237	228	225	77	131	208
Racetracks	4	15	2	0	0	0	0	0	0	0
Phone gaming	0	0	0	0	25	30	28	25	49	74
Others	0	0	0	0	0	0	0	0	0	0
5127 Other taxes on internat. trade and transactions	1 037	3 606	21 017	379	380	435	511	211	346	407
Exchange commission	857	3 412	19 998	0	0	0	0	0	0	0
Consular fees	77	32	271	132	153	153	156	72	65	133
Others	103	162	748	247	227	281	355	139	282	274
5128 Other taxes	0	0	0	0	0	0	0	0	0	0
5130 Unallocable between 5110 and 5120	0	0	0	0	0	0	0	0	0	0
5200 Taxes on use of goods and perform activities	65	710	1 708	6 475	13 254	14 141	17 134	11 747	20 824	22 993
5210 Recurrent taxes	65	710	1 708	2 241	3 508	3 763	4 857	2 235	4 534	4 725
5211 Paid by households: motor vehicles	45	268	977	1 277	2 081	2 310	3 407	1 189	2 991	3 023
5212 Paid by others: motor vehicles	0	0	0	0	0	0	0	0	0	0
5213 Paid in respect of other goods	21	442	731	964	1 426	1 454	1 450	1 046	1 543	1 703
Licences to carry firearms	17	237	244	296	176	192	182	162	169	276
Licences to operate gambling houses	0	114	155	211	1 250	1 262	1 268	885	1 374	1 427
Licences to operate slot machines	4	60	102	458	0	0	0	0	0	0
Others	0	30	230	0	0	0	0	0	0	0
5220 Non-recurrent taxes	0	0	0	4 234	9 747	10 378	12 277	9 511	16 290	18 268
Vehicle property registration	..	..	..	4 234	9 072	9 667	11 442	8 882	15 188	17 059
Ecological taxes	..	..	..	0	675	711	835	629	1 102	1 209
5300 Unallocable between 5100 and 5200	0	0	0	0	0	0	0	0	0	0
6000 Other taxes	**159**	**429**	**1 603**	**0**	**1**	**1**	**2**	**1**	**2**	**3**
6100 Paid solely by business	0	0	0	..	0	0	0	0	0	0
6200 Other	159	429	1 603	..	1	1	2	1	2	3

.. Not available

Note: Year ending 31st December.

The data are on a cash basis.

The figures exclude local government tax revenues as the data are not available.

Fines have been identified and excluded from taxes on income and taxes on property since 1995 and from taxes on goods and services since 1990.

Heading 2000: The data exclude social security contributions to general government managed by the private sector. An additional breakdown has been available between 2006 and 2017 to distinguish between social security contributions paid by employees and those paid by employers.

Heading 3000: This heading includes the mandatory non-pensions contributions to the Instituto de Formación Técnico Profesional (INFOTEP). The tax revenue is classified under the central government. In Dominican Republic this revenue is classified under a separate unit (decentralised) considered to be different to the central government.

Heading 5211: In ECLAC data, the vehicle transfer tax is classified as a property tax (4000).

Source: Ministerio de Hacienda (Ministry of Finance); Instituto Nacional de Formación Técnico Profesional (National Institute for Technical and Vocational Training).

Table 5.13. Ecuador

Details of tax revenue

Million USD

	1990	2000	2005	2010	2017	2018	2019	2020	2021	2022
Total tax revenue	**1 078**	**2 125**	**5 724**	**11 693**	**21 036**	**22 656**	**21 501**	**18 543**	**20 647**	**24 070**
1000 Taxes on income, profits and capital gains	**139**	**268**	**1 248**	**2 924**	**4 134**	**5 246**	**4 669**	**4 503**	**4 444**	**5 315**
1100 Of individuals	..	10	27	80	180	193	197	155	143	181
1110 On income and profits	..	10	27	80	180	193	197	155	143	181
Personal income tax	..	10	27	80	176	193	197	155	143	181
Solidarity contribution on remuneration	..	0	0	0	5	0	0	0	0	0
1120 On capital gains	..	..	..	0	0	0	0	0	0	0
1200 Corporate	..	53	362	1 046	1 074	1 894	1 308	1 333	899	1 350
1210 On profits	..	53	362	1 046	1 074	1 894	1 308	1 333	899	1 350
Corporate income tax	..	53	342	474	991	1 808	1 232	1 276	832	1 284
Income tax on oil companies and others	..	0	20	572	63	81	75	57	67	65
Solidarity contribution on profits	..	0	0	0	19	4	0	0	0	0
1220 On capital gains of corporates	..	..	..	..	..	..	..	..	..	..
1300 Unallocable between 1100 and 1200	139	206	859	1 798	2 880	3 159	3 164	3 015	3 402	3 784
Withholding tax	0	190	683	1 560	2 578	2 858	2 847	2 787	3 416	3 886
Income tax advances	0	14	170	298	343	353	394	290	15	4
Income tax refunds	0	0	0	-75	-112	-132	-151	-112	-98	-180
Other income taxes (local)	1	2	6	15	71	81	74	50	69	74
2000 Social security contributions	**243**	**228**	**1 109**	**2 541**	**5 699**	**5 909**	**5 704**	**5 079**	**5 305**	**5 773**
2100 Employees	..	..	..	..	..	..	..	..	..	..
2110 On a payroll basis	..	..	..	..	..	..	..	..	..	..
2120 On an income tax basis	..	..	..	..	..	..	..	..	..	..
2200 Employers	..	..	..	..	..	..	..	..	..	..
2210 On a payroll basis	..	..	..	..	..	..	..	..	..	..
2220 On an income tax basis	..	..	..	..	..	..	..	..	..	..
2300 Self-employed or non-employed	..	..	..	..	..	..	..	..	..	..
2310 On a payroll basis	..	..	..	..	..	..	..	..	..	..
2320 On an income tax basis	..	..	..	..	..	..	..	..	..	..
2400 Unallocable between 2100, 2200 and 2300	243	228	1 109	2 541	5 699	5 909	5 704	5 079	5 305	5 773
2410 On a payroll basis	..	..	..	..	..	..	..	..	..	..
2420 On an income tax basis	..	..	..	..	..	..	..	..	..	..
3000 Taxes on payroll and workforce	**0**	**0**	**0**	**0**	**0**	**0**	**0**	**0**	**0**	**0**
4000 Taxes on property	**16**	**17**	**71**	**159**	**347**	**372**	**353**	**334**	**360**	**986**
4100 Recurrent taxes on immovable property	13	8	37	68	162	192	186	172	184	200
Rural land tax	0	0	0	3	7	2	0	0	0	0
4110 Households	0	0	0	0	..	0	0	0	0	0
4120 Others	13	8	37	66	155	190	185	172	184	200
Tax on urban properties	12	7	32	55	129	162	158	145	157	170
Tax on rural properties	1	1	6	10	26	27	27	27	27	30
4200 Recurrent taxes on net wealth	0	0	0	35	35	30	35	31	24	19
4210 Individual	..	..	..	0	0	0	0	0	0	0
4220 Corporate	..	..	..	35	35	30	35	31	24	19
Tax on foreign assets	..	..	..	35	35	30	35	31	24	19
4300 Estate, inheritance and gift taxes	0	0	1	5	26	27	24	24	40	11
4310 Estate and inheritance taxes	..	..	1	5	26	27	24	24	40	11
4320 Gift taxes	..	..	0	0	0	0	0	0	0	0
4400 Taxes on financial and capital transactions	0	0	0	0	0	0	0	0	0	0
4500 Non-recurrent taxes	0	0	0	0	19	7	0	0	0	635
4510 On net wealth	..	..	..	..	19	7	..	..	..	635
Solidarity contribution on equity	..	..	..	..	16	6	..	..	..	0
Solidarity contribution on foreign assets	..	..	..	..	3	1	..	..	..	0
Regularisation of assets abroad	..	..	..	..	0	0	..	..	..	88
Post-COVID contributions	..	..	..	..	0	0	..	..	..	547
4520 Other non-recurrent taxes	..	..	..	..	0	0	..	..	..	0
4600 Other recurrent taxes on property	3	9	33	50	106	116	108	107	112	121
5000 Taxes on goods and services	**679**	**1 609**	**3 244**	**6 066**	**10 837**	**11 108**	**10 755**	**8 608**	**10 516**	**11 994**
5100 Taxes on production, sale, transfer, etc	671	1 580	3 140	5 863	10 378	10 615	10 248	8 266	10 133	11 586
5110 General taxes	306	928	2 211	3 801	6 718	6 716	6 622	5 459	6 658	7 937
5111 Value added taxes	302	923	2 194	3 759	6 643	6 630	6 539	5 398	6 581	7 854
VAT (internal operations)	..	557	1 239	2 506	4 671	4 789	4 885	4 093	4 765	5 783
VAT (imports)	..	381	1 105	1 668	1 646	1 947	1 800	1 413	1 961	2 350
2% contribution on VAT	..	0	0	0	412	4	0	0	0	0
VAT refunds	..	-14	-149	-416	-87	-109	-146	-108	-146	-279
Other VATs (local)	..	0	0	0	0	0	0	0	0	0
5112 Sales tax	0	0	0	0	0	0	0	0	0	0
5113 Other	4	5	16	41	75	85	83	61	77	84
5120 Taxes on specific goods and services	365	652	929	2 062	3 660	3 900	3 627	2 807	3 475	3 648

	1990	2000	2005	2010	2017	2018	2019	2020	2021	2022
5121 Excises	90	89	237	508	919	955	885	715	821	865
Beer	..	29	62	119	237	239	246	209	234	274
Cigarettes	..	30	72	117	126	112	103	71	42	0
Fizzy drinks	..	9	15	40	103	94	93	79	81	79
Vehicles	..	6	17	55	67	63	42	25	31	38
Alcohol and alcoholic products	..	4	11	23	38	43	40	28	36	43
Non-returnable plastic bottles	..	0	0	0	31	35	36	29	34	40
Telephone	..	0	0	0	37	32	29	84	75	4
Water heaters	..	0	0	0	32	26	2	1	2	0
Perfumes	..	0	0	17	24	25	21	13	14	15
Non-alcoholic drinks	..	0	0	0	11	11	11	11	14	16
Other excises (internal operations)	..	0	0	0	4	5	5	4	5	6
Excises on imports	..	10	60	138	209	271	257	162	253	351
5122 Profits of fiscal monopolies	0	0	0	0	0	0	0	0	0	0
5123 Customs and import duties	227	217	547	1 153	1 475	1 559	1 414	944	1 207	1 267
5124 Taxes on exports	0	0	0	0	0	0	0	0	0	0
5125 Taxes on investment goods	0	0	0	0	0	0	0	0	0	0
5126 Taxes on specific services	26	343	145	30	169	179	188	183	235	243
Contribution to comprehensive cancer care	0	0	0	0	97	104	116	125	184	202
Prepaid television services	0	0	0	14	60	64	60	54	43	32
Club membership fees	0	0	0	0	1	1	1	0	0	0
Casino services	0	0	0	8	0	0	0	0	0	0
Telecommunications	0	0	142	0	0	0	0	0	0	0
Capital circulation tax	0	322	0	0	0	0	0	0	0	0
Departure tax	7	16	0	0	0	0	0	0	0	0
Tax on credit operations	18	2	0	1	0	0	0	0	0	0
Other service taxes (local)	1	2	3	7	10	10	11	3	8	9
5127 Other taxes on internat. trade and transactions	22	4	0	371	1 098	1 206	1 140	964	1 212	1 274
Foreign Currency Exit Tax (ISD)	0	0	..	371	1 098	1 206	1 140	964	1 212	1 274
Tax on purchase of foreign currency	22	4	..	0	0	0	0	0	0	0
5128 Other taxes	0	0	0	0	0	0	0	0	0	0
5130 Unallocable between 5110 and 5120	0	0	0	0	0	0	0	0	0	0
5200 Taxes on use of goods and perform activities	8	29	105	203	460	493	507	342	382	409
5210 Recurrent taxes	5	28	104	203	441	477	491	330	368	393
5211 Paid by households: motor vehicles	5	23	78	168	323	354	364	215	245	260
Motor vehicle tax	5	23	78	168	212	234	242	208	236	250
Environmental tax on vehicle pollution	0	0	0	0	111	119	122	7	9	9
5212 Paid by others: motor vehicles	0	0	0	0	0	0	0	0	0	0
5213 Paid in respect of other goods	1	5	26	35	118	123	127	115	123	134
5220 Non-recurrent taxes	2	1	0	0	18	16	16	11	14	16
5300 Unallocable between 5100 and 5200	0	0	0	0	0	0	0	0	0	0
6000 Other taxes	**2**	**2**	**52**	**4**	**19**	**21**	**20**	**20**	**22**	**2**
6100 Paid solely by business	0	0	0	0	0	0	0	0	0	0
6200 Other	2	2	52	4	19	21	20	20	22	2
Simplified taxation system of Ecuador (RISE)	0	0	0	6	22	23	22	20	23	5
Other tax refunds	0	0	0	-2	-3	-2	-2	-1	-1	-3
Other taxes (local)	2	2	52	1	0	0	0	0	0	0

.. Not available

Note: Year ending 31st December.

The data are on a cash basis, except for the data from the Central Bank of Ecuador which are on an accrual basis.

Central government tax revenues mainly come from the Internal Revenue Service while some are from the Central Bank of Ecuador (see details below). Local tax revenues come from the Development Bank of Ecuador. Central government tax revenue data are preliminary for 2019-22. Local government tax revenues are estimated for 2021 and 2022.

Heading 2000: The data are collected from non-financial public sector operations published by the Central Bank of Ecuador.

Heading 4510: Temporary revenues from regularisation of assets abroad and post-COVID contributions have been added in this edition.

Heading 5123: The data are collected from the general budget of the consolidated state government published by the Central Bank of Ecuador.

Heading 5126: This heading includes the tax on credit operations from the general budget of the consolidated state government published by the Central Bank of Ecuador.

Heading 5127: This heading includes the tax on purchase of foreign currency from the general budget of the consolidated state government published by the Central Bank of Ecuador.

Source: Servicio de Rentas Internas (Internal Revenue Service); Banco Central del Ecuador (Central Bank of Ecuador); Banco de Desarrollo de Ecuador (Development Bank of Ecuador).

Table 5.14. El Salvador

Details of tax revenue

Million USD

	1990	2000	2005	2010	2017	2018	2019	2020	2021	2022
Total tax revenue	**543**	**1 669**	**2 497**	**3 447**	**5 234**	**5 545**	**5 640**	**5 404**	**6 708**	**7 430**
1000 Taxes on income, profits and capital gains	**95**	**429**	**637**	**996**	**1 799**	**1 889**	**1 959**	**1 954**	**2 259**	**2 707**
1100 Of individuals	..	..	312	590	759	795	836	820	923	1 060
1110 On income and profits	..	..	312	590	759	795	836	820	923	1 060
1120 On capital gains	..	..	..	..	..	..	..	..	..	..
1200 Corporate	..	..	356	420	870	914	922	934	1 078	1 334
1210 On profits	..	..	356	420	870	914	922	934	1 078	1 334
Corporate income tax	..	..	356	420	804	845	848	848	1 004	1 334
Special Contribution - Public security (large taxpayers)	..	..	0	0	67	70	74	85	74	0
1220 On capital gains of corporates	..	..	..	..	..	..	..	..	..	..
1300 Unallocable between 1100 and 1200	95	429	-31	-14	170	180	201	201	258	313
Withholding income tax	..	..	0	41	209	220	249	239	299	387
Income tax refunds	..	..	-31	-55	-39	-40	-48	-38	-41	-74
2000 Social security contributions	**104**	**325**	**339**	**470**	**684**	**705**	**722**	**700**	**771**	**834**
2100 Employees	..	75	126	165	239	246	251	246	271	293
2110 On a payroll basis	..	75	126	165	239	246	251	246	271	293
2120 On an income tax basis	..	0	0	0	0	0	0	0	0	0
2200 Employers	..	176	213	306	444	459	471	454	500	541
2210 On a payroll basis	..	176	213	306	444	459	471	454	500	541
2220 On an income tax basis	..	0	0	0	0	0	0	0	0	0
2300 Self-employed or non-employed	..	13	0	0	0	0	0	0	0	0
2310 On a payroll basis	..	13	..	..	..	..	..	..	..	..
2320 On an income tax basis	..	0	..	..	..	..	..	..	..	..
2400 Unallocable between 2100, 2200 and 2300	104	62	0	0	0	0	0	0	0	0
2410 On a payroll basis	104	62	..	..	..	..	..	..	..	..
2420 On an income tax basis	0	0	..	..	..	..	..	..	..	..
3000 Taxes on payroll and workforce	**0**	**0**	**16**	**21**	**36**	**37**	**38**	**36**	**40**	**42**
4000 Taxes on property	**26**	**12**	**18**	**19**	**112**	**119**	**44**	**27**	**47**	**58**
4100 Recurrent taxes on immovable property	0	0	2	3	5	6	7	6	8	11
4110 Households	..	..	..	..	..	..	..	..	..	..
4120 Others	..	..	..	..	..	..	..	..	..	..
4200 Recurrent taxes on net wealth	16	0	0	0	0	0	0	0	0	0
4210 Individual	..	..	..	..	..	..	..	..	..	..
4220 Corporate	..	..	..	..	..	..	..	..	..	..
4300 Estate, inheritance and gift taxes	0	0	0	0	0	0	0	0	0	0
4310 Estate and inheritance taxes	..	..	..	..	..	..	..	..	..	..
4320 Gift taxes	..	..	..	..	..	..	..	..	..	..
4400 Taxes on financial and capital transactions	10	12	16	16	108	113	37	21	39	47
Property transfers	10	12	16	16	23	24	29	21	39	47
Checks and electronic transfers of funds	0	0	0	0	53	56	5	0	0	0
Withholding for liquidity control	0	0	0	0	32	34	3	0	0	0
4500 Non-recurrent taxes	0	0	0	0	0	0	0	0	0	0
4510 On net wealth	..	..	..	..	..	..	..	..	..	..
4520 Other non-recurrent taxes	..	..	..	..	..	..	..	..	..	..
4600 Other recurrent taxes on property	0	0	0	0	0	0	0	0	0	0
5000 Taxes on goods and services	**259**	**903**	**1 450**	**1 878**	**2 512**	**2 694**	**2 778**	**2 585**	**3 493**	**3 682**
5100 Taxes on production, sale, transfer, etc	259	903	1 447	1 863	2 484	2 663	2 747	2 561	3 453	3 637
5110 General taxes	133	714	1 104	1 433	1 904	2 054	2 109	2 033	2 771	2 944
5111 Value added taxes	0	714	1 104	1 433	1 904	2 054	2 109	2 033	2 771	2 944
5112 Sales tax	0	0	0	0	0	0	0	0	0	0
5113 Other	133	0	0	0	0	0	0	0	0	0
5120 Taxes on specific goods and services	127	189	343	431	580	608	638	528	682	694
5121 Excises	65	49	162	224	357	367	393	336	379	361
Alcoholic beverages	..	..	14	22	24	24	25	34	40	33
Cigarettes	..	..	23	38	27	24	24	25	27	27
Soft drinks	..	..	33	31	49	49	52	50	62	64
Beer	..	..	26	29	65	73	82	67	92	101
Weapons, ammunition and explosives	..	..	1	1	1	1	1	1	1	2
Ad-valorem on fuels	..	..	0	0	8	7	8	7	5	0
Special contribution- Sugar	..	..	1	1	1	1	1	1	1	1
Special contribution- Public transportation	..	..	0	35	45	47	48	23	49	25
Special contribution- FOVIAL	..	..	66	69	89	93	96	83	104	108
Special contribution- Public security	..	..	0	0	49	48	55	43	1	0
5122 Profits of fiscal monopolies	0	0	0	0	0	0	0	0	0	0
5123 Customs and import duties	61	141	181	151	211	227	232	187	291	319

	1990	2000	2005	2010	2017	2018	2019	2020	2021	2022
5124 Taxes on exports	0	0	0	0	0	0	0	0	0	0
5125 Taxes on investment goods	0	0	0	0	0	0	0	0	0	0
5126 Taxes on specific services	0	0	0	56	13	14	13	5	11	14
5127 Other taxes on internat. trade and transactions	0	0	0	0	0	0	0	0	0	0
5128 Other taxes	0	0	0	0	0	0	0	0	0	0
5130 Unallocable between 5110 and 5120	0	0	0	0	0	0	0	0	0	0
5200 Taxes on use of goods and perform activities	0	0	3	15	28	32	31	24	40	45
5210 Recurrent taxes	..	..	3	7	14	17	15	12	17	20
5211 Paid by households: motor vehicles	..	..	0	0	0	0	0	0	0	0
5212 Paid by others: motor vehicles	..	..	0	0	0	0	0	0	0	0
5213 Paid in respect of other goods	..	..	3	7	14	17	15	12	17	20
5220 Non-recurrent taxes	..	..	0	7	14	15	16	12	23	24
5300 Unallocable between 5100 and 5200	0	0	0	0	0	0	0	0	0	0
6000 Other taxes	**58**	**0**	**37**	**63**	**90**	**101**	**98**	**102**	**99**	**107**
6100 Paid solely by business	0	0	0	0	0	0	0	0	0	0
6200 Other	58	0	37	63	90	101	98	102	99	107

.. Not available

Note: Year ending 31st December.

The data are on a cash basis.

Central government tax revenue data are preliminary for 2022.

Heading 1000: Disaggregated individual and corporate income taxes are not available before 2002.

Heading 2000: The figures include social security contributions paid to the Salvadoran Institute of Social Security (ISSS), National Public Employees Pension Institute (INPEP), Social Security Institute of the Armed Forces (IPSFA) and Salvadoran Institute of Teacher Welfare (ISBM). The figures exclude payments to privately managed pension funds (AFPs) and may include a small amount of voluntary contributions which is undistinguishable from the public social security contribution data.

Heading 3000: Vocational training contributions to the Instituto Salvadoreño de Formación Profesional (INSAFORP) are included in heading 3000. The tax revenue is classified under the central government. In El Salvador this revenue is classified under a separate unit considered to be different to the central government.

Source: Dirección General de Tesorería en Ministerio de Hacienda (General Treasury Directorate in Ministry of Finance); Dirección General de Contabilidad Gubernamental en Ministerio de Hacienda (General Directorate of Government Accounting in Ministry of Finance); División de Análisis Financiero y Estadístico en Ministerio de Hacienda (Financial Analysis and Statistics Division in Ministry of Finance); Instituto Salvadoreño del Seguro Social (Salvadoran Social Security Institute); Centro Interamericano de Administraciones Tributarias (Inter-American Center of Tax Administrations).

Table 5.15. Guatemala

Details of tax revenue

Million GTQ

	1990	2000	2005	2010	2017	2018	2019	2020	2021	2022
Total tax revenue	**2 646**	**16 531**	**27 187**	**41 537**	**69 691**	**72 505**	**77 121**	**74 529**	**94 113**	**105 942**
1000 Taxes on income, profits and capital gains	**507**	**3 293**	**4 401**	**7 745**	**16 313**	**16 236**	**17 100**	**16 751**	**23 291**	**25 658**
1100 Of individuals	25	143	645	1 225	2 468	2 603	2 813	2 816	4 769	3 892
1110 On income and profits	25	143	645	1 225	2 468	2 603	2 813	2 816	4 769	3 892
1120 On capital gains	..	..	..	..	..	..	..	..	..	..
1200 Corporate	482	3 149	3 756	6 520	13 846	13 633	14 287	13 935	18 522	21 765
1210 On profits	482	3 149	3 756	6 520	13 846	13 633	14 287	13 935	18 522	21 765
Corporate income tax	482	1 858	3 730	6 518	13 839	13 633	14 285	13 933	18 519	21 763
Commercial and agricultural enterprises	0	1 291	26	2	6	0	2	2	3	2
1220 On capital gains of corporates	..	..	..	..	..	..	..	..	..	..
1300 Unallocable between 1100 and 1200	0	0	0	0	0	0	0	0	0	0
2000 Social security contributions	**436**	**2 569**	**4 072**	**6 312**	**11 523**	**12 102**	**12 957**	**12 742**	**14 314**	**15 539**
2100 Employees	..	..	..	..	..	..	..	..	..	..
2110 On a payroll basis	..	..	..	..	..	..	..	..	..	..
2120 On an income tax basis	..	..	..	..	..	..	..	..	..	..
2200 Employers	..	..	..	..	..	..	..	..	..	..
2210 On a payroll basis	..	..	..	..	..	..	..	..	..	..
2220 On an income tax basis	..	..	..	..	..	..	..	..	..	..
2300 Self-employed or non-employed	..	..	..	..	..	..	..	..	..	..
2310 On a payroll basis	..	..	..	..	..	..	..	..	..	..
2320 On an income tax basis	..	..	..	..	..	..	..	..	..	..
2400 Unallocable between 2100, 2200 and 2300	436	2 569	4 072	6 312	11 523	12 102	12 957	12 742	14 314	15 539
2410 On a payroll basis	436	2 569	4 072	6 312	11 523	12 102	12 957	12 742	14 314	15 539
2420 On an income tax basis	0	0	0	0	0	0	0	0	0	0
3000 Taxes on payroll and workforce	**0**	**0**	**0**	**447**	**862**	**903**	**933**	**859**	**1 038**	**1 102**
Contributions to INTECAP	..	..	..	233	449	469	484	448	537	586
Contributions to IRTRA	..	..	..	214	413	434	449	411	501	516
4000 Taxes on property	**149**	**347**	**663**	**1 202**	**1 247**	**1 354**	**1 177**	**1 115**	**1 405**	**1 537**
4100 Recurrent taxes on immovable property	0	153	342	621	710	865	685	712	839	915
4110 Households	..	0	0	0	0	0	0	0	0	0
4120 Others	..	153	342	621	710	865	685	712	839	915
Property tax	..	6	1	1	1	2	2	1	2	1
Property tax (municipal)	..	147	341	620	709	863	683	711	837	914
4200 Recurrent taxes on net wealth	0	0	0	0	0	0	0	0	0	0
4210 Individual	..	..	..	..	..	..	..	..	..	..
4220 Corporate	..	..	..	..	..	..	..	..	..	..
4300 Estate, inheritance and gift taxes	0	0	0	0	0	0	0	0	0	0
4310 Estate and inheritance taxes	..	..	..	..	..	..	..	..	..	..
4320 Gift taxes	..	..	..	..	..	..	..	..	..	..
4400 Taxes on financial and capital transactions	149	194	321	581	537	489	492	403	567	622
Stamp duty	104	182	313	572	508	463	451	392	542	586
Tax on property transfer	45	12	8	10	29	26	40	11	25	36
4500 Non-recurrent taxes	0	0	0	0	0	0	0	0	0	0
4510 On net wealth	..	..	..	..	..	..	..	..	..	..
4520 Other non-recurrent taxes	..	..	..	..	..	..	..	..	..	..
4600 Other recurrent taxes on property	0	0	0	0	0	0	0	0	0	0
5000 Taxes on goods and services	**1 554**	**10 317**	**16 402**	**23 255**	**35 365**	**37 253**	**40 124**	**37 993**	**48 666**	**55 975**
5100 Taxes on production, sale, transfer, etc	1 526	10 131	16 083	22 750	34 539	36 372	39 215	37 090	47 655	54 905
5110 General taxes	762	6 259	10 753	16 980	26 187	27 733	29 920	28 760	36 985	43 404
5111 Value added taxes	762	6 259	10 753	16 980	26 187	27 733	29 920	28 760	36 985	43 404
VAT domestic	361	2 903	4 250	7 995	14 380	14 573	15 897	15 992	18 226	20 215
VAT imports	401	4 189	7 953	11 127	14 148	15 560	16 331	14 955	21 461	26 131
Tax credit refunds	0	-834	-1 450	-2 142	-2 342	-2 401	-2 307	-2 187	-2 702	-2 941
5112 Sales tax	0	0	0	0	0	0	0	0	0	0
5113 Other	0	0	0	0	0	0	0	0	0	0
5120 Taxes on specific goods and services	764	3 872	5 330	5 770	8 353	8 640	9 294	8 330	10 670	11 500
5121 Excises	258	1 797	1 262	3 101	5 471	5 621	6 106	5 662	6 879	7 132
Tobacco and derivatives	76	205	312	347	348	337	363	299	333	346
Beer	0	97	122	159	314	322	365	387	471	526
Alcoholic beverages	0	77	76	97	96	103	109	104	130	154
Soft drinks	0	15	172	220	348	365	396	405	458	479
Other beverages	77	12	2	2	0	0	0	0	0	1
Cement	0	0	93	99	114	123	131	147	183	186
Oil and derivatives	105	1 389	485	2 179	3 296	3 417	3 743	3 485	4 066	4 039
IPRIMA	0	0	0	0	953	953	999	836	1 238	1 402
5122 Profits of fiscal monopolies	0	0	0	0	0	0	0	0	0	0
5123 Customs and import duties	506	1 806	3 715	2 368	2 455	2 576	2 712	2 487	3 485	3 903
5124 Taxes on exports	0	0	0	0	0	0	0	0	0	0

	1990	2000	2005	2010	2017	2018	2019	2020	2021	2022
5125 Taxes on investment goods	0	0	0	0	0	0	0	0	0	0
5126 Taxes on specific services	0	269	354	301	427	443	477	181	305	466
Departure tax	..	135	197	224	300	312	338	117	214	323
INGUATE	..	40	56	73	120	125	132	57	83	134
Transportation and communications	..	94	100	3	7	6	7	7	8	9
5127 Other taxes on internat. trade and transactions	0	0	0	0	0	0	0	0	0	0
5128 Other taxes	0	0	0	0	0	0	0	0	0	0
5130 Unallocable between 5110 and 5120	0	0	0	0	0	0	0	0	0	0
5200 Taxes on use of goods and perform activities	28	186	319	505	826	881	909	903	1 011	1 071
5210 Recurrent taxes	28	186	319	505	826	881	909	903	1 011	1 071
5211 Paid by households: motor vehicles	0	0	0	0	0	0	0	0	0	0
5212 Paid by others: motor vehicles	28	186	319	505	826	881	909	903	1 011	1 071
5213 Paid in respect of other goods	0	0	0	0	0	0	0	0	0	0
5220 Non-recurrent taxes	0	0	0	0	0	0	0	0	0	0
5300 Unallocable between 5100 and 5200	0	0	0	0	0	0	0	0	0	0
6000 Other taxes	**0**	**7**	**1 649**	**2 575**	**4 380**	**4 656**	**4 830**	**5 070**	**5 399**	**6 130**
6100 Paid solely by business	..	0	0	0	0	0	0	0	0	0
6200 Other	..	7	1 649	2 575	4 380	4 656	4 830	5 070	5 399	6 130
Extraordinary and temporary solidarity tax in support of peace agreements	..	0	1 647	44	28	10	63	3	9	11
Solidarity tax	..	0	0	2 530	4 352	4 646	4 766	5 067	5 389	6 119
Extraordinary and temporary solidarity tax	..	2	0	0	0	0	0	0	0	0
Other indirect taxes	..	4	1	1	0	0	0	0	0	1

.. Not available

Note: Year ending 31st December.

The data are on a cash basis.

Local government tax revenues include revenues from the municipal property tax (IUSI).

Heading 1000: Personal and corporate income taxes also include taxes on income from financial products.

Heading 2000: Figures include contributions to the Guatemalan Social Security Institute (IGSS) and payments by public employees to the government's pension fund.

Heading 3000: Contributions to INTECAP and contributions to IRTRA are included in heading 3000. The tax revenues are classified under the central government. In Guatemala these revenues are classified under a separate unit considered to be different to the central government.

Heading 4400: Before 2000, tax on property transfer under heading 4400 also includes central government property tax under heading 4120 as they cannot be distinguished.

Heading 5121: Other beverages contain all alcoholic and non-alcoholic beverages before 2000.

Source: Superintendencia de Administración Tributaria (Superintendency of Tax Administration); Ministerio de Finanzas Públicas (Ministry of Public Finance); Contraloría General de Cuentas (General Comptroller's Office).

Table 5.16. Guyana

Details of tax revenue

Million GYD

	1990	2000	2005	2010	2017	2018	2019	2020	2021	2022
Total tax revenue	**5 232**	**42 750**	**60 319**	**111 906**	**191 513**	**220 421**	**250 240**	**243 507**	**282 401**	**324 376**
1000 Taxes on income, profits and capital gains	**1 752**	**16 179**	**23 843**	**39 561**	**68 088**	**78 956**	**94 504**	**105 756**	**124 088**	**164 802**
1100 Of individuals	333	7 734	11 139	17 816	26 564	32 037	35 249	39 711	46 962	58 903
1110 On income and profits	333	7 734	11 139	17 816	26 564	32 037	35 249	39 711	46 962	58 903
Personal	306	7 157	11 139	15 419	21 669	25 808	29 213	34 688	42 907	54 881
Self-employed	27	577	0	2 397	4 895	6 229	6 036	5 024	4 054	4 022
1120 On capital gains	..	..	..	..	..	..	..	..	..	..
1200 Corporate	1 375	8 266	12 555	21 427	41 183	46 198	58 346	64 992	75 897	104 581
1210 On profits	1 375	8 266	12 555	21 427	41 183	46 198	58 346	64 992	75 897	104 581
1220 On capital gains of corporates	..	..	..	..	..	..	..	..	..	..
1300 Unallocable between 1100 and 1200	43	179	149	317	341	721	908	1 053	1 229	1 318
2000 Social security contributions	**191**	**4 868**	**6 670**	**10 047**	**19 911**	**21 178**	**23 728**	**24 706**	**26 725**	**31 353**
2100 Employees	..	..	..	..	..	..	..	..	..	..
2110 On a payroll basis	..	..	..	..	..	..	..	..	..	..
2120 On an income tax basis	..	..	..	..	..	..	..	..	..	..
2200 Employers	..	..	..	..	..	..	..	..	..	..
2210 On a payroll basis	..	..	..	..	..	..	..	..	..	..
2220 On an income tax basis	..	..	..	..	..	..	..	..	..	..
2300 Self-employed or non-employed	..	..	..	..	..	..	..	..	..	..
2310 On a payroll basis	..	..	..	..	..	..	..	..	..	..
2320 On an income tax basis	..	..	..	..	..	..	..	..	..	..
2400 Unallocable between 2100, 2200 and 2300	191	4 868	6 670	10 047	19 911	21 178	23 728	24 706	26 725	31 353
2410 On a payroll basis	..	..	..	..	..	..	..	..	..	..
2420 On an income tax basis	..	..	..	..	..	..	..	..	..	..
3000 Taxes on payroll and workforce	**0**	**0**	**0**	**0**	**0**	**0**	**0**	**0**	**0**	**0**
4000 Taxes on property	**53**	**701**	**828**	**2 068**	**4 027**	**4 875**	**4 917**	**4 390**	**5 581**	**6 543**
4100 Recurrent taxes on immovable property	40	681	807	1 562	3 579	4 377	4 312	3 847	4 907	5 853
4110 Households	0	0	0	0	781	1 016	933	892	1 030	1 235
4120 Others	40	681	807	1 562	2 798	3 361	3 379	2 956	3 877	4 619
4200 Recurrent taxes on net wealth	0	0	0	0	0	0	0	0	0	0
4210 Individual	..	..	..	..	..	..	..	..	..	..
4220 Corporate	..	..	..	..	..	..	..	..	..	..
4300 Estate, inheritance and gift taxes	13	20	21	31	39	44	41	44	67	91
4310 Estate and inheritance taxes	13	20	21	31	39	44	41	44	67	91
4320 Gift taxes	0	0	0	0	0	0	0	0	0	0
4400 Taxes on financial and capital transactions	0	0	0	476	409	454	565	499	607	598
Stamp duties	..	..	..	476	409	454	565	499	607	598
4500 Non-recurrent taxes	0	0	0	0	0	0	0	0	0	0
4510 On net wealth	..	..	..	..	..	..	..	..	..	..
4520 Other non-recurrent taxes	..	..	..	..	..	..	..	..	..	..
4600 Other recurrent taxes on property	0	0	0	0	0	0	0	0	0	0
5000 Taxes on goods and services	**2 200**	**20 798**	**27 940**	**59 360**	**97 502**	**113 216**	**124 952**	**106 683**	**124 040**	**119 641**
5100 Taxes on production, sale, transfer, etc	2 162	20 530	27 414	58 846	96 386	111 770	123 710	105 489	122 857	118 411
5110 General taxes	1 399	14 861	21 396	27 044	42 728	48 155	52 735	49 907	48 452	56 998
5111 Value added taxes	0	0	0	27 044	42 423	48 036	52 676	49 844	48 363	56 830
Imports	..	..	..	14 877	23 261	27 819	29 302	22 934	21 134	23 255
Domestic supply	..	..	..	12 168	19 162	20 216	23 374	26 910	27 228	33 575
5112 Sales tax	0	0	0	0	0	0	0	0	0	0
5113 Other	1 399	14 861	21 396	0	305	119	60	63	90	168
5120 Taxes on specific goods and services	763	5 669	6 019	31 802	53 659	63 615	70 975	55 582	74 404	61 413
5121 Excises	32	609	1 211	22 070	35 162	41 659	45 979	35 941	48 793	31 139
Motor vehicle (imports)	..	..	..	7 702	5 443	6 781	7 977	8 188	14 917	13 708
Petroleum products (imports)	..	..	..	9 437	21 745	26 359	29 124	19 290	24 019	6 801
Tobacco (imports)	..	..	..	1 077	1 078	1 204	1 427	1 256	1 179	1 314
Alcoholic beverages (imports)	..	..	..	719	844	867	785	589	1 010	1 175
Alcoholic beverages (domestic)	..	..	..	2 358	4 348	4 468	4 486	4 599	5 275	5 394
Purchase tax - motor cars	..	..	..	0	0	0	0	0	0	0
Environmental tax	..	..	..	777	1 703	1 979	2 179	2 019	2 392	2 747
5122 Profits of fiscal monopolies	0	0	0	0	0	0	0	0	0	0
5123 Customs and import duties	544	3 943	3 635	8 302	16 273	19 321	22 140	18 624	23 737	27 125
5124 Taxes on exports	94	7	7	7	23	33	29	27	29	84
5125 Taxes on investment goods	0	0	0	0	0	0	0	0	0	0
5126 Taxes on specific services	92	1 110	1 166	1 423	2 201	2 603	2 827	990	1 845	3 064
Entertainment tax	12	27	2	0	0	0	0	0	0	0
Travel tax	80	1 084	1 164	1 423	2 201	2 603	2 827	990	1 845	3 064
5127 Other taxes on internat. trade and transactions	0	0	0	0	0	0	0	0	0	0
5128 Other taxes	0	0	0	0	0	0	0	0	0	0
5130 Unallocable between 5110 and 5120	0	0	0	0	0	0	0	0	0	0

	1990	2000	2005	2010	2017	2018	2019	2020	2021	2022
5200 Taxes on use of goods and perform activities	38	268	525	514	1 116	1 446	1 242	1 194	1 183	1 230
5210 Recurrent taxes	38	268	525	514	1 116	1 446	1 242	1 194	1 183	1 230
5211 Paid by households: motor vehicles	27	239	274	475	1 039	1 095	1 150	1 135	1 112	1 165
5212 Paid by others: motor vehicles	0	0	0	0	0	0	0	0	0	0
5213 Paid in respect of other goods	12	29	251	39	77	352	92	60	70	65
Other licences	12	29	251	39	77	352	92	60	70	65
5220 Non-recurrent taxes	0	0	0	0	0	0	0	0	0	0
5300 Unallocable between 5100 and 5200	0	0	0	0	0	0	0	0	0	0
6000 Other taxes	**1 037**	**204**	**1 039**	**870**	**1 985**	**2 196**	**2 139**	**1 972**	**1 968**	**2 037**
6100 Paid solely by business	0	0	0	0	0	0	0	0	0	0
6200 Other	1 037	204	1 039	870	1 985	2 196	2 139	1 972	1 968	2 037

.. Not available

Note: Year ending 31st December.

The data are on a cash basis.

Data on local government tax revenues include payments of local taxes by public corporations. Tax revenue data are government revised estimates for 2022.

Heading 2000: The figures include contributions to the National Insurance Scheme.

Source: Ministry of Finance; Bank of Guyana; National Insurance Scheme.

Table 5.17. Honduras

Details of tax revenue

Million HNL

	1990	2000	2005	2010	2017	2018	2019	2020	2021	2022
Total tax revenue	**2 118**	**18 299**	**32 974**	**54 544**	**117 659**	**126 062**	**131 995**	**112 448**	**145 066**	**166 126**
1000 Taxes on income, profits and capital gains	**431**	**2 907**	**7 037**	**13 232**	**33 055**	**36 071**	**34 533**	**25 587**	**35 209**	**48 289**
1100 Of individuals	157	992	2 312	4 528	10 533	11 368	11 365	11 214	14 258	17 478
1110 On income and profits	157	992	2 312	4 528	10 533	11 368	11 365	11 214	14 258	17 478
1120 On capital gains	..	..	..	..	..	..	..	..	..	..
1200 Corporate	274	1 916	4 725	8 705	22 522	24 702	23 167	14 373	20 951	30 811
1210 On profits	274	1 916	4 725	8 705	22 522	24 702	23 167	14 373	20 951	30 811
Corporate income tax	274	1 916	4 121	7 400	20 668	22 083	20 538	12 731	18 286	26 509
Income tax surcharge	0	0	604	1 305	1 841	2 601	2 612	1 620	2 646	4 277
Special contribution of the cooperative sector	0	0	0	0	14	19	17	21	19	25
1220 On capital gains of corporates	..	..	..	..	..	..	..	..	..	..
1300 Unallocable between 1100 and 1200	0	0	0	0	0	0	0	0	0	0
2000 Social security contributions	**179**	**1 727**	**4 416**	**8 671**	**17 911**	**19 302**	**21 068**	**23 138**	**23 994**	**25 284**
2100 Employees	..	..	..	..	..	..	..	..	..	..
2110 On a payroll basis	..	..	..	..	..	..	..	..	..	..
2120 On an income tax basis	..	..	..	..	..	..	..	..	..	..
2200 Employers	..	..	..	..	..	..	..	..	..	..
2210 On a payroll basis	..	..	..	..	..	..	..	..	..	..
2220 On an income tax basis	..	..	..	..	..	..	..	..	..	..
2300 Self-employed or non-employed	..	..	..	..	..	..	..	..	..	..
2310 On a payroll basis	..	..	..	..	..	..	..	..	..	..
2320 On an income tax basis	..	..	..	..	..	..	..	..	..	..
2400 Unallocable between 2100, 2200 and 2300	179	1 727	4 416	8 671	17 911	19 302	21 068	23 138	23 994	25 284
2410 On a payroll basis	179	1 727	4 416	8 671	17 911	19 302	21 068	23 138	23 994	25 284
2420 On an income tax basis	0	0	0	0	0	0	0	0	0	0
3000 Taxes on payroll and workforce	**0**	**0**	**0**	**485**	**925**	**1 025**	**1 005**	**935**	**1 081**	**1 215**
4000 Taxes on property	**16**	**266**	**631**	**994**	**3 046**	**3 243**	**3 428**	**2 954**	**4 119**	**4 881**
4100 Recurrent taxes on immovable property	16	189	170	254	344	435	446	282	586	720
4110 Households	..	..	..	..	..	..	..	..	..	..
4120 Others	..	..	..	..	..	..	..	..	..	..
4200 Recurrent taxes on net wealth	0	78	144	359	349	278	341	328	469	439
4210 Individual	..	..	..	..	..	..	..	..	..	..
4220 Corporate	..	..	..	..	..	..	..	..	..	..
4300 Estate, inheritance and gift taxes	0	0	0	0	0	0	0	0	0	0
4310 Estate and inheritance taxes	..	..	..	..	..	..	..	..	..	..
4320 Gift taxes	..	..	..	..	..	..	..	..	..	..
4400 Taxes on financial and capital transactions	0	0	0	0	2 353	2 531	2 641	2 344	3 064	3 722
4500 Non-recurrent taxes	0	0	316	380	0	0	0	0	0	0
4510 On net wealth	..	..	0	0	..	..	..	..	..	..
4520 Other non-recurrent taxes	..	..	316	380	..	..	..	..	..	..
4600 Other recurrent taxes on property	0	0	0	0	0	0	0	0	0	0
5000 Taxes on goods and services	**1 401**	**12 436**	**19 032**	**28 937**	**60 580**	**64 017**	**66 742**	**55 520**	**75 817**	**80 525**
5100 Taxes on production, sale, transfer, etc	1 401	12 436	19 032	28 937	60 580	64 017	66 742	55 520	75 817	80 525
5110 General taxes	344	5 146	9 565	16 050	39 228	41 562	42 891	35 815	49 264	56 067
5111 Value added taxes	344	5 146	9 565	16 050	39 228	41 562	42 891	35 815	49 264	56 067
5112 Sales tax	0	0	0	0	0	0	0	0	0	0
5113 Other	0	0	0	0	0	0	0	0	0	0
5120 Taxes on specific goods and services	1 057	7 290	9 468	12 887	21 352	22 454	23 851	19 705	26 553	24 458
5121 Excises	256	4 592	6 322	8 458	16 405	17 011	18 285	15 598	20 048	16 664
Beer	70	376	338	376	974	1 150	1 339	1 164	1 754	1 766
Soft drinks	25	240	268	514	938	979	1 075	1 073	1 332	1 351
Liquors	32	48	69	121	192	227	217	206	297	318
Petroleum products	43	347	0	0	0	0	0	0	0	0
Cigarettes	57	369	437	607	563	565	514	471	531	647
Fuel tax	0	2 954	4 916	6 288	12 773	13 061	14 131	11 951	14 919	11 004
Other	28	258	295	551	965	1 028	1 010	733	1 215	1 578
5122 Profits of fiscal monopolies	0	0	0	0	0	0	0	0	0	0
5123 Customs and import duties	498	2 083	2 174	2 505	4 244	4 485	4 474	3 282	5 288	6 501
Petroleum	0	297	0	0	0	0	0	0	0	0
Other	498	1 786	2 174	2 505	4 244	4 485	4 474	3 282	5 288	6 501
5124 Taxes on exports	217	6	0	0	79	90	18	10	76	21
Bananas	39	5	..	..	0	0	0	0	0	0
Coffee	1	0	..	..	0	0	0	0	0	0
Temporary export tax	163	0	..	..	0	0	0	0	0	0
Special contribution of the mining sector	0	0	..	..	79	90	18	10	76	21
Other	15	1	..	..	0	0	0	0	0	0
5125 Taxes on investment goods	0	0	0	0	0	0	0	0	0	0

	1990	2000	2005	2010	2017	2018	2019	2020	2021	2022
5126 Taxes on specific services	0	0	0	0	84	80	49	41	44	42
Special contribution of mobile services	..	..	..	..	55	49	35	36	36	35
Special contribution of the food and services sector	..	..	..	..	25	26	9	3	5	2
Special contribution of casino games and slot machines	..	..	..	..	4	4	5	2	3	5
5127 Other taxes on internat. trade and transactions	0	0	0	0	0	0	0	0	0	0
5128 Other taxes	87	610	971	1 924	539	789	1 025	774	1 097	1 230
5130 Unallocable between 5110 and 5120	0	0	0	0	0	0	0	0	0	0
5200 Taxes on use of goods and perform activities	0	0	0	0	0	0	0	0	0	0
5210 Recurrent taxes	..	..	..	..	..	..	..	..	..	..
5211 Paid by households: motor vehicles	..	..	..	..	..	..	..	..	..	..
5212 Paid by others: motor vehicles	..	..	..	..	..	..	..	..	..	..
5213 Paid in respect of other goods	..	..	..	..	..	..	..	..	..	..
5220 Non-recurrent taxes	..	..	..	..	..	..	..	..	..	..
5300 Unallocable between 5100 and 5200	0	0	0	0	0	0	0	0	0	0
6000 Other taxes	**91**	**962**	**1 858**	**2 225**	**2 142**	**2 404**	**5 220**	**4 315**	**4 847**	**5 931**
6100 Paid solely by business	0	0	0	0	0	0	0	0	0	0
6200 Other	91	962	1 858	2 225	2 142	2 404	5 220	4 315	4 847	5 931

.. Not available

Note: Year ending 31st December.

The data are on a cash basis.

Figures for local tax revenues may include non-tax revenues and central government transfers which are not considered as tax revenues according to the OECD classification, described in the Interpretative Guide, but it has not been possible to distinguish the different components within the aggregate data.

Heading 3000: The employer contributions to the National Institute of Vocational Training (INFOP) are included in heading 3000. The tax revenue is classified under the central government. In Honduras this revenue is classified under a separate unit considered to be different to the central government.

Source: Servicio de Administración de Rentas (Revenue Administration Service); Secretaría de Finanzas (Ministry of Finance).

Table 5.18. Jamaica

Details of tax revenue

Million JMD

	1990	2000	2005	2010	2017	2018	2019	2020	2021	2022
Total tax revenue	**7 748**	**87 713**	**163 154**	**287 139**	**517 091**	**562 009**	**602 592**	**544 211**	**616 467**	**768 574**
1000 Taxes on income, profits and capital gains	**3 639**	**35 457**	**62 702**	**105 917**	**129 925**	**144 581**	**155 140**	**155 632**	**167 112**	**206 743**
1100 Of individuals	1 687	17 441	36 043	54 798	60 306	62 644	69 323	72 692	77 756	96 902
1110 On income and profits	1 687	17 441	36 043	54 798	60 306	62 644	69 323	72 692	77 756	96 902
PAYE	1 489	16 515	34 223	50 828	54 879	57 472	63 716	67 228	72 416	90 077
Other individuals	198	926	1 820	3 969	5 427	5 [illegible]73	5 607	5 464	5 340	6 825
1120 On capital gains	..	..	..	..	..	..	..	..	..	..
1200 Corporate	1 280	7 627	13 134	33 091	61 401	62 504	67 623	61 823	68 791	79 485
1210 On profits	1 280	7 627	13 134	33 091	61 401	62 504	67 623	61 823	68 791	79 485
Bauxite/alumina	134	430	446	866	0	0	0	0	0	0
Other companies	1 146	7 197	12 688	32 224	60 431	61 427	67 251	61 665	68 646	79 355
Minimum business tax	0	0	0	0	970	1 077	372	159	145	129
1220 On capital gains of corporates	..	..	..	..	..	..	..	..	..	..
1300 Unallocable between 1100 and 1200	672	10 389	13 525	18 028	8 218	19 433	18 194	21 117	20 565	30 356
Tax on dividends	68	854	248	1 059	1 801	1 987	2 368	2 757	2 536	3 379
Tax on interests	605	9 535	13 277	16 970	6 417	17 446	15 827	18 360	18 029	26 977
2000 Social security contributions	**..**	**..**	**4 924**	**8 199**	**19 249**	**21 033**	**24 569**	**25 076**	**31 671**	**42 531**
2100 Employees	..	..	..	..	..	..	..	..	..	..
2110 On a payroll basis	..	..	..	..	..	..	..	..	..	..
2120 On an income tax basis	..	..	..	..	..	..	..	..	..	..
2200 Employers	..	..	..	..	..	..	..	..	..	..
2210 On a payroll basis	..	..	..	..	..	..	..	..	..	..
2220 On an income tax basis	..	..	..	..	..	..	..	..	..	..
2300 Self-employed or non-employed	..	..	..	..	..	..	..	..	..	..
2310 On a payroll basis	..	..	..	..	..	..	..	..	..	..
2320 On an income tax basis	..	..	..	..	..	..	..	..	..	..
2400 Unallocable between 2100, 2200 and 2300	..	..	4 924	8 199	19 249	21 033	24 569	25 076	31 671	42 531
2410 On a payroll basis	..	..	..	..	..	..	..	..	..	..
2420 On an income tax basis	..	..	..	..	..	..	..	..	..	..
3000 Taxes on payroll and workforce	**305**	**3 821**	**7 193**	**12 792**	**25 865**	**28 541**	**31 294**	**30 813**	**32 063**	**38 188**
4000 Taxes on property	**965**	**4 262**	**10 796**	**9 939**	**23 583**	**24 793**	**19 117**	**15 600**	**18 155**	**21 115**
4100 Recurrent taxes on immovable property	67	639	1 455	2 600	8 523	8 478	9 020	7 996	9 546	9 716
4110 Households	67	639	1 455	2 600	8 523	8 478	9 020	7 996	9 546	9 716
Municipal property tax	0	639	1 455	2 600	8 523	8 478	9 020	7 996	9 546	9 716
Other property taxes	67	0	0	0	0	0	0	0	0	0
4120 Others	0	0	0	0	0	0	0	0	0	0
4200 Recurrent taxes on net wealth	0	0	0	0	0	0	0	0	0	0
4210 Individual	..	..	..	..	..	..	..	..	..	..
4220 Corporate	..	..	..	..	..	..	..	..	..	..
4300 Estate, inheritance and gift taxes	0	0	0	0	0	0	0	0	0	0
4310 Estate and inheritance taxes	..	..	..	..	..	..	..	..	..	..
4320 Gift taxes	..	..	..	..	..	..	..	..	..	..
4400 Taxes on financial and capital transactions	898	3 623	9 341	7 339	15 060	16 315	10 097	7 603	8 609	11 399
Stamp duty	898	3 623	9 341	7 339	15 060	16 315	10 097	7 603	8 609	11 399
4500 Non-recurrent taxes	0	0	0	0	0	0	0	0	0	0
4510 On net wealth	..	..	..	..	..	..	..	..	..	..
4520 Other non-recurrent taxes	..	..	..	..	..	..	..	..	..	..
4600 Other recurrent taxes on property	0	0	0	0	0	0	0	0	0	0
5000 Taxes on goods and services	**2 824**	**43 907**	**77 065**	**149 544**	**316 601**	**340 651**	**370 321**	**315 268**	**365 499**	**457 446**
5100 Taxes on production, sale, transfer, etc	2 760	43 107	75 954	147 500	311 911	335 [illegible]89	363 429	308 011	357 080	448 649
5110 General taxes	297	22 356	45 602	84 409	171 584	187 576	203 297	177 354	199 638	253 358
5111 Value added taxes	293	22 356	45 602	82 407	168 112	183 646	199 150	173 480	194 725	246 993
General consumption tax	293	22 356	45 602	82 407	168 112	183 646	199 150	173 480	194 725	246 993
5112 Sales tax	4	0	0	0	0	0	0	0	0	0
Sales tax on used cars	4	..	..	..	..	..	..	..	..	..
5113 Other	0	0	0	2 002	3 472	3 930	4 147	3 873	4 913	6 364
Environmental levy	..	..	..	2 002	3 472	3 930	4 147	3 873	4 913	6 364
5120 Taxes on specific goods and services	2 463	20 752	30 352	63 091	140 327	147 613	160 133	130 658	157 442	195 291
5121 Excises	1 158	9 751	12 387	38 112	75 152	75 [illegible]69	80 773	69 949	84 782	96 588
Special consumption tax	1 115	9 751	12 387	38 112	75 112	75 [illegible]03	80 693	69 852	84 704	96 475
Quarry tax	0	0	0	0	39	66	80	97	78	113
Other excises	44	0	0	0	0	0	0	0	0	0
5122 Profits of fiscal monopolies	0	0	0	0	0	0	0	0	0	0
5123 Customs and import duties	782	8 498	14 999	19 959	37 737	41 243	44 809	40 420	47 762	60 695
5124 Taxes on exports	0	0	0	0	0	0	0	0	0	0
5125 Taxes on investment goods	0	0	0	0	0	0	0	0	0	0

	1990	2000	2005	2010	2017	2018	2019	2020	2021	2022
5126 Taxes on specific services	523	2 503	2 966	5 020	27 438	31 202	34 550	20 289	24 898	38 009
Travel tax	86	1 999	1 914	3 512	18 659	20 114	21 954	9 108	12 624	23 274
Telephone call tax	86	0	0	0	3 543	3 247	3 568	3 619	3 414	3 252
Betting, gaming and lottery	50	504	1 052	1 508	2 639	5 205	6 152	6 163	7 229	8 401
Accommodation tax	87	0	0	0	2 598	2 636	2 877	1 400	1 631	3 082
Bank and trust	204	0	0	0	0	0	0	0	0	0
Entertainment tax	11	0	0	0	0	0	0	0	0	0
5127 Other taxes on internat. trade and transactions	0	0	0	0	0	0	0	0	0	0
5128 Other taxes	0	0	0	0	0	0	0	0	0	0
5130 Unallocable between 5110 and 5120	0	0	0	0	0	0	0	0	0	0
5200 Taxes on use of goods and perform activities	64	800	1 111	2 045	4 690	5 463	6 892	7 257	8 419	8 797
5210 Recurrent taxes	64	800	1 111	2 045	4 690	5 463	6 892	7 257	8 419	8 797
5211 Paid by households: motor vehicles	47	751	935	1 775	3 768	4 334	4 863	4 528	4 864	5 668
5212 Paid by others: motor vehicles	0	0	0	0	0	0	0	0	0	0
5213 Paid in respect of other goods	17	49	176	270	922	1 129	2 029	2 728	3 555	3 129
5220 Non-recurrent taxes	0	0	0	0	0	0	0	0	0	0
5300 Unallocable between 5100 and 5200	0	0	0	0	0	0	0	0	0	0
6000 Other taxes	**16**	**266**	**475**	**748**	**1 868**	**2 410**	**2 151**	**1 824**	**1 967**	**2 551**
6100 Paid solely by business	0	0	0	0	0	0	0	0	0	0
6200 Other	16	266	475	748	1 868	2 410	2 151	1 824	1 967	2 551
Contractors levy	16	266	475	748	1 868	2 410	2 151	1 824	1 967	2 551

.. Not available

Note: Year ending 31st December, except for 1990-2003 which refer to fiscal year ending 31st March due to data availability.

The data are on a cash basis.

Heading 2000: The figures include contributions to National Insurance Scheme (NIS).

Heading 3000: Education tax in Jamaica includes contributions from employees, employers and the self-employed calculated based on their emoluments. The employer contributions account for the majority of the total contributions.

Source: Ministry of Finance and the Public Service; Tax Administration Jamaica.

Table 5.19. Mexico

Details of tax revenue

Million MXN

	1990	2000	2005	2010	2017	2013	2019	2020	2021	2022
Total tax revenue	**102 005**	**767 216**	**1 086 482**	**1 716 243**	**3 527 032**	**3 797 888**	**3 995 654**	**4 148 699**	**4 452 355**	**4 818 014**
1000 Taxes on income, profits and capital gains	**34 673**	**276 548**	**402 036**	**683 604**	**1 571 954**	**1 671 513**	**1 694 143**	**1 768 161**	**1 903 047**	**2 280 791**
1100 Of individuals	..	..	195 869	313 473	754 109	804 236	829 501	872 598	938 623	1 066 965
Tax on income of individuals	..	..	195 869	313 473	754 109	804 236	829 501	872 598	938 623	1 066 965
1110 On income and profits	..	..	..	..	..	..	..	..	..	..
1120 On capital gains	..	..	..	..	..	..	..	..	..	..
1200 Corporate	..	..	135 840	246 745	769 193	809 834	803 643	832 120	898 767	1 136 636
Tax on income of corporations	..	..	135 840	246 745	769 193	809 834	803 643	832 120	898 767	1 136 636
1210 On profits	..	..	..	..	..	..	..	..	..	..
1220 On capital gains of corporates	..	..	..	..	..	..	..	..	..	..
1300 Unallocable between 1100 and 1200	34 673	276 548	70 327	123 386	48 652	57 443	60 999	63 443	65 657	77 190
Tax on income of other individuals and corporations	..	244 841	40 780	66 937	46 004	50 878	54 686	58 196	58 306	70 239
Tax on asset	..	13 913	12 033	-624	-1 069	-396	-585	-1 245	-380	31
Credit on salary	..	17 794	17 514	9 708	1 036	1 172	1 290	479	512	107
Oil yields tax	..	0	0	2 296	0	0	0	0	0	0
IETU	..	0	0	45 069	-1 648	319	-195	-888	200	-346
Imposed by Activity Exploration and extraction of hydrocarbon	..	0	0	0	4 330	5 470	5 803	6 902	7 019	7 160
2000 Social security contributions	**17 165**	**138 223**	**206 551**	**277 459**	**467 619**	**509 087**	**552 058**	**576 019**	**612 175**	**681 672**
2100 Employees	..	..	..	..	..	..	..	..	..	..
2110 On a payroll basis	..	..	..	..	..	..	..	..	..	..
2120 On an income tax basis	..	..	..	..	..	..	..	..	..	..
2200 Employers	..	..	..	..	..	..	..	..	..	..
2210 On a payroll basis	..	..	..	..	..	..	..	..	..	..
2220 On an income tax basis	..	..	..	..	..	..	..	..	..	..
2300 Self-employed or non-employed	..	..	..	..	..	..	..	..	..	..
2310 On a payroll basis	..	..	..	..	..	..	..	..	..	..
2320 On an income tax basis	..	..	..	..	..	..	..	..	..	..
2400 Unallocable between 2100, 2200 and 2300	17 165	138 223	206 551	277 459	467 619	509 087	552 058	576 019	612 175	681 672
2410 On a payroll basis	..	138 223	206 551	277 459	467 619	509 087	552 058	576 019	612 175	681 672
2420 On an income tax basis	..	0	0	0	0	0	0	0	0	0
3000 Taxes on payroll and workforce	**1 797**	**11 217**	**20 461**	**36 911**	**84 099**	**93 303**	**101 284**	**105 456**	**116 910**	**141 140**
Substitute tax on salary	..	0	0	0	0	0	0	0	0	0
Payroll tax	..	11 101	15 746	27 813	83 608	92 833	100 798	104 825	115 974	139 977
Tax on remuneration to the personal work	..	65	4 562	8 841	246	270	298	407	579	837
Tax on professions and fees	..	36	53	71	103	111	121	177	235	263
Tax on operations by contract	..	15	100	186	141	90	67	47	121	64
4000 Taxes on property	**1 914**	**13 964**	**26 796**	**38 955**	**67 836**	**77 110**	**79 262**	**79 237**	**90 204**	**90 123**
4100 Recurrent taxes on immovable property	1 036	9 948	16 641	25 724	44 680	49 445	50 540	52 728	56 146	56 112
4110 Households	0	0	0	0	0	0	0	0	0	0
4120 Others	1 036	9 948	16 641	25 724	44 680	49 445	50 540	52 728	56 146	56 112
Property tax	..	9 948	16 641	25 724	44 680	49 445	50 540	52 728	56 146	56 112
4200 Recurrent taxes on net wealth	0	0	0	0	0	0	0	0	0	0
4210 Individual	..	..	..	..	..	..	..	..	..	..
4220 Corporate	..	..	..	..	..	..	..	..	..	..
4300 Estate, inheritance and gift taxes	8	0	0	0	0	0	0	0	0	0
4310 Estate and inheritance taxes	8	..	..	..	..	..	..	..	..	..
4320 Gift taxes	0	..	..	..	..	..	..	..	..	..
4400 Taxes on financial and capital transactions	870	4 017	10 155	13 231	23 156	27 665	28 722	26 509	34 057	34 011
Alienation of immovable property	..	1 763	984	1 122	1 623	1 823	1 939	1 982	2 486	2 762
Transfer of ownership of real estate	..	2 236	5 528	5 027	7 016	8 658	8 385	12 072	11 394	15 124
Purchasing property	..	18	3 643	7 082	14 516	17 184	18 397	12 456	20 177	16 125
4500 Non-recurrent taxes	0	0	0	0	0	0	0	0	0	0
4510 On net wealth	..	..	..	..	..	..	..	..	..	..
4520 Other non-recurrent taxes	..	..	..	..	..	..	..	..	..	..
4600 Other recurrent taxes on property	0	0	0	0	0	0	0	0	0	0
5000 Taxes on goods and services	**44 837**	**319 612**	**418 945**	**651 915**	**1 283 049**	**1 381 659**	**1 504 252**	**1 544 156**	**1 647 926**	**1 496 589**
5100 Taxes on production, sale, transfer, etc	44 171	310 325	403 158	630 123	1 262 770	1 364 208	1 486 758	1 527 674	1 630 615	1 479 144
5110 General taxes	26 635	189 606	318 432	504 509	816 048	922 238	933 327	987 525	1 123 699	1 221 803
5111 Value added taxes	26 635	189 606	318 432	504 509	816 048	922 238	933 327	987 525	1 123 699	1 221 803
5112 Sales tax	0	0	0	0	0	0	0	0	0	0
5113 Other	0	0	0	0	0	0	0	0	0	0
5120 Taxes on specific goods and services	17 519	120 720	84 726	125 614	446 722	441 970	553 432	540 149	506 917	257 341
5121 Excises	10 072	86 163	55 286	86 098	378 537	353 577	470 993	469 040	410 450	132 593
Special tax on production and services	..	81 544	49 627	81 427	367 834	347 436	460 496	460 674	399 154	117 533
Tax on new automobiles	..	4 619	5 659	4 671	10 703	11 142	10 497	8 366	11 296	15 060
Tax on luxury goods and services	..	0	0	0	0	0	0	0	0	0
5122 Profits of fiscal monopolies	0	0	0	0	0	0	0	0	0	0

	1990	2000	2005	2010	2017	2018	2019	2020	2021	2022
5123 Customs and import duties	6 998	33 285	27 512	26 602	53 793	67 232	66 295	59 247	77 236	95 901
Step customs officer	..	423	692	2 071	1 463	1 690	1 554	1 309	1 697	2 229
Import taxes	..	32 861	26 820	24 531	52 330	65 543	64 741	57 938	75 539	93 672
5124 Taxes on exports	75	4	0	0	0	0	0	0	0	0
Tax on exports	..	4	0	0	0	0	0	0	0	0
5125 Taxes on investment goods	0	0	0	0	0	0	0	0	0	0
5126 Taxes on specific services	132	1 042	1 578	10 958	7 778	8 692	9 196	5 625	9 265	13 575
IDE	..	0	0	8 022	-739	-629	-405	-252	-135	-152
Tax on lodging	..	504	798	1 384	3 598	3 945	4 254	2 500	4 119	6 411
Public entertainment tax	..	240	349	462	839	909	924	467	393	1 149
Tax on lotteries, raffles and gambling	..	267	417	923	2 717	2 947	3 403	2 114	3 799	3 921
Tax on commercials	..	4	15	166	1 082	1 231	376	0	0	0
Various indirect taxes	..	28	0	1	282	288	644	795	1 089	2 247
5127 Other taxes on internat. trade and transactions	0	0	0	0	0	0	0	0	0	0
5128 Other taxes	242	226	350	1 956	6 613	7 468	6 947	6 238	9 966	15 271
Mining fees	..	226	350	1 956	6 613	7 468	6 947	6 238	9 966	15 271
5130 Unallocable between 5110 and 5120	17	0	0	0	0	0	0	0	0	0
5200 Taxes on use of goods and perform activities	666	9 287	15 787	21 793	20 279	17 451	17 494	16 482	17 311	17 445
5210 Recurrent taxes	666	9 287	15 787	21 793	20 279	17 451	17 494	16 482	17 311	17 445
5211 Paid by households: motor vehicles	567	8 878	15 237	21 319	19 530	16 533	16 624	15 699	16 422	16 311
Tax on motor vehicules	..	8 878	15 237	21 319	19 530	16 533	16 624	15 699	16 422	16 311
5212 Paid by others: motor vehicles	0	301	357	281	554	640	645	437	605	705
Tax on federal auto transport	..	301	357	281	554	640	645	437	605	705
5213 Paid in respect of other goods	99	108	193	193	194	278	225	347	285	429
Sport fishing	..	40	80	59	71	73	73	55	69	87
Sport hunting	..	3	0	0	0	0	0	0	0	0
Tax on commercial activities	..	63	113	50	28	115	41	159	39	97
Trade in books and magazines	..	0	0	0	0	0	0	0	0	0
Tax on industrial activities	..	2	0	82	77	73	92	113	113	51
Mining	..	0	0	1	18	17	17	19	64	194
5220 Non-recurrent taxes	0	0	0	0	0	0	0	0	0	0
5300 Unallocable between 5100 and 5200	0	0	0	0	0	0	0	0	0	0
6000 Other taxes	**1 619**	**7 651**	**11 693**	**27 398**	**52 475**	**65 217**	**64 654**	**75 671**	**82 092**	**127 699**
6100 Paid solely by business	0	0	0	0	0	0	0	0	0	0
6200 Other	1 619	7 651	11 693	27 398	52 475	65 217	64 654	75 671	82 092	127 699
Accessories	..	5 504	9 543	22 206	32 153	45 864	41 063	56 793	54 231	83 591
Unallocable between 1000 and 5000 caused in exercices fiscal previous liquidation slopes or of payment	..	374	-927	30	281	400	79	218	304	328
Additional state and local taxes	..	1 773	3 077	5 162	20 042	18 952	23 512	18 660	27 558	43 780

.. Not available

Note: Year ending 31st December.

The data are on a cash basis.

Heading 1000: In ECLAC data, income taxes are presented net of credit on salary figures.

Heading 2000: In ECLAC data, social security contributions are presented net of transfers from the Federal government for the payment of IMSS (Mexican Social Security Institute) pensions.

Source: Ministry of Finance, Economic Department.

Table 5.20. Nicaragua

Details of tax revenue

Million NIO

	1990	2000	2005	2010	2017	2018	2019	2020	2021	2022
Total tax revenue	..	**9 300**	**18 353**	**36 162**	**98 803**	**95 459**	**107 333**	**110 648**	**134 518**	**156 174**
1000 Taxes on income, profits and capital gains	..	**1 144**	**3 902**	**8 351**	**28 557**	**29 258**	**33 036**	**32 470**	**40 753**	**50 714**
1100 Of individuals	..	299	925	1 857	6 468	6 780	6 561	5 833	7 753	9 648
1110 On income and profits	..	299	925	1 857	6 468	6 780	6 561	5 833	7 753	9 648
1120 On capital gains	..	..	..	..	..	..	..	..	..	..
1200 Corporate	..	845	2 977	6 494	22 089	22 478	26 475	25 637	33 000	41 066
1210 On profits	..	845	2 977	6 494	22 089	22 478	26 475	25 637	33 000	41 066
1220 On capital gains of corporates	..	..	..	..	..	..	..	..	..	..
1300 Unallocable between 1100 and 1200	..	0	0	0	0	0	0	0	0	0
2000 Social security contributions	..	**1 678**	**3 363**	**8 090**	**23 868**	**24 624**	**27 586**	**29 014**	**32 054**	**35 571**
2100 Employees	..	..	..	..	..	..	..	..	..	..
2110 On a payroll basis	..	..	..	..	..	..	..	..	..	..
2120 On an income tax basis	..	..	..	..	..	..	..	..	..	..
2200 Employers	..	..	..	..	..	..	..	..	..	..
2210 On a payroll basis	..	..	..	..	..	..	..	..	..	..
2220 On an income tax basis	..	..	..	..	..	..	..	..	..	..
2300 Self-employed or non-employed	..	..	..	..	..	..	..	..	..	..
2310 On a payroll basis	..	..	..	..	..	..	..	..	..	..
2320 On an income tax basis	..	..	..	..	..	..	..	..	..	..
2400 Unallocable between 2100, 2200 and 2300	..	1 678	3 363	8 090	23 868	24 624	27 586	29 014	32 054	35 571
2410 On a payroll basis	..	1 678	3 363	8 090	23 868	24 624	27 586	29 014	32 054	35 571
2420 On an income tax basis	..	0	0	0	0	0	0	0	0	0
3000 Taxes on payroll and workforce	..	**0**	**0**	**0**	**0**	**0**	**0**	**0**	**0**	**0**
4000 Taxes on property	..	**11**	**227**	**423**	**896**	**961**	**1 196**	**1 401**	**1 778**	**1 815**
4100 Recurrent taxes on immovable property	..	0	211	403	808	881	1 129	1 346	1 707	1 726
4110 Households	..	..	..	..	..	..	..	..	..	..
4120 Others	..	..	..	..	..	..	..	..	..	..
4200 Recurrent taxes on net wealth	..	0	0	0	0	0	0	0	0	0
4210 Individual	..	..	..	..	..	..	..	..	..	..
4220 Corporate	..	..	..	..	..	..	..	..	..	..
4300 Estate, inheritance and gift taxes	..	0	0	0	0	0	0	0	0	0
4310 Estate and inheritance taxes	..	..	..	..	..	..	..	..	..	..
4320 Gift taxes	..	..	..	..	..	..	..	..	..	..
4400 Taxes on financial and capital transactions	..	11	17	20	88	80	67	55	71	90
Stamp duties	..	11	17	20	88	80	67	55	71	90
4500 Non-recurrent taxes	..	0	0	0	0	0	0	0	0	0
4510 On net wealth	..	..	..	..	..	..	..	..	..	..
4520 Other non-recurrent taxes	..	..	..	..	..	..	..	..	..	..
4600 Other recurrent taxes on property	..	0	0	0	0	0	0	0	0	0
5000 Taxes on goods and services	..	**5 584**	**10 649**	**18 951**	**44 563**	**39 817**	**44 608**	**46 487**	**58 693**	**66 654**
5100 Taxes on production, sale, transfer, etc	..	5 584	10 485	18 608	43 619	38 782	43 674	45 505	57 630	65 415
5110 General taxes	..	2 931	6 359	11 932	29 201	25 792	27 933	29 002	37 772	43 273
5111 Value added taxes	..	2 931	5 599	10 353	25 551	21 905	24 116	24 990	32 998	38 081
5112 Sales tax	..	0	0	0	0	0	0	0	0	0
5113 Other	..	0	761	1 579	3 650	3 888	3 817	4 012	4 774	5 192
5120 Taxes on specific goods and services	..	2 653	4 126	6 676	14 419	12 990	15 741	16 503	19 858	22 142
5121 Excises	..	2 034	3 227	5 541	11 764	10 931	13 616	14 163	16 549	18 191
Alcoholic beverages	..	84	102	198	355	353	583	702	626	713
Beer	..	203	340	645	1 649	1 663	1 857	1 939	2 269	2 401
Cigarettes	..	70	143	45	0	0	0	0	0	0
Soft drinks	..	123	128	248	545	523	470	539	611	753
Petroleum products	..	1 359	1 756	2 699	5 534	5 395	5 589	5 561	6 846	6 900
Gaming machines	..	0	0	0	0	90	120	118	137	147
Excises on imports	..	196	734	1 559	3 541	2 763	4 805	5 083	5 794	7 057
Other excises	..	-1	25	148	140	145	193	222	267	221
5122 Profits of fiscal monopolies	..	0	0	0	0	0	0	0	0	0
5123 Customs and import duties	..	619	899	1 135	2 654	2 058	2 125	2 340	3 309	3 950
Custom duties	..	452	880	1 094	2 623	2 058	2 125	2 340	3 309	3 950
Temporary protection duty	..	96	0	0	0	0	0	0	0	0
On products originating in Colombia or Honduras	..	72	18	41	31	0	0	0	0	1
5124 Taxes on exports	..	0	0	0	0	0	0	0	0	0
5125 Taxes on investment goods	..	0	0	0	0	0	0	0	0	0
5126 Taxes on specific services	..	0	0	0	0	0	0	0	0	0
5127 Other taxes on internat. trade and transactions	..	0	0	0	0	0	0	0	0	0
5128 Other taxes	..	0	0	0	0	0	0	0	0	0
5130 Unallocable between 5110 and 5120	..	0	0	0	0	0	0	0	0	0
5200 Taxes on use of goods and perform activities	..	0	163	343	943	1 035	934	982	1 063	1 239
5210 Recurrent taxes	..	..	18	20	59	59	61	63	68	80

	1990	2000	2005	2010	2017	2018	2019	2020	2021	2022
5211 Paid by households: motor vehicles	..	..	18	20	59	59	61	63	68	80
5212 Paid by others: motor vehicles	..	..	0	0	0	0	0	0	0	0
5213 Paid in respect of other goods	..	..	0	0	0	0	0	0	0	0
5220 Non-recurrent taxes	..	..	145	323	884	976	874	919	994	1 159
5300 Unallocable between 5100 and 5200	..	0	0	0	0	0	0	0	0	0
6000 Other taxes	**..**	**0**	**212**	**347**	**919**	**798**	**907**	**1 275**	**1 240**	**1 420**
6100 Paid solely by business	..	..	0	0	0	0	0	0	0	0
6200 Other	..	..	212	347	919	798	907	1 275	1 240	1 420

.. Not available

Note: Year ending 31st December.

The data are on a cash basis.

Comparable statistics for 1990 cannot be shown due to the devaluation of the Nicaraguan cordoba.

Figures for local tax revenues are estimated for 2022 as data are not available. Data for social security contributions have been preliminary since 2014.

Heading 1000: The split between PIT (heading 1100) and CIT (heading 1200) in 2022 is estimated.

Source: Ministerio de Hacienda y Crédito Público (Ministry of Finance and Public Credit); Centro Interamericano de Administraciones Tributarias (Inter-American Centre of Tax Administrations).

Table 5.21. Panama

Details of tax revenue

Million PAB

	1990	2000	2005	2010	2017	2018	2019	2020	2021	2022
Total tax revenue	**948**	**1 942**	**2 257**	**4 815**	**9 366**	**9 631**	**9 382**	**7 240**	**8 106**	**10 038**
1000 Taxes on income, profits and capital gains	**217**	**485**	**563**	**1 317**	**2 451**	**2 672**	**2 445**	**1 880**	**1 998**	**2 808**
1100 Of individuals	140	295	303	440	1 088	1 193	1 135	965	1 101	1 418
1110 On income and profits	140	295	303	440	1 088	1 193	1 135	965	1 101	1 418
Payroll	115	222	227	353	931	1 049	992	838	967	1 269
Personal income tax	14	20	24	35	68	54	49	32	38	46
Panama Canal Authority withholding	10	53	52	52	89	90	94	94	97	103
1120 On capital gains	..	..	..	..	..	..	..	..	..	..
1200 Corporate	66	159	213	603	943	955	902	595	582	954
1210 On profits	66	159	213	603	943	955	902	595	582	954
Colón Free Zone	5	3	4	20	41	53	45	30	41	69
Corporate income tax	61	155	208	584	902	901	857	565	541	885
1220 On capital gains of corporates	..	..	..	..	..	..	..	..	..	..
1300 Unallocable between 1100 and 1200	11	31	47	273	420	524	407	320	315	435
Dividends and complimentary tax	11	31	47	166	253	307	266	218	210	269
Capital gains	0	0	0	107	167	217	142	102	105	167
2000 Social security contributions	**325**	**742**	**827**	**1 637**	**3 654**	**3 797**	**3 894**	**3 225**	**3 570**	**4 217**
2100 Employees	..	..	..	..	..	..	..	..	..	..
2110 On a payroll basis	..	..	..	..	..	..	..	..	..	..
2120 On an income tax basis	..	..	..	..	..	..	..	..	..	..
2200 Employers	..	..	..	..	..	..	..	..	..	..
2210 On a payroll basis	..	..	..	..	..	..	..	..	..	..
2220 On an income tax basis	..	..	..	..	..	..	..	..	..	..
2300 Self-employed or non-employed	..	..	..	..	..	..	..	..	..	..
2310 On a payroll basis	..	..	..	..	..	..	..	..	..	..
2320 On an income tax basis	..	..	..	..	..	..	..	..	..	..
2400 Unallocable between 2100, 2200 and 2300	325	742	827	1 637	3 654	3 797	3 894	3 225	3 570	4 217
2410 On a payroll basis	..	..	..	..	..	..	..	..	..	..
2420 On an income tax basis	..	..	..	..	..	..	..	..	..	..
3000 Taxes on payroll and workforce	**0**	**36**	**36**	**59**	**127**	**130**	**138**	**103**	**113**	**131**
Education insurance	..	36	36	59	127	130	138	103	113	131
4000 Taxes on property	**32**	**43**	**77**	**138**	**251**	**244**	**169**	**126**	**180**	**208**
4100 Recurrent taxes on immovable property	28	34	56	108	207	209	134	104	145	160
4110 Households	28	34	56	108	207	209	134	104	145	160
4120 Others	0	0	0	0	0	0	0	0	0	0
4200 Recurrent taxes on net wealth	0	0	0	0	0	0	0	0	0	0
4210 Individual	..	..	..	..	..	..	..	..	..	..
4220 Corporate	..	..	..	..	..	..	..	..	..	..
4300 Estate, inheritance and gift taxes	0	0	0	0	0	0	0	0	0	0
4310 Estate and inheritance taxes	..	..	..	..	..	..	..	..	..	..
4320 Gift taxes	..	..	..	..	..	..	..	..	..	..
4400 Taxes on financial and capital transactions	3	9	21	30	44	36	35	22	35	48
4500 Non-recurrent taxes	0	0	0	0	0	0	0	0	0	0
4510 On net wealth	..	..	..	..	..	..	..	..	..	..
4520 Other non-recurrent taxes	..	..	..	..	..	..	..	..	..	..
4600 Other recurrent taxes on property	0	0	0	0	0	0	0	0	0	0
5000 Taxes on goods and services	**349**	**608**	**726**	**1 623**	**2 849**	**2 754**	**2 705**	**1 887**	**2 221**	**2 648**
5100 Taxes on production, sale, transfer, etc	332	546	643	1 473	2 570	2 474	2 425	1 661	1 974	2 365
5110 General taxes	80	69	138	766	1 529	1 477	1 436	979	1 152	1 407
5111 Value added taxes	80	69	138	766	1 529	1 477	1 436	979	1 152	1 407
ITBMS on sales	31	69	138	399	983	957	954	659	710	863
ITBMS on imports	49	0	0	367	546	519	482	320	442	543
5112 Sales tax	0	0	0	0	0	0	0	0	0	0
5113 Other	0	0	0	0	0	0	0	0	0	0
5120 Taxes on specific goods and services	251	477	505	707	1 041	997	939	682	822	959
5121 Excises	0	141	106	239	480	449	438	301	368	431
Petroleum products	..	109	69	97	190	163	196	123	151	152
Beer	..	18	22	31	49	53	54	47	47	57
Cigarette	..	0	0	0	21	24	26	20	17	20
Wine and liquor	..	12	11	11	6	13	17	13	15	23
Soft drinks	..	2	3	6	7	11	11	7	6	6
Automobiles	..	0	0	0	182	149	138	69	105	142
Other excises	..	0	1	95	25	27	26	23	27	30
5122 Profits of fiscal monopolies	0	0	0	0	0	0	0	0	0	0
5123 Customs and import duties	125	298	364	390	358	338	319	215	286	323
5124 Taxes on exports	13	0	0	0	0	0	0	0	0	0
5125 Taxes on investment goods	0	0	0	0	0	0	0	0	0	0

	1990	2000	2005	2010	2017	2018	2019	2020	2021	2022
5126 Taxes on specific services	1	37	35	78	203	211	203	166	168	205
Insurance premiums	0	17	20	47	86	90	86	88	80	101
Cable and telecommunications	0	16	7	17	40	42	40	37	36	36
Gambling	0	0	1	1	52	53	50	16	29	42
Banks, financial institutions and exchange houses	0	2	7	12	25	26	26	25	23	26
Commercial activities and services	1	3	0	0	0	0	0	0	0	0
5127 Other taxes on internat. trade and transactions	0	0	0	0	0	0	0	0	0	0
5128 Other taxes	0	0	0	0	0	0	0	0	0	0
5130 Unallocable between 5110 and 5120	0	0	0	0	0	0	0	0	0	0
5200 Taxes on use of goods and perform activities	15	62	83	151	279	280	280	227	247	283
Other indirect taxes	0	0	0	36	69	66	61	42	50	60
5210 Recurrent taxes	12	58	75	115	210	214	219	184	197	222
5211 Paid by households: motor vehicles	0	7	8	0	0	0	0	0	0	0
5212 Paid by others: motor vehicles	0	5	4	0	0	0	0	0	0	0
5213 Paid in respect of other goods	12	46	63	115	210	214	219	184	197	222
Commercial licences	12	19	32	75	121	124	126	107	119	125
Permission to conduct commercial and service activities	0	25	29	38	84	86	89	73	75	94
Permission to conduct industrial activities	0	2	2	2	4	4	4	3	3	4
Others	0	0	1	0	0	0	0	0	0	0
5220 Non-recurrent taxes	4	4	7	0	0	0	0	0	0	0
Building and construction	0	4	7	..	..	..	..	..	..	..
Ship registration	4	0	0	..	..	..	..	..	..	..
5300 Unallocable between 5100 and 5200	2	0	0	0	0	0	0	0	0	0
6000 Other taxes	**26**	**27**	**27**	**41**	**34**	**34**	**30**	**20**	**24**	**28**
6100 Paid solely by business	0	0	0	0	0	0	0	0	0	0
6200 Other	26	27	27	41	34	34	30	20	24	28
Stamp duties	17	27	27	41	34	34	30	20	24	28
Others	9	0	0	0	0	0	0	0	0	0

.. Not available

Note: Year ending 31st December.

The data are on a cash basis.

Tax revenue data are exclusive of fiscal documents ("documentos fiscales") which are considered as wastable tax credits according to the OECD classification described in the Interpretative Guide. Central government tax revenue data for 2022 are preliminary. Local government tax revenue and social security contributions data for 2022 are estimated.

Heading 2000: Social security contributions include regular and special contributions and professional risks premium collected by the Caja de Seguro Social (CSS).

Heading 3000: In ECLAC data, education insurance is classified as "Other taxes" (6000).

Heading 5126: In CIAT and ECLAC data, tax on banks, financial institutions and exchange houses is classified as a property tax (4000).

Heading 6200: Stamp duties before 2000 include tax on telephone calls and cables which cannot be distinguished due to data availability.

Source: Contraloría General de la República de Panamá (Comptroller General of the Republic of Panama); Ministerio de Economía y Finanzas de Panamá (Ministry of Economy and Finance of Panama) Caja de Seguro Social (Social Security Fund); Centro Interamericano de Administraciones Tributarias (Inter-American Centre of Tax Administrations).

Table 5.22. Paraguay

Details of tax revenue

Million PYG

	1990	2000	2005	2010	2017	2018	2019	2020	2021	2022
Total tax revenue	**608 021**	**3 587 451**	**7 078 832**	**15 638 531**	**30 731 221**	**31 954 693**	**33 008 733**	**32 441 314**	**37 556 283**	**42 759 988**
1000 Taxes on income, profits and capital gains	**73 726**	**470 388**	**938 886**	**2 096 498**	**5 086 803**	**5 265 609**	**6 022 875**	**6 010 196**	**6 920 734**	**8 736 495**
1100 Of individuals	..	15 042	22 477	31 263	526 704	626 525	620 038	536 357	364 990	437 426
1110 On income and profits	..	15 042	22 477	31 263	526 704	626 525	620 038	536 357	364 990	437 426
IRAGRO-IMAGRO	..	15 042	22 477	30 113	326 555	360 003	327 328	277 061	14 567	3 475
Personal income tax	..	0	0	1 150	200 150	266 523	292 710	259 296	350 422	433 951
1120 On capital gains	..	..	..	..	..	..	..	..	..	..
1200 Corporate	..	455 346	916 409	2 065 235	4 560 099	4 639 084	5 402 837	5 473 839	6 555 744	8 299 069
1210 On profits	..	455 346	916 409	2 065 235	4 560 099	4 639 084	5 402 837	5 473 839	6 555 744	8 299 069
Income tax on small businesses	..	0	0	9 380	22 848	25 540	26 824	28 852	1 907	416
Single tax	..	4 238	5 802	715	2	-	0	0	0	0
Single tax on maquiladoras companies	..	0	289	3 310	20 194	27 070	31 201	35 229	53 255	59 260
IRACIS	..	451 108	910 318	2 051 830	4 517 056	4 586 475	5 344 811	1 302 426	215 069	115 514
Business income tax (IRE)	..	0	0	0	0	0	0	3 239 933	5 288 814	6 984 251
Tax on dividends and income (IDU)	..	0	0	0	0	0	0	867 399	996 698	1 139 627
1220 On capital gains of corporates	..	..	..	..	..	..	..	..	..	..
1300 Unallocable between 1100 and 1200	73 726	0	0	0	0	0	0	0	0	0
Others	73 726	..	..	..	..	..	..	..	..	..
2000 Social security contributions	**28 882**	**919 533**	**1 591 980**	**3 552 640**	**8 052 403**	**8 209 087**	**8 729 492**	**8 954 858**	**10 335 479**	**12 326 174**
2100 Employees	..	..	..	..	..	..	..	..	..	..
2110 On a payroll basis	..	..	..	..	..	..	..	..	..	..
2120 On an income tax basis	..	..	..	..	..	..	..	..	..	..
2200 Employers	..	..	..	..	..	..	..	..	..	..
2210 On a payroll basis	..	..	..	..	..	..	..	..	..	..
2220 On an income tax basis	..	..	..	..	..	..	..	..	..	..
2300 Self-employed or non-employed	..	..	..	..	..	..	..	..	..	..
2310 On a payroll basis	..	..	..	..	..	..	..	..	..	..
2320 On an income tax basis	..	..	..	..	..	..	..	..	..	..
2400 Unallocable between 2100, 2200 and 2300	28 882	919 533	1 591 980	3 552 640	8 052 403	8 209 087	8 729 492	8 954 858	10 335 479	12 326 174
2410 On a payroll basis	28 882	919 533	1 591 980	3 552 640	8 052 403	8 209 087	8 729 492	8 954 858	10 335 479	12 326 174
2420 On an income tax basis	0	0	0	0	0	0	0	0	0	0
3000 Taxes on payroll and workforce	**0**	**0**	**0**	**0**	**0**	**0**	**0**	**0**	**0**	**0**
4000 Taxes on property	**17 162**	**71 777**	**192 393**	**276 119**	**565 323**	**415 570**	**443 521**	**401 222**	**488 894**	**498 303**
4100 Recurrent taxes on immovable property	17 162	0	0	258 423	529 986	389 962	417 177	375 800	457 759	459 869
4110 Households	17 162	..	..	258 423	529 986	389 962	417 177	375 800	457 759	459 869
Real estate tax	17 162	..	..	249 697	501 873	359 235	378 712	342 625	408 189	414 357
Tax on vacant lots	0	..	..	2 925	13 600	17 411	20 985	19 608	25 876	24 577
Large estate and land tax	0	..	..	5 801	14 513	13 315	17 480	13 566	23 694	20 935
4120 Others	0	..	..	0	0	0	0	0	0	0
4200 Recurrent taxes on net wealth	0	0	0	0	0	0	0	0	0	0
4210 Individual	..	..	..	..	..	..	..	..	..	..
4220 Corporate	..	..	..	..	..	..	..	..	..	..
4300 Estate, inheritance and gift taxes	0	0	0	0	0	0	0	0	0	0
4310 Estate and inheritance taxes	..	..	..	..	..	..	..	..	..	..
4320 Gift taxes	..	..	..	..	..	..	..	..	..	..
4400 Taxes on financial and capital transactions	0	71 777	192 393	15 955	33 872	24 583	24 912	24 857	30 556	38 309
Real estate transfer tax	..	0	0	11 766	26 263	17 228	17 216	13 595	21 025	29 922
Municipal Seal and Stamp Paper Tax	..	0	0	3 857	7 464	7 326	7 346	11 205	9 466	8 159
Registration and stamp duties	..	71 777	192 393	332	144	30	350	57	65	228
4500 Non-recurrent taxes	0	0	0	0	0	0	0	0	0	0
4510 On net wealth	..	..	..	..	..	..	..	..	..	..
4520 Other non-recurrent taxes	..	..	..	..	..	..	..	..	..	..
4600 Other recurrent taxes on property	0	0	0	1 742	1 466	1 025	1 432	565	579	124
5000 Taxes on goods and services	**438 444**	**2 080 878**	**4 313 729**	**9 462 461**	**16 813 348**	**17 901 774**	**17 610 929**	**16 929 091**	**19 548 577**	**20 912 305**
5100 Taxes on production, sale, transfer, etc	438 444	2 080 878	4 309 832	9 245 877	16 356 200	17 550 296	17 230 758	16 557 669	19 123 598	20 500 842
5110 General taxes	0	1 150 496	2 478 998	5 991 694	11 221 710	11 851 395	11 794 402	11 787 033	13 705 814	14 986 187
5111 Value added taxes	0	1 150 496	2 478 998	5 991 694	11 221 710	11 851 395	11 794 402	11 787 033	13 705 814	14 986 187
5112 Sales tax	..	0	0	0	0	0	0	0	0	0
5113 Other	..	0	0	0	0	0	0	0	0	0
5120 Taxes on specific goods and services	438 444	930 382	1 830 834	3 254 183	5 134 490	5 698 901	5 436 356	4 770 635	5 417 784	5 514 654
5121 Excises	300 219	456 561	949 962	1 710 531	2 890 013	3 156 091	2 992 813	2 773 235	2 989 115	2 657 727
Fuels	41 087	316 694	688 773	1 126 143	2 032 235	2 300 311	2 084 712	2 032 124	2 301 115	1 953 770
Other excises	259 132	136 194	249 239	537 887	843 123	841 900	886 475	724 578	664 820	380 785
Animal health and quality service	0	3 673	11 950	46 501	14 656	13 881	13 875	16 533	23 163	323 173
Livestock trade	0	0	0	0	0	0	7 751	0	17	0
5122 Profits of fiscal monopolies	0	0	0	0	0	0	0	0	0	0
5123 Customs and import duties	138 225	473 821	880 872	1 524 252	2 206 934	2 512 883	2 420 302	1 984 697	2 409 292	2 836 933
5124 Taxes on exports	0	0	0	0	0	0	0	0	0	0

	1990	2000	2005	2010	2017	2018	2019	2020	2021	2022
5125 Taxes on investment goods	0	0	0	0	0	0	0	0	0	0
5126 Taxes on specific services	0	0	0	19 401	37 542	29 927	23 241	12 704	19 377	19 994
Advertising	..	..	..	5 249	9 489	7 387	6 741	6 384	7 979	7 359
Public transport	..	..	..	4 363	4 080	4 196	3 420	1 255	2 079	345
Gambling	..	..	..	16	7 131	6 448	6 617	2 666	4 006	6 724
Advertising and gambling	..	..	..	8 884	14 821	9 796	4 447	1 317	2 502	3 430
Other taxes on specific services	..	..	..	888	2 021	2 099	2 017	1 082	2 810	2 137
5127 Other taxes on internat. trade and transactions	0	0	0	0	0	0	0	0	0	0
5128 Other taxes	0	0	0	0	0	0	0	0	0	0
5130 Unallocable between 5110 and 5120	0	0	0	0	0	0	0	0	0	0
5200 Taxes on use of goods and perform activities	0	0	3 897	216 347	426 115	350 893	379 208	370 331	423 107	404 159
5210 Recurrent taxes	..	..	0	183 622	365 303	315 178	329 087	334 724	365 717	355 371
5211 Paid by households: motor vehicles	..	..	..	0	0	0	0	0	0	0
5212 Paid by others: motor vehicles	..	..	..	52 365	109 084	106 872	109 402	103 274	116 044	111 493
Motor vehicle licences	..	..	..	52 365	109 084	106 872	109 402	103 274	116 044	111 493
5213 Paid in respect of other goods	..	..	..	131 257	256 219	208 305	219 685	231 450	249 673	243 878
Licencing fees	..	..	..	126 965	250 528	203 605	214 555	225 717	245 516	241 700
slaughter tax	..	..	..	4 271	5 395	4 635	4 991	5 585	3 958	1 833
Tax to the owners of animals	..	..	..	21	296	65	140	148	199	345
5220 Non-recurrent taxes	..	..	3 897	32 725	60 812	35 715	50 121	35 607	57 390	48 788
Tax on construction	..	..	0	31 696	60 092	34 999	49 375	34 930	56 728	48 067
Luxury automobile tax	..	..	3 897	91	7	0	0	0	0	0
Trademarks registration	..	..	0	938	713	716	746	677	662	721
5300 Unallocable between 5100 and 5200	0	0	0	237	31 034	585	962	1 092	1 872	7 304
6000 Other taxes	**49 807**	**44 875**	**41 844**	**250 812**	**213 344**	**162 652**	**201 917**	**145 946**	**262 599**	**286 711**
6100 Paid solely by business	0	0	0	0	0	0	0	0	0	0
6200 Other	49 807	44 875	41 844	250 812	213 344	162 652	201 917	145 946	262 599	286 711
Taxes replaced	0	0	0	0	0	0	0	0	0	0
Other	49 807	44 875	41 844	250 812	213 344	162 652	201 917	145 946	262 599	286 711

.. Not available

Note: Year ending 31st December.

The data are on a cash basis.

The figures for years before 2006 exclude local government tax revenues as the data are not available. This affects data in categories 4000, 5000 and 6000.

Heading 2000: Social security contributions before 1999 do not include social security contributions collected by decentralised institutions as the data are not available. Contributions to the health system in 2021 and 2022 have been added in this edition.

Source: Subsecretaría de Estado de Tributación, Ministerio de Hacienda del Paraguay (Tax Undersecretary, Ministry of Finance of Paraguay); Centro Interamericano de Administraciones Tributarias (Inter-American Centre of Tax Administrations).

Table 5.23. Peru

Details of tax revenue

Million PEN

	1990	2000	2005	2010	2017	2018	2019	2020	2021	2022
Total tax revenue	**637**	**26 771**	**40 663**	**74 803**	**107 932**	**123 178**	**129 398**	**110 581**	**159 235**	**180 010**
1000 Taxes on income, profits and capital gains	**37**	**5 078**	**11 950**	**27 317**	**40 750**	**45 312**	**48 162**	**41 290**	**61 112**	**75 444**
1100 Of individuals	3	2 117	3 327	6 518	13 008	13 598	14 744	13 182	16 765	18 325
First category	..	167	181	160	532	580	624	503	616	679
Second category	..	7	250	869	1 581	1 772	2 412	1 767	3 835	3 605
Fourth category	..	234	395	521	894	960	1 023	1 002	1 328	1 410
Fifth category	..	1 641	2 369	4 735	8 444	9 162	9 760	9 178	10 237	11 600
Tax debt payments	..	68	130	233	1 558	1 125	926	733	749	1 030
1110 On income and profits	..	..	..	..	..	..	..	..	..	..
1120 On capital gains	..	..	..	..	..	..	..	..	..	..
1200 Corporate	32	2 526	8 391	19 561	25 508	30 164	30 858	24 520	41 415	54 751
1210 On profits	32	2 526	8 391	19 561	25 508	30 164	30 858	24 520	41 415	54 751
Third category	..	2 023	5 316	14 652	15 499	17 268	17 679	13 804	22 786	29 821
Income tax on mining	..	0	0	0	638	770	545	430	1 802	1 608
Income tax special regime	..	47	55	118	323	344	354	271	406	458
Other incomes corporate	..	18	41	148	1 137	1 584	1 666	1 388	2 206	2 571
Tax debt payments	..	438	1 908	2 856	3 327	5 244	5 438	3 863	8 291	13 992
Temporary tax on net assets	..	0	1 073	1 788	4 585	4 953	5 176	4 764	5 926	6 302
1220 On capital gains of corporates	..	..	..	..	..	..	..	..	..	..
1300 Unallocable between 1100 and 1200	1	436	232	1 239	2 233	1 550	2 560	3 588	2 932	2 368
Income tax on non-residents	1	487	542	1 511	3 462	3 560	4 135	5 658	4 425	4 755
Income tax refunds	0	-51	-310	-272	-1 228	-2 009	-1 575	-2 071	-1 493	-2 387
2000 Social security contributions	**50**	**3 185**	**4 024**	**7 929**	**13 677**	**14 873**	**15 453**	**14 680**	**16 407**	**17 877**
2100 Employees	..	566	692	2 433	3 732	4 150	4 137	3 864	4 193	4 471
2110 On a payroll basis	..	566	669	1 665	3 597	3 874	3 959	3 681	3 988	4 121
2120 On an income tax basis	..	0	23	768	135	275	179	182	206	350
Solidarity contribution for pension plan	..	..	23	768	135	275	179	182	206	350
2200 Employers	..	2 515	3 285	5 454	9 878	10 653	11 245	10 767	12 166	13 353
2210 On a payroll basis	..	2 432	3 140	5 216	9 591	10 299	10 883	10 344	11 680	12 795
2220 On an income tax basis	..	83	144	238	287	354	362	423	486	558
2300 Self-employed or non-employed	..	95	36	42	66	70	70	49	48	54
2310 On a payroll basis	..	0	0	0	0	0	0	0	0	0
2320 On an income tax basis	..	95	36	42	66	70	70	49	48	54
2400 Unallocable between 2100, 2200 and 2300	50	9	12	0	1	1	0	0	0	0
2410 On a payroll basis	50	9	12	0	1	1	..	..	..	..
2420 On an income tax basis	0	0	0	0	0	0	..	..	..	..
3000 Taxes on payroll and workforce	**0**	**1 176**	**7**	**57**	**91**	**99**	**99**	**96**	**101**	**113**
Extraordinary solidarity tax (IES)	..	1 151	14	3	0	1	0	1	0	2
IES refunds	..	-2	-7	-2	-2	0	-3	0	0	0
National Housing Fund (FONAVI)	..	27	0	0	0	0	0	0	0	0
Contributions to SENATI	..	0	0	56	93	98	102	96	100	111
4000 Taxes on property	**87**	**323**	**1 342**	**2 231**	**2 573**	**2 680**	**3 063**	**2 418**	**3 266**	**3 560**
4100 Recurrent taxes on immovable property	0	298	461	727	1 718	1 748	2 026	1 749	2 266	2 391
4110 Households	..	..	..	..	..	..	..	..	..	..
4120 Others	..	..	..	..	..	..	..	..	..	..
4200 Recurrent taxes on net wealth	49	0	0	0	0	0	0	0	0	0
4210 Individual	..	..	..	..	..	..	..	..	..	..
4220 Corporate	..	..	..	..	..	..	..	..	..	..
4300 Estate, inheritance and gift taxes	0	0	0	0	0	0	0	0	0	0
4310 Estate and inheritance taxes	..	..	..	..	..	..	..	..	..	..
4320 Gift taxes	..	..	..	..	..	..	..	..	..	..
4400 Taxes on financial and capital transactions	38	25	804	1 504	855	932	1 037	669	1 000	1 169
Financial transactions tax	0	0	706	944	175	200	224	207	271	309
Real estate transfer tax	0	25	98	560	680	732	813	463	728	861
Tax Law Decree 519	38	0	0	0	0	0	0	0	0	0
4500 Non-recurrent taxes	0	0	0	0	0	0	0	0	0	0
4510 On net wealth	..	..	..	..	..	..	..	..	..	..
4520 Other non-recurrent taxes	..	..	..	..	..	..	..	..	..	..
4600 Other recurrent taxes on property	0	0	76	0	0	0	0	0	0	0
5000 Taxes on goods and services	**454**	**16 263**	**22 674**	**36 353**	**50 061**	**58 551**	**60 366**	**51 218**	**74 387**	**80 862**
5100 Taxes on production, sale, transfer, etc	454	16 239	22 619	36 199	49 774	58 257	60 064	50 977	74 104	80 539
5110 General taxes	109	9 646	15 109	29 094	41 036	49 038	49 197	42 375	62 780	68 418
5111 Value added taxes	109	9 646	15 109	29 094	41 036	49 038	49 197	42 375	62 780	68 418
VAT (internal)	69	6 992	10 587	19 629	32 114	35 125	37 892	32 708	42 608	47 375
VAT (imports)	41	4 961	7 715	15 908	22 529	25 541	25 613	22 671	35 490	40 930
VAT refunds	0	-2 307	-3 193	-6 442	-13 606	-11 628	-14 307	-13 004	-15 318	-19 887
5112 Sales tax	0	0	0	0	0	0	0	0	0	0
5113 Other	0	0	0	0	0	0	0	0	0	0

	1990	2000	2005	2010	2017	2018	2019	2020	2021	2022
5120 Taxes on specific goods and services	345	6 593	7 510	7 105	8 737	9 219	10 867	8 602	11 324	12 121
5121 Excises	232	3 518	4 193	4 875	6 588	7 011	8 668	7 231	9 568	9 766
Fuels	151	2 145	2 607	2 410	2 604	2 565	3 212	2 950	3 648	3 000
Gasoline sales tax	3	97	140	210	363	437	456	316	548	799
Other excises	78	1 304	1 459	2 258	3 711	4 295	5 005	3 971	5 490	6 026
Excise tax refunds	0	-28	-12	-4	-91	-286	-4	-5	-119	-58
5122 Profits of fiscal monopolies	0	0	0	0	0	0	0	0	0	0
5123 Customs and import duties	64	2 960	3 143	1 803	1 448	1 455	1 424	1 159	1 465	1 806
5124 Taxes on exports	2	0	0	0	0	0	0	0	0	0
5125 Taxes on investment goods	0	0	0	0	0	0	0	0	0	0
5126 Taxes on specific services	0	115	174	427	702	754	774	212	291	548
Casinos and slot machines	..	81	49	187	297	318	310	69	125	204
Tourism tax	..	0	74	105	174	193	215	72	83	183
Municipal taxes on services	..	34	50	135	230	243	250	70	83	162
5127 Other taxes on internat. trade and transactions	48	0	0	0	0	0	0	0	0	0
5128 Other taxes	0	0	0	0	0	0	0	0	0	0
5130 Unallocable between 5110 and 5120	0	0	0	0	0	0	0	0	0	0
5200 Taxes on use of goods and perform activities	0	25	55	154	288	294	302	241	284	323
5210 Recurrent taxes	..	25	55	154	288	294	302	241	284	323
5211 Paid by households: motor vehicles	..	..	..	..	..	..	..	..	..	..
5212 Paid by others: motor vehicles	..	..	..	..	..	..	..	..	..	..
5213 Paid in respect of other goods	..	..	..	..	..	..	..	..	..	..
5220 Non-recurrent taxes	..	0	0	0	0	0	0	0	0	0
5300 Unallocable between 5100 and 5200	0	0	0	0	0	0	0	0	0	0
6000 Other taxes	**9**	**745**	**666**	**914**	**780**	**1 662**	**2 254**	**878**	**3 962**	**2 154**
6100 Paid solely by business	0	84	73	108	140	133	135	93	109	114
Single simplified regime	..	84	73	108	140	133	135	93	109	114
University Development Fund	..	0	0	0	0	0	0	0	0	0
6200 Other	9	662	594	806	639	1 529	2 119	785	3 853	2 040
Tax debt payments	9	542	397	714	1 109	1 320	1 843	1 165	4 437	2 345
Other taxes	0	133	266	280	785	1 225	1 389	868	1 031	1 271
Other tax refunds	0	-14	-69	-188	-1 255	-1 016	-1 112	-1 249	-1 615	-1 577

.. Not available

Note: Year ending 31st December.

The data are on a cash basis.

The figures for years up to 2000 exclude local government tax revenues as the data are not available.

Heading 1210: Revenues from Régimen MYPE Tributario (RMT) have been included under heading 1210 in this edition. RMT is a regime introduced in 2017, specifically created for micro and small businesses with the aim of promoting their growth.

Heading 2000: All contributions pertaining to pensions are only made by employees and contributions to healthcare are made by employers. The exceptions are special regimes which apply to self-employed and are levied on an income basis.

Heading 3000: Contributions to SENATI are included in heading 3000. The tax revenue is classified under the central government. In Peru this revenue is classified under a separate unit considered to be different to the central government.

Heading 5123: Import tax refunds are classified under 6200 because they cannot be distinguished from other tax refunds.

Source: Superintendencia Nacional de Aduanas y de Administración Tributaria (National Superintendence of Customs and Tax Administration - SUNAT); Banco de la Nación (Bank of the Nation); Ministerio de Economía y Finanzas (Ministry of Economy and Finance); Servicio Nacional de Adiestramiento en Trabajo Industrial (National Industrial Work Training Service).

Table 5.24. Saint Lucia

Details of tax revenue

Million XCD

	1990	2000	2005	2010	2017	2018	2019	2020	2021	2022
Total tax revenue	..	**480**	**612**	**828**	**1 107**	**1 157**	**1 180**	**923**	**1 047**	**1 162**
1000 Taxes on income, profits and capital gains	..	**137**	**157**	**224**	**247**	**269**	**258**	**228**	**229**	**246**
1100 Of individuals	..	49	58	83	124	131	134	115	130	135
1110 On income and profits	..	49	58	83	124	131	134	115	130	135
Personal income tax	..	49	58	83	104	113	116	99	112	115
Arrears on personal income tax	..	0	0	0	21	18	18	16	18	20
1120 On capital gains	..	..	..	..	..	..	..	..	..	..
1200 Corporate	..	63	60	95	102	115	111	97	84	98
1210 On profits	..	63	60	95	102	115	111	97	84	98
Corporate income tax	..	63	60	95	89	92	93	81	67	73
Arrears on corporate income tax	..	0	0	0	13	23	18	16	17	25
1220 On capital gains of corporates	..	..	..	..	..	..	..	..	..	..
1300 Unallocable between 1100 and 1200	..	26	39	46	21	23	13	17	15	13
Withholdings	..	7	17	14	24	28	16	20	18	18
Arrears	..	25	30	42	7	5	7	5	4	5
Tax Refunds	..	-6	-8	-10	-10	-10	-9	-8	-7	-10
2000 Social security contributions	..	**48**	**63**	**92**	**114**	**120**	**127**	**118**	**125**	**154**
2100 Employees	..	..	..	..	..	..	..	..	..	..
2110 On a payroll basis	..	..	..	..	..	..	..	..	..	..
2120 On an income tax basis	..	..	..	..	..	..	..	..	..	..
2200 Employers	..	..	..	..	..	..	..	..	..	..
2210 On a payroll basis	..	..	..	..	..	..	..	..	..	..
2220 On an income tax basis	..	..	..	..	..	..	..	..	..	..
2300 Self-employed or non-employed	..	..	0	1	1	1	1	1	1	1
2310 On a payroll basis	..	..	0	1	1	1	1	1	1	1
2320 On an income tax basis	..	..	0	0	0	0	0	0	0	0
2400 Unallocable between 2100, 2200 and 2300	..	48	63	91	113	119	126	117	124	153
2410 On a payroll basis	..	48	63	91	113	119	126	117	124	153
2420 On an income tax basis	..	0	0	0	0	0	0	0	0	0
3000 Taxes on payroll and workforce	..	**0**	**0**	**0**	**0**	**0**	**0**	**0**	**0**	**0**
4000 Taxes on property	..	**11**	**24**	**19**	**26**	**26**	**25**	**20**	**31**	**27**
4100 Recurrent taxes on immovable property	..	2	6	3	12	10	8	7	8	8
4110 Households	..	..	..	..	..	..	..	..	..	..
4120 Others	..	..	..	..	..	..	..	..	..	..
4200 Recurrent taxes on net wealth	..	0	0	0	0	0	0	0	0	0
4210 Individual	..	..	..	..	..	..	..	..	..	..
4220 Corporate	..	..	..	..	..	..	..	..	..	..
4300 Estate, inheritance and gift taxes	..	0	0	0	0	0	0	0	0	0
4310 Estate and inheritance taxes	..	..	..	..	..	..	..	..	..	..
4320 Gift taxes	..	..	..	..	..	..	..	..	..	..
4400 Taxes on financial and capital transactions	..	9	18	16	14	17	18	13	23	18
4500 Non-reccurrent taxes	..	0	0	0	0	0	0	0	0	0
4510 On net wealth	..	..	..	..	..	..	..	..	..	..
4520 Other non-recurrent taxes	..	..	..	..	..	..	..	..	..	..
4600 Other recurrent taxes on property	..	0	0	0	0	0	0	0	0	0
5000 Taxes on goods and services	..	**284**	**368**	**493**	**720**	**742**	**770**	**556**	**662**	**734**
5100 Taxes on production, sale, transfer, etc	..	277	353	467	694	715	742	548	655	726
5110 General taxes	..	101	112	119	318	329	339	241	306	335
5111 Value added taxes	..	0	0	0	318	329	339	241	306	335
VAT (domestic)	..	..	..	..	176	181	184	..	..	..
VAT (imports)	..	..	..	..	142	148	156	..	..	..
5112 Sales tax	..	101	112	119	0	0	0	0	0	0
Consumption tax (domestic)	..	11	8	6	..	..	..	0	..	..
Consumption tax (Imports)	..	90	104	114	..	..	..	0	..	..
5113 Other	..	0	0	0	0	0	0	0	0	0
5120 Taxes on specific goods and services	..	176	240	348	376	385	402	307	349	390
5121 Excises	..	34	13	85	128	134	140	121	111	129
Excise tax (domestic)	..	28	6	14	5	5	5	3	3	4
Excise tax (imports)	..	0	0	68	103	109	114	99	88	103
Fuel Surcharge	..	3	3	4	21	20	21	18	20	22
Surcharge on international calls	..	4	4	0	0	0	0	0	0	0
5122 Profits of fiscal monopolies	..	0	0	0	0	0	0	0	0	0
5123 Customs and import duties	..	108	178	187	202	206	205	161	203	221
Import Duty	..	64	90	101	121	123	122	92	116	126
Thruput Charge	..	1	2	6	5	4	4	4	4	4
Service Charge (imports) and security charges	..	33	86	64	76	79	80	65	83	90
Environmental Levy	..	9	0	16	0	0	0	0	0	0
5124 Taxes on exports	..	0	0	0	0	0	0	0	0	0

	1990	2000	2005	2010	2017	2018	2019	2020	2021	2022
5125 Taxes on investment goods	..	0	0	0	0	0	0	0	0	0
5126 Taxes on specific services	..	34	49	76	46	45	57	25	35	40
Hotel occupancy tax	..	23	29	34	0	0	1	0	0	0
Insurance premium tax	..	4	5	7	9	9	10	10	10	10
Cellular tax	..	0	8	18	0	0	0	0	0	0
Passenger facility fee	..	0	2	5	4	3	3	1	1	2
Travel tax	..	3	5	4	5	5	4	1	1	2
Airport tax	..	5	1	9	29	28	39	13	22	26
5127 Other taxes on internat. trade and transactions	..	0	0	0	0	0	0	0	0	0
5128 Other taxes	..	0	0	0	0	0	0	0	0	0
5130 Unallocable between 5110 and 5120	..	0	0	0	0	0	0	0	0	0
5200 Taxes on use of goods and to perform activities	..	7	16	26	26	28	28	8	7	9
5210 Recurrent taxes	..	7	16	26	26	28	28	8	7	9
5211 Paid by households: motor vehicles	..	0	0	0	0	0	0	0	0	0
5212 Paid by others: motor vehicles	..	0	0	0	0	0	0	0	0	0
5213 Paid in respect of other goods	..	7	16	26	26	28	28	8	7	9
5220 Non-recurrent taxes	..	0	0	0	0	0	0	0	0	0
5300 Unallocable between 5100 and 5200	..	0	0	0	0	0	0	0	0	0
6000 Other taxes	**..**	**0**	**0**	**0**	**0**	**0**	**0**	**0**	**0**	**0**
6100 Paid solely by business	..	..	..	..	..	..	..	..	..	..
6200 Other	..	..	..	..	..	..	..	..	..	..

.. Not available

Note: Year ending 31st March. For example, the data for 2022 represent April 2022 to March 2023.

The data are on a cash basis.

The figures do not include local tax revenues because data are not available. Central government tax revenue data are government revised estimates for 2021 and budget estimates for 2022.

Heading 2000: Social security contributions follow financial year from July to June, instead of April to March. For example, social security contributions in 2022 are between 1st July 2021 and 30th June 2022. Data is estimated for 2021 and 2022.

Heading 5123: Data for security charge are estimated for 2020-22.

Heading 5213: Data from 2020 include some of the licences and fees under taxes on use of goods and permissions in Estimates of Revenue and Expenditure 2022-2023 from the Department of Finance.

Source: The Central Statistical Office of Saint Lucia; Department of Finance of Saint Lucia; National Insurance Corporation of Saint Lucia.

Table 5.25. Trinidad and Tobago

Details of tax revenue

Million TTD

	1990	2000	2005	2010	2017	2018	2019	2020	2021	2022
Total tax revenue	**4 923**	**10 953**	**27 665**	**39 720**	**31 164**	**36 813**	**38 417**	**31 258**	**34 745**	**45 599**
1000 Taxes on income, profits and capital gains	**2 595**	**6 224**	**20 010**	**27 213**	**16 133**	**19 413**	**22 391**	**15 332**	**17 206**	**30 756**
1100 Of individuals	669	2 325	4 452	4 674	6 570	6 842	7 215	6 209	5 816	6 191
1110 On income and profits	669	2 325	4 452	4 674	6 570	6 842	7 215	6 209	5 816	6 191
Health surcharge	92	149	187	185	218	184	191	170	166	178
Insurance surrender tax	6	7	15	22	48	57	65	59	65	78
Individuals (Ch. 75:01)	571	2 169	4 250	4 467	6 303	6 601	6 960	5 980	5 585	5 936
1120 On capital gains	..	..	..	..	..	..	..	..	..	..
1200 Corporate	1 856	3 704	15 023	21 659	8 736	11 713	13 816	8 186	10 384	23 499
1210 On profits	1 856	3 704	15 023	21 659	8 736	11 713	13 816	8 186	10 384	23 499
Oil companies	1 439	2 441	10 806	13 834	1 116	2 093	3 755	1 762	3 104	10 447
Other companies	383	1 041	3 166	6 630	6 919	3 858	8 694	5 641	6 292	10 477
Business levy	0	65	146	206	603	608	649	571	650	630
National recovery impost	34	0	0	0	0	0	0	0	0	0
Unemployment Fund	0	157	905	989	99	153	718	211	339	1 945
1220 On capital gains of corporates	..	..	..	..	..	..	..	..	..	..
1300 Unallocable between 1100 and 1200	70	195	536	881	827	858	1 360	938	1 005	1 067
2000 Social security contributions	**183**	**702**	**1 173**	**2 645**	**4 608**	**4 670**	**4 706**	**4 686**	**4 510**	**4 530**
2100 Employees	..	..	..	..	..	..	..	..	..	..
2110 On a payroll basis	..	..	..	..	..	..	..	..	..	..
2120 On an income tax basis	..	..	..	..	..	..	..	..	..	..
2200 Employers	..	..	..	..	..	..	..	..	..	..
2210 On a payroll basis	..	..	..	..	..	..	..	..	..	..
2220 On an income tax basis	..	..	..	..	..	..	..	..	..	..
2300 Self-employed or non-employed	..	..	..	..	..	..	..	..	..	..
2310 On a payroll basis	..	..	..	..	..	..	..	..	..	..
2320 On an income tax basis	..	..	..	..	..	..	..	..	..	..
2400 Unallocable between 2100, 2200 and 2300	183	702	1 173	2 645	4 608	4 670	4 706	4 686	4 510	4 530
2410 On a payroll basis	..	..	..	..	..	..	..	..	..	..
2420 On an income tax basis	..	..	..	..	..	..	..	..	..	..
3000 Taxes on payroll and workforce	**0**	**0**	**0**	**0**	**0**	**0**	**0**	**0**	**0**	**0**
4000 Taxes on property	**90**	**175**	**307**	**194**	**322**	**362**	**405**	**260**	**289**	**359**
4100 Recurrent taxes on immovable property	39	64	63	22	3	4	50	2	2	2
4110 Households	..	..	..	..	..	..	..	..	..	..
4120 Others	..	..	..	..	..	..	..	..	..	..
4200 Recurrent taxes on net wealth	0	0	0	0	0	0	0	0	0	0
4210 Individual	..	..	..	..	..	..	..	..	..	..
4220 Corporate	..	..	..	..	..	..	..	..	..	..
4300 Estate, inheritance and gift taxes	1	0	0	0	0	0	0	0	0	0
4310 Estate and inheritance taxes	1	..	..	..	..	..	..	..	..	..
4320 Gift taxes	0	..	..	..	..	..	..	..	..	..
4400 Taxes on financial and capital transactions	49	111	245	172	319	359	356	258	287	357
Stamp duties	49	111	245	172	319	359	356	258	287	357
4500 Non-recurrent taxes	0	0	0	0	0	0	0	0	0	0
4510 On net wealth	..	..	..	..	..	..	..	..	..	..
4520 Other non-recurrent taxes	..	..	..	..	..	..	..	..	..	..
4600 Other recurrent taxes on property	0	0	0	0	0	0	0	0	0	0
5000 Taxes on goods and services	**2 055**	**3 852**	**6 175**	**9 667**	**10 101**	**12 368**	**10 915**	**10 980**	**12 740**	**9 954**
5100 Taxes on production, sale, transfer, etc	1 973	3 603	5 948	9 282	9 675	12 024	10 612	10 752	12 480	9 687
5110 General taxes	980	1 890	3 149	6 358	5 876	8 087	6 836	7 417	9 173	6 006
5111 Value added taxes	927	1 890	2 963	6 032	5 050	7 245	5 848	6 682	8 296	4 665
5112 Sales tax	54	0	0	0	1	0	0	0	0	0
5113 Other	0	0	186	325	825	842	988	734	877	1 341
Green Fund	..	..	186	325	803	813	957	689	811	1 284
Tax on online purchases	..	..	0	0	22	23	31	46	66	58
5120 Taxes on specific goods and services	993	1 713	2 799	2 924	3 798	3 933	3 777	3 336	3 307	3 681
5121 Excises	481	801	1 072	708	739	793	680	703	707	760
Alcohol products	..	..	..	156	150	183	187	205	209	245
Beer	..	..	..	202	202	202	173	197	208	205
Petroleum products	..	..	..	105	102	98	23	6	0	0
Cigarette products	..	..	..	243	253	269	262	274	288	308
Malt beverages	..	..	..	2	33	41	35	21	2	1
5122 Profits of fiscal monopolies	0	0	0	0	0	0	0	0	0	0
5123 Customs and import duties	260	748	1 473	1 905	2 684	2 732	2 672	2 301	2 287	2 596
5124 Taxes on exports	0	0	0	0	0	0	0	0	0	0
5125 Taxes on investment goods	0	0	0	0	0	0	0	0	0	0

	1990	2000	2005	2010	2017	2018	2019	2020	2021	2022
5126 Taxes on specific services	49	163	253	311	375	411	425	331	313	324
Insurance premium tax	0	56	98	167	163	170	180	159	175	166
Transaction tax on financial services	0	23	33	53	93	97	103	92	90	100
Hotel room tax	0	23	42	46	52	52	55	34	20	33
Betting and entertainment taxes	4	17	9	12	0	0	0	0	0	0
Other taxes on goods and services	45	44	72	33	67	93	86	46	27	26
5127 Other taxes on internat. trade and transactions	202	0	0	1	1	0	0	0	0	0
5128 Other taxes	0	0	0	0	0	0	0	0	0	0
5130 Unallocable between 5110 and 5120	0	0	0	0	0	0	0	0	0	0
5200 Taxes on use of goods and perform activities	81	249	227	386	426	344	303	228	260	267
5210 Recurrent taxes	81	249	227	386	426	344	303	228	260	267
Motor vehicle taxes and duties	76	239	217	375	415	334	291	221	251	256
5211 Paid by households: motor vehicles	..	..	..	..	..	..	..	..	..	..
5212 Paid by others: motor vehicles	..	..	..	..	..	..	..	..	..	..
5213 Paid in respect of other goods	5	10	10	10	11	11	12	7	9	11
Liquor and miscellaneous business licence fees	5	10	10	10	11	11	12	7	9	11
5220 Non-recurrent taxes	0	0	0	0	0	0	0	0	0	0
5300 Unallocable between 5100 and 5200	0	0	0	0	0	0	0	0	0	0
6000 Other taxes	**0**	**0**	**0**	**0**	**0**	**0**	**0**	**0**	**0**	**0**
6100 Paid solely by business	..	..	..	..	..	..	..	..	..	..
6200 Other	..	..	..	..	..	..	..	..	..	..

.. Not available

Note: Fiscal year ending on 30th September. For example, the data for 2022 represent October 2021 to September 2022.

The data are on a cash basis.

The figures exclude local government tax revenues as the data are not available.

Heading 1100: Income taxes on individuals include "Individuals (Ch. 75:01)" and lottery winnings tax.

Heading 2000: Social security contributions follow financial year from July to June, instead of October to September. For example, social security contributions in 2022 are between 1st July 2021 and 30th June 2022. The figures include total contribution income of National Insurance Board minus refunds. A small amount of voluntary contributions have been identified and removed from the figures since 2013.

Heading 5126: Other taxes on goods and services under heading 5126 include mainly club gaming tax which is charged on all gambling tables and other gambling devices from a licenced gambling operator.

Source: Ministry of Finance; The National Insurance Board.

Table 5.26. Uruguay

Details of tax revenue

Million UYU

	1990	2000	2005	2010	2017	2018	2019	2020	2021	2022
Total tax revenue	**2 399**	**64 183**	**106 251**	**212 907**	**494 901**	**534 519**	**573 642**	**600 332**	**684 851**	**778 260**
1000 Taxes on income, profits and capital gains	**114**	**8 698**	**13 831**	**42 583**	**125 295**	**140 527**	**149 920**	**159 783**	**178 797**	**207 294**
1100 Of individuals	0	3 597	3 285	19 148	68 948	78 571	85 847	91 819	98 825	113 351
Personal income tax (IRP)	..	3 597	3 285	0	0	0	0	0	0	0
1110 On income and profits	..	..	..	16 790	60 570	69 083	75 944	80 407	84 910	96 142
IRPF second category	..	..	..	14 643	54 327	61 077	67 254	70 295	74 209	84 803
Social security assistance	..	..	..	2 651	9 448	11 091	12 336	14 198	15 355	16 315
Personal income tax refunds	..	..	..	-504	-3 204	-3 085	-3 646	-4 086	-4 653	-4 977
1120 On capital gains	..	..	..	2 358	8 377	9 488	9 903	11 412	13 915	17 209
IRPF first category	..	..	..	2 358	8 377	9 488	9 903	11 412	13 915	17 209
1200 Corporate	114	5 102	10 546	21 772	51 169	56 316	58 071	61 487	71 500	82 729
1210 On profits	114	5 102	10 546	21 772	51 169	56 316	58 071	61 487	71 500	82 729
Income tax for economic activities (IRAE)	0	0	0	21 437	51 081	56 316	58 071	61 487	71 500	82 729
Industry and commerce income tax (IRIC)	97	5 096	10 516	333	88	0	0	0	0	0
Agricultural income tax (IRA)	10	3	30	2	0	0	0	0	0	0
Tax on agricultural activities (IMAGRO)	7	3	0	0	0	0	0	0	0	0
1220 On capital gains of corporates	..	..	..	..	..	..	..	..	..	..
1300 Unallocable between 1100 and 1200	0	0	0	1 662	5 179	5 639	6 002	6 477	8 472	11 214
Non-resident income tax (IRNR)	..	..	..	1 662	5 179	5 639	6 002	6 477	8 472	11 214
2000 Social security contributions	**717**	**17 679**	**21 425**	**49 742**	**131 545**	**139 561**	**151 589**	**150 185**	**165 500**	**196 064**
2100 Employees	..	..	..	..	..	..	..	..	..	..
2110 On a payroll basis	..	..	..	..	..	..	..	..	..	..
2120 On an income tax basis	..	..	..	..	..	..	..	..	..	..
2200 Employers	..	..	..	..	..	..	..	..	..	..
2210 On a payroll basis	..	..	..	..	..	..	..	..	..	..
2220 On an income tax basis	..	..	..	..	..	..	..	..	..	..
2300 Self-employed or non-employed	..	..	..	..	..	..	..	..	..	..
2310 On a payroll basis	..	..	..	..	..	..	..	..	..	..
2320 On an income tax basis	..	..	..	..	..	..	..	..	..	..
2400 Unallocable between 2100, 2200 and 2300	717	17 679	21 425	49 742	131 545	139 561	151 589	150 185	165 500	196 064
2410 On a payroll basis	717	17 679	21 425	49 742	131 545	139 561	151 589	150 185	165 500	196 064
2420 On an income tax basis	0	0	0	0	0	0	0	0	0	0
3000 Taxes on payroll and workforce	**0**	**0**	**0**	**0**	**0**	**0**	**0**	**0**	**0**	**0**
4000 Taxes on property	**213**	**5 508**	**12 159**	**18 965**	**38 460**	**40 508**	**44 178**	**46 785**	**52 387**	**59 925**
4100 Recurrent taxes on immovable property	87	3 248	5 586	8 140	18 180	19 648	21 056	22 672	24 921	28 140
Primary education tax	0	378	852	1 064	2 781	2 961	3 271	3 474	3 822	4 224
Farm property tax	0	155	1	189	764	728	750	941	968	1 127
Property tax surcharge	0	0	0	0	543	476	471	610	562	601
Primary education tax refunds	0	0	0	0	0	-3	-2	-1	-1	-2
Other property taxes	87	2 715	4 733	6 887	14 092	15 485	16 567	17 649	19 570	22 189
4110 Households	..	..	..	..	..	..	..	..	..	..
4120 Others	..	..	..	..	..	..	..	..	..	..
4200 Recurrent taxes on net wealth	94	1 769	4 942	8 760	17 057	17 473	19 717	20 335	22 357	25 740
4210 Individual	64	108	336	382	711	760	707	676	579	519
4220 Corporate	30	1 661	4 605	8 378	16 346	16 713	19 010	19 659	21 778	25 221
Corporate wealth tax	28	1 507	4 382	8 165	16 345	16 713	19 010	19 659	21 778	25 221
Tax on financial investment companies (ISAFI)	1	154	224	213	1	1	0	1	0	0
4300 Estate, inheritance and gift taxes	0	0	0	0	0	0	0	0	0	0
4310 Estate and inheritance taxes	..	..	..	..	..	..	..	..	..	..
4320 Gift taxes	..	..	..	..	..	..	..	..	..	..
4400 Taxes on financial and capital transactions	31	476	1 259	1 740	2 662	2 819	2 841	3 193	4 341	4 995
Property transfer tax (ITP)	11	372	886	1 347	1 927	1 984	1 859	2 120	2 866	3 553
Tax on transfer of rights over athletes	0	0	47	3	0	0	0	0	0	0
Auction tax	20	104	326	390	735	835	982	1 073	1 475	1 442
4500 Non-recurrent taxes	0	0	0	0	0	0	0	0	0	0
4510 On net wealth	..	..	..	..	..	..	..	..	..	..
4520 Other non-recurrent taxes	..	..	..	..	..	..	..	..	..	..
4600 Other recurrent taxes on property	1	15	372	326	560	567	564	585	768	1 050
Corporation control tax (ICOSA)	1	15	176	325	560	567	564	585	768	1 050
Financial system control tax (ICOSIFI)	0	0	196	0	0	0	0	0	0	0
5000 Taxes on goods and services	**1 358**	**32 139**	**57 834**	**100 282**	**196 669**	**210 711**	**224 394**	**239 924**	**284 206**	**310 465**
5100 Taxes on production, sale, transfer, etc	1 301	29 562	54 763	96 494	186 355	199 329	212 218	227 247	269 210	294 061
5110 General taxes	660	18 009	34 641	69 951	129 663	137 400	145 846	157 644	184 834	199 428
5111 Value added taxes	660	17 995	31 696	69 921	129 663	137 400	145 846	157 644	184 834	199 428
5112 Sales tax	1	14	2 945	30	0	0	0	0	0	0
Social security financing tax (COFIS)	0	0	2 905	30	..	..	..	..	..	..
Other sales taxes	1	14	40	0	..	..	..	..	..	..
5113 Other	0	0	0	0	0	0	0	0	0	0

	1990	2000	2005	2010	2017	2018	2019	2020	2021	2022
5120 Taxes on specific goods and services	641	11 553	20 122	26 543	56 692	61 928	66 372	69 604	84 376	94 633
5121 Excises	393	7 896	11 447	17 300	37 779	39 214	42 183	44 212	51 646	58 274
Fuels	203	4 067	4 900	6 551	17 129	18 662	20 094	22 157	23 720	18 047
Tobacco products	80	1 741	2 705	4 236	6 995	7 518	7 703	7 944	8 303	8 640
Motor vehicles	20	656	977	2 289	4 313	3 789	3 799	4 626	7 289	7 437
Non-alcoholic beverages	19	464	532	1 172	2 547	2 687	2 754	2 879	2 964	3 297
Agricultural products	4	299	1 182	1 349	2 369	2 636	2 998	3 256	4 548	5 222
Beer	8	205	308	602	1 357	1 526	1 494	1 688	1 773	2 032
Advances of import excises	0	27	9	-136	1 372	704	1 591	-465	0	0
Greases and lubricants	5	119	289	390	623	652	677	815	1 380	1 374
Alcoholic beverages	22	212	352	562	766	617	677	714	1 024	1 125
Other excises	32	106	193	283	309	423	397	598	644	11 098
5122 Profits of fiscal monopolies	0	0	0	0	0	0	0	0	0	0
5123 Customs and import duties	214	1 967	5 195	8 478	17 198	20 878	22 124	23 099	29 923	33 304
5124 Taxes on exports	1	32	243	325	664	770	858	908	1 374	1 430
5125 Taxes on investment goods	0	0	0	0	0	0	0	0	0	0
5126 Taxes on specific services	34	1 392	2 748	440	1 052	1 067	1 207	1 384	1 433	1 624
Bank asset tax (IMABA)	31	1 092	1 152	2	0	0	0	0	0	0
Income tax for insurance companies	3	76	298	366	902	916	1 004	1 270	1 333	1 447
Other services taxes	0	224	1 298	72	150	152	202	115	100	177
5127 Other taxes on internat. trade and transactions	0	265	489	0	0	0	0	0	0	0
5128 Other taxes	0	0	0	0	0	0	0	0	0	0
5130 Unallocable between 5110 and 5120	0	0	0	0	0	0	0	0	0	0
5200 Taxes on use of goods and perform activities	57	2 576	3 071	3 788	10 313	11 382	12 176	12 677	14 996	16 404
5210 Recurrent taxes	57	2 576	3 071	3 788	10 313	11 382	12 176	12 677	14 996	16 404
5211 Paid by households: motor vehicles	0	0	0	0	0	0	0	0	0	0
5212 Paid by others: motor vehicles	57	2 576	3 071	3 788	10 313	11 382	12 176	12 677	14 996	16 404
5213 Paid in respect of other goods	0	0	0	0	0	0	0	0	0	0
5220 Non-recurrent taxes	0	0	0	0	0	0	0	0	0	0
5300 Unallocable between 5100 and 5200	0	0	0	0	0	0	0	0	0	0
6000 Other taxes	**-3**	**159**	**1 003**	**1 335**	**2 933**	**3 212**	**3 560**	**3 655**	**3 960**	**4 512**
6100 Paid solely by business	-10	-145	533	586	925	980	1 039	1 033	1 099	1 205
Small business tax (minimum VAT)	0	296	457	586	925	980	1 039	1 033	1 099	1 205
Credit card tax	0	0	76	0	0	0	0	0	0	0
Other tax refunds	-10	-440	0	0	0	0	0	0	0	0
6200 Other	7	303	470	748	2 008	2 232	2 521	2 623	2 861	3 306

.. Not available

Note: Year ending 31st December.

The data are on a cash basis.

Figures for local tax revenues are estimated for 2022 as data are not available.

Heading 2000: Figures for 1990-98 are estimated by the General Tax Directorate (DGI). The figures have included income from Social Security Bank (BPS) published by the Ministry of Economy and Finance since 1999.

Heading 5112: The tax on the sale of goods by public auctions recorded under other sales taxes is classified in category 4000 in ECLAC data.

Source: Dirección General Impositiva (General Tax Directorate); Ministerio de Economia y Finanzas (Ministry of Economy and Finance).

Table 5.27. Venezuela

Details of tax revenue

VES

	1990	2000	2005	2010	2017	2018	2019	2020	2021	2022
Total tax revenue	**4 115**	**108 486**	**482 849**	**1 200 840**	..	..	..	..	..	..
1000 Taxes on income, profits and capital gains	**3 444**	**46 856**	**185 291**	**368 365**	..	..	..	..	..	..
1100 Of individuals	..	..	..	..	..	..	..	..	..	..
1110 On income and profits	..	..	..	..	..	..	..	..	..	..
1120 On capital gains	..	..	..	..	..	..	..	..	..	..
1200 Corporate	3 148	33 683	111 839	86 998	..	..	..	..	..	..
1210 On profits	3 148	33 683	111 839	86 998	..	..	..	..	..	..
Oil	3 148	33 683	111 839	86 998	..	..	..	..	..	..
1220 On capital gains of corporates	..	..	..	..	..	..	..	..	..	..
1300 Unallocable between 1100 and 1200	297	13 173	73 452	281 367	31 378 510	..	..	..	..	..
2000 Social security contributions	**202**	**5 905**	**18 899**	**96 896**	..	..	..	..	..	..
2100 Employees	..	..	..	..	..	..	..	..	..	..
2110 On a payroll basis	..	..	..	..	..	..	..	..	..	..
2120 On an income tax basis	..	..	..	..	..	..	..	..	..	..
2200 Employers	..	..	..	..	..	..	..	..	..	..
2210 On a payroll basis	..	..	..	..	..	..	..	..	..	..
2220 On an income tax basis	..	..	..	..	..	..	..	..	..	..
2300 Self-employed or non-employed	..	..	..	..	..	..	..	..	..	..
2310 On a payroll basis	..	..	..	..	..	..	..	..	..	..
2320 On an income tax basis	..	..	..	..	..	..	..	..	..	..
2400 Unallocable between 2100, 2200 and 2300	202	5 905	18 899	96 896	..	..	..	..	..	..
2410 On a payroll basis	..	..	..	..	..	..	..	..	..	..
2420 On an income tax basis	..	..	..	..	..	..	..	..	..	..
3000 Taxes on payroll and workforce	**0**	**0**	**0**	**0**	**0**	..	..	..	..	..
4000 Taxes on property	**11**	**3 999**	**28 338**	**2 217**	**24 353 035**	..	..	..	..	..
4100 Recurrent taxes on immovable property	0	0	0	0	0	..	..	..	..	..
4110 Households	..	..	..	..	..	..	..	..	..	..
4120 Others	..	..	..	..	..	..	..	..	..	..
4200 Recurrent taxes on net wealth	0	0	0	0	0	..	..	..	..	..
4210 Individual	..	..	..	..	..	..	..	..	..	..
4220 Corporate	..	..	..	..	..	..	..	..	..	..
4300 Estate, inheritance and gift taxes	11	191	552	2 217	361 298	..	..	..	..	..
4310 Estate and inheritance taxes	11	191	552	2 217	361 298	..	..	..	..	..
4320 Gift taxes	0	0	0	0	0	..	..	..	..	..
4400 Taxes on financial and capital transactions	0	3 808	27 786	0	23 991 737	..	..	..	..	..
Bank debits	..	2 918	27 429	..	0	..	..	..	..	..
Registration of immovable property rights	..	890	357	..	0	..	..	..	..	..
Tax on Large Financial Transactions (IGTF)	..	0	0	..	23 991 737	..	..	..	..	..
4500 Non-recurrent taxes	0	0	0	0	0	..	..	..	..	..
4510 On net wealth	..	..	..	..	..	..	..	..	..	..
4520 Other non-recurrent taxes	..	..	..	..	..	..	..	..	..	..
4600 Other recurrent taxes on property	0	0	0	0	0	..	..	..	..	..
5000 Taxes on goods and services	**457**	**51 726**	**250 322**	**733 363**	**148 669 517**	..	..	..	..	..
5100 Taxes on production, sale, transfer, etc	457	51 726	250 322	733 363	148 669 517	..	..	..	..	..
5110 General taxes	0	32 716	195 132	561 005	112 990 174	..	..	..	..	..
5111 Value added taxes	0	32 716	195 132	561 005	112 990 174	..	..	..	..	..
5112 Sales tax	..	0	0	0	0	..	..	..	..	..
5113 Other	..	0	0	0	0	..	..	..	..	..
5120 Taxes on specific goods and services	457	19 011	55 190	172 357	35 679 343	..	..	..	..	..
5121 Excises	157	7 742	16 036	88 722	29 679 186	..	..	..	..	..
Oil	57	4 679	4 718	12 798	0	..	..	..	..	..
Alcoholic beverages	58	852	4 270	21 915	14 113 397	..	..	..	..	..
Tobacco	42	2 201	7 038	54 009	15 565 789	..	..	..	..	..
Matches	0	9	11	0	0	..	..	..	..	..
5122 Profits of fiscal monopolies	0	0	0	0	0	..	..	..	..	..
5123 Customs and import duties	300	9 716	36 522	81 333	5 986 482	..	..	..	..	..
5124 Taxes on exports	0	0	0	0	0	..	..	..	..	..
5125 Taxes on investment goods	0	0	0	0	0	..	..	..	..	..
5126 Taxes on specific services	0	1 552	2 631	2 302	13 675	..	..	..	..	..
Telecommunications	0	1 505	2 370	0	0	..	..	..	..	..
Casinos, bingo and slot machines	0	47	261	2 302	13 675	..	..	..	..	..
5127 Other taxes on internat. trade and transactions	0	0	0	0	0	..	..	..	..	..
5128 Other taxes	0	0	0	0	0	..	..	..	..	..
5130 Unallocable between 5110 and 5120	0	0	0	0	0	..	..	..	..	..
5200 Taxes on use of goods and perform activities	0	0	0	0	0	..	..	..	..	..
5210 Recurrent taxes	..	..	..	..	..	..	..	..	..	..
5211 Paid by households: motor vehicles	..	..	..	..	..	..	..	..	..	..
5212 Paid by others: motor vehicles	..	..	..	..	..	..	..	..	..	..

	1990	2000	2005	2010	2017	2018	2019	2020	2021	2022
5213 Paid in respect of other goods	..	..	..	..	..	..	..	..	..	..
5220 Non-recurrent taxes	..	..	..	..	..	..	..	..	..	..
5300 Unallocable between 5100 and 5200	0	0	0	0	0	..	..	..	..	..
6000 Other taxes	**0**	**0**	**0**	**0**	**1 225 170**	**..**	**..**	**..**	**..**	**..**
6100 Paid solely by business	..	..	..	..	0	..	..	..	..	..
6200 Other	..	..	..	..	1 225 170	..	..	..	..	..

.. Not available

Note: Year ending 31st December.

The data are on a cash basis.

Tax data are not available from 2018.

The figures exclude state and local government tax revenues as the data are not available.

The figures between 2015 and 2017 should be interpreted with caution as they have been affected by the high rate of inflation over this period.

Total tax revenue data were not available since 2014 due to missing data for social security contributions since 2014 and oil revenues since 2016 (classified in heading 1210 taxes on corporate profits).

Source: Servicio Nacional Integrado de Administración Aduanera (National Integrated Service of Customs); Ministerio de Finanzas (Ministry of Finance).

6 Country tables, tax revenues by sub-sectors of general government, 1990-2022

Revenues of Latin American, Caribbean and OECD countries have been attributed to the different levels of government according to the revised guidelines set out in the final version of the 2008 System of National Accounts (SNA). Under this, revenues are generally attributed to the level of government that exercises the authority to impose the tax or has the final discretion to set and vary the tax rate.

In all of the following tables a ("..") indicates not available. The main series in this volume cover the years 1990 to 2022.

Figures referring to 1991-99, 2001-04, 2006-09, 2011-14 and 2016-21 in Tables 6.1 to 6.27 have been omitted because of lack of space. Complete series are, however, available on line at http://dx.doi.org/10.1787/data-00641-en.

Table 6.1. Antigua and Barbuda, tax revenues by sub-sectors of government

Million XCD

	Federal government					State/Regional				
	1990	2000	2010	2021	2022	1990	2000	2010	2021	2022
1000 Taxes on income, profits and capital gains	..	**38**	**92**	**83**	**71**	..	..	..	..	..
1100 Of individuals	..	0	33	0	0	..	..	..	..	..
1200 Corporate	..	37	59	83	71	..	..	..	..	..
1300 Unallocable between 1100 and 1200	..	0	0	0	0	..	..	..	..	..
2000 Social security contributions	..	**0**	**0**	**0**	**0**	..	..	..	..	..
2100 Employees	..	..	..	..	..	..	..	..	..	..
2200 Employers	..	..	..	..	..	..	..	..	..	..
2300 Self-employed or non-employed	..	..	..	..	..	..	..	..	..	..
2400 Unallocable between 2100, 2200 and 2300	..	..	..	..	..	..	..	..	..	..
3000 Taxes on payroll and workforce	..	**0**	**0**	**0**	**0**	..	..	..	..	..
4000 Taxes on property	..	**13**	**49**	**93**	**96**	..	..	..	..	..
4100 Recurrent taxes on immovable property	..	0	18	24	32	..	..	..	..	..
4200 Recurrent taxes on net wealth	..	0	0	0	0	..	..	..	..	..
4300 Estate, inheritance and gift taxes	..	0	0	0	0	..	..	..	..	..
4400 Taxes on financial and capital transactions	..	13	32	69	64	..	..	..	..	..
4500 Non-recurrent taxes	..	0	0	0	0	..	..	..	..	..
4600 Other recurrent taxes on property	..	0	0	0	0	..	..	..	..	..
5000 Taxes on goods and services	..	**217**	**435**	**490**	**585**	..	..	..	..	..
5100 Taxes on production, sale, transfer, etc	..	217	429	487	581	..	..	..	..	..
5110 General taxes	..	0	179	315	396	..	..	..	..	..
5120 Taxes on specific goods and services	..	217	250	171	186	..	..	..	..	..
5130 Unallocable between 5110 and 5120	..	0	0	0	0	..	..	..	..	..
5200 Taxes on use of goods and perform activities	..	0	6	3	4	..	..	..	..	..
5300 Unallocable between 5100 and 5200	..	0	0	1	0	..	..	..	..	..
6000 Other taxes	..	**0**	**0**	**0**	**0**	..	..	..	..	..
6100 Paid solely by business	..	..	..	..	..	..	..	..	..	..
6200 Other	..	..	..	..	..	..	..	..	..	..
Total tax revenue	..	**268**	**577**	**667**	**752**	..	..	..	..	..

Million XCD

	Local government					Social security funds[1]				
	1990	2000	2010	2021	2022	1990	2000	2010	2021	2022
1000 Taxes on income, profits and capital gains	..	..	..	..	..	..	..	**0**	**0**	**0**
1100 Of individuals	..	..	..	..	..	..	..	..	..	..
1200 Corporate	..	..	..	..	..	..	..	..	..	..
1300 Unallocable between 1100 and 1200	..	..	..	..	..	..	..	..	..	..
2000 Social security contributions	..	..	..	..	..	..	..	**83**	**131**	**156**
2100 Employees	..	..	..	..	..	..	..	..	..	..
2200 Employers	..	..	..	..	..	..	..	..	..	..
2300 Self-employed or non-employed	..	..	..	..	..	..	..	..	..	..
2400 Unallocable between 2100, 2200 and 2300	..	..	..	..	..	..	..	83	131	156
3000 Taxes on payroll and workforce	..	..	..	..	..	..	..	**0**	**0**	**0**
4000 Taxes on property	..	..	..	..	..	..	..	**0**	**0**	**0**
4100 Recurrent taxes on immovable property	..	..	..	..	..	..	..	..	..	..
4200 Recurrent taxes on net wealth	..	..	..	..	..	..	..	..	..	..
4300 Estate, inheritance and gift taxes	..	..	..	..	..	..	..	..	..	..
4400 Taxes on financial and capital transactions	..	..	..	..	..	..	..	..	..	..
4500 Non-recurrent taxes	..	..	..	..	..	..	..	..	..	..
4600 Other recurrent taxes on property	..	..	..	..	..	..	..	..	..	..
5000 Taxes on goods and services	..	..	..	..	..	..	..	**0**	**0**	**0**
5100 Taxes on production, sale, transfer, etc	..	..	..	..	..	..	..	..	..	..
5110 General taxes	..	..	..	..	..	..	..	..	..	..
5120 Taxes on specific goods and services	..	..	..	..	..	..	..	..	..	..
5130 Unallocable between 5110 and 5120	..	..	..	..	..	..	..	..	..	..
5200 Taxes on use of goods and perform activities	..	..	..	..	..	..	..	..	..	..
5300 Unallocable between 5100 and 5200	..	..	..	..	..	..	..	..	..	..
6000 Other taxes	..	..	..	..	..	..	..	**0**	**0**	**0**
6100 Paid solely by business	..	..	..	..	..	..	..	..	..	..
6200 Other	..	..	..	..	..	..	..	..	..	..
Total tax revenue	..	..	..	..	..	..	..	**83**	**131**	**156**

.. Not available

1. Figures for 2019-22 are estimated.

Table 6.2. Argentina, tax revenues by sub-sectors of government

Million ARS

	Federal government					State/Regional				
	1990	2000	2010	2021	2022	1990	2000	2010	2021	2022
1000 Taxes on income, profits and capital gains	**542**	**11 303**	**78 427**	**2 351 998**	**4 727 878**	**0**	**0**	**0**	**0**	**0**
1100 Of individuals	141	3 937	23 980	1 004 641	2 083 662	..	..	..	..	..
1200 Corporate	357	6 575	50 664	1 151 704	2 398 339	..	..	..	..	..
1300 Unallocable between 1100 and 1200	43	792	3 783	195 653	245 876	..	..	..	..	..
2000 Social security contributions[1]	**0**	**0**	**0**	**0**	**0**	**0**	**0**	**0**	**0**	**0**
2100 Employees	..	..	..	..	..	..	..	..	..	..
2200 Employers	..	..	..	..	..	..	..	..	..	..
2300 Self-employed or non-employed	..	..	..	..	..	..	..	..	..	..
2400 Unallocable between 2100, 2200 and 2300	..	..	..	..	..	..	..	..	..	..
3000 Taxes on payroll and workforce	**0**	**0**	**0**	**0**	**0**	**0**	**0**	**0**	**0**	**0**
4000 Taxes on property	**616**	**1 254**	**32 674**	**1 043 679**	**1 786 657**	**549**	**2 614**	**10 864**	**373 956**	**614 364**
4100 Recurrent taxes on immovable property	0	0	0	0	0	419	1 809	5 035	170 405	262 053
4200 Recurrent taxes on net wealth	246	1 084	5 248	283 469	428 916	0	0	0	0	0
4300 Estate, inheritance and gift taxes	0	0	0	0	0	0	0	0	0	0
4400 Taxes on financial and capital transactions	330	100	27 423	760 209	1 357 741	130	804	5 829	203 551	352 310
4500 Non-recurrent taxes	40	70	3	0	0	0	0	0	0	0
4600 Other recurrent taxes on property	0	0	0	0	0	0	0	0	0	0
5000 Taxes on goods and services	**4 669**	**27 592**	**198 346**	**5 310 281**	**9 335 993**	**967**	**6 947**	**54 746**	**1 900 411**	**3 502 540**
5100 Taxes on production, sale, transfer, etc	4 671	28 174	201 402	5 376 231	9 445 963	791	6 114	51 148	1 778 442	3 312 564
5110 General taxes	1 594	19 009	116 386	3 243 608	5 831 330	791	6 114	51 148	1 778 442	3 312 564
5120 Taxes on specific goods and services	3 077	9 166	85 016	2 132 623	3 614 634	0	0	0	0	0
5130 Unallocable between 5110 and 5120	0	0	0	0	0	0	0	0	0	0
5200 Taxes on use of goods and perform activities[2]	..	..	..	..	..	177	833	3 598	121 969	189 977
5300 Unallocable between 5100 and 5200	-3	-583	-3 056	-65 950	-109 970	0	0	0	0	0
6000 Other taxes	**214**	**395**	**2 386**	**36 762**	**58 005**	**78**	**1 309**	**3 110**	**44 440**	**72 233**
6100 Paid solely by business	0	354	2 093	31 500	39 721	0	0	0	0	0
6200 Other[3]	214	41	294	5 262	18 284	78	1 309	3 110	44 440	72 233
Total tax revenue	**6 040**	**40 544**	**311 834**	**8 742 720**	**15 908 533**	**1 594**	**10 870**	**68 720**	**2 318 806**	**4 189 137**

Million ARS

	Local government					Social security funds				
	1990	2000	2010	2021	2022	1990	2000	2010	2021	2022
1000 Taxes on income, profits and capital gains	..	..	..	..	..	**0**	**0**	**0**	**0**	**0**
1100 Of individuals	..	..	..	..	..	..	..	..	..	..
1200 Corporate	..	..	..	..	..	..	..	..	..	..
1300 Unallocable between 1100 and 1200	..	..	..	..	..	..	..	..	..	..
2000 Social security contributions[1]	..	..	..	..	..	**2 583**	**9 670**	**102 460**	**2 398 126**	**4 331 972**
2100 Employees	..	..	..	..	..	..	2 486	37 990	967 274	1 719 052
2200 Employers	..	..	..	..	..	..	6 069	54 713	1 356 354	2 492 899
2300 Self-employed or non-employed	..	..	..	..	..	98	1 115	9 757	74 498	120 021
2400 Unallocable between 2100, 2200 and 2300	..	..	..	..	..	2 485	0	0	0	0
3000 Taxes on payroll and workforce	..	..	..	..	..	**0**	**0**	**0**	**0**	**0**
4000 Taxes on property	..	..	..	..	..	**0**	**0**	**0**	**0**	**0**
4100 Recurrent taxes on immovable property	..	..	..	..	..	..	..	..	..	..
4200 Recurrent taxes on net wealth	..	..	..	..	..	..	..	..	..	..
4300 Estate, inheritance and gift taxes	..	..	..	..	..	..	..	..	..	..
4400 Taxes on financial and capital transactions	..	..	..	..	..	..	..	..	..	..
4500 Non-recurrent taxes	..	..	..	..	..	..	..	..	..	..
4600 Other recurrent taxes on property	..	..	..	..	..	..	..	..	..	..
5000 Taxes on goods and services	..	..	..	..	..	**0**	**0**	**0**	**0**	**0**
5100 Taxes on production, sale, transfer, etc	..	..	..	..	..	..	..	..	..	..
5110 General taxes	..	..	..	..	..	..	..	..	..	..
5120 Taxes on specific goods and services	..	..	..	..	..	..	..	..	..	..
5130 Unallocable between 5110 and 5120	..	..	..	..	..	..	..	..	..	..
5200 Taxes on use of goods and perform activities[2]	..	..	..	..	..	..	..	..	..	..
5300 Unallocable between 5100 and 5200	..	..	..	..	..	..	..	..	..	..
6000 Other taxes	..	..	..	..	..	**0**	**0**	**0**	**0**	**0**
6100 Paid solely by business	..	..	..	..	..	..	..	..	..	..
6200 Other[3]	..	..	..	..	..	..	..	..	..	..
Total tax revenue	..	..	..	..	..	**2 583**	**9 670**	**102 460**	**2 398 126**	**4 331 972**

.. Not available

1. The figures may be under-estimated as they exclude certain types of social security contributions for which data are not readily available.
2. In ECLAC data, tax on ownership of motor vehicles is classified in category 4000.
3. The tax debt payments in 2016 include revenue following the implementation of a new voluntary disclosure regime in July 2016 (Law 27260).

Table 6.3. Bahamas, tax revenues by sub-sectors of government

Million BSD

	Federal government					State/Regional				
	1990	2000	2010	2021	2022	1990	2000	2010	2021	2022
1000 Taxes on income, profits and capital gains	**0**	**0**	**0**	**0**	**0**	..	..	..	..	..
1100 Of individuals	0	0	0	0	0	..	..	..	..	..
1200 Corporate	0	0	0	0	0	..	..	..	..	..
1300 Unallocable between 1100 and 1200	0	0	0	0	0	..	..	..	..	..
2000 Social security contributions	**0**	**0**	**0**	**0**	**0**	..	..	..	..	..
2100 Employees	..	..	..	..	..	..	..	..	..	..
2200 Employers	..	..	..	..	..	..	..	..	..	..
2300 Self-employed or non-employed	..	..	..	..	..	..	..	..	..	..
2400 Unallocable between 2100, 2200 and 2300	..	..	..	..	..	..	..	..	..	..
3000 Taxes on payroll and workforce	**0**	**0**	**0**	**0**	**0**	..	..	..	..	..
4000 Taxes on property	**56**	**208**	**269**	**203**	**241**	..	..	..	..	..
4100 Recurrent taxes on immovable property	19	32	92	143	147	..	..	..	..	..
4200 Recurrent taxes on net wealth	0	0	0	0	0	..	..	..	..	..
4300 Estate, inheritance and gift taxes	0	0	0	0	0	..	..	..	..	..
4400 Taxes on financial and capital transactions	37	176	177	60	94	..	..	..	..	..
4500 Non-recurrent taxes	0	0	0	0	0	..	..	..	..	..
4600 Other recurrent taxes on property	0	0	0	0	0	..	..	..	..	..
5000 Taxes on goods and services	**386**	**620**	**780**	**1 408**	**1 917**	..	..	..	..	..
5100 Taxes on production, sale, transfer, etc	354	552	657	1 253	1 745	..	..	..	..	..
5110 General taxes	0	0	0	740	1 136	..	..	..	..	..
5120 Taxes on specific goods and services	354	552	657	513	609	..	..	..	..	..
5130 Unallocable between 5110 and 5120	0	0	0	0	0	..	..	..	..	..
5200 Taxes on use of goods and perform activities	32	69	123	155	172	..	..	..	..	..
5300 Unallocable between 5100 and 5200	0	0	0	0	0	..	..	..	..	..
6000 Other taxes	**-4**	**21**	**60**	**0**	**0**	..	..	..	..	..
6100 Paid solely by business	0	0	0	..	..	..	..	..	..	..
6200 Other	-4	21	60	..	..	..	..	..	..	..
Total tax revenue	**438**	**849**	**1 109**	**1 612**	**2 158**	..	..	..	..	..

Million BSD

	Local government					Social security funds[1]				
	1990	2000	2010	2021	2022	1990	2000	2010	2021	2022
1000 Taxes on income, profits and capital gains	..	..	..	..	..	**0**	**0**	**0**	**0**	**0**
1100 Of individuals	..	..	..	..	..	..	..	..	..	..
1200 Corporate	..	..	..	..	..	..	..	..	..	..
1300 Unallocable between 1100 and 1200	..	..	..	..	..	..	..	..	..	..
2000 Social security contributions	..	..	..	..	..	**66**	**115**	**167**	**219**	**267**
2100 Employees	..	..	..	..	..	..	..	60	..	..
2200 Employers	..	..	..	..	..	..	..	104	..	..
2300 Self-employed or non-employed	..	..	..	..	..	..	..	3	..	..
2400 Unallocable between 2100, 2200 and 2300	..	..	..	..	..	66	115	0	219	267
3000 Taxes on payroll and workforce	..	..	..	..	..	**0**	**0**	**0**	**0**	**0**
4000 Taxes on property	..	..	..	..	..	**0**	**0**	**0**	**0**	**0**
4100 Recurrent taxes on immovable property	..	..	..	..	..	..	..	..	..	..
4200 Recurrent taxes on net wealth	..	..	..	..	..	..	..	..	..	..
4300 Estate, inheritance and gift taxes	..	..	..	..	..	..	..	..	..	..
4400 Taxes on financial and capital transactions	..	..	..	..	..	..	..	..	..	..
4500 Non-recurrent taxes	..	..	..	..	..	..	..	..	..	..
4600 Other recurrent taxes on property	..	..	..	..	..	..	..	..	..	..
5000 Taxes on goods and services	..	..	..	..	..	**0**	**0**	**0**	**0**	**0**
5100 Taxes on production, sale, transfer, etc	..	..	..	..	..	..	..	..	..	..
5110 General taxes	..	..	..	..	..	..	..	..	..	..
5120 Taxes on specific goods and services	..	..	..	..	..	..	..	..	..	..
5130 Unallocable between 5110 and 5120	..	..	..	..	..	..	..	..	..	..
5200 Taxes on use of goods and perform activities	..	..	..	..	..	..	..	..	..	..
5300 Unallocable between 5100 and 5200	..	..	..	..	..	..	..	..	..	..
6000 Other taxes	..	..	..	..	..	**0**	**0**	**0**	..	..
6100 Paid solely by business	..	..	..	..	..	..	..	..	..	..
6200 Other	..	..	..	..	..	..	..	..	..	..
Total tax revenue	..	..	..	..	..	**66**	**115**	**167**	**219**	**267**

.. Not available

1. The data for social security contributions are estimated for 2021 and 2022.

Table 6.4. Barbados, tax revenues by sub-sectors of government

Million BBD

	Federal government					State/Regional				
	1990	2000	2010	2021	2022	1990	2000	2010	2021	2022
1000 Taxes on income, profits and capital gains	**250**	**599**	**766**	**897**	**1 023**	..	..	..	..	..
1100 Of individuals	140	293	395	385	393	..	..	..	..	..
1200 Corporate	95	269	294	451	549	..	..	..	..	..
1300 Unallocable between 1100 and 1200	15	37	76	61	81	..	..	..	..	..
2000 Social security contributions	**0**	**0**	**0**	**0**	**0**	..	..	..	..	..
2100 Employees	..	..	..	..	..	..	..	..	..	..
2200 Employers	..	..	..	..	..	..	..	..	..	..
2300 Self-employed or non-employed	..	..	..	..	..	..	..	..	..	..
2400 Unallocable between 2100, 2200 and 2300	..	..	..	..	..	..	..	..	..	..
3000 Taxes on payroll and workforce	**0**	**0**	**0**	**0**	**0**	..	..	..	..	..
4000 Taxes on property	**147**	**108**	**130**	**219**	**239**	..	..	..	..	..
4100 Recurrent taxes on immovable property	46	95	118	205	217	..	..	..	..	..
4200 Recurrent taxes on net wealth	0	0	0	0	0	..	..	..	..	..
4300 Estate, inheritance and gift taxes	0	0	0	0	0	..	..	..	..	..
4400 Taxes on financial and capital transactions	101	13	12	13	22	..	..	..	..	..
4500 Non-recurrent taxes	0	0	0	0	0	..	..	..	..	..
4600 Other recurrent taxes on property	0	0	0	0	0	..	..	..	..	..
5000 Taxes on goods and services	**495**	**889**	**1 276**	**1 531**	**1 761**	..	..	..	..	..
5100 Taxes on production, sale, transfer, etc	424	788	1 105	1 459	1 686	..	..	..	..	..
5110 General taxes	197	492	768	885	1 023	..	..	..	..	..
5120 Taxes on specific goods and services	227	296	337	575	663	..	..	..	..	..
5130 Unallocable between 5110 and 5120	0	0	0	0	0	..	..	..	..	..
5200 Taxes on use of goods and perform activities	71	101	171	72	75	..	..	..	..	..
5300 Unallocable between 5100 and 5200	0	0	0	0	0	..	..	..	..	..
6000 Other taxes	**0**	**0**	**0**	**0**	**0**	..	..	..	..	..
6100 Paid solely by business	..	..	..	..	..	..	..	..	..	..
6200 Other	..	..	..	..	..	..	..	..	..	..
Total tax revenue	**892**	**1 596**	**2 171**	**2 646**	**3 022**	..	..	..	..	..

Million BBD

	Local government					Social security funds				
	1990	2000	2010	2021	2022	1990	2000	2010	2021	2022
1000 Taxes on income, profits and capital gains	..	..	..	..	..	**0**	**0**	**0**	**0**	**0**
1100 Of individuals	..	..	..	..	..	..	..	..	..	..
1200 Corporate	..	..	..	..	..	..	..	..	..	..
1300 Unallocable between 1100 and 1200	..	..	..	..	..	..	..	..	..	..
2000 Social security contributions	..	..	..	..	..	**134**	**295**	**565**	**595**	**621**
2100 Employees	..	..	..	..	..	..	..	..	..	..
2200 Employers	..	..	..	..	..	..	..	..	..	..
2300 Self-employed or non-employed	..	..	..	..	..	..	..	..	..	..
2400 Unallocable between 2100, 2200 and 2300	..	..	..	..	..	134	295	565	595	621
3000 Taxes on payroll and workforce	..	..	..	..	..	**0**	**0**	**0**	**0**	**0**
4000 Taxes on property	..	..	..	..	..	**0**	**0**	**0**	**0**	**0**
4100 Recurrent taxes on immovable property	..	..	..	..	..	..	..	..	..	..
4200 Recurrent taxes on net wealth	..	..	..	..	..	..	..	..	..	..
4300 Estate, inheritance and gift taxes	..	..	..	..	..	..	..	..	..	..
4400 Taxes on financial and capital transactions	..	..	..	..	..	..	..	..	..	..
4500 Non-recurrent taxes	..	..	..	..	..	..	..	..	..	..
4600 Other recurrent taxes on property	..	..	..	..	..	..	..	..	..	..
5000 Taxes on goods and services	..	..	..	..	..	**0**	**0**	**0**	**0**	**0**
5100 Taxes on production, sale, transfer, etc	..	..	..	..	..	..	..	..	..	..
5110 General taxes	..	..	..	..	..	..	..	..	..	..
5120 Taxes on specific goods and services	..	..	..	..	..	..	..	..	..	..
5130 Unallocable between 5110 and 5120	..	..	..	..	..	..	..	..	..	..
5200 Taxes on use of goods and perform activities	..	..	..	..	..	..	..	..	..	..
5300 Unallocable between 5100 and 5200	..	..	..	..	..	..	..	..	..	..
6000 Other taxes	..	..	..	..	..	**0**	**0**	**0**	**0**	**0**
6100 Paid solely by business	..	..	..	..	..	..	..	..	..	..
6200 Other	..	..	..	..	..	..	..	..	..	..
Total tax revenue	..	..	..	..	..	**134**	**295**	**565**	**595**	**621**

.. Not available

Table 6.5. Belize, tax revenues by sub-sectors of government

Million BZD

	Federal government					State/Regional				
	1990	2000	2010	2021	2022	1990	2000	2010	2021	2022
1000 Taxes on income, profits and capital gains	**37**	**76**	**248**	**224**	**345**	..	..	..	..	..
1100 Of individuals	21	19	52	78	121	..	..	..	..	..
1200 Corporate	12	51	189	126	211	..	..	..	..	..
1300 Unallocable between 1100 and 1200	4	6	7	20	13	..	..	..	..	..
2000 Social security contributions	**0**	**0**	**0**	**0**	**0**	..	..	..	..	..
2100 Employees	..	..	..	..	..	..	..	..	..	..
2200 Employers	..	..	..	..	..	..	..	..	..	..
2300 Self-employed or non-employed	..	..	..	..	..	..	..	..	..	..
2400 Unallocable between 2100, 2200 and 2300	..	..	..	..	..	..	..	..	..	..
3000 Taxes on payroll and workforce	**0**	**0**	**0**	**0**	**0**	..	..	..	..	..
4000 Taxes on property	**33**	**11**	**16**	**54**	**35**	..	..	..	..	..
4100 Recurrent taxes on immovable property	0	0	0	0	0	..	..	..	..	..
4200 Recurrent taxes on net wealth	0	0	0	0	0	..	..	..	..	..
4300 Estate, inheritance and gift taxes	0	0	0	0	0	..	..	..	..	..
4400 Taxes on financial and capital transactions	33	11	16	54	35	..	..	..	..	..
4500 Non-recurrent taxes	0	0	0	0	0	..	..	..	..	..
4600 Other recurrent taxes on property	0	0	0	0	0	..	..	..	..	..
5000 Taxes on goods and services	**97**	**211**	**409**	**724**	**815**	..	..	..	..	..
5100 Taxes on production, sale, transfer, etc	94	207	400	715	806	..	..	..	..	..
5110 General taxes	0	82	199	306	397	..	..	..	..	..
5120 Taxes on specific goods and services	94	125	200	409	409	..	..	..	..	..
5130 Unallocable between 5110 and 5120	0	0	0	0	0	..	..	..	..	..
5200 Taxes on use of goods and perform activities	3	4	9	9	9	..	..	..	..	..
5300 Unallocable between 5100 and 5200	0	0	0	0	0	..	..	..	..	..
6000 Other taxes	**0**	**0**	**0**	**0**	**0**	..	..	..	..	..
6100 Paid solely by business	..	..	..	..	..	..	..	..	..	..
6200 Other	..	..	..	..	..	..	..	..	..	..
Total tax revenue	**167**	**298**	**673**	**1 002**	**1 196**	..	..	..	..	..

Million BZD

	Local government					Social security funds				
	1990	2000	2010	2021	2022	1990	2000	2010	2021	2022
1000 Taxes on income, profits and capital gains	**0**	**0**	**0**	**0**	**0**	**0**	**0**	**0**	**0**	**0**
1100 Of individuals	..	..	..	..	..	..	..	..	..	..
1200 Corporate	..	..	..	..	..	..	..	..	..	..
1300 Unallocable between 1100 and 1200	..	..	..	..	..	..	..	..	..	..
2000 Social security contributions	**0**	**0**	**0**	**0**	**0**	**10**	**18**	**60**	**117**	**144**
2100 Employees	..	..	..	..	..	..	..	..	..	..
2200 Employers	..	..	..	..	..	..	..	..	..	..
2300 Self-employed or non-employed	..	..	..	..	..	..	..	..	..	..
2400 Unallocable between 2100, 2200 and 2300	..	..	..	..	..	10	18	60	117	144
3000 Taxes on payroll and workforce	**0**	**0**	**0**	**0**	**0**	**0**	**0**	**0**	**0**	**0**
4000 Taxes on property	**1**	**2**	**7**	**9**	**7**	**0**	**0**	**0**	**0**	**0**
4100 Recurrent taxes on immovable property	1	2	7	9	6	..	..	..	..	..
4200 Recurrent taxes on net wealth	0	0	0	0	0	..	..	..	..	..
4300 Estate, inheritance and gift taxes	0	0	0	0	0	..	..	..	..	..
4400 Taxes on financial and capital transactions	0	0	0	0	0	..	..	..	..	..
4500 Non-recurrent taxes	0	0	0	0	0	..	..	..	..	..
4600 Other recurrent taxes on property	0	0	0	0	0	..	..	..	..	..
5000 Taxes on goods and services	**0**	**0**	**0**	**0**	**0**	**0**	**0**	**0**	**0**	**0**
5100 Taxes on production, sale, transfer, etc	..	..	..	..	..	..	..	..	..	..
5110 General taxes	..	..	..	..	..	..	..	..	..	..
5120 Taxes on specific goods and services	..	..	..	..	..	..	..	..	..	..
5130 Unallocable between 5110 and 5120	..	..	..	..	..	..	..	..	..	..
5200 Taxes on use of goods and perform activities	..	..	..	..	..	..	..	..	..	..
5300 Unallocable between 5100 and 5200	..	..	..	..	..	..	..	..	..	..
6000 Other taxes	**0**	**0**	**0**	**0**	**0**	**0**	**0**	**0**	**0**	**0**
6100 Paid solely by business	..	..	..	..	..	..	..	..	..	..
6200 Other	..	..	..	..	..	..	..	..	..	..
Total tax revenue	**1**	**2**	**7**	**9**	**7**	**10**	**18**	**60**	**117**	**144**

.. Not available

Table 6.6. Bolivia, tax revenues by sub-sectors of government

Million BOB

	Federal government					State/Regional				
	1990	2000	2010	2021	2022	1990	2000	2010	2021	2022
1000 Taxes on income, profits and capital gains	**68**	**1 209**	**6 294**	**7 644**	**10 397**	..	..	..	..	..
1100 Of individuals	68	214	263	457	502	..	..	..	..	..
1200 Corporate	0	995	6 031	7 187	9 896	..	..	..	..	..
1300 Unallocable between 1100 and 1200	0	0	0	0	0	..	..	..	..	..
2000 Social security contributions	**0**	**0**	**0**	**0**	**0**	..	..	..	..	..
2100 Employees	..	..	..	..	..	..	..	..	..	..
2200 Employers	..	..	..	..	..	..	..	..	..	..
2300 Self-employed or non-employed	..	..	..	..	..	..	..	..	..	..
2400 Unallocable between 2100, 2200 and 2300	..	..	..	..	..	..	..	..	..	..
3000 Taxes on payroll and workforce	**0**	**0**	**0**	**0**	**0**	..	..	..	..	..
4000 Taxes on property	**1**	**3**	**367**	**743**	**767**	..	..	..	..	..
4100 Recurrent taxes on immovable property	0	0	0	0	0	..	..	..	..	..
4200 Recurrent taxes on net wealth	0	0	0	241	205	..	..	..	..	..
4300 Estate, inheritance and gift taxes	1	3	20	0	0	..	..	..	..	..
4400 Taxes on financial and capital transactions	0	0	347	502	561	..	..	..	..	..
4500 Non-recurrent taxes	0	0	0	0	0	..	..	..	..	..
4600 Other recurrent taxes on property	0	0	0	0	0	..	..	..	..	..
5000 Taxes on goods and services	**907**	**6 656**	**17 791**	**32 190**	**36 806**	..	..	..	..	..
5100 Taxes on production, sale, transfer, etc	907	6 656	17 791	32 190	36 806	..	..	..	..	..
5110 General taxes	584	3 953	12 541	24 307	27 953	..	..	..	..	..
5120 Taxes on specific goods and services	324	2 702	5 250	7 883	8 853	..	..	..	..	..
5130 Unallocable between 5110 and 5120	0	0	0	0	0	..	..	..	..	..
5200 Taxes on use of goods and perform activities	0	0	0	0	0	..	..	..	..	..
5300 Unallocable between 5100 and 5200	0	0	0	0	0	..	..	..	..	..
6000 Other taxes	**30**	**42**	**451**	**2 997**	**3 526**	..	..	..	..	..
6100 Paid solely by business	4	6	12	29	30	..	..	..	..	..
6200 Other	26	36	439	2 968	3 496	..	..	..	..	..
Total tax revenue	**1 005**	**7 910**	**24 903**	**43 574**	**51 496**	..	..	..	..	..

Million BOB

	Local government[1]					Social security funds[2]				
	1990	2000	2010	2021	2022	1990	2000	2010	2021	2022
1000 Taxes on income, profits and capital gains	..	**0**	**0**	**0**	**0**	..	**0**	**0**	**0**	**0**
1100 Of individuals	..	..	..	..	..	..	..	..	..	..
1200 Corporate	..	..	..	..	..	..	..	..	..	..
1300 Unallocable between 1100 and 1200	..	..	..	..	..	..	..	..	..	..
2000 Social security contributions	..	**0**	**0**	**0**	**0**	..	**666**	**5 265**	**16 814**	**17 351**
2100 Employees	..	..	..	..	..	..	..	..	..	..
2200 Employers	..	..	..	..	..	..	..	..	..	..
2300 Self-employed or non-employed	..	..	..	..	..	..	..	..	..	..
2400 Unallocable between 2100, 2200 and 2300	..	..	..	..	..	..	666	5 265	16 814	17 351
3000 Taxes on payroll and workforce	..	**0**	**0**	**0**	**0**	..	**0**	**0**	**0**	**0**
4000 Taxes on property	..	**0**	**0**	**0**	**0**	..	**0**	**0**	**0**	**0**
4100 Recurrent taxes on immovable property	..	..	..	..	..	..	..	..	..	..
4200 Recurrent taxes on net wealth	..	..	..	..	..	..	..	..	..	..
4300 Estate, inheritance and gift taxes	..	..	..	..	..	..	..	..	..	..
4400 Taxes on financial and capital transactions	..	..	..	..	..	..	..	..	..	..
4500 Non-recurrent taxes	..	..	..	..	..	..	..	..	..	..
4600 Other recurrent taxes on property	..	..	..	..	..	..	..	..	..	..
5000 Taxes on goods and services	..	**0**	**0**	**0**	**0**	..	**0**	**0**	**0**	**0**
5100 Taxes on production, sale, transfer, etc	..	..	..	..	..	..	..	..	..	..
5110 General taxes	..	..	..	..	..	..	..	..	..	..
5120 Taxes on specific goods and services	..	..	..	..	..	..	..	..	..	..
5130 Unallocable between 5110 and 5120	..	..	..	..	..	..	..	..	..	..
5200 Taxes on use of goods and perform activities	..	..	..	..	..	..	..	..	..	..
5300 Unallocable between 5100 and 5200	..	..	..	..	..	..	..	..	..	..
6000 Other taxes	..	**575**	**1 381**	**2 815**	**3 166**	..	**0**	**0**	**0**	**0**
6100 Paid solely by business	..	0	0	0	0	..	..	..	..	..
6200 Other	..	575	1 381	2 815	3 166	..	..	..	..	..
Total tax revenue	..	**575**	**1 381**	**2 815**	**3 166**	..	**666**	**5 265**	**16 814**	**17 351**

.. Not available

1. The figures exclude local government tax revenues for the period 1990-1993 as the data are not available.
2. The data for social security contributions include contributions to Bolivia's pension system (since its nationalisation in 2010) and healthcare related funds.

Table 6.7. Brazil, tax revenues by sub-sectors of government

Million BRL

	Federal government					State/Regional				
	1990	2000	2010	2021	2022	1990	2000	2010	2021	2022
1000 Taxes on income, profits and capital gains	**1**	**68 667**	**258 738**	**698 098**	**910 191**	**0**	**0**	**0**	**0**	**0**
1100 Of individuals	0	3 406	87 828	262 008	303 290	..	..	..	..	..
1200 Corporate	0	25 430	128 255	322 527	437 358	..	..	..	..	..
1300 Unallocable between 1100 and 1200	0	39 831	42 656	113 564	169 543	..	..	..	..	..
2000 Social security contributions	**0**	**0**	**0**	**0**	**0**	**0**	**0**	**0**	**0**	**0**
2100 Employees	..	..	..	..	..	..	..	..	..	..
2200 Employers	..	..	..	..	..	..	..	..	..	..
2300 Self-employed or non-employed	..	..	..	..	..	..	..	..	..	..
2400 Unallocable between 2100, 2200 and 2300	..	..	..	..	..	..	..	..	..	..
3000 Taxes on payroll and workforce	**0**	**5 437**	**21 348**	**47 320**	**54 297**	**0**	**0**	**0**	**0**	**0**
4000 Taxes on property	**0**	**17 726**	**27 044**	**51 168**	**61 583**	**0**	**329**	**3 166**	**14 201**	**14 613**
4100 Recurrent taxes on immovable property	0	234	485	2 167	2 594	0	0	437	1 221	1 218
4200 Recurrent taxes on net wealth	0	0	0	0	0	0	0	0	0	0
4300 Estate, inheritance and gift taxes	0	0	0	0	0	0	329	2 518	12 330	12 874
4400 Taxes on financial and capital transactions	0	17 492	26 559	49 001	58 989	0	0	210	651	521
4500 Non-recurrent taxes	0	0	0	0	0	0	0	0	0	0
4600 Other recurrent taxes on property	0	0	0	0	0	0	0	0	0	0
5000 Taxes on goods and services	**1**	**75 502**	**256 256**	**503 599**	**477 900**	**1**	**87 573**	**290 506**	**706 483**	**758 941**
5100 Taxes on production, sale, transfer, etc	1	75 502	250 857	489 218	477 897	1	82 279	269 140	654 722	695 012
5110 General taxes[1]	0	48 358	182 188	345 672	350 333	1	82 279	269 056	654 490	694 786
5120 Taxes on specific goods and services	0	27 144	68 669	143 547	127 564	0	0	84	232	226
5130 Unallocable between 5110 and 5120	0	0	0	0	0	0	0	0	0	0
5200 Taxes on use of goods and perform activities	0	0	5 399	14 380	3	0	5 294	21 367	51 762	63 928
5300 Unallocable between 5100 and 5200	0	0	0	0	0	0	0	0	0	0
6000 Other taxes	**0**	**1 479**	**480**	**144**	**19 196**	**0**	**322**	**0**	**0**	**4**
6100 Paid solely by business	0	0	0	0	0	0	0	..	..	0
6200 Other	0	1 479	480	144	19 196	0	322	..	..	4
Total tax revenue	**1**	**168 811**	**563 866**	**1 300 329**	**1 523 167**	**1**	**88 224**	**293 672**	**720 685**	**773 557**

Million BRL

	Local government					Social security funds				
	1990	2000	2010	2021	2022	1990	2000	2010	2021	2022
1000 Taxes on income, profits and capital gains	**0**	**0**	**0**	**0**	**0**	**0**	**0**	**0**	**0**	**0**
1100 Of individuals	..	..	..	..	..	..	..	..	..	..
1200 Corporate	..	..	..	..	..	..	..	..	..	..
1300 Unallocable between 1100 and 1200	..	..	..	..	..	..	..	..	..	..
2000 Social security contributions	**0**	**0**	**0**	**0**	**0**	**1**	**83 469**	**316 530**	**694 877**	**798 214**
2100 Employees	..	..	..	..	..	..	..	75 509	182 011	..
2200 Employers	..	..	..	..	..	0	18 709	240 280	499 361	156 298
2300 Self-employed or non-employed	..	..	..	..	..	..	..	..	..	..
2400 Unallocable between 2100, 2200 and 2300	..	..	..	..	..	1	64 760	741	13 505	641 917
3000 Taxes on payroll and workforce	**0**	**0**	**0**	**0**	**0**	**0**	**0**	**0**	**0**	**0**
4000 Taxes on property	**0**	**5 469**	**23 285**	**76 475**	**83 849**	**0**	**0**	**0**	**0**	**0**
4100 Recurrent taxes on immovable property	0	4 519	17 444	55 899	63 109	..	..	..	..	..
4200 Recurrent taxes on net wealth	0	0	0	0	0	..	..	..	..	..
4300 Estate, inheritance and gift taxes	0	0	0	0	0	..	..	..	..	..
4400 Taxes on financial and capital transactions	0	950	5 840	20 576	20 739	..	..	..	..	..
4500 Non-recurrent taxes	0	0	0	0	0	..	..	..	..	..
4600 Other recurrent taxes on property	0	0	0	0	0	..	..	..	..	..
5000 Taxes on goods and services	**0**	**6 106**	**35 873**	**100 366**	**119 774**	**0**	**0**	**0**	**0**	**0**
5100 Taxes on production, sale, transfer, etc	0	6 106	35 873	100 366	119 774	..	..	..	..	..
5110 General taxes[1]	0	6 106	32 756	88 694	107 218	..	..	..	..	..
5120 Taxes on specific goods and services	0	0	3 117	11 672	12 555	..	..	..	..	..
5130 Unallocable between 5110 and 5120	0	0	0	0	0	..	..	..	..	..
5200 Taxes on use of goods and perform activities	0	0	0	0	0	..	..	..	..	..
5300 Unallocable between 5100 and 5200	0	0	0	0	0	..	..	..	..	..
6000 Other taxes	**0**	**377**	**0**	**0**	**370**	**0**	**0**	**0**	**0**	**0**
6100 Paid solely by business	0	0	..	..	0	..	..	..	..	..
6200 Other	0	377	..	..	370	..	..	..	..	..
Total tax revenue	**0**	**11 952**	**59 158**	**176 841**	**203 992**	**1**	**83 469**	**316 530**	**694 877**	**798 214**

.. Not available

1. The PASEP (Programme of Formation of the Patrimony of the Public Servants) contributions are added to the PIS (Social Integration Programme) contributions in heading 5110 for the years prior to 2000.

Table 6.8. Chile, tax revenues by sub-sectors of government

Million CLP

	Federal government					State/Regional				
	1990	2000	2010	2021	2022	1990	2000	2010	2021	2022
1000 Taxes on income, profits and capital gains	**412 974**	**1 841 630**	**8 329 060**	**20 456 920**	**27 491 879**	..	..	..	..	..
1100 Of individuals	99 154	604 100	1 492 837	5 780 432	6 626 617	..	..	..	..	..
1200 Corporate	219 586	882 896	4 448 745	9 145 873	14 900 568	..	..	..	..	..
1300 Unallocable between 1100 and 1200	94 233	354 634	2 387 478	5 530 616	5 964 694	..	..	..	..	..
2000 Social security contributions	**66 738**	**232 728**	**371 386**	**511 529**	**548 558**	..	..	..	..	..
2100 Employees	61 200	209 907	310 558	382 461	398 535	..	..	..	..	..
2200 Employers	5 538	22 821	60 828	129 068	150 023	..	..	..	..	..
2300 Self-employed or non-employed	0	0	0	0	0	..	..	..	..	..
2400 Unallocable between 2100, 2200 and 2300	0	0	0	0	0	..	..	..	..	..
3000 Taxes on payroll and workforce	**0**	**0**	**0**	**0**	**0**	..	..	..	..	..
4000 Taxes on property	**59 682**	**255 371**	**245 044**	**909 034**	**1 218 087**	..	..	..	..	..
4100 Recurrent taxes on immovable property	10 331	3 578	8 805	26 388	36 158	..	..	..	..	..
4200 Recurrent taxes on net wealth	0	0	0	0	0	..	..	..	..	..
4300 Estate, inheritance and gift taxes	3 444	10 906	39 338	291 830	416 219	..	..	..	..	..
4400 Taxes on financial and capital transactions	45 907	240 886	196 901	590 816	765 709	..	..	..	..	..
4500 Non-recurrent taxes	0	0	0	0	0	..	..	..	..	..
4600 Other recurrent taxes on property	0	0	0	0	0	..	..	..	..	..
5000 Taxes on goods and services	**1 063 677**	**4 719 255**	**10 330 378**	**26 318 567**	**27 756 629**	..	..	..	..	..
5100 Taxes on production, sale, transfer, etc	1 060 304	4 684 525	10 294 165	26 135 885	27 545 053	..	..	..	..	..
5110 General taxes	664 421	3 306 350	8 399 926	22 785 935	24 515 246	..	..	..	..	..
5120 Taxes on specific goods and services[1]	395 883	1 378 175	1 894 239	3 349 951	3 029 807	..	..	..	..	..
5130 Unallocable between 5110 and 5120	0	0	0	0	0	..	..	..	..	..
5200 Taxes on use of goods and perform activities	3 374	34 730	36 213	182 681	211 576	..	..	..	..	..
5300 Unallocable between 5100 and 5200	0	0	0	0	0	..	..	..	..	..
6000 Other taxes	**-23 356**	**-112 195**	**-61 117**	**-785 585**	**-485 934**	..	..	..	..	..
6100 Paid solely by business	0	0	0	0	0	..	..	..	..	..
6200 Other	-23 356	-112 195	-61 117	-785 585	-485 934	..	..	..	..	..
Total tax revenue	**1 579 715**	**6 936 788**	**19 214 751**	**47 410 465**	**56 529 219**	..	..	..	..	..

Million CLP

	Local government					Social security funds				
	1990	2000	2010	2021	2022	1990	2000	2010	2021	2022
1000 Taxes on income, profits and capital gains	**0**	**0**	**0**	**0**	**0**	**0**	**0**	**0**	**0**	**0**
1100 Of individuals	..	..	..	..	..	..	..	..	..	..
1200 Corporate	..	..	..	..	..	..	..	..	..	..
1300 Unallocable between 1100 and 1200	..	..	..	..	..	..	..	..	..	..
2000 Social security contributions	**0**	**0**	**0**	**0**	**0**	**92 821**	**344 030**	**1 122 601**	**2 303 561**	**2 036 863**
2100 Employees	..	..	..	..	..	92 821	344 030	1 122 601	2 303 561	2 036 863
2200 Employers	..	..	..	..	..	0	0	0	0	0
2300 Self-employed or non-employed	..	..	..	..	..	0	0	0	0	0
2400 Unallocable between 2100, 2200 and 2300	..	..	..	..	..	0	0	0	0	0
3000 Taxes on payroll and workforce	**0**	**0**	**0**	**0**	**0**	**0**	**0**	**0**	**0**	**0**
4000 Taxes on property	**49 637**	**298 666**	**653 563**	**1 697 887**	**1 987 188**	**0**	**0**	**0**	**0**	**0**
4100 Recurrent taxes on immovable property	49 637	298 666	653 563	1 697 887	1 987 188	..	..	..	..	..
4200 Recurrent taxes on net wealth	0	0	0	0	0	..	..	..	..	..
4300 Estate, inheritance and gift taxes	0	0	0	0	0	..	..	..	..	..
4400 Taxes on financial and capital transactions	0	0	0	0	0	..	..	..	..	..
4500 Non-recurrent taxes	0	0	0	0	0	..	..	..	..	..
4600 Other recurrent taxes on property	0	0	0	0	0	..	..	..	..	..
5000 Taxes on goods and services	**55 045**	**322 514**	**854 778**	**2 051 419**	**2 321 158**	**0**	**0**	**0**	**0**	**0**
5100 Taxes on production, sale, transfer, etc	13 705	105 302	238 739	493 510	533 528	..	..	..	..	..
5110 General taxes	0	0	0	0	0	..	..	..	..	..
5120 Taxes on specific goods and services[1]	13 705	105 302	238 739	493 510	533 528	..	..	..	..	..
5130 Unallocable between 5110 and 5120	0	0	0	0	0	..	..	..	..	..
5200 Taxes on use of goods and perform activities	41 340	217 212	616 039	1 557 909	1 787 630	..	..	..	..	..
5300 Unallocable between 5100 and 5200	0	0	0	0	0	..	..	..	..	..
6000 Other taxes	**0**	**0**	**0**	**0**	**0**	**0**	**0**	**0**	**0**	**0**
6100 Paid solely by business	..	..	..	..	..	..	..	..	..	..
6200 Other	..	..	..	..	..	..	..	..	..	..
Total tax revenue	**104 682**	**621 180**	**1 508 341**	**3 749 307**	**4 308 346**	**92 821**	**344 030**	**1 122 601**	**2 303 561**	**2 036 863**

.. Not available

1. ECLAC classifies Oil Prices Stabilisation Fund (FEPP) revenues as non-tax revenues.

Table 6.9. Colombia, tax revenues by sub-sectors of government

Million COP

	Federal government					State/Regional[1]				
	1990	2000	2010	2021	2022	1990	2000	2010	2021	2022
1000 Taxes on income, profits and capital gains	**771 694**	**7 103 525**	**26 218 852**	**73 222 876**	**95 891 679**	**0**	**0**	**0**	**0**	**0**
1100 Of individuals	47 210	1 499 345	5 192 384	15 758 043	18 984 236	..	..	..	..	..
1200 Corporate	359 758	5 119 828	20 405 209	54 418 742	72 985 286	..	..	..	..	..
1300 Unallocable between 1100 and 1200	364 726	484 352	621 258	3 046 091	3 922 156	..	..	..	..	..
2000 Social security contributions	**0**	**0**	**0**	**0**	**0**	**0**	**0**	**0**	**0**	**0**
2100 Employees	..	..	..	..	..	..	..	..	..	..
2200 Employers	..	..	..	..	..	..	..	..	..	..
2300 Self-employed or non-employed	..	..	..	..	..	..	..	..	..	..
2400 Unallocable between 2100, 2200 and 2300	..	..	..	..	..	..	..	..	..	..
3000 Taxes on payroll and workforce	**0**	**1 286 803**	**4 022 503**	**3 927 070**	**4 421 997**	**0**	**0**	**0**	**0**	**0**
4000 Taxes on property	**0**	**1 036 584**	**5 196 303**	**11 008 836**	**12 588 105**	**0**	**0**	**0**	**0**	**0**
4100 Recurrent taxes on immovable property	..	0	0	0	0	..	..	..	..	..
4200 Recurrent taxes on net wealth	..	0	1 970 530	1 032 058	73 113	..	..	..	..	..
4300 Estate, inheritance and gift taxes	..	0	0	0	0	..	..	..	..	..
4400 Taxes on financial and capital transactions	..	1 036 584	3 225 773	9 831 204	12 281 751	..	..	..	..	..
4500 Non-recurrent taxes	..	0	0	145 573	233 241	..	..	..	..	..
4600 Other recurrent taxes on property	..	0	0	0	0	..	..	..	..	..
5000 Taxes on goods and services	**1 035 934**	**11 108 594**	**35 382 852**	**78 060 059**	**103 250 678**	**263 429**	**1 481 725**	**3 406 301**	**8 435 850**	**9 802 283**
5100 Taxes on production, sale, transfer, etc	1 035 934	11 108 594	35 382 852	78 060 059	103 250 678	263 429	1 349 930	3 032 733	7 173 147	8 350 507
5110 General taxes	583 078	8 445 776	28 811 682	69 883 378	91 744 973	0	0	0	0	0
5120 Taxes on specific goods and services	452 856	2 662 818	6 571 170	8 176 681	11 505 705	263 429	1 349 930	3 032 733	7 173 147	8 350 507
5130 Unallocable between 5110 and 5120	0	0	0	0	0	0	0	0	0	0
5200 Taxes on use of goods and perform activities	0	0	0	0	0	0	131 795	373 568	1 262 703	1 451 776
5300 Unallocable between 5100 and 5200	0	0	0	0	0	0	0	0	0	0
6000 Other taxes	**78 306**	**480 784**	**483 762**	**506 938**	**923 110**	**0**	**241 471**	**1 374 970**	**3 263 710**	**4 053 893**
6100 Paid solely by business	0	0	0	0	0	..	0	0	0	0
6200 Other	78 306	480 784	483 762	506 938	923 110	..	241 471	1 374 970	3 263 710	4 053 893
Total tax revenue	**1 885 934**	**21 016 290**	**71 304 272**	**166 725 777**	**217 075 569**	**263 429**	**1 723 196**	**4 781 271**	**11 699 560**	**13 856 177**

Million COP

	Local government[1]					Social security funds[2]				
	1990	2000	2010	2021	2022	1990	2000	2010	2021	2022
1000 Taxes on income, profits and capital gains	**0**	**0**	**0**	**0**	**0**	**0**	**0**	**0**	**0**	**0**
1100 Of individuals	..	..	..	..	..	..	..	..	..	..
1200 Corporate	..	..	..	..	..	..	..	..	..	..
1300 Unallocable between 1100 and 1200	..	..	..	..	..	..	..	..	..	..
2000 Social security contributions	**0**	**0**	**0**	**0**	**0**	**203 596**	**4 989 000**	**11 478 085**	**22 844 403**	**23 907 649**
2100 Employees	..	..	..	..	..	..	..	..	..	..
2200 Employers	..	..	..	..	..	..	..	..	..	..
2300 Self-employed or non-employed	..	..	..	..	..	..	..	..	..	..
2400 Unallocable between 2100, 2200 and 2300	..	..	..	..	..	203 596	4 989 000	11 478 085	22 844 403	23 907 649
3000 Taxes on payroll and workforce	**0**	**0**	**0**	**0**	**0**	**0**	**0**	**0**	**0**	**0**
4000 Taxes on property	**56 160**	**991 070**	**3 338 935**	**9 039 961**	**9 794 710**	**0**	**0**	**0**	**0**	**0**
4100 Recurrent taxes on immovable property	56 160	991 070	3 338 935	9 039 961	9 794 710	..	..	..	..	..
4200 Recurrent taxes on net wealth	0	0	0	0	0	..	..	..	..	..
4300 Estate, inheritance and gift taxes	0	0	0	0	0	..	..	..	..	..
4400 Taxes on financial and capital transactions	0	0	0	0	0	..	..	..	..	..
4500 Non-recurrent taxes	0	0	0	0	0	..	..	..	..	..
4600 Other recurrent taxes on property	0	0	0	0	0	..	..	..	..	..
5000 Taxes on goods and services	**89 290**	**1 590 132**	**5 622 489**	**12 769 452**	**16 283 133**	**0**	**0**	**0**	**0**	**0**
5100 Taxes on production, sale, transfer, etc	89 290	1 590 132	5 622 489	11 989 065	15 449 352	..	..	..	..	..
5110 General taxes	89 290	1 140 090	4 522 121	10 217 878	13 360 416	..	..	..	..	..
5120 Taxes on specific goods and services	0	450 042	1 100 368	1 771 188	2 088 936	..	..	..	..	..
5130 Unallocable between 5110 and 5120	0	0	0	0	0	..	..	..	..	..
5200 Taxes on use of goods and perform activities	0	0	0	780 387	833 781	..	..	..	..	..
5300 Unallocable between 5100 and 5200	0	0	0	0	0	..	..	..	..	..
6000 Other taxes	**81 017**	**288 942**	**1 930 282**	**6 401 692**	**7 766 603**	**0**	**0**	**0**	**0**	**0**
6100 Paid solely by business	0	0	0	0	0	..	..	..	..	..
6200 Other	81 017	288 942	1 930 282	6 401 692	7 766 603	..	..	..	..	..
Total tax revenue	**226 467**	**2 870 144**	**10 891 707**	**28 211 104**	**33 844 446**	**203 596**	**4 989 000**	**11 478 085**	**22 844 403**	**23 907 649**

.. Not available

1. The data correspond to the reported consolidated revenues of the territorial entities (departments and municipalities).
2. All of the health contributions pertaining to FOSYGA (Solidarity and Guarantee Fund) are classified as social security contributions from 2013. Prior to 2013, only the portion of the contributions used to finance the subsidised regime was included and the part to finance the contributory regime was classified in the social security sector as "other incomes".

Table 6.10. Costa Rica, tax revenues by sub-sectors of government

Million CRC

	Federal government					State/Regional				
	1990	2000	2010	2021	2022	1990	2000	2010	2021	2022
1000 Taxes on income, profits and capital gains	**11 820**	**128 805**	**748 093**	**2 063 810**	**2 430 200**	..	..	..	..	..
1100 Of individuals	..	..	202 849	622 772	691 305	..	..	..	..	..
1200 Corporate	..	..	450 312	970 546	1 188 835	..	..	..	..	..
1300 Unallocable between 1100 and 1200	11 820	128 805	94 932	470 492	550 059	..	..	..	..	..
2000 Social security contributions[1]	**1 345**	**18 677**	**61 193**	**469 195**	**515 732**	..	..	..	..	..
2100 Employees	..	..	..	..	..	..	..	..	..	..
2200 Employers	0	0	0	0	0	..	..	..	..	..
2300 Self-employed or non-employed	..	..	..	..	..	..	..	..	..	..
2400 Unallocable between 2100, 2200 and 2300	1 345	18 677	61 193	469 195	515 732	..	..	..	..	..
3000 Taxes on payroll and workforce	**0**	**0**	**0**	**0**	**0**	..	..	..	..	..
4000 Taxes on property	**366**	**3 007**	**18 270**	**63 314**	**71 009**	..	..	..	..	..
4100 Recurrent taxes on immovable property	0	0	3 527	5 108	5 206	..	..	..	..	..
4200 Recurrent taxes on net wealth	0	0	0	0	0	..	..	..	..	..
4300 Estate, inheritance and gift taxes	0	0	0	0	0	..	..	..	..	..
4400 Taxes on financial and capital transactions	366	3 007	14 743	58 206	65 802	..	..	..	..	..
4500 Non-recurrent taxes	0	0	0	0	0	..	..	..	..	..
4600 Other recurrent taxes on property	0	0	0	0	0	..	..	..	..	..
5000 Taxes on goods and services	**52 248**	**444 870**	**1 696 593**	**3 337 270**	**3 519 484**	..	..	..	..	..
5100 Taxes on production, sale, transfer, etc	49 867	425 630	1 598 789	3 146 482	3 326 853	..	..	..	..	..
5110 General taxes	21 326	222 775	920 298	2 065 623	2 217 743	..	..	..	..	..
5120 Taxes on specific goods and services[2]	28 541	202 856	678 491	1 080 859	1 109 110	..	..	..	..	..
5130 Unallocable between 5110 and 5120	0	0	0	0	0	..	..	..	..	..
5200 Taxes on use of goods and perform activities	2 380	19 240	97 804	190 789	192 631	..	..	..	..	..
5300 Unallocable between 5100 and 5200	0	0	0	0	0	..	..	..	..	..
6000 Other taxes[3]	**9 251**	**23 956**	**92 452**	**83 185**	**394 676**	..	..	..	..	..
6100 Paid solely by business	0	0	0	0	0	..	..	..	..	..
6200 Other	9 251	23 956	92 452	83 185	394 676	..	..	..	..	..
Total tax revenue	**75 030**	**619 314**	**2 616 600**	**6 016 775**	**6 931 100**	..	..	..	..	..

Million CRC

	Local government					Social security funds				
	1990	2000	2010	2021	2022	1990	2000	2010	2021	2022
1000 Taxes on income, profits and capital gains	**0**	**0**	**0**	**0**	**0**	**0**	**0**	**0**	**0**	**0**
1100 Of individuals	..	..	..	..	..	..	..	..	..	..
1200 Corporate	..	..	..	..	..	..	..	..	..	..
1300 Unallocable between 1100 and 1200	..	..	..	..	..	..	..	..	..	..
2000 Social security contributions[1]	**0**	**0**	**0**	**0**	**0**	**32 645**	**278 392**	**1 389 338**	**3 136 535**	**3 409 960**
2100 Employees	..	..	..	..	..	..	..	..	..	..
2200 Employers	..	..	..	..	..	3 447	37 313	207 206	389 183	412 852
2300 Self-employed or non-employed	..	..	..	..	..	..	..	..	..	..
2400 Unallocable between 2100, 2200 and 2300	..	..	..	..	..	29 198	241 079	1 182 132	2 747 353	2 997 108
3000 Taxes on payroll and workforce	**0**	**0**	**0**	**0**	**0**	**7 575**	**61 796**	**260 664**	**569 339**	**639 737**
4000 Taxes on property	**1 200**	**5 390**	**45 436**	**145 217**	**149 733**	**0**	**0**	**0**	**0**	**0**
4100 Recurrent taxes on immovable property	1 200	5 390	45 436	145 171	149 724	..	..	..	..	..
4200 Recurrent taxes on net wealth	0	0	0	0	0	..	..	..	..	..
4300 Estate, inheritance and gift taxes	0	0	0	0	0	..	..	..	..	..
4400 Taxes on financial and capital transactions	0	0	0	0	0	..	..	..	..	..
4500 Non-recurrent taxes	0	0	0	46	8	..	..	..	..	..
4600 Other recurrent taxes on property	0	0	0	0	0	..	..	..	..	..
5000 Taxes on goods and services	**1 262**	**11 981**	**70 321**	**151 265**	**155 239**	**0**	**0**	**0**	**0**	**0**
5100 Taxes on production, sale, transfer, etc	0	83	1 513	3 916	3 919	..	..	..	..	..
5110 General taxes	..	0	0	0	0	..	..	..	..	..
5120 Taxes on specific goods and services[2]	..	83	1 513	3 916	3 919	..	..	..	..	..
5130 Unallocable between 5110 and 5120	..	0	0	0	0	..	..	..	..	..
5200 Taxes on use of goods and perform activities	1 262	11 898	68 808	147 349	151 320	..	..	..	..	..
5300 Unallocable between 5100 and 5200	0	0	0	0	0	..	..	..	..	..
6000 Other taxes[3]	**0**	**1 242**	**8**	**133**	**198**	**0**	**0**	**0**	**0**	**0**
6100 Paid solely by business	..	0	0	0	0	..	..	..	..	..
6200 Other	..	1 242	8	133	198	..	..	..	..	..
Total tax revenue	**2 461**	**18 613**	**115 765**	**296 615**	**305 170**	**40 220**	**340 187**	**1 650 002**	**3 705 874**	**4 049 697**

.. Not available

1. The data include social security contributions paid by the governments for their employees as well as the contributions for special regimes (teachers and magistrates). In ECLAC data, social security contributions also include INA (National Institute of Apprenticeship), IMAS (Joint Social Aid Institute) and FODESAF (Social Development and Family Allowances Fund).
2. In ECLAC data, the tax on ownership of vehicles, aircraft and boats is classified in category 4000.
3. The tax revenue of decentralised bodies is classified under the central government. In Costa Rica this revenue is classified under a separate unit (decentralised) considered to be different to the central government.

Table 6.11. Cuba, tax revenues by sub-sectors of government

Million CUP

	Federal government[1]					State/Regional				
	1990	2000	2010	2021	2022	1990	2000	2010	2021	2022
1000 Taxes on income, profits and capital gains	..	..	**1 857**	..	..	..	..	..	..	..
1100 Of individuals	..	..	0	..	..	..	..	..	..	..
1200 Corporate	..	..	1 857	..	..	..	..	..	..	..
1300 Unallocable between 1100 and 1200	..	..	0	..	..	..	..	..	..	..
2000 Social security contributions	..	..	**0**	..	..	..	..	..	..	..
2100 Employees	..	..	..	..	..	..	..	..	..	..
2200 Employers	..	..	..	..	..	..	..	..	..	..
2300 Self-employed or non-employed	..	..	..	..	..	..	..	..	..	..
2400 Unallocable between 2100, 2200 and 2300	..	..	..	..	..	..	..	..	..	..
3000 Taxes on payroll and workforce	..	..	**289**	..	..	..	..	..	..	..
4000 Taxes on property	..	..	**0**	..	..	..	..	..	..	..
4100 Recurrent taxes on immovable property	..	..	..	..	..	..	..	..	..	..
4200 Recurrent taxes on net wealth	..	..	..	..	..	..	..	..	..	..
4300 Estate, inheritance and gift taxes	..	..	..	..	..	..	..	..	..	..
4400 Taxes on financial and capital transactions	..	..	..	..	..	..	..	..	..	..
4500 Non-recurrent taxes	..	..	..	..	..	..	..	..	..	..
4600 Other recurrent taxes on property	..	..	..	..	..	..	..	..	..	..
5000 Taxes on goods and services	..	..	**5 757**	..	..	..	..	..	..	..
5100 Taxes on production, sale, transfer, etc	..	..	5 757	..	..	..	..	..	..	..
5110 General taxes	..	..	4 924	..	..	..	..	..	..	..
5120 Taxes on specific goods and services	..	..	833	..	..	..	..	..	..	..
5130 Unallocable between 5110 and 5120	..	..	0	..	..	..	..	..	..	..
5200 Taxes on use of goods and perform activities	..	..	0	..	..	..	..	..	..	..
5300 Unallocable between 5100 and 5200	..	..	0	..	..	..	..	..	..	..
6000 Other taxes	..	..	**569**	..	..	..	..	..	..	..
6100 Paid solely by business	..	..	..	..	..	..	..	..	..	..
6200 Other	..	..	..	..	..	..	..	..	..	..
Total tax revenue	..	..	**8 472**	..	..	..	..	..	..	..

Million CUP

	Local government[2]					Social security funds				
	1990	2000	2010	2021	2022	1990	2000	2010	2021	2022
1000 Taxes on income, profits and capital gains	..	..	**1 746**	..	..	**0**	**0**	**0**	**0**	**0**
1100 Of individuals	..	..	554	..	..	..	..	..	..	..
1200 Corporate	..	..	1 193	..	..	..	..	..	..	..
1300 Unallocable between 1100 and 1200	..	..	0	..	..	..	..	..	..	..
2000 Social security contributions	..	..	**0**	..	..	**691**	**1 181**	**2 974**	**24 155**	**16 727**
2100 Employees	..	..	..	..	..	..	..	..	..	..
2200 Employers	..	..	..	..	..	..	..	..	..	..
2300 Self-employed or non-employed	..	..	..	..	..	..	..	..	..	..
2400 Unallocable between 2100, 2200 and 2300	..	..	..	..	..	691	1 181	2 974	24 155	16 727
3000 Taxes on payroll and workforce	..	..	**4 125**	..	..	**0**	**0**	**0**	**0**	**0**
4000 Taxes on property	..	..	**0**	..	..	**0**	**0**	**0**	**0**	**0**
4100 Recurrent taxes on immovable property	..	..	..	..	..	..	..	..	..	..
4200 Recurrent taxes on net wealth	..	..	..	..	..	..	..	..	..	..
4300 Estate, inheritance and gift taxes	..	..	..	..	..	..	..	..	..	..
4400 Taxes on financial and capital transactions	..	..	..	..	..	..	..	..	..	..
4500 Non-recurrent taxes	..	..	..	..	..	..	..	..	..	..
4600 Other recurrent taxes on property	..	..	..	..	..	..	..	..	..	..
5000 Taxes on goods and services	..	..	**6 526**	..	..	**0**	**0**	**0**	**0**	**0**
5100 Taxes on production, sale, transfer, etc	..	..	6 526	..	..	..	..	..	..	..
5110 General taxes	..	..	5 601	..	..	..	..	..	..	..
5120 Taxes on specific goods and services	..	..	925	..	..	..	..	..	..	..
5130 Unallocable between 5110 and 5120	..	..	0	..	..	..	..	..	..	..
5200 Taxes on use of goods and perform activities	..	..	0	..	..	..	..	..	..	..
5300 Unallocable between 5100 and 5200	..	..	0	..	..	..	..	..	..	..
6000 Other taxes	..	..	**106**	..	..	**0**	**0**	**0**	**0**	**0**
6100 Paid solely by business	..	..	..	..	..	..	..	..	..	..
6200 Other	..	..	..	..	..	..	..	..	..	..
Total tax revenue	..	..	**12 503**	..	..	**691**	**1 181**	**2 974**	**24 155**	**16 727**

.. Not available

1. The figures include central government tax revenues between 2002 and 2012. Central tax revenues are not available for other years.

2. The figures include local government tax revenues between 2002 and 2012. Local tax revenues are not available for other years.

Table 6.12. Dominican Republic, tax revenues by sub-sectors of government

Million DOP

	Federal government					State/Regional				
	1990	2000	2010	2021	2022	1990	2000	2010	2021	2022
1000 Taxes on income, profits and capital gains	**1 650**	**10 517**	**52 653**	**263 082**	**276 183**	..	..	..	..	..
1100 Of individuals	..	4 088	17 088	69 026	87 200	..	..	..	..	..
1200 Corporate	..	4 605	21 325	150 695	140 603	..	..	..	..	..
1300 Unallocable between 1100 and 1200	1 650	1 824	14 241	43 361	48 380	..	..	..	..	..
2000 Social security contributions	**0**	**0**	**0**	**0**	**0**	..	..	..	..	..
2100 Employees	..	..	..	..	..	..	..	..	..	..
2200 Employers	..	..	..	..	..	..	..	..	..	..
2300 Self-employed or non-employed	..	..	..	..	..	..	..	..	..	..
2400 Unallocable between 2100, 2200 and 2300	..	..	..	..	..	..	..	..	..	..
3000 Taxes on payroll and workforce[1]	**0**	**0**	**1 385**	**3 810**	**3 811**	..	..	..	..	..
4000 Taxes on property	**74**	**644**	**12 416**	**45 798**	**45 061**	..	..	..	..	..
4100 Recurrent taxes on immovable property	9	115	555	4 171	4 438	..	..	..	..	..
4200 Recurrent taxes on net wealth	0	0	2 449	8 396	8 615	..	..	..	..	..
4300 Estate, inheritance and gift taxes	11	96	231	1 308	1 389	..	..	..	..	..
4400 Taxes on financial and capital transactions	40	377	8 658	30 206	28 611	..	..	..	..	..
4500 Non-recurrent taxes	3	32	488	1 642	1 929	..	..	..	..	..
4600 Other recurrent taxes on property	11	25	35	76	81	..	..	..	..	..
5000 Taxes on goods and services	**4 484**	**35 672**	**174 457**	**465 072**	**542 443**	..	..	..	..	..
5100 Taxes on production, sale, transfer, etc	4 418	34 962	167 983	444 248	519 450	..	..	..	..	..
5110 General taxes	970	9 912	81 226	261 207	310 788	..	..	..	..	..
5120 Taxes on specific goods and services	3 449	25 051	86 757	183 041	208 662	..	..	..	..	..
5130 Unallocable between 5110 and 5120	0	0	0	0	0	..	..	..	..	..
5200 Taxes on use of goods and perform activities	65	710	6 475	20 824	22 993	..	..	..	..	..
5300 Unallocable between 5100 and 5200	0	0	0	0	0	..	..	..	..	..
6000 Other taxes	**159**	**429**	**0**	**2**	**3**	..	..	..	..	..
6100 Paid solely by business	0	0	..	0	0	..	..	..	..	..
6200 Other	159	429	..	2	3	..	..	..	..	..
Total tax revenue	**6 367**	**47 263**	**240 910**	**777 763**	**867 501**	..	..	..	..	..

Million DOP

	Local government					Social security funds[2]				
	1990	2000	2010	2021	2022	1990	2000	2010	2021	2022
1000 Taxes on income, profits and capital gains	..	..	..	..	..	**0**	**0**	**0**	**0**	**0**
1100 Of individuals	..	..	..	..	..	..	..	..	..	..
1200 Corporate	..	..	..	..	..	..	..	..	..	..
1300 Unallocable between 1100 and 1200	..	..	..	..	..	..	..	..	..	..
2000 Social security contributions	..	..	..	..	..	**53**	**490**	**1 845**	**3 420**	**4 923**
2100 Employees	..	..	..	..	..	..	..	1 720	..	..
2200 Employers	..	..	..	..	..	..	..	125	..	..
2300 Self-employed or non-employed	..	..	..	..	..	..	..	0	..	..
2400 Unallocable between 2100, 2200 and 2300	..	..	..	..	..	53	490	0	3 420	4 923
3000 Taxes on payroll and workforce[1]	..	..	..	..	..	**0**	**0**	**0**	**0**	**0**
4000 Taxes on property	..	..	..	..	..	**0**	**0**	**0**	**0**	**0**
4100 Recurrent taxes on immovable property	..	..	..	..	..	..	..	..	..	..
4200 Recurrent taxes on net wealth	..	..	..	..	..	..	..	..	..	..
4300 Estate, inheritance and gift taxes	..	..	..	..	..	..	..	..	..	..
4400 Taxes on financial and capital transactions	..	..	..	..	..	..	..	..	..	..
4500 Non-recurrent taxes	..	..	..	..	..	..	..	..	..	..
4600 Other recurrent taxes on property	..	..	..	..	..	..	..	..	..	..
5000 Taxes on goods and services	..	..	..	..	..	**0**	**0**	**0**	**0**	**0**
5100 Taxes on production, sale, transfer, etc	..	..	..	..	..	..	..	..	..	..
5110 General taxes	..	..	..	..	..	..	..	..	..	..
5120 Taxes on specific goods and services	..	..	..	..	..	..	..	..	..	..
5130 Unallocable between 5110 and 5120	..	..	..	..	..	..	..	..	..	..
5200 Taxes on use of goods and perform activities	..	..	..	..	..	..	..	..	..	..
5300 Unallocable between 5100 and 5200	..	..	..	..	..	..	..	..	..	..
6000 Other taxes	..	..	..	..	..	**0**	**0**	**0**	**0**	**0**
6100 Paid solely by business	..	..	..	..	..	..	..	..	..	..
6200 Other	..	..	..	..	..	..	..	..	..	..
Total tax revenue	..	..	..	..	..	**53**	**490**	**1 845**	**3 420**	**4 923**

.. Not available

1. This heading includes the mandatory non-pensions contributions to the Instituto de Formación Técnico Profesional (INFOTEP). The tax revenue is classified under the central government. In Dominican Republic this revenue is classified under a separate unit (decentralised) considered to be different to the central government.
2. The figures exclude social security contributions to general government managed by the private sector.

Table 6.13. Ecuador, tax revenues by sub-sectors of government

Million USD

	Federal government					State/Regional				
	1990	2000	2010	2021	2022	1990	2000	2010	2021	2022
1000 Taxes on income, profits and capital gains	**138**	**267**	**2 909**	**4 376**	**5 241**	..	..	..	..	..
1100 Of individuals	..	10	80	143	181	..	..	..	..	..
1200 Corporate	..	53	1 046	899	1 350	..	..	..	..	..
1300 Unallocable between 1100 and 1200	138	204	1 783	3 333	3 710	..	..	..	..	..
2000 Social security contributions	**0**	**0**	**0**	**0**	**0**	..	..	..	..	..
2100 Employees	..	..	..	..	..	..	..	..	..	..
2200 Employers	..	..	..	..	..	..	..	..	..	..
2300 Self-employed or non-employed	..	..	..	..	..	..	..	..	..	..
2400 Unallocable between 2100, 2200 and 2300	..	..	..	..	..	..	..	..	..	..
3000 Taxes on payroll and workforce	**0**	**0**	**0**	**0**	**0**	..	..	..	..	..
4000 Taxes on property	**0**	**0**	**43**	**64**	**665**	..	..	..	..	..
4100 Recurrent taxes on immovable property	..	..	3	0	0	..	..	..	..	..
4200 Recurrent taxes on net wealth	..	..	35	24	19	..	..	..	..	..
4300 Estate, inheritance and gift taxes	..	..	5	40	11	..	..	..	..	..
4400 Taxes on financial and capital transactions	..	..	0	0	0	..	..	..	..	..
4500 Non-recurrent taxes	..	..	0	0	635	..	..	..	..	..
4600 Other recurrent taxes on property	..	..	0	0	0	..	..	..	..	..
5000 Taxes on goods and services	**668**	**1 596**	**5 969**	**10 275**	**11 733**	..	..	..	..	..
5100 Taxes on production, sale, transfer, etc	665	1 574	5 814	10 048	11 493	..	..	..	..	..
5110 General taxes	302	923	3 759	6 581	7 854	..	..	..	..	..
5120 Taxes on specific goods and services	363	651	2 054	3 467	3 640	..	..	..	..	..
5130 Unallocable between 5110 and 5120	0	0	0	0	0	..	..	..	..	..
5200 Taxes on use of goods and perform activities	3	22	156	227	240	..	..	..	..	..
5300 Unallocable between 5100 and 5200	0	0	0	0	0	..	..	..	..	..
6000 Other taxes	**0**	**0**	**4**	**22**	**2**	..	..	..	..	..
6100 Paid solely by business	..	..	0	0	0	..	..	..	..	..
6200 Other	..	..	4	22	2	..	..	..	..	..
Total tax revenue	**806**	**1 863**	**8 925**	**14 736**	**17 640**	..	..	..	..	..

Million USD

	Local government[1]					Social security funds				
	1990	2000	2010	2021	2022	1990	2000	2010	2021	2022
1000 Taxes on income, profits and capital gains	**1**	**2**	**15**	**69**	**74**	**0**	**0**	**0**	**0**	**0**
1100 Of individuals	..	..	0	0	0	..	..	..	..	..
1200 Corporate	..	..	..	..	..	..	..	..	..	..
1300 Unallocable between 1100 and 1200	1	2	15	69	74	..	..	..	..	..
2000 Social security contributions	**0**	**0**	**0**	**0**	**0**	**243**	**228**	**2 541**	**5 305**	**5 773**
2100 Employees	..	..	..	..	..	..	..	..	..	..
2200 Employers	..	..	..	..	..	..	..	..	..	..
2300 Self-employed or non-employed	..	..	..	..	..	..	..	..	..	..
2400 Unallocable between 2100, 2200 and 2300	..	..	..	..	..	243	228	2 541	5 305	5 773
3000 Taxes on payroll and workforce	**0**	**0**	**0**	**0**	**0**	**0**	**0**	**0**	**0**	**0**
4000 Taxes on property	**16**	**17**	**116**	**296**	**321**	**0**	**0**	**0**	**0**	**0**
4100 Recurrent taxes on immovable property	13	8	66	184	200	..	..	..	..	..
4200 Recurrent taxes on net wealth	0	0	0	0	0	..	..	..	..	..
4300 Estate, inheritance and gift taxes	0	0	0	0	0	..	..	..	..	..
4400 Taxes on financial and capital transactions	0	0	0	0	0	..	..	..	..	..
4500 Non-recurrent taxes	0	0	0	0	0	..	..	..	..	..
4600 Other recurrent taxes on property	3	9	50	112	121	..	..	..	..	..
5000 Taxes on goods and services	**10**	**13**	**97**	**241**	**261**	**0**	**0**	**0**	**0**	**0**
5100 Taxes on production, sale, transfer, etc	6	6	49	85	92	..	..	..	..	..
5110 General taxes	4	5	41	77	84	..	..	..	..	..
5120 Taxes on specific goods and services	1	2	8	8	9	..	..	..	..	..
5130 Unallocable between 5110 and 5120	0	0	0	0	0	..	..	..	..	..
5200 Taxes on use of goods and perform activities	5	7	48	156	169	..	..	..	..	..
5300 Unallocable between 5100 and 5200	0	0	0	0	0	..	..	..	..	..
6000 Other taxes	**2**	**2**	**1**	**0**	**0**	**0**	**0**	**0**	**0**	**0**
6100 Paid solely by business	0	0	0	0	0	..	..	..	..	..
6200 Other	2	2	1	0	0	..	..	..	..	..
Total tax revenue	**29**	**34**	**228**	**606**	**656**	**243**	**228**	**2 541**	**5 305**	**5 773**

.. Not available

1. Local tax revenue data in 2021 and 2022 are estimated.

Table 6.14. El Salvador, tax revenues by sub-sectors of government

Million USD

	Federal government					State/Regional				
	1990	2000	2010	2021	2022	1990	2000	2010	2021	2022
1000 Taxes on income, profits and capital gains	**95**	**429**	**996**	**2 259**	**2 707**	..	..	..	..	..
1100 Of individuals	..	..	590	923	1 060	..	..	..	..	..
1200 Corporate	..	..	420	1 078	1 334	..	..	..	..	..
1300 Unallocable between 1100 and 1200	95	429	-14	258	313	..	..	..	..	..
2000 Social security contributions	**0**	**0**	**0**	**0**	**0**	..	..	..	..	..
2100 Employees	..	..	..	..	..	..	..	..	..	..
2200 Employers	..	..	..	..	..	..	..	..	..	..
2300 Self-employed or non-employed	..	..	..	..	..	..	..	..	..	..
2400 Unallocable between 2100, 2200 and 2300	..	..	..	..	..	..	..	..	..	..
3000 Taxes on payroll and workforce[1]	**0**	**0**	**21**	**40**	**42**	..	..	..	..	..
4000 Taxes on property	**26**	**12**	**16**	**39**	**47**	..	..	..	..	..
4100 Recurrent taxes on immovable property	0	0	0	0	0	..	..	..	..	..
4200 Recurrent taxes on net wealth	16	0	0	0	0	..	..	..	..	..
4300 Estate, inheritance and gift taxes	0	0	0	0	0	..	..	..	..	..
4400 Taxes on financial and capital transactions	10	12	16	39	47	..	..	..	..	..
4500 Non-recurrent taxes	0	0	0	0	0	..	..	..	..	..
4600 Other recurrent taxes on property	0	0	0	0	0	..	..	..	..	..
5000 Taxes on goods and services	**259**	**903**	**1 871**	**3 476**	**3 661**	..	..	..	..	..
5100 Taxes on production, sale, transfer, etc	259	903	1 863	3 453	3 637	..	..	..	..	..
5110 General taxes	133	714	1 433	2 771	2 944	..	..	..	..	..
5120 Taxes on specific goods and services	127	189	431	682	694	..	..	..	..	..
5130 Unallocable between 5110 and 5120	0	0	0	0	0	..	..	..	..	..
5200 Taxes on use of goods and perform activities	0	0	7	23	24	..	..	..	..	..
5300 Unallocable between 5100 and 5200	0	0	0	0	0	..	..	..	..	..
6000 Other taxes	**58**	**0**	**0**	**0**	**0**	..	..	..	..	..
6100 Paid solely by business	0	0	..	..	..	..	..	..	..	..
6200 Other	58	0	..	..	..	..	..	..	..	..
Total tax revenue	**438**	**1 344**	**2 903**	**5 814**	**6 457**	..	..	..	..	..

Million USD

	Local government					Social security funds[2]				
	1990	2000	2010	2021	2022	1990	2000	2010	2021	2022
1000 Taxes on income, profits and capital gains	..	..	**0**	**0**	**0**	**0**	**0**	**0**	**0**	**0**
1100 Of individuals	..	..	..	..	..	..	..	..	..	..
1200 Corporate	..	..	..	..	..	..	..	..	..	..
1300 Unallocable between 1100 and 1200	..	..	..	..	..	..	..	..	..	..
2000 Social security contributions	..	..	**0**	**0**	**0**	**104**	**325**	**470**	**771**	**834**
2100 Employees	..	..	..	..	..	..	75	165	271	293
2200 Employers	..	..	..	..	..	..	176	306	500	541
2300 Self-employed or non-employed	..	..	..	..	..	..	13	0	0	0
2400 Unallocable between 2100, 2200 and 2300	..	..	..	..	..	104	62	0	0	0
3000 Taxes on payroll and workforce[1]	..	..	**0**	**0**	**0**	**0**	**0**	**0**	**0**	**0**
4000 Taxes on property	..	..	**3**	**8**	**11**	**0**	**0**	**0**	**0**	**0**
4100 Recurrent taxes on immovable property	..	..	3	8	11	..	..	..	..	..
4200 Recurrent taxes on net wealth	..	..	0	0	0	..	..	..	..	..
4300 Estate, inheritance and gift taxes	..	..	0	0	0	..	..	..	..	..
4400 Taxes on financial and capital transactions	..	..	0	0	0	..	..	..	..	..
4500 Non-recurrent taxes	..	..	0	0	0	..	..	..	..	..
4600 Other recurrent taxes on property	..	..	0	0	0	..	..	..	..	..
5000 Taxes on goods and services	..	..	**7**	**17**	**20**	**0**	**0**	**0**	**0**	**0**
5100 Taxes on production, sale, transfer, etc	..	..	0	0	0	..	..	..	..	..
5110 General taxes	..	..	..	..	..	..	..	..	..	..
5120 Taxes on specific goods and services	..	..	..	..	..	..	..	..	..	..
5130 Unallocable between 5110 and 5120	..	..	..	..	..	..	..	..	..	..
5200 Taxes on use of goods and perform activities	..	..	7	17	20	..	..	..	..	..
5300 Unallocable between 5100 and 5200	..	..	0	0	0	..	..	..	..	..
6000 Other taxes	..	..	**63**	**99**	**107**	**0**	**0**	**0**	**0**	**0**
6100 Paid solely by business	..	..	0	0	0	..	..	..	..	..
6200 Other	..	..	63	99	107	..	..	..	..	..
Total tax revenue	..	..	**74**	**124**	**138**	**104**	**325**	**470**	**771**	**834**

.. Not available

1. Vocational training contributions to the Instituto Salvadoreño de Formación Profesional (INSAFORP) are included in heading 3000. The tax revenue is classified under the central government. In El Salvador this revenue is classified under a separate unit considered to be different to the central government.
2. Social security contributions are those paid to the Salvadoran Institute of Social Security (ISSS), National Public Employees Pension Institute (INPEP), Social Security Institute of the Armed Forces (IPSFA) and Salvadoran Institute of Teacher Welfare (ISBM). The figures exclude contributions to the privately managed regime and may include a small amount of voluntary contributions which is undistinguishable from the public social security contribution data.

Table 6.15. Guatemala, tax revenues by sub-sectors of government

Million GTQ

	Federal government					State/Regional				
	1990	2000	2010	2021	2022	1990	2000	2010	2021	2022
1000 Taxes on income, profits and capital gains	**507**	**3 293**	**7 745**	**23 291**	**25 658**	**..**	**..**	**..**	**..**	**..**
1100 Of individuals	25	143	1 225	4 769	3 892	..	..	..	..	..
1200 Corporate	482	3 149	6 520	18 522	21 765	..	..	..	..	..
1300 Unallocable between 1100 and 1200	0	0	0	0	0	..	..	..	..	..
2000 Social security contributions	**0**	**0**	**0**	**0**	**0**	**..**	**..**	**..**	**..**	**..**
2100 Employees	..	..	..	..	..	..	..	..	..	..
2200 Employers	..	..	..	..	..	..	..	..	..	..
2300 Self-employed or non-employed	..	..	..	..	..	..	..	..	..	..
2400 Unallocable between 2100, 2200 and 2300	..	..	..	..	..	..	..	..	..	..
3000 Taxes on payroll and workforce[1]	**0**	**0**	**447**	**1 038**	**1 102**	**..**	**..**	**..**	**..**	**..**
4000 Taxes on property	**149**	**199**	**582**	**568**	**623**	**..**	**..**	**..**	**..**	**..**
4100 Recurrent taxes on immovable property	0	6	1	2	1	..	..	..	..	..
4200 Recurrent taxes on net wealth	0	0	0	0	0	..	..	..	..	..
4300 Estate, inheritance and gift taxes	0	0	0	0	0	..	..	..	..	..
4400 Taxes on financial and capital transactions	149	194	581	567	622	..	..	..	..	..
4500 Non-recurrent taxes	0	0	0	0	0	..	..	..	..	..
4600 Other recurrent taxes on property	0	0	0	0	0	..	..	..	..	..
5000 Taxes on goods and services	**1 554**	**10 317**	**23 255**	**48 666**	**55 975**	**..**	**..**	**..**	**..**	**..**
5100 Taxes on production, sale, transfer, etc	1 526	10 131	22 750	47 655	54 905	..	..	..	..	..
5110 General taxes	762	6 259	16 980	36 985	43 404	..	..	..	..	..
5120 Taxes on specific goods and services	764	3 872	5 770	10 670	11 500	..	..	..	..	..
5130 Unallocable between 5110 and 5120	0	0	0	0	0	..	..	..	..	..
5200 Taxes on use of goods and perform activities	28	186	505	1 011	1 071	..	..	..	..	..
5300 Unallocable between 5100 and 5200	0	0	0	0	0	..	..	..	..	..
6000 Other taxes	**0**	**7**	**2 575**	**5 399**	**6 130**	**..**	**..**	**..**	**..**	**..**
6100 Paid solely by business	..	0	0	0	0	..	..	..	..	..
6200 Other	..	7	2 575	5 399	6 130	..	..	..	..	..
Total tax revenue	**2 210**	**13 815**	**34 605**	**78 962**	**89 489**	**..**	**..**	**..**	**..**	**..**

Million GTQ

	Local government					Social security funds[2]				
	1990	2000	2010	2021	2022	1990	2000	2010	2021	2022
1000 Taxes on income, profits and capital gains	**..**	**0**	**0**	**0**	**0**	**0**	**0**	**0**	**0**	**0**
1100 Of individuals	..	..	..	..	..	..	..	..	..	..
1200 Corporate	..	..	..	..	..	..	..	..	..	..
1300 Unallocable between 1100 and 1200	..	..	..	..	..	..	..	..	..	..
2000 Social security contributions	**..**	**0**	**0**	**0**	**0**	**436**	**2 569**	**6 312**	**14 314**	**15 539**
2100 Employees	..	..	..	..	..	..	..	..	..	..
2200 Employers	..	..	..	..	..	..	..	..	..	..
2300 Self-employed or non-employed	..	..	..	..	..	..	..	..	..	..
2400 Unallocable between 2100, 2200 and 2300	..	..	..	..	..	436	2 569	6 312	14 314	15 539
3000 Taxes on payroll and workforce[1]	**..**	**0**	**0**	**0**	**0**	**0**	**0**	**0**	**0**	**0**
4000 Taxes on property	**..**	**147**	**620**	**837**	**914**	**0**	**0**	**0**	**0**	**0**
4100 Recurrent taxes on immovable property	..	147	620	837	914	..	..	..	..	..
4200 Recurrent taxes on net wealth	..	0	0	0	0	..	..	..	..	..
4300 Estate, inheritance and gift taxes	..	0	0	0	0	..	..	..	..	..
4400 Taxes on financial and capital transactions	..	0	0	0	0	..	..	..	..	..
4500 Non-recurrent taxes	..	0	0	0	0	..	..	..	..	..
4600 Other recurrent taxes on property	..	0	0	0	0	..	..	..	..	..
5000 Taxes on goods and services	**..**	**0**	**0**	**0**	**0**	**0**	**0**	**0**	**0**	**0**
5100 Taxes on production, sale, transfer, etc	..	..	..	..	..	..	..	..	..	..
5110 General taxes	..	..	..	..	..	..	..	..	..	..
5120 Taxes on specific goods and services	..	..	..	..	..	..	..	..	..	..
5130 Unallocable between 5110 and 5120	..	..	..	..	..	..	..	..	..	..
5200 Taxes on use of goods and perform activities	..	..	..	..	..	..	..	..	..	..
5300 Unallocable between 5100 and 5200	..	..	..	..	..	..	..	..	..	..
6000 Other taxes	**..**	**0**	**0**	**0**	**0**	**0**	**0**	**0**	**0**	**0**
6100 Paid solely by business	..	..	..	..	..	..	..	..	..	..
6200 Other	..	..	..	..	..	..	..	..	..	..
Total tax revenue	**..**	**147**	**620**	**837**	**914**	**436**	**2 569**	**6 312**	**14 314**	**15 539**

.. Not available

1. Contributions to INTECAP and contributions to RTRA are included in heading 3000. The tax revenues are classified under the central government. In Guatemala these revenues are classified uncer a separate unit considered to be different to the central government.

2. Corresponds to social security contributions to the Guatemalan Social Security Institute (IGSS) and payments by public employees to the government's pension fund.

Table 6.16. Guyana, tax revenues by sub-sectors of government

Million GYD

	Federal government[1]					State/Regional				
	1990	2000	2010	2021	2022	1990	2000	2010	2021	2022
1000 Taxes on income, profits and capital gains	**1 752**	**16 179**	**39 561**	**124 088**	**164 802**	..	..	..	..	..
1100 Of individuals	333	7 734	17 816	46 962	58 903	..	..	..	..	..
1200 Corporate	1 375	8 266	21 427	75 897	104 581	..	..	..	..	..
1300 Unallocable between 1100 and 1200	43	179	317	1 229	1 318	..	..	..	..	..
2000 Social security contributions	**0**	**0**	**0**	**0**	**0**	..	..	..	..	..
2100 Employees	..	..	..	..	..	..	..	..	..	..
2200 Employers	..	..	..	..	..	..	..	..	..	..
2300 Self-employed or non-employed	..	..	..	..	..	..	..	..	..	..
2400 Unallocable between 2100, 2200 and 2300	..	..	..	..	..	..	..	..	..	..
3000 Taxes on payroll and workforce	**0**	**0**	**0**	**0**	**0**	..	..	..	..	..
4000 Taxes on property	**53**	**701**	**2 068**	**5 581**	**6 543**	..	..	..	..	..
4100 Recurrent taxes on immovable property	40	681	1 562	4 907	5 853	..	..	..	..	..
4200 Recurrent taxes on net wealth	0	0	0	0	0	..	..	..	..	..
4300 Estate, inheritance and gift taxes	13	20	31	67	91	..	..	..	..	..
4400 Taxes on financial and capital transactions	0	0	476	607	598	..	..	..	..	..
4500 Non-recurrent taxes	0	0	0	0	0	..	..	..	..	..
4600 Other recurrent taxes on property	0	0	0	0	0	..	..	..	..	..
5000 Taxes on goods and services	**2 200**	**20 798**	**59 360**	**124 040**	**119 641**	..	..	..	..	..
5100 Taxes on production, sale, transfer, etc	2 162	20 530	58 846	122 857	118 411	..	..	..	..	..
5110 General taxes	1 399	14 861	27 044	48 452	56 998	..	..	..	..	..
5120 Taxes on specific goods and services	763	5 669	31 802	74 404	61 413	..	..	..	..	..
5130 Unallocable between 5110 and 5120	0	0	0	0	0	..	..	..	..	..
5200 Taxes on use of goods and perform activities	38	268	514	1 183	1 230	..	..	..	..	..
5300 Unallocable between 5100 and 5200	0	0	0	0	0	..	..	..	..	..
6000 Other taxes	**1 037**	**204**	**757**	**1 925**	**1 878**	..	..	..	..	..
6100 Paid solely by business	0	0	0	0	0	..	..	..	..	..
6200 Other	1 037	204	757	1 925	1 878	..	..	..	..	..
Total tax revenue	**5 041**	**37 882**	**101 746**	**255 633**	**292 863**	..	..	..	..	..

Million GYD

	Local government[2]					Social security funds[3]				
	1990	2000	2010	2021	2022	1990	2000	2010	2021	2022
1000 Taxes on income, profits and capital gains	..	..	**0**	**0**	**0**	**0**	**0**	**0**	**0**	**0**
1100 Of individuals	..	..	..	..	..	..	..	..	..	..
1200 Corporate	..	..	..	..	..	..	..	..	..	..
1300 Unallocable between 1100 and 1200	..	..	..	..	..	..	..	..	..	..
2000 Social security contributions	..	..	**0**	**0**	**0**	**191**	**4 868**	**10 047**	**26 725**	**31 353**
2100 Employees	..	..	..	..	..	..	..	..	..	..
2200 Employers	..	..	..	..	..	..	..	..	..	..
2300 Self-employed or non-employed	..	..	..	..	..	..	..	..	..	..
2400 Unallocable between 2100, 2200 and 2300	..	..	..	..	..	191	4 868	10 047	26 725	31 353
3000 Taxes on payroll and workforce	..	..	**0**	**0**	**0**	**0**	**0**	**0**	**0**	**0**
4000 Taxes on property	..	..	**0**	**0**	**0**	**0**	**0**	**0**	**0**	**0**
4100 Recurrent taxes on immovable property	..	..	..	..	..	..	..	..	..	..
4200 Recurrent taxes on net wealth	..	..	..	..	..	..	..	..	..	..
4300 Estate, inheritance and gift taxes	..	..	..	..	..	..	..	..	..	..
4400 Taxes on financial and capital transactions	..	..	..	..	..	..	..	..	..	..
4500 Non-recurrent taxes	..	..	..	..	..	..	..	..	..	..
4600 Other recurrent taxes on property	..	..	..	..	..	..	..	..	..	..
5000 Taxes on goods and services	..	..	**0**	**0**	**0**	**0**	**0**	**0**	**0**	**0**
5100 Taxes on production, sale, transfer, etc	..	..	..	..	..	..	..	..	..	..
5110 General taxes	..	..	..	..	..	..	..	..	..	..
5120 Taxes on specific goods and services	..	..	..	..	..	..	..	..	..	..
5130 Unallocable between 5110 and 5120	..	..	..	..	..	..	..	..	..	..
5200 Taxes on use of goods and perform activities	..	..	..	..	..	..	..	..	..	..
5300 Unallocable between 5100 and 5200	..	..	..	..	..	..	..	..	..	..
6000 Other taxes	..	..	**113**	**43**	**159**	**0**	**0**	**0**	**0**	**0**
6100 Paid solely by business	..	..	0	0	0	..	..	..	..	..
6200 Other	..	..	113	43	159	..	..	..	..	..
Total tax revenue	..	..	**113**	**43**	**159**	**191**	**4 868**	**10 047**	**26 725**	**31 353**

.. Not available

1. Central government tax revenues are based on Budget Estimates by the Ministry of Finance.

2. Local government tax revenues include payments of local taxes by public corporations.

3. Social security figures include contributions to National Insurance Scheme.

Table 6.17. Honduras, tax revenues by sub-sectors of government

Million HNL

	Federal government					State/Regional				
	1990	2000	2010	2021	2022	1990	2000	2010	2021	2022
1000 Taxes on income, profits and capital gains	**431**	**2 907**	**13 232**	**35 209**	**48 289**	**..**	**..**	**..**	**..**	**..**
1100 Of individuals	157	992	4 528	14 258	17 478	..	..	..	..	..
1200 Corporate	274	1 916	8 705	20 951	30 811	..	..	..	..	..
1300 Unallocable between 1100 and 1200	0	0	0	0	0	..	..	..	..	..
2000 Social security contributions	**0**	**0**	**0**	**0**	**0**	**..**	**..**	**..**	**..**	**..**
2100 Employees	..	..	..	..	..	..	..	..	..	..
2200 Employers	..	..	..	..	..	..	..	..	..	..
2300 Self-employed or non-employed	..	..	..	..	..	..	..	..	..	..
2400 Unallocable between 2100, 2200 and 2300	..	..	..	..	..	..	..	..	..	..
3000 Taxes on payroll and workforce[1]	**0**	**0**	**485**	**1 081**	**1 215**	**..**	**..**	**..**	**..**	**..**
4000 Taxes on property	**16**	**266**	**994**	**4 119**	**4 881**	**..**	**..**	**..**	**..**	**..**
4100 Recurrent taxes on immovable property	16	189	254	586	720	..	..	..	..	..
4200 Recurrent taxes on net wealth	0	78	359	469	439	..	..	..	..	..
4300 Estate, inheritance and gift taxes	0	0	0	0	0	..	..	..	..	..
4400 Taxes on financial and capital transactions	0	0	0	3 064	3 722	..	..	..	..	..
4500 Non-recurrent taxes	0	0	380	0	0	..	..	..	..	..
4600 Other recurrent taxes on property	0	0	0	0	0	..	..	..	..	..
5000 Taxes on goods and services	**1 401**	**12 436**	**28 937**	**75 817**	**80 525**	**..**	**..**	**..**	**..**	**..**
5100 Taxes on production, sale, transfer, etc	1 401	12 436	28 937	75 817	80 525	..	..	..	..	..
5110 General taxes	344	5 146	16 050	49 264	56 067	..	..	..	..	..
5120 Taxes on specific goods and services	1 057	7 290	12 887	26 553	24 458	..	..	..	..	..
5130 Unallocable between 5110 and 5120	0	0	0	0	0	..	..	..	..	..
5200 Taxes on use of goods and perform activities	0	0	0	0	0	..	..	..	..	..
5300 Unallocable between 5100 and 5200	0	0	0	0	0	..	..	..	..	..
6000 Other taxes	**1**	**2**	**9**	**11**	**13**	**..**	**..**	**..**	**..**	**..**
6100 Paid solely by business	0	0	0	0	0	..	..	..	..	..
6200 Other	1	2	9	11	13	..	..	..	..	..
Total tax revenue	**1 849**	**15 612**	**43 657**	**116 236**	**134 924**	**..**	**..**	**..**	**..**	**..**

Million HNL

	Local government[2]					Social security funds				
	1990	2000	2010	2021	2022	1990	2000	2010	2021	2022
1000 Taxes on income, profits and capital gains	**0**	**0**	**0**	**0**	**0**	**0**	**0**	**0**	**0**	**0**
1100 Of individuals	..	..	..	..	..	..	..	..	..	..
1200 Corporate	..	..	..	..	..	..	..	..	..	..
1300 Unallocable between 1100 and 1200	..	..	..	..	..	..	..	..	..	..
2000 Social security contributions	**0**	**0**	**0**	**0**	**0**	**179**	**1 727**	**8 671**	**23 994**	**25 284**
2100 Employees	..	..	..	..	..	..	..	..	..	..
2200 Employers	..	..	..	..	..	..	..	..	..	..
2300 Self-employed or non-employed	..	..	..	..	..	..	..	..	..	..
2400 Unallocable between 2100, 2200 and 2300	..	..	..	..	..	179	1 727	8 671	23 994	25 284
3000 Taxes on payroll and workforce[1]	**0**	**0**	**0**	**0**	**0**	**0**	**0**	**0**	**0**	**0**
4000 Taxes on property	**0**	**0**	**0**	**0**	**0**	**0**	**0**	**0**	**0**	**0**
4100 Recurrent taxes on immovable property	..	..	..	..	..	..	..	..	..	..
4200 Recurrent taxes on net wealth	..	..	..	..	..	..	..	..	..	..
4300 Estate, inheritance and gift taxes	..	..	..	..	..	..	..	..	..	..
4400 Taxes on financial and capital transactions	..	..	..	..	..	..	..	..	..	..
4500 Non-recurrent taxes	..	..	..	..	..	..	..	..	..	..
4600 Other recurrent taxes on property	..	..	..	..	..	..	..	..	..	..
5000 Taxes on goods and services	**0**	**0**	**0**	**0**	**0**	**0**	**0**	**0**	**0**	**0**
5100 Taxes on production, sale, transfer, etc	..	..	..	..	..	..	..	..	..	..
5110 General taxes	..	..	..	..	..	..	..	..	..	..
5120 Taxes on specific goods and services	..	..	..	..	..	..	..	..	..	..
5130 Unallocable between 5110 and 5120	..	..	..	..	..	..	..	..	..	..
5200 Taxes on use of goods and perform activities	..	..	..	..	..	..	..	..	..	..
5300 Unallocable between 5100 and 5200	..	..	..	..	..	..	..	..	..	..
6000 Other taxes	**90**	**960**	**2 216**	**4 836**	**5 918**	**0**	**0**	**0**	**0**	**0**
6100 Paid solely by business	0	0	0	0	0	..	..	..	..	..
6200 Other	90	960	2 216	4 836	5 918	..	..	..	..	..
Total tax revenue	**90**	**960**	**2 216**	**4 836**	**5 918**	**179**	**1 727**	**8 671**	**23 994**	**25 284**

.. Not available

1. The employer contributions to National Institute of Vocational Training (INFOP) are included in heading 3000. The tax revenue is classified under the central government. In Honduras this revenue is classified under a separate unit considered to be different to the central government.
2. The figures may include non-tax revenues and central government transfers but it has not been possible to distinguish the different components of local government tax revenues.

Table 6.18. Jamaica, tax revenues by sub-sectors of government

Million JMD

	Federal government[1]					State/Regional				
	1990	2000	2010	2021	2022	1990	2000	2010	2021	2022
1000 Taxes on income, profits and capital gains	**3 639**	**35 457**	**105 917**	**167 112**	**206 743**	..	..	..	..	..
1100 Of individuals	1 687	17 441	54 798	77 756	96 902	..	..	..	..	..
1200 Corporate	1 280	7 627	33 091	68 791	79 485	..	..	..	..	..
1300 Unallocable between 1100 and 1200	672	10 389	18 028	20 565	30 356	..	..	..	..	..
2000 Social security contributions	**0**	**0**	**0**	**0**	**0**	..	..	..	..	..
2100 Employees	..	..	..	..	..	..	..	..	..	..
2200 Employers	..	..	..	..	..	..	..	..	..	..
2300 Self-employed or non-employed	..	..	..	..	..	..	..	..	..	..
2400 Unallocable between 2100, 2200 and 2300	..	..	..	..	..	..	..	..	..	..
3000 Taxes on payroll and workforce	**305**	**3 821**	**12 792**	**32 063**	**38 188**	..	..	..	..	..
4000 Taxes on property	**965**	**3 623**	**7 339**	**8 609**	**11 399**	..	..	..	..	..
4100 Recurrent taxes on immovable property	67	0	0	0	0	..	..	..	..	..
4200 Recurrent taxes on net wealth	0	0	0	0	0	..	..	..	..	..
4300 Estate, inheritance and gift taxes	0	0	0	0	0	..	..	..	..	..
4400 Taxes on financial and capital transactions	898	3 623	7 339	8 609	11 399	..	..	..	..	..
4500 Non-recurrent taxes	0	0	0	0	0	..	..	..	..	..
4600 Other recurrent taxes on property	0	0	0	0	0	..	..	..	..	..
5000 Taxes on goods and services	**2 824**	**43 907**	**149 544**	**365 499**	**457 446**	..	..	..	..	..
5100 Taxes on production, sale, transfer, etc	2 760	43 107	147 500	357 080	448 649	..	..	..	..	..
5110 General taxes	297	22 356	84 409	199 638	253 358	..	..	..	..	..
5120 Taxes on specific goods and services	2 463	20 752	63 091	157 442	195 291	..	..	..	..	..
5130 Unallocable between 5110 and 5120	0	0	0	0	0	..	..	..	..	..
5200 Taxes on use of goods and perform activities	64	800	2 045	8 419	8 797	..	..	..	..	..
5300 Unallocable between 5100 and 5200	0	0	0	0	0	..	..	..	..	..
6000 Other taxes	**16**	**266**	**748**	**1 967**	**2 551**	..	..	..	..	..
6100 Paid solely by business	0	0	0	0	0	..	..	..	..	..
6200 Other	16	266	748	1 967	2 551	..	..	..	..	..
Total tax revenue	**7 748**	**87 074**	**276 340**	**575 251**	**716 327**	..	..	..	..	..

Million JMD

	Local government[1]					Social security funds[1]				
	1990	2000	2010	2021	2022	1990	2000	2010	2021	2022
1000 Taxes on income, profits and capital gains	..	**0**	**0**	**0**	**0**	..	..	**0**	**0**	**0**
1100 Of individuals	..	..	..	..	..	..	..	..	..	..
1200 Corporate	..	..	..	..	..	..	..	..	..	..
1300 Unallocable between 1100 and 1200	..	..	..	..	..	..	..	..	..	..
2000 Social security contributions	..	**0**	**0**	**0**	**0**	..	..	**8 199**	**31 671**	**42 531**
2100 Employees	..	..	..	..	..	..	..	..	..	..
2200 Employers	..	..	..	..	..	..	..	..	..	..
2300 Self-employed or non-employed	..	..	..	..	..	..	..	..	..	..
2400 Unallocable between 2100, 2200 and 2300	..	..	..	..	..	..	..	8 199	31 671	42 531
3000 Taxes on payroll and workforce	..	**0**	**0**	**0**	**0**	..	..	**0**	**0**	**0**
4000 Taxes on property	..	**639**	**2 600**	**9 546**	**9 716**	..	..	**0**	**0**	**0**
4100 Recurrent taxes on immovable property	..	639	2 600	9 546	9 716	..	..	..	..	..
4200 Recurrent taxes on net wealth	..	0	0	0	0	..	..	..	..	..
4300 Estate, inheritance and gift taxes	..	0	0	0	0	..	..	..	..	..
4400 Taxes on financial and capital transactions	..	0	0	0	0	..	..	..	..	..
4500 Non-recurrent taxes	..	0	0	0	0	..	..	..	..	..
4600 Other recurrent taxes on property	..	0	0	0	0	..	..	..	..	..
5000 Taxes on goods and services	..	**0**	**0**	**0**	**0**	..	..	**0**	**0**	**0**
5100 Taxes on production, sale, transfer, etc	..	..	..	..	..	..	..	..	..	..
5110 General taxes	..	..	..	..	..	..	..	..	..	..
5120 Taxes on specific goods and services	..	..	..	..	..	..	..	..	..	..
5130 Unallocable between 5110 and 5120	..	..	..	..	..	..	..	..	..	..
5200 Taxes on use of goods and perform activities	..	..	..	..	..	..	..	..	..	..
5300 Unallocable between 5100 and 5200	..	..	..	..	..	..	..	..	..	..
6000 Other taxes	..	**0**	**0**	**0**	**0**	..	..	**0**	**0**	**0**
6100 Paid solely by business	..	..	..	..	..	..	..	..	..	..
6200 Other	..	..	..	..	..	..	..	..	..	..
Total tax revenue	..	**639**	**2 600**	**9 546**	**9 716**	..	..	**8 199**	**31 671**	**42 531**

.. Not available

1. The figures refer to fiscal year ending 31st March for 1990-2003 and then calendar year ending 31st December.

Table 6.19. Mexico, tax revenues by sub-sectors of government

Million MXN

	Federal government					State/Regional				
	1990	2000	2010	2021	2022	1990	2000	2010	2021	2022
1000 Taxes on income, profits and capital gains[1]	**34 668**	**276 548**	**683 604**	**1 903 047**	**2 280 791**	**3**	**0**	**0**	**0**	**0**
1100 Of individuals	..	..	313 473	938 623	1 066 965	..	..	..	..	..
1200 Corporate	..	..	246 745	898 767	1 136 636	..	..	..	..	..
1300 Unallocable between 1100 and 1200	34 668	276 548	123 386	65 657	77 190	3	..	..	..	..
2000 Social security contributions	**0**	**0**	**0**	**0**	**0**	**0**	**0**	**0**	**0**	**0**
2100 Employees	..	..	..	..	..	..	..	..	..	..
2200 Employers	..	..	..	..	..	..	..	..	..	..
2300 Self-employed or non-employed	..	..	..	..	..	..	..	..	..	..
2400 Unallocable between 2100, 2200 and 2300	..	..	..	..	..	..	..	..	..	..
3000 Taxes on payroll and workforce	**818**	**0**	**0**	**0**	**0**	**972**	**11 215**	**36 818**	**116 910**	**141 140**
4000 Taxes on property	**3**	**0**	**0**	**0**	**0**	**894**	**7 018**	**13 137**	**30 097**	**33 508**
4100 Recurrent taxes on immovable property	0	..	..	..	..	482	5 238	8 522	19 407	21 898
4200 Recurrent taxes on net wealth	0	..	..	..	..	0	0	0	0	0
4300 Estate, inheritance and gift taxes	0	..	..	..	..	7	0	0	0	0
4400 Taxes on financial and capital transactions	3	..	..	..	..	405	1 781	4 615	10 690	11 610
4500 Non-recurrent taxes	0	..	..	..	..	0	0	0	0	0
4600 Other recurrent taxes on property	0	..	..	..	..	0	0	0	0	0
5000 Taxes on goods and services	**44 605**	**318 065**	**645 623**	**1 621 889**	**1 466 208**	**118**	**1 346**	**5 805**	**25 401**	**29 519**
5100 Taxes on production, sale, transfer, etc	44 029	309 283	627 187	1 621 215	1 465 417	45	910	2 470	8 779	12 939
5110 General taxes	26 635	189 606	504 509	1 123 699	1 221 803	0	0	0	0	0
5120 Taxes on specific goods and services	17 394	119 677	122 678	497 517	243 614	30	910	2 470	8 779	12 939
5130 Unallocable between 5110 and 5120	0	0	0	0	0	15	0	0	0	0
5200 Taxes on use of goods and perform activities	576	8 782	18 436	673	792	73	436	3 335	16 622	16 580
5300 Unallocable between 5100 and 5200	0	0	0	0	0	0	0	0	0	0
6000 Other taxes	**1 340**	**5 878**	**22 236**	**54 534**	**83 919**	**165**	**907**	**2 546**	**10 209**	**14 515**
6100 Paid solely by business	0	0	0	0	0	0	0	0	0	0
6200 Other	1 340	5 878	22 236	54 534	83 919	165	907	2 546	10 209	14 515
Total tax revenue	**81 434**	**600 491**	**1 351 463**	**3 579 470**	**3 830 919**	**2 152**	**20 485**	**58 307**	**182 616**	**218 683**

Million MXN

	Local government					Social security funds[2]				
	1990	2000	2010	2021	2022	1990	2000	2010	2021	2022
1000 Taxes on income, profits and capital gains[1]	**2**	**0**	**0**	**0**	**0**	**0**	**0**	**0**	**0**	**0**
1100 Of individuals	..	..	..	..	..	..	..	..	..	..
1200 Corporate	..	..	..	..	..	..	..	..	..	..
1300 Unallocable between 1100 and 1200	2	..	..	..	..	..	..	..	..	..
2000 Social security contributions	**0**	**0**	**0**	**0**	**0**	**17 165**	**138 223**	**277 459**	**612 175**	**681 672**
2100 Employees	..	..	..	..	..	..	..	..	..	..
2200 Employers	..	..	..	..	..	..	..	..	..	..
2300 Self-employed or non-employed	..	..	..	..	..	..	..	..	..	..
2400 Unallocable between 2100, 2200 and 2300	..	..	..	..	..	17 165	138 223	277 459	612 175	681 672
3000 Taxes on payroll and workforce	**7**	**2**	**93**	**0**	**0**	**0**	**0**	**0**	**0**	**0**
4000 Taxes on property	**1 017**	**6 946**	**25 818**	**60 107**	**56 615**	**0**	**0**	**0**	**0**	**0**
4100 Recurrent taxes on immovable property	554	4 710	17 202	36 739	34 214	..	..	..	..	..
4200 Recurrent taxes on net wealth	0	0	0	0	0	..	..	..	..	..
4300 Estate, inheritance and gift taxes	1	0	0	0	0	..	..	..	..	..
4400 Taxes on financial and capital transactions	462	2 236	8 616	23 368	22 401	..	..	..	..	..
4500 Non-recurrent taxes	0	0	0	0	0	..	..	..	..	..
4600 Other recurrent taxes on property	0	0	0	0	0	..	..	..	..	..
5000 Taxes on goods and services	**114**	**202**	**487**	**637**	**861**	**0**	**0**	**0**	**0**	**0**
5100 Taxes on production, sale, transfer, etc	97	133	466	622	788	..	..	..	..	..
5110 General taxes	0	0	0	0	0	..	..	..	..	..
5120 Taxes on specific goods and services	95	133	466	622	788	..	..	..	..	..
5130 Unallocable between 5110 and 5120	2	0	0	0	0	..	..	..	..	..
5200 Taxes on use of goods and perform activities	17	69	21	15	73	..	..	..	..	..
5300 Unallocable between 5100 and 5200	0	0	0	0	0	..	..	..	..	..
6000 Other taxes	**114**	**866**	**2 616**	**17 349**	**29 264**	**0**	**0**	**0**	**0**	**0**
6100 Paid solely by business	0	0	0	0	0	..	..	..	..	..
6200 Other	114	866	2 616	17 349	29 264	..	..	..	..	..
Total tax revenue	**1 254**	**8 016**	**29 014**	**78 094**	**86 741**	**17 165**	**138 223**	**277 459**	**612 175**	**681 672**

.. Not available

1. In ECLAC data, income taxes are presented net of credit on salary figures.
2. In ECLAC data, social security contributions are presented net of transfers from the Federal government for the payment of IMSS (Mexican Social Security Institute) pensions.

Table 6.20. Nicaragua, tax revenues by sub-sectors of government

Million NIO

	Federal government					State/Regional				
	1990	2000	2010	2021	2022	1990	2000	2010	2021	2022
1000 Taxes on income, profits and capital gains	..	**1 144**	**8 351**	**40 753**	**50 714**	..	..	..	..	..
1100 Of individuals	..	299	1 857	7 753	9 648	..	..	..	..	..
1200 Corporate	..	845	6 494	33 000	41 066	..	..	..	..	..
1300 Unallocable between 1100 and 1200	..	0	0	0	0	..	..	..	..	..
2000 Social security contributions	..	**0**	**0**	**0**	**0**	..	..	..	..	..
2100 Employees	..	..	..	..	..	..	..	..	..	..
2200 Employers	..	..	..	..	..	..	..	..	..	..
2300 Self-employed or non-employed	..	..	..	..	..	..	..	..	..	..
2400 Unallocable between 2100, 2200 and 2300	..	..	..	..	..	..	..	..	..	..
3000 Taxes on payroll and workforce	..	**0**	**0**	**0**	**0**	..	..	..	..	..
4000 Taxes on property	..	**11**	**20**	**71**	**90**	..	..	..	..	..
4100 Recurrent taxes on immovable property	..	0	0	0	0	..	..	..	..	..
4200 Recurrent taxes on net wealth	..	0	0	0	0	..	..	..	..	..
4300 Estate, inheritance and gift taxes	..	0	0	0	0	..	..	..	..	..
4400 Taxes on financial and capital transactions	..	11	20	71	90	..	..	..	..	..
4500 Non-recurrent taxes	..	0	0	0	0	..	..	..	..	..
4600 Other recurrent taxes on property	..	0	0	0	0	..	..	..	..	..
5000 Taxes on goods and services	..	**5 584**	**17 029**	**53 199**	**60 591**	..	..	..	..	..
5100 Taxes on production, sale, transfer, etc	..	5 584	17 029	53 199	60 591	..	..	..	..	..
5110 General taxes	..	2 931	10 353	33 341	38 449	..	..	..	..	..
5120 Taxes on specific goods and services	..	2 653	6 676	19 858	22 142	..	..	..	..	..
5130 Unallocable between 5110 and 5120	..	0	0	0	0	..	..	..	..	..
5200 Taxes on use of goods and perform activities	..	0	0	0	0	..	..	..	..	..
5300 Unallocable between 5100 and 5200	..	0	0	0	0	..	..	..	..	..
6000 Other taxes	..	**0**	**0**	**0**	**0**	..	..	..	..	..
6100 Paid solely by business	..	..	..	..	..	..	..	..	..	..
6200 Other	..	..	..	..	..	..	..	..	..	..
Total tax revenue	..	**6 739**	**25 400**	**94 023**	**111 395**	..	..	..	..	..

Million NIO

	Local government[1]					Social security funds				
	1990	2000	2010	2021	2022	1990	2000	2010	2021	2022
1000 Taxes on income, profits and capital gains	..	**0**	**0**	**0**	**0**	..	**0**	**0**	**0**	**0**
1100 Of individuals	..	..	..	..	..	..	..	..	..	..
1200 Corporate	..	..	..	..	..	..	..	..	..	..
1300 Unallocable between 1100 and 1200	..	..	..	..	..	..	..	..	..	..
2000 Social security contributions	..	**0**	**0**	**0**	**0**	..	**1 678**	**8 090**	**32 054**	**35 571**
2100 Employees	..	..	..	..	..	..	..	..	..	..
2200 Employers	..	..	..	..	..	..	..	..	..	..
2300 Self-employed or non-employed	..	..	..	..	..	..	..	..	..	..
2400 Unallocable between 2100, 2200 and 2300	..	..	..	..	..	..	1 678	8 090	32 054	35 571
3000 Taxes on payroll and workforce	..	**0**	**0**	**0**	**0**	..	**0**	**0**	**0**	**0**
4000 Taxes on property	..	**0**	**403**	**1 707**	**1 726**	..	**0**	**0**	**0**	**0**
4100 Recurrent taxes on immovable property	..	..	403	1 707	1 726	..	..	..	..	..
4200 Recurrent taxes on net wealth	..	..	0	0	0	..	..	..	..	..
4300 Estate, inheritance and gift taxes	..	..	0	0	0	..	..	..	..	..
4400 Taxes on financial and capital transactions	..	..	0	0	0	..	..	..	..	..
4500 Non-recurrent taxes	..	..	0	0	0	..	..	..	..	..
4600 Other recurrent taxes on property	..	..	0	0	0	..	..	..	..	..
5000 Taxes on goods and services	..	**0**	**1 922**	**5 494**	**6 063**	..	**0**	**0**	**0**	**0**
5100 Taxes on production, sale, transfer, etc	..	..	1 579	4 431	4 824	..	..	..	..	..
5110 General taxes	..	..	1 579	4 431	4 824	..	..	..	..	..
5120 Taxes on specific goods and services	..	..	0	0	0	..	..	..	..	..
5130 Unallocable between 5110 and 5120	..	..	0	0	0	..	..	..	..	..
5200 Taxes on use of goods and perform activities	..	..	343	1 063	1 239	..	..	..	..	..
5300 Unallocable between 5100 and 5200	..	..	0	0	0	..	..	..	..	..
6000 Other taxes	..	**0**	**347**	**1 240**	**1 420**	..	**0**	**0**	**0**	**0**
6100 Paid solely by business	..	..	0	0	0	..	..	..	..	..
6200 Other	..	..	347	1 240	1 420	..	..	..	..	..
Total tax revenue	..	**882**	**2 672**	**8 440**	**9 209**	..	**1 678**	**8 090**	**32 054**	**35 571**

.. Not available

Note: Comparable statistics for 1990 cannot be shown due to the devaluation of the Nicaraguan cordoba.

1. Local tax revenue data in 2022 are estimated.

Table 6.21. Panama, tax revenues by sub-sectors of government

Million PAB

	Federal government[3]					State/Regional				
	1990	2000	2010	2021	2022	1990	2000	2010	2021	2022
1000 Taxes on income, profits and capital gains	**217**	**485**	**1 317**	**1 998**	**2 808**	..	..	..	..	..
1100 Of individuals	140	295	440	1 101	1 418	..	..	..	..	..
1200 Corporate	66	159	603	582	954	..	..	..	..	..
1300 Unallocable between 1100 and 1200	11	31	273	315	435	..	..	..	..	..
2000 Social security contributions	**0**	**0**	**0**	**0**	**0**	..	..	..	..	..
2100 Employees	..	..	..	..	..	..	..	..	..	..
2200 Employers	..	..	..	..	..	..	..	..	..	..
2300 Self-employed or non-employed	..	..	..	..	..	..	..	..	..	..
2400 Unallocable between 2100, 2200 and 2300	..	..	..	..	..	..	..	..	..	..
3000 Taxes on payroll and workforce[1]	**0**	**36**	**59**	**113**	**131**	..	..	..	..	..
4000 Taxes on property	**32**	**43**	**138**	**180**	**208**	..	..	..	..	..
4100 Recurrent taxes on immovable property	28	34	108	145	160	..	..	..	..	..
4200 Recurrent taxes on net wealth	0	0	0	0	0	..	..	..	..	..
4300 Estate, inheritance and gift taxes	0	0	0	0	0	..	..	..	..	..
4400 Taxes on financial and capital transactions	3	9	30	35	48	..	..	..	..	..
4500 Non-recurrent taxes	0	0	0	0	0	..	..	..	..	..
4600 Other recurrent taxes on property	0	0	0	0	0	..	..	..	..	..
5000 Taxes on goods and services	**349**	**565**	**1 547**	**2 093**	**2 490**	..	..	..	..	..
5100 Taxes on production, sale, transfer, etc	332	546	1 473	1 974	2 365	..	..	..	..	..
5110 General taxes	80	69	766	1 152	1 407	..	..	..	..	..
5120 Taxes on specific goods and services[2]	251	477	707	822	959	..	..	..	..	..
5130 Unallocable between 5110 and 5120	0	0	0	0	0	..	..	..	..	..
5200 Taxes on use of goods and perform activities	15	19	75	119	125	..	..	..	..	..
5300 Unallocable between 5100 and 5200	2	0	0	0	0	..	..	..	..	..
6000 Other taxes	**26**	**27**	**41**	**24**	**28**	..	..	..	..	..
6100 Paid solely by business	0	0	0	0	0	..	..	..	..	..
6200 Other	26	27	41	24	28	..	..	..	..	..
Total tax revenue	**624**	**1 157**	**3 102**	**4 408**	**5 664**	..	..	..	..	..

Million PAB

	Local government[4]					Social security funds[5]				
	1990	2000	2010	2021	2022	1990	2000	2010	2021	2022
1000 Taxes on income, profits and capital gains	..	**0**	**0**	**0**	**0**	**0**	**0**	**0**	**0**	**0**
1100 Of individuals	..	..	..	..	..	..	..	..	..	..
1200 Corporate	..	..	..	..	..	..	..	..	..	..
1300 Unallocable between 1100 and 1200	..	..	..	..	..	..	..	..	..	..
2000 Social security contributions	..	**0**	**0**	**0**	**0**	**325**	**742**	**1 637**	**3 570**	**4 217**
2100 Employees	..	..	..	..	..	..	..	..	..	..
2200 Employers	..	..	..	..	..	..	..	..	..	..
2300 Self-employed or non-employed	..	..	..	..	..	..	..	..	..	..
2400 Unallocable between 2100, 2200 and 2300	..	..	..	..	..	325	742	1 637	3 570	4 217
3000 Taxes on payroll and workforce[1]	..	**0**	**0**	**0**	**0**	**0**	**0**	**0**	**0**	**0**
4000 Taxes on property	..	**0**	**0**	**0**	**0**	**0**	**0**	**0**	**0**	**0**
4100 Recurrent taxes on immovable property	..	0	..	..	..	..	..	..	..	..
4200 Recurrent taxes on net wealth	..	0	..	..	..	..	..	..	..	..
4300 Estate, inheritance and gift taxes	..	0	..	..	..	..	..	..	..	..
4400 Taxes on financial and capital transactions	..	0	..	..	..	..	..	..	..	..
4500 Non-recurrent taxes	..	0	..	..	..	..	..	..	..	..
4600 Other recurrent taxes on property	..	0	..	..	..	..	..	..	..	..
5000 Taxes on goods and services	..	**43**	**76**	**128**	**158**	**0**	**0**	**0**	**0**	**0**
5100 Taxes on production, sale, transfer, etc	..	0	0	0	0	..	..	..	..	..
5110 General taxes	..	0	..	..	..	..	..	..	..	..
5120 Taxes on specific goods and services[2]	..	0	..	..	..	..	..	..	..	..
5130 Unallocable between 5110 and 5120	..	0	..	..	..	..	..	..	..	..
5200 Taxes on use of goods and perform activities	..	43	76	128	158	..	..	..	..	..
5300 Unallocable between 5100 and 5200	..	0	0	0	0	..	..	..	..	..
6000 Other taxes	..	**0**	**0**	**0**	**0**	**0**	**0**	**0**	**0**	**0**
6100 Paid solely by business	..	0	..	..	..	..	..	..	..	..
6200 Other	..	0	..	..	..	..	..	..	..	..
Total tax revenue	..	**43**	**76**	**128**	**158**	**325**	**742**	**1 637**	**3 570**	**4 217**

.. Not available

1. In ECLAC data, education insurance is classified as "Other taxes" (6000).
2. In CIAT and ECLAC data, the tax on banks, financial institutions and currency exchange is classified as a property tax (4000).
3. The figures exclude documentos fiscales as they are not considered as tax revenues according to the OECD classification, described in the interpretative guide.
4. Local tax revenue data in 2022 are estimated.
5. Social security contributions include regular and special contributions and professional risks premium collected by the Caja de Seguro Social (CSS). Figures in 2022 are estimated.

Table 6.22. Paraguay, tax revenues by sub-sectors of government

Million PYG

	Federal government					State/Regional				
	1990	2000	2010	2021	2022	1990	2000	2010	2021	2022
1000 Taxes on income, profits and capital gains	**73 726**	**470 388**	**2 096 498**	**6 920 734**	**8 736 495**	..	..	..	..	..
1100 Of individuals	..	15 042	31 263	364 990	437 426	..	..	..	..	..
1200 Corporate	..	455 346	2 065 235	6 555 744	8 299 069	..	..	..	..	..
1300 Unallocable between 1100 and 1200	73 726	0	0	0	0	..	..	..	..	..
2000 Social security contributions	**0**	**0**	**0**	**0**	**0**	..	..	..	..	..
2100 Employees	..	..	..	..	..	..	..	..	..	..
2200 Employers	..	..	..	..	..	..	..	..	..	..
2300 Self-employed or non-employed	..	..	..	..	..	..	..	..	..	..
2400 Unallocable between 2100, 2200 and 2300	..	..	..	..	..	..	..	..	..	..
3000 Taxes on payroll and workforce	**0**	**0**	**0**	**0**	**0**	..	..	..	..	..
4000 Taxes on property	**17 162**	**71 777**	**332**	**65**	**141**	..	..	..	..	..
4100 Recurrent taxes on immovable property	17 162	0	0	0	0	..	..	..	..	..
4200 Recurrent taxes on net wealth	0	0	0	0	0	..	..	..	..	..
4300 Estate, inheritance and gift taxes	0	0	0	0	0	..	..	..	..	..
4400 Taxes on financial and capital transactions	0	71 777	332	65	141	..	..	..	..	..
4500 Non-recurrent taxes	0	0	0	0	0	..	..	..	..	..
4600 Other recurrent taxes on property	0	0	0	0	0	..	..	..	..	..
5000 Taxes on goods and services	**438 444**	**2 080 878**	**9 226 584**	**19 108 227**	**20 487 571**	..	..	..	..	..
5100 Taxes on production, sale, transfer, etc	438 444	2 080 878	9 226 493	19 108 227	20 487 571	..	..	..	..	..
5110 General taxes	0	1 150 496	5 991 694	13 705 814	14 986 187	..	..	..	..	..
5120 Taxes on specific goods and services	438 444	930 382	3 234 799	5 402 413	5 501 384	..	..	..	..	..
5130 Unallocable between 5110 and 5120	0	0	0	0	0	..	..	..	..	..
5200 Taxes on use of goods and perform activities	0	0	91	0	0	..	..	..	..	..
5300 Unallocable between 5100 and 5200	0	0	0	0	0	..	..	..	..	..
6000 Other taxes	**49 807**	**44 875**	**109 001**	**210 427**	**191 917**	..	..	..	..	..
6100 Paid solely by business	0	0	0	0	0	..	..	..	..	..
6200 Other	49 807	44 875	109 001	210 427	191 917	..	..	..	..	..
Total tax revenue	**579 139**	**2 667 918**	**11 432 415**	**26 239 453**	**29 416 125**	..	..	..	..	..

Million PYG

	Local government[1]					Social security funds[2]				
	1990	2000	2010	2021	2022	1990	2000	2010	2021	2022
1000 Taxes on income, profits and capital gains	..	..	**0**	**0**	**0**	**0**	**0**	**0**	**0**	**0**
1100 Of individuals	..	..	..	..	..	..	..	..	..	..
1200 Corporate	..	..	..	..	..	..	..	..	..	..
1300 Unallocable between 1100 and 1200	..	..	..	..	..	..	..	..	..	..
2000 Social security contributions	..	..	**0**	**0**	**0**	**28 882**	**919 533**	**3 552 640**	**10 335 479**	**12 326 174**
2100 Employees	..	..	..	..	..	..	..	..	..	..
2200 Employers	..	..	..	..	..	..	..	..	..	..
2300 Self-employed or non-employed	..	..	..	..	..	..	..	..	..	..
2400 Unallocable between 2100, 2200 and 2300	..	..	..	..	..	28 882	919 533	3 552 640	10 335 479	12 326 174
3000 Taxes on payroll and workforce	..	..	**0**	**0**	**0**	**0**	**0**	**0**	**0**	**0**
4000 Taxes on property	..	..	**275 787**	**488 829**	**498 161**	**0**	**0**	**0**	**0**	**0**
4100 Recurrent taxes on immovable property	..	..	258 423	457 759	459 869	..	..	..	..	..
4200 Recurrent taxes on net wealth	..	..	0	0	0	..	..	..	..	..
4300 Estate, inheritance and gift taxes	..	..	0	0	0	..	..	..	..	..
4400 Taxes on financial and capital transactions	..	..	15 623	30 491	38 168	..	..	..	..	..
4500 Non-recurrent taxes	..	..	0	0	0	..	..	..	..	..
4600 Other recurrent taxes on property	..	..	1 742	579	124	..	..	..	..	..
5000 Taxes on goods and services	..	..	**235 877**	**440 350**	**424 734**	**0**	**0**	**0**	**0**	**0**
5100 Taxes on production, sale, transfer, etc	..	..	19 384	15 371	13 270	..	..	..	..	..
5110 General taxes	..	..	0	0	0	..	..	..	..	..
5120 Taxes on specific goods and services	..	..	19 384	15 371	13 270	..	..	..	..	..
5130 Unallocable between 5110 and 5120	..	..	0	0	0	..	..	..	..	..
5200 Taxes on use of goods and perform activities	..	..	216 256	423 107	404 159	..	..	..	..	..
5300 Unallocable between 5100 and 5200	..	..	237	1 872	7 304	..	..	..	..	..
6000 Other taxes	..	..	**141 811**	**52 172**	**94 794**	**0**	**0**	**0**	**0**	**0**
6100 Paid solely by business	..	..	0	0	0	..	..	..	..	..
6200 Other	..	..	141 811	52 172	94 794	..	..	..	..	..
Total tax revenue	..	..	**653 476**	**981 351**	**1 017 689**	**28 882**	**919 533**	**3 552 640**	**10 335 479**	**12 326 174**

.. Not available

1. The figures for years before 2006 exclude local government tax revenues as the data are not available.

2. Social security contributions before 1999 do not include contributions collected by decentralised institutions as the data are not available.

Table 6.23. Peru, tax revenues by sub-sectors of government

Million PEN

	Federal government					State/Regional				
	1990	2000	2010	2021	2022	1990	2000	2010	2021	2022
1000 Taxes on income, profits and capital gains	**37**	**5 078**	**27 317**	**61 112**	**75 444**	..	..	..	..	..
1100 Of individuals	3	2 117	6 518	16 765	18 325	..	..	..	..	..
1200 Corporate	32	2 526	19 561	41 415	54 751	..	..	..	..	..
1300 Unallocable between 1100 and 1200	1	436	1 239	2 932	2 368	..	..	..	..	..
2000 Social security contributions	**0**	**0**	**0**	**0**	**0**	..	..	..	..	..
2100 Employees	..	..	..	..	..	..	..	..	..	..
2200 Employers	..	..	..	..	..	..	..	..	..	..
2300 Self-employed or non-employed	..	..	..	..	..	..	..	..	..	..
2400 Unallocable between 2100, 2200 and 2300	..	..	..	..	..	..	..	..	..	..
3000 Taxes on payroll and workforce[1]	**0**	**1 176**	**57**	**101**	**113**	..	..	..	..	..
4000 Taxes on property	**87**	**0**	**944**	**271**	**309**	..	..	..	..	..
4100 Recurrent taxes on immovable property	0	0	0	0	0	..	..	..	..	..
4200 Recurrent taxes on net wealth	49	0	0	0	0	..	..	..	..	..
4300 Estate, inheritance and gift taxes	0	0	0	0	0	..	..	..	..	..
4400 Taxes on financial and capital transactions	38	0	944	271	309	..	..	..	..	..
4500 Non-recurrent taxes	0	0	0	0	0	..	..	..	..	..
4600 Other recurrent taxes on property	0	0	0	0	0	..	..	..	..	..
5000 Taxes on goods and services	**454**	**16 205**	**36 064**	**74 021**	**80 377**	..	..	..	..	..
5100 Taxes on production, sale, transfer, etc	454	16 205	36 064	74 021	80 377	..	..	..	..	..
5110 General taxes	109	9 646	29 094	62 780	68 418	..	..	..	..	..
5120 Taxes on specific goods and services	345	6 558	6 970	11 241	11 959	..	..	..	..	..
5130 Unallocable between 5110 and 5120	0	0	0	0	0	..	..	..	..	..
5200 Taxes on use of goods and perform activities	0	0	0	0	0	..	..	..	..	..
5300 Unallocable between 5100 and 5200	0	0	0	0	0	..	..	..	..	..
6000 Other taxes	**9**	**697**	**888**	**3 910**	**2 098**	..	..	..	..	..
6100 Paid solely by business	0	84	108	109	114	..	..	..	..	..
6200 Other	9	614	780	3 801	1 984	..	..	..	..	..
Total tax revenue	**587**	**23 156**	**65 270**	**139 414**	**158 341**	..	..	..	..	..

Million PEN

	Local government[2]					Social security funds				
	1990	2000	2010	2021	2022	1990	2000	2010	2021	2022
1000 Taxes on income, profits and capital gains	..	**0**	**0**	**0**	**0**	**0**	**0**	**0**	**0**	**0**
1100 Of individuals	..	..	..	..	..	..	..	..	..	..
1200 Corporate	..	..	..	..	..	..	..	..	..	..
1300 Unallocable between 1100 and 1200	..	..	..	..	..	..	..	..	..	..
2000 Social security contributions	..	**0**	**0**	**0**	**0**	**50**	**3 185**	**7 929**	**16 407**	**17 877**
2100 Employees	..	..	..	..	..	..	566	2 433	4 193	4 471
2200 Employers	..	..	..	..	..	..	2 515	5 454	12 166	13 353
2300 Self-employed or non-employed	..	..	..	..	..	..	95	42	48	54
2400 Unallocable between 2100, 2200 and 2300	..	..	..	..	..	50	9	0	0	0
3000 Taxes on payroll and workforce[1]	..	**0**	**0**	**0**	**0**	**0**	**0**	**0**	**0**	**0**
4000 Taxes on property	..	**323**	**1 287**	**2 994**	**3 251**	**0**	**0**	**0**	**0**	**0**
4100 Recurrent taxes on immovable property	..	298	727	2 266	2 391	..	..	..	..	..
4200 Recurrent taxes on net wealth	..	0	0	0	0	..	..	..	..	..
4300 Estate, inheritance and gift taxes	..	0	0	0	0	..	..	..	..	..
4400 Taxes on financial and capital transactions	..	25	560	728	861	..	..	..	..	..
4500 Non-recurrent taxes	..	0	0	0	0	..	..	..	..	..
4600 Other recurrent taxes on property	..	0	0	0	0	..	..	..	..	..
5000 Taxes on goods and services	..	**59**	**290**	**366**	**485**	**0**	**0**	**0**	**0**	**0**
5100 Taxes on production, sale, transfer, etc	..	34	135	83	162	..	..	..	..	..
5110 General taxes	..	0	0	0	0	..	..	..	..	..
5120 Taxes on specific goods and services	..	34	135	83	162	..	..	..	..	..
5130 Unallocable between 5110 and 5120	..	0	0	0	0	..	..	..	..	..
5200 Taxes on use of goods and perform activities	..	25	154	284	323	..	..	..	..	..
5300 Unallocable between 5100 and 5200	..	0	0	0	0	..	..	..	..	..
6000 Other taxes	..	**48**	**26**	**52**	**55**	**0**	**0**	**0**	**0**	**0**
6100 Paid solely by business	..	0	0	0	0	..	..	..	..	..
6200 Other	..	48	26	52	55	..	..	..	..	..
Total tax revenue	..	**430**	**1 603**	**3 413**	**3 792**	**50**	**3 185**	**7 929**	**16 407**	**17 877**

.. Not available

1. Contributions to SENATI are included in heading 3000. The tax revenue is classified under the central government. In Peru this revenue is classified under a separate unit considered to be different to the central government.
2. The figures for years up to 2000 exclude local government tax revenues as the data are not available.

Table 6.24. Saint Lucia, tax revenues by sub-sectors of government

Million XCD

	Federal government					State/Regional				
	1990	2000	2010	2021	2022	1990	2000	2010	2021	2022
1000 Taxes on income, profits and capital gains	..	**137**	**224**	**229**	**246**	..	..	..	..	..
1100 Of individuals	..	49	83	130	135	..	..	..	..	..
1200 Corporate	..	63	95	84	98	..	..	..	..	..
1300 Unallocable between 1100 and 1200	..	26	46	15	13	..	..	..	..	..
2000 Social security contributions	..	**0**	**0**	**0**	**0**	..	..	..	..	..
2100 Employees	..	..	..	..	..	..	..	..	..	..
2200 Employers	..	..	..	..	..	..	..	..	..	..
2300 Self-employed or non-employed	..	..	..	..	..	..	..	..	..	..
2400 Unallocable between 2100, 2200 and 2300	..	..	..	..	..	..	..	..	..	..
3000 Taxes on payroll and workforce	..	**0**	**0**	**0**	**0**	..	..	..	..	..
4000 Taxes on property	..	**11**	**19**	**31**	**27**	..	..	..	..	..
4100 Recurrent taxes on immovable property	..	2	3	8	8	..	..	..	..	..
4200 Recurrent taxes on net wealth	..	0	0	0	0	..	..	..	..	..
4300 Estate, inheritance and gift taxes	..	0	0	0	0	..	..	..	..	..
4400 Taxes on financial and capital transactions	..	9	16	23	18	..	..	..	..	..
4500 Non-recurrent taxes	..	0	0	0	0	..	..	..	..	..
4600 Other recurrent taxes on property	..	0	0	0	0	..	..	..	..	..
5000 Taxes on goods and services	..	**284**	**493**	**662**	**734**	..	..	..	..	..
5100 Taxes on production, sale, transfer, etc	..	277	467	655	726	..	..	..	..	..
5110 General taxes	..	101	119	306	335	..	..	..	..	..
5120 Taxes on specific goods and services	..	176	348	349	390	..	..	..	..	..
5130 Unallocable between 5110 and 5120	..	0	0	0	0	..	..	..	..	..
5200 Taxes on use of goods and perform activities	..	7	26	7	9	..	..	..	..	..
5300 Unallocable between 5100 and 5200	..	0	0	0	0	..	..	..	..	..
6000 Other taxes	..	**0**	**0**	**0**	**0**	..	..	..	..	..
6100 Paid solely by business	..	..	..	..	..	..	..	..	..	..
6200 Other	..	..	..	..	..	..	..	..	..	..
Total tax revenue	..	**432**	**737**	**922**	**1 007**	..	..	..	..	..

Million XCD

	Local government					Social security funds[1]				
	1990	2000	2010	2021	2022	1990	2000	2010	2021	2022
1000 Taxes on income, profits and capital gains	..	..	..	..	..	..	**0**	**0**	**0**	**0**
1100 Of individuals	..	..	..	..	..	..	..	..	..	..
1200 Corporate	..	..	..	..	..	..	..	..	..	..
1300 Unallocable between 1100 and 1200	..	..	..	..	..	..	..	..	..	..
2000 Social security contributions	..	..	..	..	..	..	**48**	**92**	**125**	**154**
2100 Employees	..	..	..	..	..	..	..	..	..	..
2200 Employers	..	..	..	..	..	..	..	..	..	..
2300 Self-employed or non-employed	..	..	..	..	..	..	..	1	1	1
2400 Unallocable between 2100, 2200 and 2300	..	..	..	..	..	..	48	91	124	153
3000 Taxes on payroll and workforce	..	..	..	..	..	..	**0**	**0**	**0**	**0**
4000 Taxes on property	..	..	..	..	..	..	**0**	**0**	**0**	**0**
4100 Recurrent taxes on immovable property	..	..	..	..	..	..	..	..	..	..
4200 Recurrent taxes on net wealth	..	..	..	..	..	..	..	..	..	..
4300 Estate, inheritance and gift taxes	..	..	..	..	..	..	..	..	..	..
4400 Taxes on financial and capital transactions	..	..	..	..	..	..	..	..	..	..
4500 Non-recurrent taxes	..	..	..	..	..	..	..	..	..	..
4600 Other recurrent taxes on property	..	..	..	..	..	..	..	..	..	..
5000 Taxes on goods and services	..	..	..	..	..	..	**0**	**0**	**0**	**0**
5100 Taxes on production, sale, transfer, etc	..	..	..	..	..	..	..	..	..	..
5110 General taxes	..	..	..	..	..	..	..	..	..	..
5120 Taxes on specific goods and services	..	..	..	..	..	..	..	..	..	..
5130 Unallocable between 5110 and 5120	..	..	..	..	..	..	..	..	..	..
5200 Taxes on use of goods and perform activities	..	..	..	..	..	..	..	..	..	..
5300 Unallocable between 5100 and 5200	..	..	..	..	..	..	..	..	..	..
6000 Other taxes	..	..	..	..	..	..	**0**	**0**	**0**	**0**
6100 Paid solely by business	..	..	..	..	..	..	..	..	..	..
6200 Other	..	..	..	..	..	..	..	..	..	..
Total tax revenue	..	..	..	..	..	..	**48**	**92**	**125**	**154**

.. Not available

1. The data for social security contributions are estimated for 2021 and 2022.

Table 6.25. Trinidad and Tobago, tax revenues by sub-sectors of government

Million TTD

	Federal government					State/Regional				
	1990	2000	2010	2021	2022	1990	2000	2010	2021	2022
1000 Taxes on income, profits and capital gains	**2 595**	**6 224**	**27 213**	**17 206**	**30 756**	..	..	..	..	..
1100 Of individuals	669	2 325	4 674	5 816	6 191	..	..	..	..	..
1200 Corporate	1 856	3 704	21 659	10 384	23 499	..	..	..	..	..
1300 Unallocable between 1100 and 1200	70	195	881	1 005	1 067	..	..	..	..	..
2000 Social security contributions	**0**	**0**	**0**	**0**	**0**	..	..	..	..	..
2100 Employees	..	..	..	..	..	..	..	..	..	..
2200 Employers	..	..	..	..	..	..	..	..	..	..
2300 Self-employed or non-employed	..	..	..	..	..	..	..	..	..	..
2400 Unallocable between 2100, 2200 and 2300	..	..	..	..	..	..	..	..	..	..
3000 Taxes on payroll and workforce	**0**	**0**	**0**	**0**	**0**	..	..	..	..	..
4000 Taxes on property	**90**	**175**	**194**	**289**	**359**	..	..	..	..	..
4100 Recurrent taxes on immovable property	39	64	22	2	2	..	..	..	..	..
4200 Recurrent taxes on net wealth	0	0	0	0	0	..	..	..	..	..
4300 Estate, inheritance and gift taxes	1	0	0	0	0	..	..	..	..	..
4400 Taxes on financial and capital transactions	49	111	172	287	357	..	..	..	..	..
4500 Non-recurrent taxes	0	0	0	0	0	..	..	..	..	..
4600 Other recurrent taxes on property	0	0	0	0	0	..	..	..	..	..
5000 Taxes on goods and services	**2 055**	**3 852**	**9 667**	**12 740**	**9 954**	..	..	..	..	..
5100 Taxes on production, sale, transfer, etc	1 973	3 603	9 282	12 480	9 687	..	..	..	..	..
5110 General taxes	980	1 890	6 358	9 173	6 006	..	..	..	..	..
5120 Taxes on specific goods and services	993	1 713	2 924	3 307	3 681	..	..	..	..	..
5130 Unallocable between 5110 and 5120	0	0	0	0	0	..	..	..	..	..
5200 Taxes on use of goods and perform activities	81	249	386	260	267	..	..	..	..	..
5300 Unallocable between 5100 and 5200	0	0	0	0	0	..	..	..	..	..
6000 Other taxes	**0**	**0**	**0**	**0**	**0**	..	..	..	..	..
6100 Paid solely by business	..	..	..	..	..	..	..	..	..	..
6200 Other	..	..	..	..	..	..	..	..	..	..
Total tax revenue	**4 740**	**10 251**	**37 074**	**30 235**	**41 069**	..	..	..	..	..

Million TTD

	Local government					Social security funds[1]				
	1990	2000	2010	2021	2022	1990	2000	2010	2021	2022
1000 Taxes on income, profits and capital gains	..	..	..	..	..	**0**	**0**	**0**	**0**	**0**
1100 Of individuals	..	..	..	..	..	..	..	..	..	..
1200 Corporate	..	..	..	..	..	..	..	..	..	..
1300 Unallocable between 1100 and 1200	..	..	..	..	..	..	..	..	..	..
2000 Social security contributions	..	..	..	..	..	**183**	**702**	**2 645**	**4 510**	**4 530**
2100 Employees	..	..	..	..	..	..	..	..	..	..
2200 Employers	..	..	..	..	..	..	..	..	..	..
2300 Self-employed or non-employed	..	..	..	..	..	..	..	..	..	..
2400 Unallocable between 2100, 2200 and 2300	..	..	..	..	..	183	702	2 645	4 510	4 530
3000 Taxes on payroll and workforce	..	..	..	..	..	**0**	**0**	**0**	**0**	**0**
4000 Taxes on property	..	..	..	..	..	**0**	**0**	**0**	**0**	**0**
4100 Recurrent taxes on immovable property	..	..	..	..	..	..	..	..	..	..
4200 Recurrent taxes on net wealth	..	..	..	..	..	..	..	..	..	..
4300 Estate, inheritance and gift taxes	..	..	..	..	..	..	..	..	..	..
4400 Taxes on financial and capital transactions	..	..	..	..	..	..	..	..	..	..
4500 Non-recurrent taxes	..	..	..	..	..	..	..	..	..	..
4600 Other recurrent taxes on property	..	..	..	..	..	..	..	..	..	..
5000 Taxes on goods and services	..	..	..	..	..	**0**	**0**	**0**	**0**	**0**
5100 Taxes on production, sale, transfer, etc	..	..	..	..	..	..	..	..	..	..
5110 General taxes	..	..	..	..	..	..	..	..	..	..
5120 Taxes on specific goods and services	..	..	..	..	..	..	..	..	..	..
5130 Unallocable between 5110 and 5120	..	..	..	..	..	..	..	..	..	..
5200 Taxes on use of goods and perform activities	..	..	..	..	..	..	..	..	..	..
5300 Unallocable between 5100 and 5200	..	..	..	..	..	..	..	..	..	..
6000 Other taxes	..	..	..	..	..	**0**	**0**	**0**	**0**	**0**
6100 Paid solely by business	..	..	..	..	..	..	..	..	..	..
6200 Other	..	..	..	..	..	..	..	..	..	..
Total tax revenue	..	..	..	..	..	**183**	**702**	**2 645**	**4 510**	**4 530**

.. Not available

1. The figures follow financial year from July tc June.

Table 6.26. Uruguay, tax revenues by sub-sectors of government

Million UYU

	Federal government					State/Regional				
	1990	2000	2010	2021	2022	1990	2000	2010	2021	2022
1000 Taxes on income, profits and capital gains	**114**	**8 698**	**42 583**	**178 797**	**207 294**	..	..	..	..	..
1100 Of individuals	0	3 597	19 148	98 825	113 351	..	..	..	..	..
1200 Corporate	114	5 102	21 772	71 500	82 729	..	..	..	..	..
1300 Unallocable between 1100 and 1200	0	0	1 662	8 472	11 214	..	..	..	..	..
2000 Social security contributions	**0**	**0**	**0**	**0**	**0**	..	..	..	..	..
2100 Employees	..	..	..	..	..	..	..	..	..	..
2200 Employers	..	..	..	..	..	..	..	..	..	..
2300 Self-employed or non-employed	..	..	..	..	..	..	..	..	..	..
2400 Unallocable between 2100, 2200 and 2300	..	..	..	..	..	..	..	..	..	..
3000 Taxes on payroll and workforce	**0**	**0**	**0**	**0**	**0**	..	..	..	..	..
4000 Taxes on property	**105**	**2 690**	**11 688**	**31 343**	**36 294**	..	..	..	..	..
4100 Recurrent taxes on immovable property	0	533	1 252	5 352	5 951	..	..	..	..	..
4200 Recurrent taxes on net wealth	94	1 769	8 760	22 357	25 740	..	..	..	..	..
4300 Estate, inheritance and gift taxes	0	0	0	0	0	..	..	..	..	..
4400 Taxes on financial and capital transactions	11	372	1 350	2 866	3 553	..	..	..	..	..
4500 Non-recurrent taxes	0	0	0	0	0	..	..	..	..	..
4600 Other recurrent taxes on property	1	15	326	768	1 050	..	..	..	..	..
5000 Taxes on goods and services	**1 301**	**29 556**	**96 432**	**269 110**	**293 884**	..	..	..	..	..
5100 Taxes on production, sale, transfer, etc	1 301	29 556	96 432	269 110	293 884	..	..	..	..	..
5110 General taxes[1]	660	18 009	69 951	184 834	199 428	..	..	..	..	..
5120 Taxes on specific goods and services	641	11 546	26 480	84 275	94 456	..	..	..	..	..
5130 Unallocable between 5110 and 5120	0	0	0	0	0	..	..	..	..	..
5200 Taxes on use of goods and perform activities	0	0	0	0	0	..	..	..	..	..
5300 Unallocable between 5100 and 5200	0	0	0	0	0	..	..	..	..	..
6000 Other taxes	**-10**	**-145**	**586**	**1 099**	**1 205**	..	..	..	..	..
6100 Paid solely by business	-10	-145	586	1 099	1 205	..	..	..	..	..
6200 Other	0	0	0	0	0	..	..	..	..	..
Total tax revenue	**1 510**	**40 799**	**151 289**	**480 349**	**538 678**	..	..	..	..	..

Million UYU

	Local government[2]					Social security funds[3]				
	1990	2000	2010	2021	2022	1990	2000	2010	2021	2022
1000 Taxes on income, profits and capital gains	**0**	**0**	**0**	**0**	**0**	**0**	**0**	**0**	**0**	**0**
1100 Of individuals	..	..	..	..	..	..	..	..	..	..
1200 Corporate	..	..	..	..	..	..	..	..	..	..
1300 Unallocable between 1100 and 1200	..	..	..	..	..	..	..	..	..	..
2000 Social security contributions	**0**	**0**	**0**	**0**	**0**	**717**	**17 679**	**49 742**	**165 500**	**196 064**
2100 Employees	..	..	..	..	..	..	..	..	..	..
2200 Employers	..	..	..	..	..	..	..	..	..	..
2300 Self-employed or non-employed	..	..	..	..	..	..	..	..	..	..
2400 Unallocable between 2100, 2200 and 2300	..	..	..	..	..	717	17 679	49 742	165 500	196 064
3000 Taxes on payroll and workforce	**0**	**0**	**0**	**0**	**0**	**0**	**0**	**0**	**0**	**0**
4000 Taxes on property	**107**	**2 819**	**7 277**	**21 045**	**23 631**	**0**	**0**	**0**	**0**	**0**
4100 Recurrent taxes on immovable property	87	2 715	6 887	19 570	22 189	..	..	..	..	..
4200 Recurrent taxes on net wealth	0	0	0	0	0	..	..	..	..	..
4300 Estate, inheritance and gift taxes	0	0	0	0	0	..	..	..	..	..
4400 Taxes on financial and capital transactions	20	104	390	1 475	1 442	..	..	..	..	..
4500 Non-recurrent taxes	0	0	0	0	0	..	..	..	..	..
4600 Other recurrent taxes on property	0	0	0	0	0	..	..	..	..	..
5000 Taxes on goods and services	**57**	**2 583**	**3 851**	**15 097**	**16 581**	**0**	**0**	**0**	**0**	**0**
5100 Taxes on production, sale, transfer, etc	0	7	63	100	177	..	..	..	..	..
5110 General taxes[1]	0	0	0	0	0	..	..	..	..	..
5120 Taxes on specific goods and services	0	7	63	100	177	..	..	..	..	..
5130 Unallocable between 5110 and 5120	0	0	0	0	0	..	..	..	..	..
5200 Taxes on use of goods and perform activities	57	2 576	3 788	14 996	16 404	..	..	..	..	..
5300 Unallocable between 5100 and 5200	0	0	0	0	0	..	..	..	..	..
6000 Other taxes	**7**	**303**	**748**	**2 861**	**3 306**	**0**	**0**	**0**	**0**	**0**
6100 Paid solely by business	0	0	0	0	0	..	..	..	..	..
6200 Other	7	303	748	2 861	3 306	..	..	..	..	..
Total tax revenue	**171**	**5 705**	**11 876**	**39 002**	**43 518**	**717**	**17 679**	**49 742**	**165 500**	**196 064**

.. Not available

1. The tax on the sale of goods by public auctions under this heading is classified in category 4000 in ECLAC data.
2. Local tax revenue data in 2022 are estimated.
3. Figures for 1990-98 are estimated by the General Tax Directorate (DGI). Since 1999 the figures include income from Social Security Bank (BPS) published by the Ministry of Economy and Finance.

Table 6.27. Venezuela, tax revenues by sub-sectors of government

VES

	Federal government[2]					State/Regional				
	1990	2000	2010	2021	2022	1990	2000	2010	2021	2022
1000 Taxes on income, profits and capital gains	**3 444**	**46 856**	**368 365**	..	..	..	..	..	..	..
1100 Of individuals	..	..	..	..	..	..	..	..	..	..
1200 Corporate[1]	3 148	33 683	86 998	..	..	..	..	..	..	..
1300 Unallocable between 1100 and 1200	297	13 173	281 367	..	..	..	..	..	..	..
2000 Social security contributions	**0**	**0**	**0**	..	..	..	..	..	..	..
2100 Employees	..	..	..	..	..	..	..	..	..	..
2200 Employers	..	..	..	..	..	..	..	..	..	..
2300 Self-employed or non-employed	..	..	..	..	..	..	..	..	..	..
2400 Unallocable between 2100, 2200 and 2300	..	..	..	..	..	..	..	..	..	..
3000 Taxes on payroll and workforce	**0**	**0**	**0**	..	..	..	..	..	..	..
4000 Taxes on property	**11**	**3 999**	**2 217**	..	..	..	..	..	..	..
4100 Recurrent taxes on immovable property	0	0	0	..	..	..	..	..	..	..
4200 Recurrent taxes on net wealth	0	0	0	..	..	..	..	..	..	..
4300 Estate, inheritance and gift taxes	11	191	2 217	..	..	..	..	..	..	..
4400 Taxes on financial and capital transactions	0	3 808	0	..	..	..	..	..	..	..
4500 Non-recurrent taxes	0	0	0	..	..	..	..	..	..	..
4600 Other recurrent taxes on property	0	0	0	..	..	..	..	..	..	..
5000 Taxes on goods and services	**457**	**51 726**	**733 363**	..	..	..	..	..	..	..
5100 Taxes on production, sale, transfer, etc	457	51 726	733 363	..	..	..	..	..	..	..
5110 General taxes	0	32 716	561 005	..	..	..	..	..	..	..
5120 Taxes on specific goods and services	457	19 011	172 357	..	..	..	..	..	..	..
5130 Unallocable between 5110 and 5120	0	0	0	..	..	..	..	..	..	..
5200 Taxes on use of goods and perform activities	0	0	0	..	..	..	..	..	..	..
5300 Unallocable between 5100 and 5200	0	0	0	..	..	..	..	..	..	..
6000 Other taxes	**0**	**0**	**0**	..	..	..	..	..	..	..
6100 Paid solely by business	..	..	..	..	..	..	..	..	..	..
6200 Other	..	..	..	..	..	..	..	..	..	..
Total tax revenue	**3 913**	**102 581**	**1 103 944**	..	..	..	..	..	..	..

VES

	Local government					Social security funds[2, 3]				
	1990	2000	2010	2021	2022	1990	2000	2010	2021	2022
1000 Taxes on income, profits and capital gains	..	..	..	..	..	**0**	**0**	**0**	..	..
1100 Of individuals	..	..	..	..	..	..	..	..	..	..
1200 Corporate[1]	..	..	..	..	..	..	..	..	..	..
1300 Unallocable between 1100 and 1200	..	..	..	..	..	..	..	..	..	..
2000 Social security contributions	..	..	..	..	..	**202**	**5 905**	**96 896**	..	..
2100 Employees	..	..	..	..	..	..	..	..	..	..
2200 Employers	..	..	..	..	..	..	..	..	..	..
2300 Self-employed or non-employed	..	..	..	..	..	..	..	..	..	..
2400 Unallocable between 2100, 2200 and 2300	..	..	..	..	..	202	5 905	96 896	..	..
3000 Taxes on payroll and workforce	..	..	..	..	..	**0**	**0**	**0**	..	..
4000 Taxes on property	..	..	..	..	..	**0**	**0**	**0**	..	..
4100 Recurrent taxes on immovable property	..	..	..	..	..	..	..	..	..	..
4200 Recurrent taxes on net wealth	..	..	..	..	..	..	..	..	..	..
4300 Estate, inheritance and gift taxes	..	..	..	..	..	..	..	..	..	..
4400 Taxes on financial and capital transactions	..	..	..	..	..	..	..	..	..	..
4500 Non-recurrent taxes	..	..	..	..	..	..	..	..	..	..
4600 Other recurrent taxes on property	..	..	..	..	..	..	..	..	..	..
5000 Taxes on goods and services	..	..	..	..	..	**0**	**0**	**0**	..	..
5100 Taxes on production, sale, transfer, etc	..	..	..	..	..	..	..	..	..	..
5110 General taxes	..	..	..	..	..	..	..	..	..	..
5120 Taxes on specific goods and services	..	..	..	..	..	..	..	..	..	..
5130 Unallocable between 5110 and 5120	..	..	..	..	..	..	..	..	..	..
5200 Taxes on use of goods and perform activities	..	..	..	..	..	..	..	..	..	..
5300 Unallocable between 5100 and 5200	..	..	..	..	..	..	..	..	..	..
6000 Other taxes	..	..	..	..	..	**0**	**0**	**0**	..	..
6100 Paid solely by business	..	..	..	..	..	..	..	..	..	..
6200 Other	..	..	..	..	..	..	..	..	..	..
Total tax revenue	..	..	..	..	..	**202**	**5 905**	**96 896**	..	..

.. Not available

1. Data for revenues from taxes on oil profits (classified under heading 1200) are not available from 2016.
2. Tax data are not available from 2018. The figures between 2015 and 2017 should be interpreted with caution as they have been affected by the high rate of inflation over this period.
3. Data on social security contributions are not available from 2014.

Annex A. The OECD classification of taxes and interpretative guide

Table of Contents[1]

A.1 The OECD Classification of Taxes

1. 1000. Taxes on income, profits and capital gains

- 1100. Taxes on income, profits and capital gains of individuals
  - 1110. On income and profits
  - 1120. On capital gains
- 1200. Corporate taxes on income, profits and capital gains
  - 1210. On income and profits
  - 1220. On capital gains
- 1300. Unallocable as between 1100 and 1200

2. 2000. Social security contributions

- 2100. Employees
  - 2110. On a payroll basis
  - 2120. On an income tax basis
- 2200. Employers
  - 2210. On a payroll basis
  - 2220. On an income tax basis
- 2300. Self-employed or non-employed
  - 2310. On a payroll basis
  - 2320. On an income tax basis
- 2400 Unallocable as between 2100, 2200 and 2300
  - 2410. On a payroll basis
  - 2420. On an income tax basis

3. 3000. Taxes on payroll and workforce

4. 4000. Taxes on property

- 4100. Recurrent taxes on immovable property
  - 4110. Households
  - 4120. Other
- 4200. Recurrent taxes on net wealth
  - 4210. Individual
  - 4220. Corporate
- 4300. Estate, inheritance and gift taxes
  - 4310. Estate and inheritance taxes
  - 4320. Gift taxes
- 4400. Taxes on financial and capital transactions

4500. Other non-recurrent taxes on property

4510. On net wealth

4520. Other non-recurrent taxes

4600. Other recurrent taxes on property

5. 5000. Taxes on goods and services

5100. Taxes on production, sale, transfer, leasing and delivery of goods and rendering of services

5110. General taxes

5111. Value added taxes

5112. Sales taxes

5113. Turnover and other general taxes on goods and services

5120. Taxes on specific goods and services

5121. Excises

5122. Profits of fiscal monopolies

5123. Customs and import duties

5124. Taxes on exports

5125. Taxes on investment goods

5126. Taxes on specific services

5127. Other taxes on international trade and transactions

5128. Other taxes on specific goods and services

5130. Unallocable as between 5110 and 5120

5200. Taxes on use of goods, or on permission to use goods or perform activities

5210. Recurrent taxes

5211. Paid by households in respect of motor vehicles

5212. Paid by others in respect of motor vehicles

5213. Other recurrent taxes

5220. Non-recurrent taxes

5300. Unallocable as between 5100 and 5200

6. **6000. Other taxes**

6100. Paid solely by business

6200. Paid by other than business or unidentifiable

A.2 Coverage

General criteria

1. In the OECD classification, the term "taxes" is confined to compulsory unrequited payments to the general government or to a supranational authority. Taxes are unrequited in the sense that benefits provided by government to taxpayers are not normally in proportion to their payments.

2. The term "tax" does not include fines, penalties and compulsory loans paid to government. Borderline cases between tax and non-tax revenues in relation to certain fees and charges are discussed in §12–15.

3. General government consists of the central administration, agencies whose operations are under its effective control, state and local governments and their administrations, certain social security schemes and autonomous governmental entities, excluding public enterprises. This definition of government follows that of the 2008 *System of National Accounts* (SNA).[2] In that publication, the general government sector and its sub-sectors are defined in Chapter 4, paragraphs 4.117 to 4.165.

4. Extra-budgetary units are part of the general government system. These are general government entities with individual budgets that are not fully covered by the main or general budget. These entities operate under the authority or control of a central, state, or local government. Extra-budgetary entities may have their own revenue sources, which may be supplemented by grants (transfers) from the general budget or from other sources. Even though their budgets may be subject to approval by the legislature, similar to that of budgetary accounts, they have discretion over the volume and composition of their spending. Such entities may be established to carry out specific government functions, such as road construction, or the nonmarket production of health or education services. Budgetary arrangements vary widely across countries, and various terms are used to describe these entities, but they are often referred to as "extra-budgetary funds" or "decentralised agencies."

5. Compulsory, unrequited payments collected by national governments and paid to supranational authorities are also included as taxes under the definition in paragraph 1. Taxes that are collected by national governments and paid to a supranational authority are included as tax revenues at the level of the supranational authority in the SNA2008 (paragraphs 22.60-61, 22.88 and 22.99 refer) and the ESA2010 (paragraph 20.165 refers). In Revenue Statistics, these taxes include customs duties, contributions to the EU Single Resolution Fund, and any other taxes collected by EU member states on behalf of the European Union. They are included in the tax revenue amounts in the country tables (Chapter 5) of the country in which they are collected and are attributed to the supranational level of government (see §102).

6. In countries where the church forms part of general government, church taxes are included, provided they meet the criteria set out in §1 above. As the data refer to receipts of general government and to supranational authorities, levies paid to non-government bodies, welfare agencies or social insurance schemes outside general government, trade unions or trade associations, even where such levies are compulsory, are excluded. Compulsory payments to general government earmarked for such bodies are, however, included, provided that the government is not simply acting in an agency capacity.[3] Profits from fiscal monopolies are distinguished from those of other public enterprises and are treated as taxes because they reflect the exercise of the taxing power of the state by the use of monopoly powers (see §66–68), as are profits received by the government from the purchase and sale of foreign exchange at different rates (see §76).

7. Taxes paid by governments (e.g., social security contributions and payroll taxes paid by governments in their capacity as an employer, consumption taxes on their purchases or taxes on their property) are not excluded from the data provided. However, where it is possible to identify the amounts of revenue involved,[4] they are shown in Table 5.40 of this Report.

8. The relationship between this classification and that of the System of National Accounts (SNA) is set out in Sections A.9 and A.11 below. Because of the differences between the two classifications, the data shown in national accounts are sometimes calculated or classified differently from the practice set out in this guide. These and other differences are mentioned where appropriate (e.g., in §31 below) but it is not possible to refer to all of them. There may also be some differences between this classification and that employed domestically by certain national administrations (e.g., see §13 below), so that OECD and national statistics data may not always be consistent: any such differences, however, are likely to be very slight in terms of amounts of revenues involved.

Social security contributions

9. Compulsory social security contributions, as defined in §40, and paid to general government, are treated here as tax revenues. They may, however, differ from other taxes in that the receipt of social security benefits depends, in most countries, upon appropriate contributions having been made, although the size of the benefits is not necessarily related to the amount of the contributions. Better comparability between countries is obtained by treating social security contributions as taxes, but they are listed under a separate heading so that they can be distinguished in any analysis.

10. The strict dividing line between tax revenues (compulsory unrequited payments to general government or a supranational authority) and non-tax compulsory payments (NTCPs) (payments that are either requited or made to other institutions) is clearly defined. However, within the range of different compulsory payments to governments existing across countries, it is not always straightforward in practice to decide whether specific payments are either taxes or NTCPs. For example, compulsory pension savings that are controlled by general government and that accumulate on an individual account earning a market return or a rate that compensates for inflation would at first sight be categorised as NTCPs as opposed to taxes. However, even these payments might still be 'unrequited' and therefore classify as taxes instead of NTCPs (for example if these pension savings are not paid out when the taxpayer dies before reaching the pension age and the funds are then used to provide a minimum pension to all taxpayers that are insured). These issues result in the social security revenue figures reported for most countries being based on the premise that all types of compulsory payments to general government are judged to some extent to have a re-distributional element. It should be noted that this conclusion is based on a typically broad interpretation of the term 'unrequited' in the tax definition.

11. Social security contributions which are either voluntary or not payable to general government (see §1) are not treated as taxes, though in some countries, as indicated in the country footnotes, there are difficulties in completely eliminating voluntary contributions and certain compulsory payments to the private sector from the revenue figures. Imputed social security contributions are also not treated as taxes.

Fees, user charges and licence fees

12. Apart from vehicle licence fees, which are universally regarded as taxes, it is not easy to distinguish between those fees and user charges which are to be treated as taxes and those which are not, since, whilst a fee or charge is levied in connection with a specific service or activity, the strength of the link between the fee and the service provided may vary considerably, as may the relation between the amount of the fee and the cost of providing the service. Where the recipient of a service pays a fee clearly related to the cost of providing the service, the levy may be regarded as requited and under the definition of §1 would not be considered as a tax. In the following cases, however, a levy could be considered as 'unrequited':

a) where the charge greatly exceeds the cost of providing the service;

b) where the payer of the levy is not the receiver of the benefit (e.g., a fee collected from slaughterhouses to finance a service which is provided to farmers);

c) where government is not providing a specific service in return for the levy which it receives even though a licence may be issued to the payer (e.g., where the government grants a hunting, fishing or shooting licence which is not accompanied by the right to use a specific area of government land);

d) where benefits are received only by those paying the levy but the benefits received by each individual are not necessarily in proportion to his payments (e.g., a milk marketing levy paid by dairy farmers and used to promote the consumption of milk).

e) where the payer of the levy cannot opt out from making payments (e.g. public broadcast fees where the payer is obliged to pay the levy although not consuming public broadcast service).

13. In marginal cases, however, the application of the criteria set out in §1 can be particularly difficult. The solution adopted — given the desirability of international uniformity and the relatively small amounts of revenue usually involved — is to follow the predominant practice among tax administrations rather than to allow each country to adopt its own view as to whether such levies are regarded as taxes or as non-tax revenue.[5]

14. A list of the main fees and charges in question and their normal[6] treatment in this publication is as follows:

Non-tax revenues:	court fees; driving licence fees; harbour fees; passport fees
Taxes within heading 5200	permission to perform such activities as distributing films; hunting, fishing and shooting; providing entertainment or gambling facilities; selling alcohol or tobacco; permission to own dogs or to use or own motor vehicles or guns; severance taxes

15. In practice, it may not always be possible to isolate tax receipts from non-tax revenue receipts when they are recorded together. If it is estimated that the bulk of the receipts derive from non-tax revenues, the whole amount involved is treated as a non-tax revenue; otherwise, such government receipts are included and classified according to the rules provided in §33 below.

Royalties

16. The ownership of subsoil assets in the form of deposits of minerals or fossil fuels (coal, oil, or natural gas) depends upon the way in which property rights are defined by law and also on international agreements in the case of deposits below international waters. In some cases, either the ground below which the mineral deposits are located, the deposits themselves or both may belong to a local or central government unit.

17. In such cases, these general government units may grant leases to other institutional units that permit them to extract these deposits over a specified period of time in return for a payment or series of payments. These payments are often described as 'royalties' but they are essentially rent that accrues to owners of natural resources in return for putting these assets at the disposal of other units for specified periods of time. The rent may take the form of periodic payments of fixed amounts, irrespective of the rate of extraction, or, more commonly, they may be a function of the quantity, volume, or value of the asset extracted. Enterprises engaged in exploration on government land may make payments to general government units in exchange for the right to undertake test drilling or otherwise investigate the existence and location of subsoil assets. Such payments are also recorded as rents even though no extraction may take place. These payments are therefore classified as non-tax revenues.

18. The same principles apply when other institutional units are granted leases that permit them to fell timber in natural forests on land owned by general government units. These payments are also classified as non-tax revenues.

19. These rents or royalties paid to general government should not be confused with taxes on income and profits, severance taxes, business licenses, or other taxes. If the payments are levied on the profits

from the extraction activity, then they should be classified as taxes on incomes, profits and gains (1000). In addition, any severance payments that are imposed on the extraction of minerals and fossil fuels from reserves owned privately or by another government should be classified as taxes. Payments related to the gross value of production should be classified as other taxes on goods and services (5128). Payments for a license or permit to conduct extraction operations should be classified as taxes on use of goods and on permission to use goods or perform activities (5213).

Fines and penalties

20. In principle, fines and penalties charged on overdue taxes or penalties imposed for the attempted evasion of taxes should not be recorded as tax revenues. However, it may not be possible to separate payments of fines or other penalties from the revenues from the taxes to which they relate. In this case, the fines and penalties relating to a particular tax are recorded together with the revenues from that tax and fines and penalties paid with revenue from unidentifiable taxes are classified as other taxes in Category 6000. Fines not relating to tax offences (e.g., for parking offences), or not identifiable as relating to tax offences, are also not treated as tax revenues.

A.3 Basis of reporting

Accrual or cash reporting

21. The data reported in the *Revenue Statistics* publications for recent years are predominantly recorded on an accrual basis for OECD countries, i.e. recorded at the time that the tax liability was created. Further information is provided in the footnotes to the country table in Chapter 5 of the Report.

22. However, data for earlier years and for non-OECD countries are still predominantly recorded on a cash basis, i.e. at the time at which the payment was received by government. Thus, for example, taxes withheld by employers in one year but paid to the government in the following year and taxes due in one year but actually paid in the following year are both included in the receipts of the second year. Corrective transactions, such as refunds, repayments and drawbacks, are deducted from gross revenues of the period in which they are made.

23. Data on tax revenues are recorded without offsets for the administrative expenses connected with tax collection. Similarly, where the proceeds of tax are used to subsidise particular members of the community, the subsidy is not deducted from the yield of the tax, though the tax may be shown net of subsidies in the national records of some countries.

24. As regards fiscal monopolies (heading 5122), only the amount actually transferred to the government is included in government revenues. However, if any expenditures of fiscal monopolies are considered to be government expenditures (e.g., social expenditures undertaken by fiscal monopolies at the direction of the government) they are added back for the purpose of arriving at tax revenue figures (see §66 below).

The distinction between tax and expenditure provisions[7]

25. Because this publication is concerned only with the revenue side of government operations, no account being taken of the expenditure side, a distinction has to be made between tax and expenditure provisions. Normally there is no difficulty in making this distinction as expenditures are made outside the tax system and the tax accounts and under legislation separate from the tax legislation. In borderline cases, cash flow is used to distinguish between tax provisions and expenditure provisions. Insofar as a provision affects the flow of tax payments from the taxpayer to the government, it is regarded as a tax provision and

is taken into account in the data shown in this publication. A provision which does not affect this flow is seen as an expenditure provision and is disregarded in the data recorded in this publication.

26. Tax allowances, exemptions and deductions against the tax base clearly affect the amount of tax paid to the government and are therefore considered as tax provisions. At the other extreme, those subsidies which cannot be offset against tax liability and which are clearly not connected with the assessment process, do not reduce tax revenues as recorded in this publication. Tax credits are amounts deductible from tax payable (as distinct from deductions from the tax base). Two types of tax credits are distinguished, those (referred to here as wastable tax credits) which are limited to the amount of the tax liability and therefore cannot give rise to a payment by the authorities to the taxpayer, and those (referred to as non-wastable tax credits) which are not so limited, so that the excess of the credit over the tax liability can be paid to the taxpayer.[8] A wastable tax credit, like a tax allowance, clearly affects the amount of tax paid to the government, and is therefore considered as a tax provision. The practice followed for non-wastable tax credits[9] is to distinguish between the 'tax expenditure component',[10] which is that portion of the credit that is used to reduce or eliminate a taxpayer's liability, and the 'transfer component', which is the portion that exceeds the taxpayer's liability and is paid to that taxpayer. Reported tax revenues should be reduced by the amount of the tax expenditure component but not by the amount of the transfer component. In addition, the amounts of the tax expenditure and transfer components should be reported as memorandum items in the country tables. Countries that are unable to distinguish between the tax expenditure and transfer components should indicate whether or not the tax revenues have been reduced by the total of these components, and provide any available estimates of the amounts of the two components. Further information is given in Chapter 1 of the Report, which illustrates the effect of alternative treatments of non-wastable tax credits on tax to GDP.

Calendar and fiscal years

27. National authorities whose fiscal years do not correspond to the calendar year show data, where possible, on a calendar year basis to permit maximum comparability with the data of other countries. There remain a few countries where data refer to fiscal years. For these the GDP data used in the comparative tables also correspond to the fiscal years.

A.4 General classification criteria

The main classification criteria

28. The classification of receipts among the main headings (1000, 2000, 3000, 4000, 5000 and 6000) is generally governed by the base on which the tax is levied: 1000 income, profits and capital gains; 2000 and 3000 earnings, payroll or number of employees; 4000 property; 5000 goods and services; 6000 multiple bases, other bases or unidentifiable bases. Where a tax is calculated on more than one base, the receipts are, where possible, split among the various headings (see §33 and §84). The headings 4000 and 5000 cover not only taxes where the tax base is the property, goods or services themselves but also certain related taxes. Thus, taxes on the transfer of property are included in 4400[11] and taxes on the use of goods or on permission to perform activities in 5200. In headings 4000 and 5000 a distinction is made in certain sub-headings between recurrent and non-recurrent taxes: recurrent taxes are defined as those levied at regular intervals (usually annually) and non-recurrent taxes are levied once and for all (see also §48 to §51, §54, §55 and §81 for particular applications of this distinction).

29. Earmarking of a tax for specific purposes does not affect the classification of tax receipts. However, as explained in §40 on the classification of social security contributions, the conferment of an entitlement to social benefits is crucial to the definition of the 2000 main heading.

30. The way that a tax is levied or collected (e.g., by use of stamps) does not affect classification.

Classification of taxpayers

31. In certain sub-headings, distinctions are made between different categories of taxpayers. These distinctions vary from tax to tax:

a) *Between individuals and corporations in relation to income and net wealth taxes*

The basic distinction is that corporation income taxes, as distinct from individual income taxes, are levied on the corporation as an entity, not on the individuals who own it, and without regard to the personal circumstances of these individuals. The same distinction applies to net wealth taxes on corporations and those on individuals. Taxes paid on the profits of partnerships and the income of institutions, such as life insurance or pension funds, are classified according to the same rule. They are classified as corporate taxes (1200) if they are charged on the partnership or institution as an entity without regard to the personal circumstances of the owners. Otherwise, they are treated as individual taxes (1100). Usually, there is different legislation for the corporation taxes and for the individual taxes.[12] The distinction made here between individuals and corporations does not follow the sector classification between households, enterprises, and so on of the System of National Accounts for income and outlay accounts. The SNA classification requires certain unincorporated businesses[13] to be excluded from the household sector and included with non-financial enterprises and financial institutions. The tax on the profits of these businesses, however, cannot always be separated from the tax on the other income of their owners, or can be separated only on an arbitrary basis. No attempt at this separation is made here and the whole of the individual income tax is shown together without regard to the nature of the income chargeable.

b) *Between households and others in relation to taxes on immovable property*

Here the distinction is that adopted by the SNA for the production and consumption expenditure accounts. The distinction is between households as consumers (i.e. excluding non-incorporated business) on the one hand and producers on the other hand. However, taxes on dwellings occupied by households, whether paid by owner-occupiers, tenants or landlords, are classified under households. This follows the common distinction made between taxes on domestic property versus taxes on business property. Some countries are not, however, in a position to make this distinction.

c) *Between households and others in relation to motor vehicle licences*

Here the distinction is between households as consumers on the one hand and producers on the other, as in the production and consumption expenditure accounts of the SNA.

d) *Between business and others in relation to the residual taxes (6000)*

The distinction is the same as in c) above between producers on the one hand and households as consumers on the other hand. Taxes which are included under the heading 6000 because they involve more than one tax base or because the tax base does not fall within any of the previous categories but which are identifiable as levyable only on producers and not on households are included under 'business'. The rest of the taxes which are included under the heading 6000 are shown as 'other' or non-identified.

Surcharges

32. Receipts from surcharges in respect of particular taxes are usually classified with the receipts from the relevant tax whether or not the surcharge is temporary. If, however, the surcharge has a characteristic which would render it classifiable in a different heading of the OECD list, receipts from the surcharge are classified under that heading separately from the relevant tax.

Unidentifiable tax receipts and residual sub-headings

33. A number of cases arise where taxes cannot be identified as belonging entirely to a heading or sub-heading of the OECD classification and the following practices are applied in such cases:

a) The heading is known, but it is not known how receipts should be allocated between sub-headings: receipts are classified in the appropriate residual sub-heading (1300, 2400, 4520, 4600, 5128, 5130, 5300 or 6200).

b) It is known that the bulk of receipts from a group of taxes (usually local taxes) is derived from taxes within a particular heading or sub-heading, but some of the taxes in the group whose amount cannot be precisely ascertained may be classifiable in other headings or sub-headings: receipts are shown in the heading or sub-heading under which most of the receipts fall.

c) Neither the heading nor sub-heading of a tax (usually local) can be identified: the tax is classified in 6200 unless it is known that it is a tax on business in which case it is classified in 6100.

A.5 Commentaries on items of the list

1000 — Taxes on income, profits and capital gains

34. This heading covers taxes levied on the net income or profits (i.e. gross income minus allowable tax reliefs) of individuals and enterprises. Also covered are taxes levied on the capital gains of individuals and enterprises, and gains from gambling.

35. Included in the heading are:

a) taxes levied predominantly on income or profits, though partially on other bases. Taxes on various bases which are not predominantly income or profits are classified according to the principles laid down in §33 and §84;

b) taxes on property, which are levied on a presumed or estimated income as part of an income tax (see also §48(a), (c) and (d));

c) compulsory payments to social security fund contributions that are levied on income but do not confer an entitlement to social benefits. When such contributions do confer an entitlement to social benefits, they are included in heading 2000 (see §40);

d) receipts from integrated scheduler income tax systems are classified as a whole in this heading, even though certain of the scheduler taxes may be based upon gross income and may not take into account the personal circumstances of the taxpayer.

36. The main subdivision of this heading is between levies on individuals (1100) and those on corporate enterprises (1200). Under each subdivision a distinction is made between taxes on income and profits (1110 and 1210), and taxes on capital gains (1120 and 1220). If certain receipts cannot be identified as appropriate to either 1100 or 1200, or if in practice this distinction cannot be made (e.g., because there are no reliable data on the recipients of payments from which withholding taxes are deducted) they are classified in 1300 as not-allocable.

Treatment of credits under imputation systems

37. Under imputation systems of corporate income tax, a company's shareholders are wholly or partly relieved of their liability to income tax on dividends paid by the company out of income or profits liable to corporate income tax. In countries with such systems,[14] part of the tax on the company's profits is available

to provide relief against the shareholders' own tax liability. The relief to the shareholder takes the form of a tax credit, the amount of which may be less than, equal to, or more than the shareholder's overall tax liability. If the tax credit exceeds this tax liability the excess may be payable to the shareholder. As this type of tax credit is an integral part of the imputation system of corporate income tax, any payment to the shareholders is treated as a repayment of tax and not as expenditure (compare the treatment of other tax credits described in §26).

38. As the tax credit under imputation systems (even when exceeding tax liability) is to be regarded as a tax provision, the question arises whether it should be deducted from individual income tax receipts (1110) or corporate income tax receipts (1210). In this Report, the full amount of corporate income tax paid is shown under 1210 and no imputed tax is included under 1110. Thus, the full amount of the credit reduces the amount of 1110 whether the credit results in a reduction of personal income tax liability or whether an actual refund is made because the credit exceeds the income tax liability. (Where, however, such tax credits are deducted from corporation tax in respect of dividends paid to corporations the amounts are deducted from the receipts of 1210).

1120 and 1220 — Taxes on capital gains

39. These sub-headings comprise taxes imposed on capital gains, 1120 covering those levied on the gains of individuals and 1220 those levied on the gains of corporate enterprises, where receipts from such taxes can be separately identified. In many countries, this is not the case and the receipts from such taxes are then classified with those from the income tax. Heading 1120 also includes taxes on gains from gambling.

2000 — Social security contributions

40. Classified here are all compulsory payments to general government that confer an entitlement to receive a (contingent) future social benefit. Such payments are usually earmarked to finance social benefits and are often paid to institutions of general government that provide such benefits. However, such earmarking is not part of the definition of social security contributions and is not required for a tax to be classified here. However, conferment of an entitlement is required for a tax to be classified under this heading. So, levies on income or payroll that are earmarked for social security funds but do not confer an entitlement to benefit are excluded from this heading and shown under personal income taxes (1100) or taxes on payroll and workforce (3000). Taxes on other bases, such as goods and services, which are earmarked for social security benefits are not shown here but are classified according to their respective bases because they generally confer no entitlement to social security benefits.

41. Contributions for the following types of social security benefits would, *inter alia*, be included: unemployment insurance benefits and supplements, accident, injury and sickness benefits, old-age, disability and survivors' pensions, family allowances, reimbursements for medical and hospital expenses or provision of hospital or medical services. Contributions may be levied on both employees and employers.

42. Contributions may be based on earnings or payroll ('on a payroll basis') or on net income after deductions and exemptions for personal circumstances ('on an income tax basis'), and the revenues from the two bases should be separately identified if possible. However, where contributions to a general social security scheme are on a payroll basis, but the contributions of particular groups (such as the self-employed) cannot be assessed on this basis and net income is used as a proxy for gross earnings, the receipts may still be classified as being on a payroll basis. In principle, this heading excludes voluntary contributions paid to social security schemes. When separately identifiable these are shown in the memorandum item on the financing of social security benefits. In practice, however, they cannot always be separately identified from compulsory contributions, in which case they are included in this heading.

43. Contributions to social insurance schemes which are not institutions of general government and to other types of insurance schemes, provident funds, pension funds, friendly societies or other saving schemes are not considered as social security contributions. Provident funds are arrangements under which the contributions of each employee and of the corresponding employer on his/her behalf are kept in a separate account earning interest and withdrawable under specific circumstances. Pension funds are separately organised schemes negotiated between employees and employers and carry provisions for different contributions and benefits, sometimes more directly tied to salary levels and length of service than under social security schemes. When contributions to these schemes are compulsory or quasi-compulsory (e.g., by virtue of agreement with professional and union organisations) they are shown in the memorandum item (refer to Table 5.39 of the Report).

44. Contributions by government employees and by governments in respect of their employees, to social security schemes classified within general government are included in this heading. Contributions to separate schemes for government employees, which can be regarded as replacing general social security schemes, are also regarded as taxes.[15] Where, however, a separate scheme is not seen as replacing a general scheme and has been negotiated between the government, in its role as an employer, and its employees, it is not regarded as social security and contributions to it are not regarded as taxes, even though the scheme may have been established by legislation.

45. This heading excludes 'imputed' contributions, which correspond to social benefits paid directly by employers to their employees or former employees or to their representatives (e.g., when employers are legally obliged to pay sickness benefits for a certain period).

46. Contributions are divided into those of employees (2100), employers (2200), and self-employed or non-employed (2300), and then further sub-divided according to the basis on which they are levied. Employees are defined for this purpose as all persons engaged in activities of business units, government bodies, private non-profit institutions, or other paid employment, except the proprietors and their unpaid family members in the case of unincorporated businesses. Members of the armed forces are included, irrespective of the duration and type of their service, if they contribute to social security schemes. The contributions of employers are defined as their payments on account of their employees to social security schemes. Where employees or employers are required to continue the payment of social security contributions when the employee becomes unemployed these contributions, data permitting, are shown in 2100 and 2200 respectively. Accordingly, the sub-heading 2300 is confined to contributions paid by the self-employed and by those outside of the labour force (e.g., disabled or retired individuals).

3000 — Taxes on payroll and workforce

47. These consist of taxes payable by enterprises assessed either as a proportion of the wages or salaries paid or as a fixed amount per person employed. They do not include compulsory social security contributions paid by employers or any taxes paid by employees themselves out of their wages or salaries

4000 — Taxes on property

48. This heading covers recurrent and non-recurrent taxes on the use, ownership or transfer of property. These include taxes on immovable property or net wealth, taxes on the change of ownership of property through inheritance or gift and taxes on financial and capital transactions. The following kinds of tax are excluded from this heading:

- *a)* taxes on capital gains resulting from the sale of a property (1120 or 1220);
- *b)* taxes on the use of goods or on permission to use goods or perform activities (5200); see §78;

c) taxes on immovable property levied on the basis of a presumed net income which take into account the personal circumstances of the taxpayer. They are classified as income taxes along with taxes on income and capital gains derived from property (1100);

d) taxes on the use of property for residence, where the tax is payable by either proprietor or tenant and the amount payable is a function of the user's personal circumstances (pay, dependants, and so on). They are classified as taxes on income (1100);

e) taxes on building in excess of permitted maximum density, taxes on the enlargement, construction or alteration of certain buildings beyond a permitted value and taxes on building construction. They are classified as taxes on permission to perform activities (5200);

f) taxes on the use of one's own property for special trading purposes like selling alcohol, tobacco, meat or for exploitation of land resources (e.g., United States severance taxes). They are classified as taxes on permission to perform activities (5200).

4100 — Recurrent taxes on immovable property

49. This sub-heading covers taxes levied regularly in respect of the use or ownership of immovable property.

- these taxes are levied on land and buildings;
- they can be in the form of a percentage of an assessed property value based on a national rental income, sales price, or capitalised yield; or in terms of other characteristics of real property, (for example size or location) from which a presumed rent or capital value can be derived.
- such taxes can be levied on proprietors, tenants, or both. They can also be paid by one level of government to another level of government in respect of property under the jurisdiction of the latter.
- debts are not taken into account in the assessment of these taxes, and they differ from taxes on net wealth in this respect.

50. Taxes on immovable property are further sub-divided into those paid by households (4110) and those paid by other entities (4120), according to the criteria set out in §31(*b*) above.

4200 — Recurrent taxes on net wealth

51. This sub-heading covers taxes levied regularly (in most cases annually) on net wealth, i.e. taxes on a wide range of movable and immovable property, net of debt. It is sub-divided into taxes paid by individuals (4210) and taxes paid by corporate enterprises (4220) according to the criteria set out in §31(*a*) above. If separate figures exist for receipts paid by institutions, the tax payments involved are added to those paid by corporations.

4300 — Estate, inheritance and gift taxes

52. This sub-heading is divided into taxes on estates and inheritances (4310) and taxes on gifts (4320).[16] Estate taxes are charged on the amount of the total estate whereas inheritance taxes are charged on the shares of the individual recipients; in addition the latter may take into account the relationship of the individual recipients to the deceased.

4400 — Taxes on financial and capital transactions

53. This sub-heading comprises, *inter alia*, taxes on the issue, transfer, purchase and sale of non-financial and financial assets (including foreign exchange or securities), taxes on cheques and other forms of payment, and taxes levied on specific legal transactions such as validation of contracts and the sale of immovable property. The heading does not include:

a) taxes on the use of goods or property or permission to perform certain activities (5200);

b) fees paid to cover court charges, charges for birth, marriage or death certificates, which are normally regarded as non-tax revenues (see §12);

c) taxes on capital gains (1000);

d) recurrent taxes on immovable property (4100);

e) recurrent taxes on net wealth (4200);

f) once-and-for-all levies on property or wealth (4500);

g) stamp taxes not related to financial and capital transactions

  i. Stamp taxes on the sale of specific products, such as alcoholic beverages or tobacco (5121);

  ii. Stamp taxes restricted by law to imported products (5123) or to exported products (5124); or

  iii. Stamp taxes not falling exclusively on a single category of transaction (6000).

4500 — Other non-recurrent taxes on property

54. This sub-heading covers once-and-for-all, as distinct from recurrent, levies on property. It is divided into taxes on net wealth (4510) and other non-recurrent taxes on property (4520). Heading 4510 would include taxes levied to meet emergency expenditures, or for redistribution purposes. Heading 4520 would cover taxes levied to take account of increases in land value due to permission given to develop or provision of additional local facilities by general government, any taxes on the revaluation of capital and once-and-for-all taxes on particular items of property.

4600 — Other recurrent taxes on property

55. These rarely exist in OECD member countries, but the heading would include taxes on goods such as cattle, jewellery, windows, and other external signs of wealth.

5000 — Taxes on goods and services

56. All taxes and duties levied on the production, extraction, sale, transfer, leasing or delivery of goods, and the rendering of services (5100), or in respect of the use of goods or permission to use goods or to perform activities (5200) are included here. The heading thus covers:

a) multi-stage cumulative taxes;

b) general sales taxes — whether levied at manufacture/production, wholesale or retail level;

c) value-added taxes;

d) excises;

e) taxes levied on the import and export of goods;

f) taxes levied in respect of the use of goods and taxes on permission to use goods, or perform certain activities;

g) taxes on the extraction, processing or production of minerals and other products.

57. Borderline cases between this heading and heading 4000 (taxes on property) and 6100 (other taxes on business) are referred to in §48, §53 and §80. Residual sub-headings (5300) and (5130) cover tax receipts which cannot be allocated between 5100 and 5200 and between 5110 and 5120, respectively; see §33.

5100 — Taxes on the production, sale, transfer, leasing and delivery of goods and rendering of services

58. This sub-heading consists of all taxes, levied on transactions in goods and services on the basis of their intrinsic characteristics (e.g., value, weight of tobacco, strength of alcohol, and so on) as distinct from taxes imposed on the use of goods, or permission to use goods or perform activities, which fall under 5200.

5110 — General taxes on goods and services

59. This sub-heading includes all taxes, other than import and export duties (5123 and 5124), levied on the production, leasing, transfer, delivery or sales of a wide range of goods and/or the rendering of a wide range of services, irrespective of whether they are domestically produced or imported and irrespective of the stage of production or distribution at which they are levied. It thus covers value-added taxes, sales taxes and multi-stage cumulative taxes. Receipts from border adjustments in respect of such taxes when goods are imported are added to gross receipts for this category, and repayments of such taxes when goods are exported are deducted. These taxes are subdivided into 5111 value-added taxes, 5112 sales taxes, 5113 turnover and other general taxes on goods and services.

60. Borderline cases arise between this heading and taxes on specific goods (5120) when taxes are levied on a large number of goods, for example, the United Kingdom purchase tax (repealed in 1973) and the Japanese commodity tax (repealed in 1988). In conformity with national views, the former United Kingdom purchase tax is classified as a general tax (5112) and the former Japanese commodity tax as excises (5121).

5111 — Value-added taxes

61. All general consumption taxes charged on value-added are classified in this sub-heading, irrespective of the method of deduction and the stages at which the taxes are levied. In practice, all OECD countries with value-added taxes normally allow immediate deduction of taxes on purchases by all but the final consumer and impose tax at all stages. In some countries the heading may include certain taxes, such as those on financial and insurance activities, either because receipts from them cannot be identified separately from those from the value-added tax, or because they are regarded as an integral part of the value-added tax, even though similar taxes in other countries might be classified elsewhere (e.g., 5126 as taxes on services or 4400 as taxes on financial and capital transactions).

5112 — Sales taxes

62. All general taxes levied at one stage only, whether at manufacturing or production, wholesale or retail stage are classified here.

5113 — Turnover and other general taxes on goods and services

63. These are multi-stage cumulative taxes and taxes where elements of consumption taxes are combined with multistage taxes. These taxes are levied each time a transaction takes place without deduction for taxes paid on inputs. Multi-stage taxes can be combined with elements of value-added or sales taxes.

5120 — Taxes on specific goods and services

64. Excises, profits generated and transferred from fiscal monopolies, and customs and imports duties as well as taxes on exports, foreign exchange transactions, investment goods and betting stakes and special taxes on services, which do not form part of a general tax of 5110, are included in this category.

5121 — Excises

65. Excises are taxes levied as a product specific unit tax on a predefined limited range of goods. Excises are usually levied at differentiated rates on nonessential or luxury goods, alcoholic beverages, tobacco, and energy. Excises may be imposed at any stage of production or distribution and are usually assessed as a specific charge per unit based on characteristics by reference to the value, weight, strength, or quantity of the product. Included are special taxes on individual products such as sugar, sugar beets, matches, and chocolates; taxes levied at varying rates on a certain range of goods; and taxes levied on tobacco goods, alcoholic drinks, motor fuels, and hydrocarbon oils. If a tax collected principally on imported goods also applies, or would apply, under the same law to comparable domestically produced goods, then the revenue from this tax is classified as arising from excises rather than from import duties. This principle applies even if there is no comparable domestic production or no possibility of such production. Taxes on the use of utilities such as water, electricity, gas, and energy are regarded as excises rather than taxes on specific services (5126). Excises exclude those taxes that are levied as general taxes on goods and services (5110); profits of fiscal monopolies (5122); customs and other import duties (5123); or taxes on exports (5124).

5122 — Profits of fiscal monopolies

66. This sub-heading covers that part of the profits of fiscal monopolies which is transferred to general government or which is used to finance any expenditures considered to be government expenditures (see §24). Amounts are shown when they are transferred to general government or used to make expenditures considered to be government expenditures.

67. Fiscal monopolies reflect the exercise of the taxing power of government by the use of monopoly powers. Fiscal monopolies are non-financial public enterprises exercising a monopoly in most cases over the production or distribution of tobacco, alcoholic beverages, salt, matches, playing cards and petroleum or agricultural products (i.e. on the kind of products which are likely to be, alternatively or additionally, subject to the excises of 5121), to raise the government revenues which in other countries are gathered through taxes on dealings in such commodities by private business units. The government monopoly may be at the production stage or, as in the case of government-owned and controlled liquor stores, at the distribution stage.

68. Fiscal monopolies are distinguished from public utilities such as rail transport, electricity, post offices, and other communications, which may enjoy a monopoly or quasi-monopoly position but where the primary purpose is normally to provide basic services rather than to raise revenue for government. Transfers from such other public enterprises to the government are considered as non-tax revenues. The traditional concept of fiscal monopoly is not generally extended to include state lotteries, the profits of which are usually accordingly regarded as non-tax revenues. However, they can be included as tax revenues if the prime reason for their operation is to raise revenues to finance government expenditure. Fiscal monopoly profits are distinguished from export and import monopoly profits (5127) transferred from marketing boards or other enterprises dealing with international trade.

5123 — Customs and other import duties

69. Taxes, stamp duties and surcharges restricted by law to imported products are included here. Also included are levies on imported agricultural products which are imposed in member countries of the European Union and amounts paid by certain of these countries under the Monetary Compensation Accounts (MCA) system.[17] Customs duties collected by European Union member states on behalf of the European Union are reported under this heading at the supranational level of government in the country tables (in Chapter 5 of the Report). Excluded here are taxes collected on imports as part of a general tax on goods and services, or an excise applicable to both imported and domestically produced goods.

5124 — Taxes on exports

70. In the 1970s, export duties were levied in Australia, Canada and Portugal as a regular measure and they have been used in Finland for counter-cyclical purposes. Some member countries of the European Union pay, as part of the MCA system, a levy on exports (see note 16 to §69). Where these amounts are identifiable, they are shown in this heading. This heading does not include repayments of general consumption taxes or excises or customs duties on exported goods, which should be deducted from the gross receipts under 5110, 5121 or 5123, as appropriate.

5125 — Taxes on investment goods

71. This sub-heading covers taxes on investment goods, such as machinery. These taxes may be imposed for a number of years or temporarily for counter-cyclical purposes. Taxes on industrial inputs which are also levied on consumers [e.g., the Swedish energy tax which is classified under (5121)] are not included here.

5126 — Taxes on specific services

72. All taxes assessed on the payment for specific services, such as taxes on insurance premiums, banking services, gambling and betting stakes (e.g., from horse races, football pools, lottery tickets), transport, entertainment, restaurant and advertising charges, fall into this category. Taxes on entry to casinos, races, other similar events or venues as well as stamp taxes on specific services are also classified under this heading. Taxes levied on the gross income of companies providing a specific service (e.g. transportation [including airport and other passenger taxes] insurance, banking, entertainment, restaurants, and advertising) are also classified under this heading.

73. Tax revenues from bank levies and payments to deposit insurance and financial stability schemes are also included here:

- Compulsory payments of stability fees, bank levies and deposit insurance should generally be treated as tax revenues where the payments are made to general government or supranational authorities and are allocated to the governments' consolidated or general funds so that the government is free to make immediate use of the money for the purposes that it chooses. This principle would apply regardless of whether the government is promising to make payments to guarantee the banks' customer deposits in some future contingency.
- If the compulsory payments are made to general government and placed in funds that are earmarked to be entirely channelled back to the sector of the economy that comprises the companies that are subject to the payment, they would still generally be treated as tax revenues on the grounds that the funds would be available for the government and would reduce its budget deficit, the fee is unrequited for an individual entity and the amounts raised could be unrelated to any eventual pay out to depositors or expenditure on wider support for the financial sector.

- Payments to made to the smaller long-standing schemes for insuring 'retail' deposits, where the payment levels are consistent with the costs of insurance should be classified as fee for service.
- Any payments which involve governments realising the assets of a failed institution or receiving a priority claim on its assets in liquidation in order to fund payments of compensation to customers for their lost deposits would be treated as a fee for a service as opposed to tax revenues.
- Compulsory payments that are made to funds operated outside the government sector and non-state institutions backed by the deposit takers and all payments to voluntary schemes should not be treated as tax revenues.
- Contributions made to the EU Single Resolution Fund are also included here and recorded under the supranational level of government in the country tables.

74. Excluded from this sub-heading are:

a) taxes on services forming part of a general tax on goods and services (5110);

b) taxes on electricity, gas and energy (5121 as excises);

c) taxes on individual gains from gambling (1120 as taxes on capital gains of individuals and non-corporate enterprises) and lump-sum taxes on the transfer of private lotteries or on the permission to set up lotteries (5200);[18]

d) taxes on cheques and on the issue, transfer or redemption of securities (4400 as taxes on financial and capital transactions);

e) general taxes on turnover (5113).

5127 — Other taxes on international trade and transactions

75. This sub-heading covers revenue received by the government from the purchase and sale of foreign exchange at different rates. When the government exercises monopoly powers to extract a margin between the purchase and sales price of foreign exchange, other than to cover administrative costs, the revenue derived constitutes a compulsory levy exacted in indeterminate proportions from both purchaser and seller of foreign exchange. It is the common equivalent of an import duty and export duty levied in a single exchange rate system or of a tax on the sale or purchase of foreign exchange Like the profits of fiscal monopolies and import or export monopolies transferred to government, it represents the exercise of monopoly powers for tax purposes and is included in tax revenues.

76. The sub-heading covers also the profits of export or import monopolies, which do not however exist in OECD countries, taxes on purchase or sale of foreign exchange, and any other taxes levied specifically on international trade or transactions.

5128 — Other taxes on specific goods and services

77. This item includes taxes on the extraction of minerals, fossil fuels and other exhaustible resources from deposits owned privately or by another government together with any other unallocable receipts from taxes on specific goods and services. Taxes on the extraction of exhaustible resources are usually a fixed amount per unit of quality or weight, but can be a percentage of value. The taxes are recorded when the resources are extracted. Payments from the extraction of exhaustible resources from deposits owned by the government unit receiving the payment are classified as rent.

5200 — Taxes on use of goods or on permission to use goods or perform activities

78. This sub-heading covers taxes which are levied in respect of the use of goods as distinct from taxes on the goods themselves. Unlike the latter taxes – reported under 5100 –, they are not assessed on the value of the goods but usually as fixed amounts. Taxes on permission to use goods or to perform activities are also included here, as are pollution taxes not based upon the value of particular goods. It is

sometimes difficult to distinguish between compulsory user charges and licence fees which are regarded as taxes and those which are excluded as non-tax revenues. The criteria which are employed are noted in §12–13.

79. Although the sub-heading refers to the 'use' of goods, registration of ownership rather than use may be what generates liability to tax, so that the taxes of this heading may apply to the ownership of animals or goods rather than their use (e.g., race horses, dogs and motor vehicles) and may apply even to unusable goods (e.g., unusable motor vehicles or guns).

80. Borderline cases arise with:

a) taxes on the permission to perform business activities which are levied on a combined income, payroll or turnover base and, accordingly, are classified following the rules in §84;

b) taxes on the ownership or use of property of headings 4100, 4200 and 4600. The heading 4100 is confined to taxes on the ownership or tenancy of immovable property and – unlike the taxes of 5200 – they are related to the value of the property. The net wealth taxes and taxes on chattels of 4200 and 4600 respectively are confined to the ownership rather than the use of assets, apply to groups of assets rather than particular goods and again are related to the value of the assets,

5210 — Recurrent taxes on use of goods and on permission to use goods or perform activities

81. The principal characteristic of taxes classified here is that they are levied at regular intervals and that they are usually fixed amounts. The most important item in terms of revenue receipts is vehicle licence taxes. This sub-heading also covers taxes on permission to hunt, shoot, fish or to sell certain products and taxes on the ownership of dogs , broadcast licence fees and taxes on the performance of certain services, provided that they meet the criteria set out in §12–13. The sub-divisions of 5210 are:

- user taxes on motor vehicles paid by households (5211);
- taxes on motor vehicles paid by others (5212); and
- other recurrent taxes (5213). This sub-heading covers business and professional licences paid by enterprises in order to obtain a licence to carry on a particular kind of business or profession when the levies are on a recurring basis. Licences such as taxi and casino licences are included. Dog licences and recurrent general licences for hunting, shooting and fishing where the right to carry out these activities is not granted as part of a normal commercial transaction are also included under this heading. Broadcast licence fees are included when the payer of the levy cannot opt out from making payments for public broadcast if one does not wish to watch or listen to public broadcast services (e.g. by declaring that one does not consume public broadcast services). Specific exemptions (for example, for elderly people) do not change the compulsory nature of the payment.

82. Excluded from sub-heading 5213 are:

a) licences where the right to carry out such activities is granted as part of a normal commercial transaction (e.g., the granting of the licence is accompanied by the right to use a specific area which is owned by government);

b) payments relating to the checks carried out by the government on the suitability and or safety of the business premises or equipment, or on the quality or standard of goods or services produced as a condition for granting such a licence. These payments are not unrequited and should be treated as payments for services rendered, unless the amounts charged for the licences are out of all proportion to the costs of the checks carried out by governments.

c) broadcast licence fees if users can opt out from paying broadcast licence fees in the case that they do not wish to consume these services while not affecting the ability to consume private broadcast services.

5220 — Non-recurrent taxes on use of goods and on permission to use goods or perform activities

83. This section covers non-recurrent taxes levied on the use of goods or on permission to use goods or perform activities and taxes levied each time goods are used. It includes taxes levied on the emission or discharge into the environment of noxious gases, liquids or other harmful substances.

- Payments for tradable emission permits issued by governments under cap and trade schemes should be recorded here at the time the emissions occur. No revenue should be recorded for permits that governments issue free of charge. The accrual basis of recording means that there can be a timing difference between the cash being received by government for the permits and the time the emission occurs. In the national accounts, this timing gives rise to a financial liability for government during the period.
- Payments made for the collection and disposal of waste or noxious substances by public authorities should be excluded as they constitute a sale of services to enterprises.

84. Other taxes falling under heading 5200 that are not levied recurrently are also included here. Thus, once-and-for-all payments for permission to sell liquor or tobacco or to set up betting shops are included provided they meet the criteria set out in §12–13.

6000 — Other taxes

85. Taxes levied on a base, or bases, other than those described under headings 1000, 3000, 4000 and 5000, or on bases of which cannot be considered to be related to any one of these headings, are included here. Where taxes are levied on a multiple base and it is possible to estimate the receipts related to each base the separate amounts are included under the appropriate headings. If separate amounts cannot be estimated and it is known that most of the receipts are derived from one base, the whole of the receipts are classified according to that base. Otherwise, they are classified here. Other revenues included here are presumptive taxes not included elsewhere in the classification system, taxes on individuals in the form of a poll tax or capitation tax, stamp taxes not related to financial and capital transactions nor falling exclusively on a single category of transaction, expenditure taxes where personal deductions or exemptions are applied and unidentifiable tax receipts. A subdivision is made between taxes levied wholly or predominantly on business (6100) and those levied on others (6200).

A.6 Conciliation with National Accounts

86. This section of the tables provides a re-conciliation between the OECD calculation of total tax revenues and the total of all taxes and social contributions paid to general government as recorded in the country's National Accounts. Where the country is a member of the European Union (EU), the comparison is between the OECD calculation of total tax revenues and the sum of tax revenues and social contributions recorded in the combination of the general government and the institutions of the EU sectors of the National Accounts.

A.7 Memorandum item on the financing of social security benefits

87. In view of the varying relationship between taxation and social security contributions and the cases referred to in §40 to §46, a memorandum item collects together all payments earmarked for social security-

type benefits, other than voluntary payments to the private sector. Data are presented as follows (refer Table 5.39 of the Report):

a) Taxes of 2000 series.

b) Taxes earmarked for social security benefits.

c) Voluntary contributions to the government.

d) Compulsory contributions to the private sector.

Guidance on the breakdown of (a) to (d) above is provided in §40 to §46.

A.8 Memorandum item on identifiable taxes paid by government

88. Identifiable taxes actually paid by government are presented in a memorandum item classified by the main headings of the OECD classification of taxes. In the vast majority of countries, only social security contributions and payroll taxes paid by government can be identified. These are, however, usually the most important taxes paid by governments (refer to Table 5.40 of the Report).

A.9 Relation of OECD classification of taxes to national accounting systems

89. A system of national accounts (SNA) seeks to provide a coherent framework for recording and presenting the main flows relating respectively to production, consumption, accumulation and external transactions of a given economic area, usually a country or a major region within a country. Government revenues are an important part of the transactions recorded in SNA. The final version of the 2008 SNA was jointly published by five international organisations: the United Nations, the International Monetary Fund, the European Union, the Organisation for Economic Co-operation and Development, and the World Bank in August 2009. The *System* is a comprehensive, consistent and flexible set of macroeconomic accounts. It is designed for use in countries with market economies, whatever their stage of economic development, and also in countries in transition to market economies. The important parts of the SNA's conceptual framework and its definitions of the various sectors of the economy have been reflected in the OECD's classification of taxes.

90. There are, however, some differences between the OECD classification of taxes and SNA concepts that are listed below. They arise because the aim of the former is to provide the maximum disaggregation of statistical data on what are generally regarded as taxes by tax administrations.

a) OECD includes compulsory social security contributions paid to general government in total tax revenues. Imputed and voluntary contributions plus those paid to private funds are not treated as taxes (§9 and §11 above);

b) there are different points of view on whether or not some levies and fees are classified as taxes (§12 and §13 above);

c) OECD excludes imputed taxes or subsidies resulting from the operation of official multiple exchange rates or from the central bank paying a rate of interest on required reserves that is different from other market rates;

d) there are differences in the treatment of non-wastable tax credits

91. As noted in §1 and §2, headings 1000 to 6000 of the OECD list of taxes cover all unrequited payments to general government or to a supranational authority, other than compulsory loans and fines. Such unrequited payments including fines, but excluding compulsory loans can be obtained from adding together the following figures in the 2008 SNA

- value-added type taxes (D.211);

- taxes and duties on imports, excluding VAT (D.212);
- export taxes (D.213);
- taxes on products, excluding VAT, import and export taxes (D.214);
- other taxes on production (D.29);
- taxes on income (D.51);
- other current taxes (D.59);
- actual social contributions (D.611 and D613), excluding voluntary contributions and payments to employment-related schemes that are not social security schemes
- capital taxes (D.91).

A.10 The OECD classification of taxes and the International Monetary Fund (GFS) system

92. The coverage and valuation of tax revenues in the GFS system and the 2008 SNA are very similar. Therefore, the differences between the OECD classification and that of the 2008 SNA (see §90 above) also apply to the GFS. In addition, the International Monetary Fund subdivides the OECD 5000 heading into section IV (Domestic Taxes on Goods and Services) and section V (Taxes on International Trade and Transactions). This reflects the fact that while the latter usually yield insignificant amounts of revenue in OECD countries, this is not the case in many non-OECD countries.

A.11 Comparison of the OECD classification of taxes with other international classifications

93. The table below describes an item by item comparison of the OECD classification of taxes and the classifications used in the following:

a) System of National Accounts (2008 SNA);
b) European System of Accounts (2010 ESA);
c) IMF Government Finance Statistics Manual (GFSM2014).

94. These comparisons represent those that would be expected to apply in the majority of cases. However in practice some flexibility should be used in their application. This is because in particular cases, countries can adopt varying approaches to the classification of revenues in National Accounts.

			OECD Classification	2008 SNA	2010 ESA	GFSM2014
1000			Taxes on income, profits and capital gains			
	1100		Individuals			
		1110	Income and profits	D51-8.61a	D51A	1111
		1120	Capital gains	D51-8.61c, d	D51C, D	1111
	1200		Corporations			
		1210	Income and profits	D51-8.61b	D51B	1112
		1220	Capital gains	D51-8.61c	D51C	1112
	1300		Unallocable as between 1100 and 1200			1113
2000			Social security contributions			
	2100		Employees	D613-8.85	D613	1211
	2200		Employers	D611-8.83	D611	1212
	2300		Self-employed, non-employed	D613-8.85	D613	1213
	2400		Unallocable as between 2100, 2200 and 2300			1214

3000				Taxes on payroll and workforce	D29-7.97a	D29C	112
4000				Taxes on property			
	4100			Recurrent taxes on immovable property			
		4110		Households	D59-8.63a	D59A	1131
		4120		Other	D29-7.97b	D29A	1131
	4200			Recurrent net wealth taxes			
		4210		Individual	D59-8.63b	D59A	1132
		4220		Corporations	D59-8.63b	D59A	1132
	4300			Estate, inheritance and gift taxes			
		4310		Estate and inheritance taxes	D91-10.207b	D91A	1133
		4320		Gift taxes	D91-10.207b	D91A	1133
	4400			Taxes on financial and capital transactions	D59-7.96d; D29-7.97e	D214B, C	114114; 1161
	4500			Other non-recurrent taxes on property	D91-10.207a	D91B	1135
	4600			Other recurrent taxes on property	D59-8.63c	D59A	1136
5000				Taxes on goods and services			
	5100			Taxes on production, sale and transfer of goods and services			
		5110		General taxes on goods and services			
			5111	Value-added taxes	D211-7.89	D211; D29G	11411
			5112	Sales taxes	D2122-7.94a; D214-7.96a	D21224; D214I	11412
			5113	Turnover and other general taxes on goods and services	D214-7.96a	D214I	11413
		5120		Taxes on specific goods and services			
			5121	Excises	D2122-7.94b; D214-7.96b	D21223; D214A, B, D	1142
			5122	Profits of fiscal monopolies	D214-7.96e	D214J	1143
			5123	Customs and other import duties	D2121-7.93	D2121; D21221, 2	1151
			5124	On exports	D213-7.95a	D214K	1152-4
			5125	On investment goods			
			5126	On specific services	D2122-7.94c; D214-7.96c	D21225; D214E, F, G, H; D29F	1144; 1156
			5127	Other taxes on international trade and transactions	D2122-7.94d D29-7.95b D29-7.97g D59-8.64d	D21226; D29D; D59E	1153; 1155-6
			5128	Other taxes on specific goods and services			1146
		5130		Unallocable between 5110 and 5120			
	5200			Taxes on use of goods and on permission to use goods or perform activities			
		5210		Recurrent taxes on use of goods and on permission to use goods or perform activities			
			5211	Motor vehicle taxes households	D59-8.64c	D59D	11451
			5212	Motor vehicles taxes others	D29-7.97d	D214D; D29B	11451
			5213	Other recurrent taxes on use of goods and on permission to use goods or perform activities	D29-7.97c, d, f D59-8.64c	D29B, E, F; D59D	11452
		5220		Non-recurrent taxes on permission to use goods or perform activities			11452
	5300			Unallocable as between 5100 and 5200			
6000				Other taxes			
	6100			Payable solely by business			1161
	6200			Payable by other than business, or unidentifiable	D59-8.64a, b	D59B, C	1162

A.12 Attribution of tax revenues by sub-sectors of general government

95. The OECD classification requires a breakdown of tax revenues by sub-sectors of government. The definition of each sub-sector and the criteria to be used to attribute tax revenues between these sub-sectors are set out below. They follow the guidance of the 2008 SNA and GFSM 2014.

Sub-sectors of general government to be identified

a) *Central government*

96. The central government sub-sector includes all governmental departments, offices, establishments and other bodies which are agencies or instruments of the central authority whose competence extends over the whole territory, with the exception of the administration of social security funds. Central government therefore has the authority to impose taxes on all resident and non-resident units engaged in economic activities within the country.

b) *State, provincial or regional government*

97. This sub-sector consists of intermediate units of government exercising a competence at a level below that of central government. It includes all such units operating independently of central government in a part of a country's territory encompassing a number of smaller localities, with the exception of the administration of social security funds. In unitary countries, regional governments may be considered to have a separate existence where they have substantial autonomy to raise a significant proportion of their revenues from sources within their control and their officers are independent of external administrative control in the actual operation of the unit's activities.

98. At present, federal countries comprise the majority of cases where revenues attributed to intermediate units of government are identified separately. Colombia and Spain are the only two unitary countries in this position. In the remaining unitary countries, regional revenues are included with those of local governments.

c) *Local* government

99. This sub-sector includes all other units of government exercising an independent competence in part of the territory of a country, with the exception of the administration of social security funds. It encompasses various urban and/or rural jurisdictions (e.g., local authorities, municipalities, cities, boroughs, districts).

d) *Social security funds*

100. Social security funds form a separate sub-sector of general government. The social security sub-sector is defined in the 2008 SNA by the following extracts from paragraphs 4.124 to 4.126 and 4.147:

"Social security schemes are social insurance schemes covering the community as a whole or large section of the community that are imposed and controlled by government units. The schemes cover a wide variety of programmes, providing benefits in cash or in kind for old age, invalidity or death, survivors, sickness and maternity, work injury, unemployment, family allowance, health care, etc. There is not necessarily a direct link between the amount of the contribution paid by an individual and the benefits he or she may receive." (Paragraph 4.124).

"When social security schemes are separately organised from the other activities of government units and hold their assets and liabilities separately from the latter and engage in financial transactions on their own account they qualify as institutional units that are described as social security funds." (Paragraph 4.125).

"The amounts raised, and paid out, in social security contributions and benefits may be deliberately varied in order to achieve objectives of government policy that have no direct connection with the concept of social security as a scheme to provide social benefits to members of the community. They may be raised or lowered in order to influence the level of aggregate demand in the economy, for example. Nevertheless, so long as they remain separately constituted funds, they must be treated as separate institutional units in the SNA. (Paragraph 4.126).

"The social security funds sub-sector (of general government) consists of the social security funds operating at all levels of government. Such funds are social insurance schemes covering the community as a whole or large section of the community that are imposed by government units." (Paragraph 4.147).

101. This definition of social security funds is followed in the OECD classification with the two following exceptions which are excluded

- Schemes imposed by government and operated by bodies outside the general government sector, as defined in §3 of this manual; and
- Schemes to which all contributions are voluntary.

Supranational Authorities

102. This sub-sector covers the revenue-raising operations of supra-national authorities within a country. In practice, the only relevant supranational authority in the OECD area is that of the institutions of the European Union (EU). Tax revenues collected by member countries and paid to the EU are included in the *Revenue Statistics* at the supranational level of government. Income taxes and social security contributions collected by European Institutions and paid by European civil servants who are resident of EU member countries should not be included.

Criteria to be used for the attribution of tax revenues

103. When a government collects taxes and pays them over in whole or in part to other governments, it is necessary to determine whether the revenues should be considered to be those of the collecting government which it distributes to others as grants, or those of the beneficiary governments which the collecting government receives and passes on only as their agent. The criteria to be used in the attribution of revenues are set out in §104 to §107 which replicate paragraphs 3.70 to 3.73 from the 2008 SNA.

104. In general, a tax is attributed to the government unit that

a) exercises the authority to impose the tax (either as a principal or through the delegated authority of the principal),

b) has final discretion to set and vary the rate of the tax

105. Where an amount is collected by one government for and on behalf of another government, and the latter government has the authority to impose the tax, and set and vary its rate, then the former is acting as an agent for the latter and the tax is reassigned. Any amount retained by the collecting government as a collection charge should be treated as a payment for a service. Any other amount retained by the collecting government, such as under a tax-sharing arrangement, should be treated as a current grant. If the collecting government was delegated the authority to set and vary the rate, then the amount collected should be treated as tax revenue of this government.

106. Where different governments jointly and equally set the rate of a tax and jointly and equally decide on the distribution of the proceeds, with no individual government having ultimate overriding authority, then the tax revenues are attributed to each government according to its respective share of the proceeds. If an arrangement allows one government unit to exercise ultimate overriding authority, then all of the tax revenue is attributed to that unit.

107. There may also be the circumstance where a tax is imposed under the constitutional or other authority of one government, but other governments individually set the tax rate in their jurisdictions. The proceeds of the tax generated in each respective government's jurisdiction are attributed as tax revenues of that government.

108. The levies paid by the member states of the EU take the form specific levies which include

a) custom duties and levies on agricultural goods (5123),

b) gross monetary compensation accounts (5123 if relating to imports and 5124 if relating to exports);

c) contributions to the Single Resolution Fund (5126); and

d) Steel, coal, sugar and milk levies (5128).

109. The custom duties collected by member states on behalf of the EU are recorded

- on a gross of collection fee basis;
- using figures adjusted so that duties are shown on a 'final destination' as opposed to a 'country of first entry' basis where such adjustments can be made. These adjustments concern in particular duties collected at important (sea) ports. Although the EU duties are collected by the authorities of the country of first entry, when possible these duties should be excluded from the revenue of the collecting country and be included in the revenue of the country of final destination

110. These are the specific EU levies that most clearly conform to the attribution criterion described in §102 above. Consequently, these amounts are footnoted as a memorandum item to the EU member state country tables (in Chapter 5) and are shown as supranational revenues against each of the tax headings identified in §108.

Notes

[1] References in this OECD Interpretative Guide to Sections or Parts of "this Report" refer to OECD (2023), Revenue Statistics 2023, OECD Publishing, Paris.

[2] All references to SNA are to the 2008 edition.

[3] See section A.12 of this guide for a discussion of the concept of agency capacity.

[4] It is usually possible to identify amounts of social security contributions and payroll taxes, but not other taxes paid by government.

[5] If, however, a levy which is considered as non-tax revenue by most countries is regarded as a tax — or raises substantial revenue — in one or more countries, the amounts collected are footnoted at the end of the relevant country tables, even though the amounts are not included in total tax revenues.

[6] Names, however, can frequently be misleading. For example, though a passport fee would normally be considered a non-tax revenue, if a supplementary levy on passports (as is the case in Portugal) were imposed in order to raise substantial amounts of revenue relative to the cost of providing the passport, the levy would be regarded as a tax under 5200.

[7] A more detailed explanation of this distinction can be found in the special feature, 'Current issues in reporting tax revenues', in the 2001 edition of *Revenue Statistics*.

[8] Sometimes the terms 'non-refundable' and 'refundable' are used, but it may be considered illogical to talk of 'refundable' when nothing has been paid.

[9] A different treatment, however, is accorded to non-wastable tax credits under imputation systems of corporate income tax (§37–39).

[10] This is not strictly a true tax expenditure in the formal sense. Such tax expenditures require identification of a benchmark tax system for each country or, preferably, a common international benchmark. In practice it has not been possible to reach agreement on a common international benchmark.

[11] Unless based on the profit made on a sale, in which case they would be classified as capital gains taxes under 1120 or 1220.

[12] In some countries the same legislation applies to both individual and corporate enterprises for particular taxes on income. However, the receipts from such taxes are usually allocable between individuals and enterprises and can therefore be shown in the appropriate sub-heading.

[13] For example, "… sufficiently self-contained and independent that they behave in the same way as corporations… (including) keeping a complete set of accounts" (2008 SNA, section 4.44).

[14] In Canada — a country also referred to as having an imputation system — the (wastable) tax credit for the shareholder is in respect of domestic corporation tax deemed to have been paid whether or not a corporation tax liability has arisen. As there is no integral connection between the corporation tax liability

and the credit given against income tax under such systems, these credits for dividends are treated, along with other tax credits, on the lines described in §26.

15. This may also apply where a scheme for government employees existed prior to the introduction of a general social security scheme.

16. In the 2008 SNA, these are regarded as capital transfers and not as taxes (see section A.8).

17. This is the system by which the European Union adjusts for differences between the exchange rates used to determine prices under the Common Market Agricultural Policy and actual exchange rates. Payments under the system may relate to imports or exports and where these amounts are separately identifiable they are shown under the appropriate heading (5123 or 5124). In this Report, these amounts are shown gross (i.e. without deducting any subsidies paid out under the MCA system).

18. Transfers of profits of State lotteries are regarded as non-tax revenues (see also §68).

www.ingramcontent.com/pod-product-compliance
Lightning Source LLC
Chambersburg PA
CBHW061211240926
51846CB00006B/1180

* 9 7 8 9 2 6 4 5 8 5 3 7 9 *